I shall feel very great pleasure in doing so

I have the honour to be

Your obedt

Servant

[illegible]

Dr. [illegible]

Oxford

London
49. Dover St
Aug 6. [illegible]

Sir,

I am exceedingly obliged by your communication. If I can be of any assistance to you in making the selection to which you refer,

SKETCHES

OF

THE IRISH BAR

BY THE RT. HON.

RICHARD LALOR SHEIL, M. P.

WITH MEMOIR AND NOTES

BY

R. SHELTON MACKENZIE, D.C.L.

IN TWO VOLUMES.

VOL. II.

REDFIELD

110 AND 112 NASSAU STREET, NEW YORK.

[Third Thousand.] 1854.

STEREOTYPED BY C. C. SAVAGE,
13 Chambers Street, N. Y.

CONTENTS OF VOL. II.

SKETCHES OF THE IRISH BAR.

LORD NORBURY.

THREE remarkable incidents have lately taken place. LORD NORBURY, in testimony of his long and numerous services, has been created an earl, Lord Plunket has sunk into his successor, and Lord Manners took his leave amidst a strong odor of onions, and the tears of the Irish Bar.* I had intended to make these three events the groundwork of the present article; for Lord Plunket's first appearance on the stage from which Lord Norbury had just made his exit—his wan and dejected aspect, which was, as much as his intellect, in contrast with that of his predecessor—the melancholy smile which superseded his habitually haughty and sardonic expression—the exultation of his antagonists at seeing him descend from his recent elevation, and the sympathy which the liberal portion of the Bar felt in what was considered as his fall, presented a scene of deep and extraordinary interest.

It was also my purpose (inasmuch as no reasonable expectation can be entertained that a new edition of Rose and Beattie will afford an opportunity of attaching, by way of appendix

* This Sketch was published in November, 1827, but appears to have been written before Canning's death, which took place in August, during the same year. The retirement of Lord Manners from the Chancellorship, and the appointment of Plunket as Chief-Justice of the Common Pleas, took place, under Canning's Administration, in 1827.—M.

to those immortal records of judicial wisdom, a report of Lord Manners's last judgment upon himself) to preserve some account of his lordship's final adjudication upon his own merits, and to commemorate the tear that fell upon that pathetic occasion from the "Outalissi" of the Four Courts—

"The first, the last, the only tear
That Peter Henchey shed:"

but I find that the first of the incidents to which I have referred, together with an account of the progress of Lord Norbury through the various parts which he performed in the political theatre, from his first entrance as "an Irish gentleman" in the House of Commons, to his exit as a jester from the bench, will occupy so much space, that I must confine myself to the biography of his Lordship; which, however little it may be instructive, will not, I think, be found unamusing, and falls within the scope of the articles on the Irish Bar.

In the account given by Sir Pertinax Macsycophant of his rise and progress in the world, he states that his only patrimony was a piece of parental advice, which stood him in lieu of an estate. I have heard it said, that Lord Norbury, in detailing the circumstances which attended his original advancement in life, generally commenced the narrative of his adventures with a death-bed scene of a peculiarly Irish character. His father, a gentleman of a respectable Protestant family in the county of Tipperary, called him in his last moments to his side, and after stating that, in order to sustain the ancient and venerable name of Toler in its dignity, he had devised the estate derived from a sergeant (not at law) to his eldest son, the old Cromwellian drew from under his pillow a case of silver-mounted pistols, and, delivering this "donatio mortis causâ," charged him never to omit exhibiting the promptitude of an Irish gentleman, in resorting to these forensic and parliamentary instruments of advancement.*

* Lord Norbury made frequent, if not good, use of his pistols—"barkers," as they were called in fighting parlance. He fought with several persons, one of whom was the ruffianly "Fighting Fitzgerald" who was finally hanged for murder. In those days a duel was necessary to fix a man's character. When a young man entered society, the first word was, "What family does he come

The family acres having gone to the eldest brother, our hero proceeded with his specific legacy, well oiled and primed, to Dublin, having no other fortune than the family pistols, and a couple of hundred pounds, when he was called, in the year 1770, to the Bar. The period is so remote, that no account of his earlier exploits, beyond that of his habitual substitution of the canons of chivalry for those of law, has remained. With one of his contemporaries, the late Sir Frederick Flood, I was acquainted, and I have heard that eminent person, whom the intellectual aristocracy of Wexford sent to supply the place of Mr. Fuller in the British House of Commons,* occa-

from?" the second, "Who has he *blazed* with?" When plain Mr. Toler, Lord Norbury quarrelled with Sir Jonah Barrington. It was in the House of Commons, when Barrington having accused him of having "a hand for every man and a heart for nobody" (which was true to the letter), Toler gave a sharp reply, and hurriedly retired. Barrington, who understood his look, followed. The Speaker sent in pursuit of both gentlemen. Barrington was overtaken, running down Nassau street, and, on his resistance, was bodily snatched up, in presence of a shouting mob of grinning spectators, and literally carried into the House, on a man's shoulders. Toler, caught by his coat-skirts being fastened by a door, was seized, and pulled until the skirts were separated from the garment. The Speaker called on both to give a promise that the affair should go no farther, which Barrington did at once. Toler rose to speak, *minus* his skirts, and the laughter caused by his appearance was increased when Curran gravely said that "it was offering an unparalleled insult to the House, for one honorable member to *trim* another member's *jacket*, within the precincts of Parliament, and almost in view of the Speaker himself." To the last, even when judge, Norbury was anxious to display himself in the duello. There is no doubt that his advancement was owing more to his readiness to challenge and fight, than to any merit as a lawyer. He valued his life at nothing — a very fair estimate. — M.

* Sir Frederick Flood was member for Wexford County in the Imperial Parliament, where he was much laughed at for his blunders, his ostentation, and his good temper. He used to adopt almost any suggestion, while making a speech. Praising the Wexford magistracy for their zeal, he suggested, "They ought to receive some signal mark of vice-regal favor." Egan (commonly called Bully Egan, and judge of Dublin County) jocularly whispered, "and be whipped at the cart's tail." Flood, hearing the words, completed his speech by adding — "and be whipped at the cart's tail!" He did not discover his unconscious mistake, until awakened by a shout of laughter from his auditors. Jack Fuller was an English M. P., who was the acknowledged Parliamentary buffoon, after the brilliant wit of Sheridan ceased to enliven the Legislature. Fuller was a mere joker: Sheridan a man of genius. — M.

sionally expatiate on the feats which he used to perform with Lord Norbury, with something of the spirit with which Justice Shallow records his achievements at Clement's Inn. "Oh the mad days that I have spent," Sir Frederick used to say, "and to think that so many of my old acquaintances are dead!" The details, however, of his narrations have escaped me. I had calculated that, as he was a strict disciple of Abernethy (except when he dined out), he would have equalled Cornaro in longevity; but being as abstemious in his dress as in his diet, and having denied himself the luxury of an exterior integument, Sir Frederick coughed himself, a couple of winters since, unexpectedly away. I am, therefore, unable to resort to any of Lord Norbury's original companions, for an authentic account of the first development of his genius at the Irish Bar.

If that bar had been constituted as it is at present, at the period when Lord Norbury was called, it is difficult to imagine how he could have succeeded. Destitute of knowledge, with a mind which, however shrewd and sagacious in the perception of his own interests, was unused to consider, and was almost incapable of comprehending any legal proposition, he could never have risen to any sort of eminence, where perspicuity or erudition was requisite for success. But the qualifications for distinction, at the time when Lord Norbury was called, were essentially different from what they are at present. Endowed with the lungs of Stentor, and a vivacity of temperament which sustained him in all the turbulence of Irish Nisi Prius, and superadding to his physical attributes for noise and bluster, a dauntless determination, he obtained some employment in those departments of his profession, in which merits of the kind were at that time of value. His elder brother, Daniel, was elected member for the county of Tipperary, which brought him into connection with Government; but, besides his brother's vote, he is reported to have intimated to the ministry, that upon all necessary occasions his life should be at their service. The first exploit from which his claims upon the gratitude of the local administration of the country were chiefly derived, was the "putting down," to use the technical phrase, of Mr.

Napper Tandy.* The latter was a distinguished member of the Whig Club, and was a tribune of the people.

Tandy had set up great pretensions to intrepidity, but, having come into collision with Lord Norbury, manifested so little alacrity in accepting the ready tender which was made to him by that intrepid loyalist, that the latter was considered to have gained a decided superiority. Napper Tandy remained lingering on the threshold of the arena, while the prize-fighter of the ministers rushed into it at once, and brandished his sword amidst the applauses of that party, of which he was thenceforward the champion. The friends of Napper Tandy accounted for his tardiness in calling on Lord Norbury (who declared his willingness to meet him in half an hour), by referring it to an apprehension that the House of Commons would interfere; but it seems probable that the patriot of the hour set a higher estimate upon his existence than it merited,

* James Napper Tandy was an Irishman, of good family, high education, and respectable fortune. He was a United Irishman, and retired to France, to avoid arrest in Ireland. There he received a commission, as general of brigade, in one of the expeditions against Ireland, in 1798, which came to nothing. The year following, Napper Tandy was in Hamburgh, where the English Government had spies, and the local authorities surrendered him, as a prisoner claimed by England. Napoleon, who was then first consul, reclaimed Tandy, as an officer in the army of France, and declared that if a hair of his head were touched, an English officer of equal rank, taken prisoner in France, should be hanged. The threat was a strong one, the man likely to execute it, and, instead of executing Tandy as "a traitor," England exchanged him, as a prisoner-of-war. He died in the French service. Napoleon levied a heavy fine on the city of Hamburgh for their breach of neutrality in surrendering a French officer. It should be noted that Theobald Wolfe Tone, taken in arms in Le Hoche, a French ship-of-war which took troops to Ireland in September, 1798, had as much right to be reclaimed by France, in whose military office he was, as Tandy. There was not time to do so, so rapidly did his trial and conviction follow his capture. It is known that Tone cut his throat in prison, to avoid death on the scaffold. But it is not generally known that it was seriously discussed by the Irish executive, whether, "for the sake of the example," he should not be conducted to the gallows, half-dead as he was, and executed forthwith—though to do so, it would be necessary to insert the halter within the wound, and thereby probably tear the victim's head from his body! Humanity or the fear of public execration prevailed, and Tone was suffered to die in peace, after lingering for eight days in mortal pain.—M.

while Lord Norbury rated himself at his real value, and did not "set his life at a pin's fee."

After this affair, which mainly contributed to the making of his fortunes, the minister determined to turn the principal talent which he appeared to possess, and of which he had given so conspicuous a proof, to farther account. In the Irish House of Commons, the government party, when hard pressed, converted the debate into a sort of sanguinary burletta, in which Lord Norbury, then Sergeant Toler, and Sir Boyle Roche,* of blundering memory, were their favorite performers.

* Sir Boyle Roche was an Irish Baronet, who had a seat in Parliament, and was the droll of the House. He was famous for his *bulls*—which, though the expression might be incorrect, generally involved aphorisms of sound sense. He was of respectable family—with a claim to the title of Viscount Fermoy, but never urging it. Once, when it was stated, on a money-grant, that it was unjust to saddle posterity with a debt incurred to benefit the present generation, Sir Boyle rose up and said, "Why should we beggar ourselves to benefit posterity? What has posterity done for us?" The laugh which followed rather surprised him, as he was unconscious of his blunder. He explained: "Sir, by posterity I do not mean our ancestors, but those who come immediately *after them.*"—Arguing in favor of a harsh Government measure, he urged that it would be better to give up not only a *part*, but even the *whole* of the constitution, to preserve the *remainder*."—On another occasion, as a free translation of

"Tu ne cede malis, sed contra audentior ito,"

he said "The best way to *avoid* danger, is *to meet it plump*."—Complaining of the smallness of wine-bottles, he suggested that a bill should be passed enacting that every quart-bottle should hold a quart.—He married Sir John Cave's eldest daughter, and boasted that if he had an older one, Sir John would have given her to him.—Fearing the progress of revolutionary opinions, he drew a frightful picture of the future, remarking that the House of Commons might be invaded by ruffians who, said he, "would cut us to mince-meat and throw our bleeding heads on that table, to stare us in the face."—Arguing in favor of the Union of Ireland with England, he said (rather wittily) that "there was no Levitical degrees between nations, and, on this occasion, he saw neither sin nor shame in *marrying our own sister*."—He brought in a bill for the improvement of the Dublin police, who were in the habit of sleeping on their post, at night, and introduced a clause to the effect that "every watchman should be *compelled* to sleep in the daytime." On this, another member arose and begged to be included in that clause, by name, "as he was troubled with the gout and sometimes could not sleep by night or day."—He assisted in preparing a bill to provide for the erection of a new jail in Dublin, and stated that the new prison should be built on the site and with the materials of the old one, and that the prisoners should

When Grattan had ignited the House of Commons, and succeeded in awakening some recollections of public virtue in that corrupt and prostituted assembly, or when Mr. Ponsonby, the leader of the Whig aristocracy, had, by his clear and simple exposition of the real interests of the country, brought a reluctant conviction of their duty to those who were most interested in shutting it out, finding themselves unequal to cope in eloquence with the one, or in argument with the other, the government managers produced Sir Boyle Roche and Sergeant Toler upon the scene.

On Grattan the experiment of bullying was not tried, for his firmness was too well known. Sir Boyle was, therefore, appointed to reply to him, as his absurdities were found to be useful in restoring the House to that moral tone, from which the elevating declamation of the greatest speaker of his time had for a moment raised them. Under the influence of Sir Boyle's blunders, which were in part intended, the Irish legislators recovered their characteristic pleasantry, and "made merry of a nation's woes;" while Sergeant Toler, who almost equalled Sir Boyle in absurdity, and was more naturally, be-

continue to reside in the old prison until the new one was completed! — Barrington states that the postillion of Lord Lisle having been mulcted in damages for crim. con. with Lady Lisle, and imprisoned in default of payment, and an applicant for relief as an Insolvent Debtor, which the Legislature resisted, Sir Boyle Roche argued for him (and with much plausibility) that "Lady Lisle, and not Dennis M'Carthy, must have been the real seducer," and concluded by asking "Mr. Speaker, what was this poor servant's crime? — Sure, it was only doing his master's business by his mistress's order." — Curran used to say that Sir Boyle Roche had a rival in an Irish Judge, who sagely contended, in an argument on the construction of a will, that "it appeared to him that the testator meant to keep a life interest in the estate to himself." Curran answered, "True, my Lord; testators do generally secure a life interest for themselves, but in this case, I rather think you *take the will for the deed.*" Sir Boyle Roche's bulls illustrated what may be called arguing wrongly from right premises. To illustrate this, let me add a bull by another. Two Irishmen met, after a long separation, and to an inquiry after the health of a third person, the reply was, "Oh, he's been ill. He's had the fever. It has worn him down, as thin as a thread-paper. *You* are thin, and *I* am thin, but *he* is thinner than *both of us put together.*" Here the idea is fully conveyed, but, in the hurry of clothing the thought with language, the mode of expression is incorrect. And such is that amusing thing — an Irish Bull. — M.

cause he was involuntarily extravagant, played his part, and was let loose upon Mr. Ponsonby, whose nerves were of a delicate organization, with singular effect. That eminent statesman had made a speech, recommending Catholic Emancipation, and other collateral measures, as the only means of rescuing Ireland from the ruin which impended over her. He was always remarkable for the dignified urbanity of his manners, and in the speech to which Sergeant Toler replied, scarcely any man but Toler could have found materials for personal vituperation.

The English reader will be able to form some idea of the system on which the debates of the Irish House of Commons were carried on, and to estimate Lord Norbury's powers of minacious oratory, from the following extract from the parliamentary debates: "What was it come to, that in the Irish House of Commons they should listen to one of their own members degrading the character of an Irish gentleman by language which was fitted but for hallooing a mob? Had he heard a man uttering out of those doors such language as that by which the honorable gentleman had violated the decorum of Parliament, he would have seized *the ruffian by the throat*, and dragged him to the dust! What were the House made of, who could listen in patience to such abominable sentiments? sentiments, thank God! which were acknowledged by no class of men in this country, except the execrable and infamous nest of traitors, who were known by the name of United Irishmen, who sat brooding in Belfast over their discontents and treasons, and from whose publications he could trace, word for word, every expression the honorable gentleman had used."—*Irish Parliamentary Debates, Feb.*, 1797.

Of this fragment of vituperation Mr. Ponsonby took no notice; and the object of the orator was attained, in securing himself a new title to the gratitude of those who kept a band of bravoes hired in their service, and could not have selected a more appropriate instrument than Lord Norbury for the purposes of intimidation. To his personal courage, or rather recklessness of the lives of others as well as his own, he is chiefly indebted for his promotion. It was the leading trait of his character, and, prevailing over his extravagance, invested him with a sort of spurious respectability. In the manifestations of that spirit, which had become habitual, he has persevered to the last; and even since he has been a Chief-Justice has betrayed his original tendency to settle matters after the old Irish fashion, at the distance of twelve paces. He has more than once intimated to a counsel, who was pressing him too closely with a Bill of Exceptions, that he would not seek shelter behind the bench, or merge the gentleman in the Chief-Justice; and, when a celebrated senator charged him with having fallen asleep on a trial for murder, he is reported to have declared that he would resign, in order to demand satisfaction, as "that Scotch *Broom* (Brougham) wanted nothing so much as an Irish *stick*."

In the year 1798, Lord Norbury was his Majesty's Solicitor-General. His services to Government had been hitherto confined to the display of ferocious rhetoric in the House of Commons, of which I have quoted a specimen. The civil disturbances of the country offered a new field to his genius, and afforded him an opportunity of accumulating his claims upon the gratitude of the Crown, which could not have found a more zealous, and, I will even add, a more useful servant during the rebellion. If the juries before whom the hordes who were charged with high treason were put upon their trial, had been either scrupulous or reluctant, if any questions of effectual difficulty could have arisen, and the forms of the law could have been used with any chance of success in the defence of the prisoners, if Justice had not rushed with eagerness through every impediment, and broken all ceremony down, such a Solicitor-General as Lord Norbury would have been an inapplicable and inefficient instrument; but the evidence of informers was generally so direct and simple, and so strong was the impatience of juries to precipitate themselves to a conviction, all niceties and technicalities of the law were so utterly disregarded, and it was so little requisite that the conductors of Government prosecutions should possess either acuteness or knowledge, that Lord Norbury's faculties were quite equal to the discharge of his official duty, while they were in happy adaptation to the moral character of the public tribunals, and the exigency of the time.

To strike terror into the people was the great object to be attained, and Lord Norbury had many qualifications for the purpose. He stood in a court of justice, not only as the servant of his sovereign, but as the representative, in some measure, of the powerful Cromwellian aristocracy to which his family belonged, and in whose prejudices and passions he himself vehemently participated. His whole bearing and aspect breathed a turbulent spirit of domination. His voice was deep and big; and in despite of the ludicrous associations connected with his character, when it rolled the denunciations of infuriated power through the court, derived from the terrible intimations which it conveyed, an awful and appalling character. He did not, indeed, cease to utter absurdity, but his orations were fraught with a kind of truculent bombast—a sort of sanguinary "fee, fa, fum!" while the dilation of his nostrils, and the fierceness of his look, expressed, if I may so say, the scent of a traitor's blood.* In his moments of excitation (and he is

* It may seem uncharitable to pronounce such an opinion, but there appear strong grounds for thinking that Lord Norbury, as a Judge, felt a sort of morbid pleasure in presiding at the trial, and (what under him was pretty sure to follow) the conviction of persons prosecuted by the Government. During the fatal and blood-stained year of 1798, he was Attorney-General, and had the task—if task it were to him who could say of it, "The duty I delight in physics pain"—of conducting the State Trials. In my youth, when I used to listen to old men's tales of the legal tortures and butcheries of '98, the narrators would tell how "bloody Toler" (as he was called) strained every point against prisoners, how he would insist on every quirk and quibble to convict them, how he would browbeat the witnesses, and all but threaten the juries, and how complacently, when the verdict was delivered, he would insist on the passing of a sentence of immediate—of almost instant death. Such was it, in the case of the Sheareses, mentioned in the preceding volume, where on the part of the Crown, he sternly refused their counsel the slightest pause for rest and thought, after the trial had already lasted sixteen consecutive hours; when, the verdict being returned at eight in the morning, he had the doomed brothers brought up that same afternoon, for judgment; how he insisted on their execution taking place the next morning; and how the condemnation was literally *forced*, by him, on the evidence of a single and tainted witness, the law of England requiring two to establish an overt-act of high treason. Then, too, while Lord Norbury's name was uttered with "curses both loud and deep," I used to hear of this

capable of ascending beyond the level of ordinary feeling and discourse) his spirit was strongly roused, and his countenance, swelled as it was with passion, and stained with a dark red, became the image of his intellect and of his sensibility. His eyes were inflamed with a ferocious loyalty, and the consciousness of unbounded power; and while they glared on the wretches who stood pale and trembling at the bar, or were fixed in defiance on the counsel for the prisoner, assisted, with

man's inhuman bearing toward Robert Emmett — the kindest, most chivalric, and truest man that ever breathed; who, like Lord Edward Fitzgerald, might have escaped, but, like him, declined to find safety in flight, leaving other and meaner partners in the revolt to face the peril and the death-doom. Emmett, from the first, did not deny his conspiracy against the English misrule which had reduced his country from independence to its opposite — from a kingdom to a province. All through, he was chiefly anxious to show that he never contemplated establishing French power in Ireland — of substituting one tyranny for another. In the speech which he made, after conviction, when called upon to say why judgment of death should not pass, he strongly urged this: — "Small, indeed," said he, "would be our claim to patriotism and sense, and palpable our affectation of the love of liberty, if we were to sell our country to a people who are not only slaves themselves, but the unprincipled and abandoned instruments of imposing slavery on others." In this vindication of his motives, Emmett was repeatedly and roughly interrupted by Norbury. Then came the sharp "You, my lord, are a judge. I am the supposed culprit. I am a man — you are a man also. By a revolution of power we might change places, though we never could change characters." And then the defiance: "There are men concerned in this conspiracy who are not only superior to me, but even to your own conceptions of yourself, my lord — men before the splendor of whose genius and virtues I should bow with respectful deference, and who would not deign to call you friend — who would not disgrace themselves by shaking your blood-stained hand." The Government of that day suspected that three noblemen were in this conspiracy — one of whom, on what suspicion or proof is unknown, was the late Lord Cloncurry, who was arrested. It was a belief in Ireland, from the time that Robert Emmett was executed, that Lord Norbury would meet a doom as tragical. He lived on, however, like the Thane of Cawdor, "a prosperous gentleman." Boundless wealth filled his coffers. Worldly honors crowded upon him. At last he died. But the Irish remembered how the sins of the fathers are visited on the sons. Eight years after Lord Norbury's death, his successor was shot on his own demesne of Durrow Abbey, and, to this hour, there has been no detection of the assassin. As if to make it more inexplicable, the doomed man was a good landlord — as landlords are estimated in Ireland. He was neither absentee, nor exacting, nor litigious. He was simply the representative of the blood-stained judge, and the shaft of vengeance fell upon him.— M.

their savage glare, the canons of extermination which the orator was laying down. A certain trick of expanding his cheeks, and swelling them with wind, which he puffed importantly off, set off his tempestuous adjurations, and made him look as if he were blowing all mercy and compunction away. Thus he was every way well adapted to his terrible task.

Nor was he less qualified, when, in his capacity of Solicitor-General, he was put on the commission, and went as a judge of assize. Much of the same demeanor and deportment was preserved on the bench, where the red robes in which he was arrayed heightened the impression which his face, voice, and figure, were calculated to produce.* There was, however,

* Norbury's personal appearance was very remarkable. He was more than eighty when I first saw him, and resembled a caricatured character in a pantomime rather than a grave judicial personage. Charles Phillips said of him that "the chivalry of Quixote was incased in the paunch of Sancho Panza," but Chivalry and Norbury were antipodes, not synonymes. He had a sort of animal courage, or insensibility to danger, but was innocent of the gallant delight

"Which warriors feel
In foemen worthy of their steel."

He was nearly as broad as he was long, with a large and rubicund face; small and twinkling eyes, and a curious expression of ferret-like keenness, resulting, in all likelihood, from his being perpetually on the watch for the opportunity of a joke. His laugh was so hearty as to be infectious. Like Hamlet, he was "fat and scant of breath," and, was perpetually puffing—like an asthmatic locomotive. From this, though resembling the German civilian in nothing, he had obtained the soubriquet of Puffendorf. On the bench, he would pant, and pun, and puff, chuckling with glee at the laughter he created, until, as the fun came faster and faster, and the buffo grew hotter and hotter, he would let his judicial robe fall from his shoulders, shift his judicial wig to obtain ventilation, and return it to his head, with the tails, most probably, hanging before instead of behind! On one occasion, Lady Castlereagh gave a fancy-ball, at which Lord Norbury appeared as Hawthorn, in "Love in a Village," and was extremely amusing. His dress was a green tabinet, with mother-of-pearl buttons, striped yellow and black vest, and black breeches. If showy, the attire, from its materials, was light. When Norbury next went the Circuit, as judge, this fancy-dress found its way into one of his travelling trunks. The weather was warm the sitting of the Court would last for seven or eight hours, the dress was thin —Norbury donned it, and covered with his ample judicial robes, no one could see it. By-and-by, the heat became almost intolerable. Norbury gave his wig the usual twitch to the side; then he turned up the sleeves of his robe; next, he loosened the girdle which confined it round his waist; and, lastly, when the loosened envelope had gradually opened, there was the Chief Justice seen

this difference, that his spirit of buffoonery became more conspicuous upon the bench. It should not, however, be too hastily concluded that his love of drollery in any degree disqualified him for the exercise of the judicial functions. On the contrary, his merits as a jester were among his most useful and efficient attributes as a judge. He was fanciful or turgid, just as the occasion required.

In his addresses to the jury, he was as swollen with exaggerated loyalty as the gravest supporter of Protestant Ascendency could have desired; while during the rest of the trial, he put on a demeanor of heedless hilarity, which indicated the little value which he attached to the life of an insurgent, and taught the populace at what rate human breath was estimated in his court. The effect of the tortures of Macbriar, in "Old Mortality," is greatly heightened by the merriment by which the Duke of Lauderdale exclaims, "He will make an old proverb good, for he'll scarce ride to-day, though he has had his boots on." I do not, however, believe that the indifference for human life which was indicated by Lord Norbury's judicial mirth, was at all studied or systematic, or the result of cruelty of disposition. He is naturally of a gay and pleasant cast of

in his Hawthorn dress, chuckling over the jokes with which he amused himself and the Court in the intervals between the graver business of sentencing culprits to be hanged.— He was usually very polite to prisoners. On one occasion, when he had to sentence half a dozen, he had them all brought up, in a batch, and, severally naming five of them, pronounced judgment of death. An officer of the Court reminded his Lordship that he had missed one. The convict was sent for. "My good man," said Norbury, blowing like a grampus, "I've made a mistake about you, and I really must beg your pardon [puff puff puff], I should have sentenced you with the rest [puff] and quite omitted your name [puff]—pray excuse me. The sentence of the law is [puff] that you, Darby Mahony [puff]—I really wonder how I came to pass you over—be taken hence to prison, and from prison to the place of execution [puff] and there hanged by the neck until you are dead [puff]—I do hope you will excuse my mistake—and may the Lord [puff] have mercy on your soul. That's all, my good man [puff]—turnkey, remove Darby Mahony." The victim coolly turned round as he was quitting the dock, exclaiming, "Faith, my Lord, I can't thank you for your prayers, for I never heard of any one that throve after your making them!" Norbury, who relished a retort, actually granted Darby a reprieve before leaving the assize-town, and successfully recommended him for a commutation of punishment on his return to Dublin.—M.

mind; and it is, I fancy, impossible for him to keep ludicrous notions out. It is also but justice to him to add, that his jokes were not, like the Duke of Lauderdale's, at the expense of the prisoner, who stood aghast and dismayed before him; and if they showed that he did not entertain any very profound sense of the awfulness of the transition to another state of existence, still, as they were not directed to the culprit at the bar, his witticisms gave no indications of natural savageness of heart, from which I believe him to be wholly free. His imagination was hurried away by some whimsical idea, and the moment a grotesque image presented itself, or a fantastical anecdote was recalled to his recollection, he could not keep it in, but let it involuntarily escape upon the court.

But these vagaries did not render the administration of justice in his hands less terrific; and while he himself gave way to the merriment which he could not restrain, the countenances of the crowds with which the public tribunals were filled, in their fearful expression, as well as their ghastly color, exhibited an awful contrast with his own. He could, indeed, with impunity indulge in these judicial antics amid the assemblage of pallid wretches by whom he was surrounded; when it might be justly said, in reference to them and to the moral expression of his visage and its complexion, "*Cum tot palloribus sufficeret sævus iste vultus, atque rubor, quo se contra pudorem muniebat.*" In his charges, too, he made ample compensation for the conundrums with which he interrupted the examination of witnesses; for he threw off in an instant the character of a jester, resumed the terrors of his deep and denunciating voice, and turning to the prisoners, spoke of that eternity to which he was about to despatch them, with an awfulness and solemnity which justified Lord Clare, who objected to his being created a Chief-Justice, in recommending that he should enter the church, and be made a bishop.

The proposition that those brows, on which the black cap had been so frequently and so conspicuously displayed, should be invested with a mitre, did credit to Lord Clare, who, with all his partiality for the church, was more solicitous for the dignity of the judicial than the episcopal bench; and had his suggestion been adopted, Lord Norbury, attired in lawn, would have proved an agreeable accession to the House of Lords, and while he relieved the tedium of many a weary debate with his pious jokes and his holy merriment, he would in all likelihood have looked as appropriate a successor of the apostles as their lordships of Ossory or Kilmore. If he had been created Archbishop of Dublin, what a spirit of good humor would have been infused into our polemics; how many a sacred jest would have sparkled in his jovial and laughter-stirring homilies! We should have been spared a fierce and unprovoked aggression on the religion of the people, and should never have seen a barbed and envenomed arrow shot from behind the altar, in shape of a wanton and virulent antithesis. Lord Norbury officiating as Archbishop of Dublin, presents a pleasant picture to the mind, and of a character as truly Christian as the reality affords.

Unfortunately, however, Lord Clare was overruled; and Lord Norbury, having been created a peer, was raised to the Chief-Justiceship of the Common Pleas, on the resignation of Lord Carleton.* For some time the terrors which had attended him during the rebellion, continued to be associated with his name; but at length the recollections of the civil commotions in which he had played so remarkable a part, began to subside

* Hugh Carleton, born at Cork in 1739, was called to the Irish bar after completing his education at Dublin University. He had little success for some years, but rose to the office of Solicitor-General in 1779, which he retained until the appointment of the Duke of Portland, as Viceroy. He was made Chief-Justice of the Common Pleas, in 1787; created Baron Carleton in 1789, and raised to the rank of Viscount in 1797. After the Union, and when he had quitted the judicial bench, Lord Carleton sat in the Imperial Parliament, as one of the Irish Representative peers. He was very unpopular in Ireland — chiefly owing to his harsh conduct toward the Sheareses, in 1798, when presiding at their trial, as previously related in page 99 of first volume. He allowed them nothing like fair play in compelling their advocate, Mr. Curran, to enter on their defence, at midnight, after the trial had already lasted sixteen hours. In 1803, during Emmett's insurrection, when the populace met the carriage of Lord Kilwarden, Chief-Justice of the Queen's Bench, who was rather popular, he was mistaken for Carleton, Chief-Justice of the Common Pleas, and literally killed by mistake. Lord Carleton had such a melancholy aspect and lugubrious manner that Curran declared him to be plaintiff (plaintive) in every case that came before him.—M.

—his energy in the cause of government was forgotten—none but the ridiculous points of his character stood out in any very considerable prominence, and he lost even that species of respect which results from fear.

He was Chief-Justice of the Common Pleas from the year 1800, and diligently employed the whole of that period in earning the reputation which he at length succeeded in establishing through the empire. "Lord Norbury's last joke" has long been the ordinary title to a pleasant paragraph in the English newspapers:* but it is right to add, in his vindication,

* A vast number of puns, each paragraphed as "Lord Norbury's Last," appeared in the Irish newspapers in his lifetime. Every editor who made a joke sent it upon the world as one of the Norbury family. His own jests were better than most of the imitations. A man of his rank was tried before him for arson, and acquitted. The populace shrewdly gave the name of "Moscow" to the ruins of his house. Norbury met him soon after, at a Castle levée. "Glad to meet you *here*," said the judge. "This is my last bachelor's visit, my lord: I am going to turn Benedict." Norbury looked him full in the face while he responded, "Ay, St. Paul says better marry than *burn*."—When giving judgment on a writ of right, he declared that it was insufficient for a demandant to say he "claimed by descent. Such an answer," he continued, "would be a shrewd one for a sweep, who had entered your house, by getting down the chimney; and it would be an easy, as well as a *sweeping* way, of getting in."—A marine officer having canvassed for a directorship in the National Assurance Company of Ireland (there really *was* such a body!) Lord Norbury stated that he was very eligible, no doubt, from his experience in marine risks, his having received premiums for taking lives, and for having himself escaped all damages from fire, though following a profession doubly hazardous; "but," he added, "inasmuch as the Captain does not hold the requisite number of shares to qualify him, it is clear that his want of a sufficient stock of assurance is an insurmountable bar to his election."—At Naas, on circuit, when a Counsel was making a speech, an ass brayed very loudly outside, "One at a time, gentlemen, if you please," said Norbury. Soon after, while his Lordship was addressing the jury, the same long-eared quadruped again began to give tongue. "What noise is that?" The counsel retorted, "Only the echo of the Court, my Lord!"—The Irish had great faith in Edmund Burke's patriotism, which had supported what was called "The Independence of Ireland," viz., when the army of Volunteers, associated in 1779, compelled the British Ministry to repeal the Statute of the sixth of George I., declaring that Ireland was bound by British acts of Parliament, if named therein, that the Irish House of Lords had no jurisdiction in Irish cases of appeal; and that the *dernier ressort*, in all cases, must be to the peers of Great Britain. Burke's son, Richard, was appointed on a large salary, to get up the petition to the Irish Parliament, from the Irish

that much has been attributed to him which does not belong to him; and many a dealer in illegitimate wit, who was ashamed of acknowledging his own productions, laid his spurious offspring at his lordship's door.

As he so essentially contributed to the amusement of the public, he gradually grew into the general favor, and was held in something like the reverence which is entertained by the upper galleries for an eminent actor of farce. His performances at Nisi Prius were greatly preferable, in the decline of the Dublin stage, to any theatrical exhibition; and, as he drew exceedingly full houses, Mr. Jones [patentee of Dublin Theatre] began to look at him with some jealousy, and is said to have been advised by Mr. Sergeant Goold, who had a share of £3565 *5s.* 6¾*d.* in Crow-street Theatre, to file a bill for an injunction against the Chief-Justice, for an infringement of his patent. Lord Norbury was at the head of an excellent company. The spirit of the judge extended itself naturally enough to the counsel; and men who were grave and consid-

Catholics. Ignorant or regardless of the rules of the House of Commons, young Burke determined to present the petition himself, and in the body not at the bar of the House. He had reached the Treasury bench before he was perceived, and cries of "Privilege," and a "A stranger in the House" instantly arose. The Speaker sonorously called on the sergeant-at-arms to do his duty. Dreading arrest, Burke ran toward the bar, where he was faced by the sergeant with a drawn sword; returning, he was stopped, at the table, by the clerk. A chase ensued, the members all keeping their seats, and, at last, Burke escaped behind the Speaker's chair. In the debate which ensued, the sergeant-at-arms was blamed for not having arrested Burke at the back-door. Sir Boyle Roche asked, with much naïveté, "How could the officer stop him in the rear, while he was catching him in the front?" and emphatically declared that "no man could be in two places at one time—barring he was a bird!" When the laughter at this had subsided, Norbury (then Mr. Toler) said "A few days ago, I found an incident, like what has just now occurred, in the cross-readings of the columns of a newspaper. 'Yesterday a petition was presented to the House of Commons—it fortunately missed fire and the villain ran off.'" This renewed the mirth, and no further notice was taken of Burke's escapade. I give the sally, to show how near to the confines of wit was the apt readiness of Norbury's humor.—He had his joke to the very last. His neighbor, Lord Erne, was far advanced in years and bedridden. When his own health failed, he heard of his friend's increased illness. "James," said he to his servant, "go next door, and tell Lord Erne, with my compliments, that it will be a *dead-heat* between us."—M.

erate everywhere else, threw off all soberness and propriety, and became infected with the habits of the venerable manager of the court, the moment they entered the Common Pleas. His principal performers were Messrs. Grady, Wallace, O'Connell, and Goold, who instituted a sort of rivalry in uproar, and played against each other.

With such a judge, and such auxiliaries to co-operate with him, some idea may be formed of the attractions which were held out to that numerous class who have no fixed occupation, and by whom, in the hope of laughing hunger away, the Four Courts are frequented in Dublin. Long before Lord Norbury took his seat, the galleries were densely filled with faces strangely expressive of idleness, haggardness, and humor. At about eleven his Lordship's registrar, Mr. Peter Jackson, used to slide in with an official leer; and a little after Lord Norbury entered with a grotesque waddle, and, having bowed to the Bar, cast his eyes round the court. Perceiving a full house, an obvious expression of satisfaction pervaded his countenance; and if he saw any of his acquaintance of a noble family, such as John Claudius Beresford, who had a good deal of time on his hands, in the crowd, he ordered the tipstaff to make way for him, and, in order, I presume, to add to the dignity of the proceedings, placed him beside himself on the bench.

While the jury were swearing, he either nodded familiarly to most of them, occasionally observing, "A most respectable man;" or, if the above-mentioned celebrated member of the house of Curraghmore* chanced to be next him, was engaged in so pleasant a vein of whispering, that it was conjectured, from the heartiness of his laugh, that he must have been talking of the recreations of the Riding-house, and the amusements of 1798.† The junior counsel having opened the pleadings, Lord Norbury generally exclaimed, "A very promising young man! Jackson, what is that young gentleman's name?"—"Mr. ——, my Lord."—"What, of the county of Cork?—I

* Curraghmore, in the County of Waterford. is the seat of the Marquis of Waterford, head of the Beresford family.—M.

† The Riding-house was a place in Dublin, where Beresford used to have suspected "rebels" flogged, with cruelty, to torture them into "loyalty."—M.

knew it by his air. Sir, you are a gentleman of very high pretensions, and I protest that I have never heard the many counts stated in a more dignified manner in all my life: I hope I shall find you, like the paper before me, a Daily Freeman in my court." Having despatched the junior, whom he was sure to make the luckless, but sometimes not inappropriate victim of his encomiums, he suffered the leading counsel to proceed.

As he was considered to have a strong bias toward the plaintiff, experimental attorneys brought into the Common Pleas the very worst and most discreditable adventures in litigation. The statement of the case, therefore, generally disclosed some paltry ground of action, which, however, did not prevent his Lordship from exclaiming in the outset, "A very important action indeed! If you make out your facts in evidence, Mr. Wallace, there will be serious matter for the jury." The evidence was then produced; and the witnesses often consisted of wretches vomited out of stews and cellars, whose emaciated and discolored countenances showed their want and their depravity, while their watchful and working eyes intimated that mixture of sagacity and humor by which the lower order of Irish attestators is distinguished. They generally appeared in coats and breeches, the external decency of which, as they were hired for the occasion, was ludicrously contrasted with the ragged and filthy shirt, which Mr. Henry Deane Grady, who was well acquainted with "the inner man" of an Irish witness, though not without repeated injunctions to unbutton, at last compelled them to disclose.

The cross-examinations of this gentleman were admirable pieces of the most serviceable and dexterous extravagance. He was the Scarron of the Bar; and few of the most practised and skilful of the horde of perjurers whom he was employed to encounter, could successfully withstand the exceedingly droll and comical scrutiny through which he forced them to pass. He had a sort of "Hail fellow, well met!" manner with every varlet, which enabled him to get into his heart and core, until he had completely turned him inside out, and excited such a spirit of mirth, that the knave whom he was uncovering, could not help joining in the merriment which the detection of his villany had produced.

Lord Norbury, however, when he saw Mr. Grady pushing the plaintiff to extremities, used to come to his aid, and rally the broken recollections of the witness. This interposition called the defendant's counsel into stronger action, and they were as vigorously encountered by the counsel on the other side. Interruption created remonstrance; remonstrance called forth retort; retort generated sarcasm; and at length voices were raised so loud, and the blood of the forensic combatants was so warmed, that a general scene of confusion, to which Lord Norbury most amply contributed, took place.

The uproar gradually increased till it became tremendous; and, to add to the tumult, a question of law, which threw Lord Norbury's faculties into complete chaos, was thrown into the conflict. Mr. Grady and Mr. O'Connell shouted upon one side, Mr. Wallace and Mr. Goold upon the other, and at last, Lord Norbury, the witnesses, the counsel, the parties, and the audience, were involved in one universal riot, in which it was difficult to determine whether the laughter of the audience, the exclamations of the parties, the protestations of the witnesses, the cries of the counsel, or the bellowing of Lord Norbury, predominated. At length, however, his Lordship's superiority of lungs prevailed; and, like Æolus in his cavern (of whom, with his puffed cheeks and inflamed visage, he would furnish a painter with a model), he shouted his stormy subjects into peace. These scenes repeatedly occurred during the trial, until at last both parties had closed, and a new exhibition took place. This was Lord Norbury's monologue, commonly called a charge.

He usually began by pronouncing the loftiest encomiums upon the party in the action, against whom he intended to advise the jury to give their verdict. For this the audience were well prepared; and accordingly, after he had stated that the defendant was one of the most honorable men alive, and that he knew his father, and loved him, he suddenly came, with a most singular emphasis, which he accompanied with a strange shake of his wig, to the fatal "but," which made the audience, who were in expectation of it, burst into a fit of laughter, while he proceeded to charge, as he almost uniformly did, in the plaintiff's favor. He then entered more deeply, as he said, into the case, and, flinging his judicial robe half aside, and sometimes casting off his wig, started from his seat, and threw off a wild harangue, in which neither law, method, nor argument, could be discovered. It generally consisted of narratives connected with the history of his early life, which it was impossible to associate with the subject—of jests from Joe Miller, mixed with jokes of his own manufacture, and of sarcastic allusions to any of the counsel who had endeavored to check him during the trial. He was exceedingly fond of quotations from Milton and Shakspere, which, however out of place, were very well delivered, and evinced an excellent enunciation. At the conclusion of his charge, he made some efforts to call the attention of the jury to any leading incident which particularly struck him, but what he meant it was not very easy to conjecture; and when he sat down, the whole performance exhibited a mind which resembled a whirlpool of mud, in which law, facts, arguments, and evidence, were lost in unfathomable confusion.

Some years ago, I remember, at the close of his charges a ludicrous incident, which was a kind of practical commentary, sometimes took place. A poor maniac, well known about the Hall, whose name was "Toby M'Cormick," had been a suitor in the Common Pleas, and had lost his senses in consequence of the loss of his cause. He regularly used to attend the court, to which he was attracted by an odd fantasy:—Toby had got it into his head that he was Lord Norbury himself, having merged all consciousness of his own separate being in the strong image of his Lordship which was constantly present to his mind, while, upon the other hand, he took Lord Norbury for "Toby M'Cormick;" believing that they had made a swap of their personal identities, and exchanged their existence. This strange madman, at the end of Lord Norbury's charges, used to cry out, with some imitation of his manner, "Find for the plaintiff!" and though not intended as a sarcasm upon his habits, yet it was so just a satire that Lord Norbury was half displeased, and, turning to Peter Jackson, exclaimed, "Jackson, turn Toby M'Cormick out of court!"

I feel that, in the portrait which I have endeavored to draw of the late Chief-Justice of the Irish Common Pleas in presiding at the Nisi-Prius sittings, I have not at all come up to my original. But to describe him in such a way as to match the reality, would be, perhaps, impossible. To conceive what he was, and his stupendous extravagances, it would have been necessary to see the "θηριον αυτο," and have witnessed the prodigy itself. It is no exaggeration to say, that as the wildest farce upon the stage never raised more laughter than his exhibitions from the bench, neither could any writer of dramatic drolleries, who should undertake to draw him, embody the substantial absurdity of his character in any fictitious representation. He might have defied O'Keeffe himself; for although his law was like Lingo's Latin, yet I do not think that even O'Keeffe's genius for extravagance could have done Lord Norbury justice.

In his capacity of Judge, sitting in full court, with his three coadjutors about him, he was almost as ludicrous as in his more tumultuous office of jester at Nisi Prius.* I remember

* A few of Lord Norbury's jests, which are not in general currency, may be worth mentioning here.—Sir Philip Crampton (father of the present British Minister at Washington) was a remarkably fine-looking man, tall in stature, erect in carriage, elegant in manner, graceful in movement. In 1824, when George IV. visited

"The emerald set in the ring of the sea,"

Sir Philip was Surgeon-General of Ireland, which high position he retains. At the King's Levée, he appeared in the rich military uniform of Surgeon-General. The monarch was immediately struck with his appearance, and, turning round to Lord Norbury, who stood by his side, rubicund and burly, asked, "Who is this very handsome officer?" With the merry twinkle of his eyes which always accompanied Norbury's jokes, he answered, "May it please your Majesty, he is General of *the Lancers.*"—Lord Norbury was in Tipperary taking what he used to call his health ride. One of the county gentlemen, a Mr. Pepper, joined him, but this deponent saith not whether he was mounted on "The White Horse of the Peppers." His steed, however, was handsome and spirited, and Norbury (who was an excellent judge—of horse-flesh) paid him some compliments on the animal. "Has plenty of life—eh?" Mr. Pepper answered, "So much, that he threw me over his head, the other day."—"Named him, yet?" Mr. Pepper said that he had not. "Why, then," said the joker, "considering who you are, and how he has served you, suppose you call him

when the court presented, in his person, and in that of Judge Mayne, a most amusing and laughable contrast. Never was Rochefoucault's maxim, that "gravity is a mystery of the body to hide the defects of the mind," more strongly exemplified than in the solemn figure which sat for many years on Lord Norbury's left hand, in his administration of the law. By the profound stagnation of his calm and imperturbable visage. which improved on Gratiano's description of a grave man, and not more in stillness than in color resembled "a standing pool;" by a certain shake of his head, which, moving with the mechanical oscillation of a wooden mandarin, made him look like the image of Confucius which is plastered on the dome of the Four Courts; by his long and measured sentences, which issued in tones of oracular wisdom from his dry and ashy lips;

Pepper-caster."—Going to a Levée at Dublin Castle, with another of the judges, they slipped when ascending the stairs. "Oh, my Lord," said Norbury, as he rubbed the broadest part of his person, which had been *barked* by the fall, "you and I have tried many cases in our time, but *the hardest case of all is this staircase*."—In 1816, when Prince Leopold, who was only a Serene Highness (as only the son of a King can be addressed as Royal) was about marrying the Princess Charlotte of Wales, he was complimented by her father, then Prince Regent of England, with the title of "Royal Highness." This was spoken of before Lord Norbury, who remarked that "Marriage was the true way of making a man lose his *serenity*."—A quaker named Nott opened a large shop, exactly opposite that of Kinahan, the well-known Dublin grocer, advertised his tea as cheaper and better than any in Ireland, and declared that he would not vend any sugar, as it yielded no profit. The novelty of the concern and the excellence and low price of Nott's tea and coffee drew many customers to him and diminished the sales of Kinahan, his *vis-a-vis* neighbor. Lord Norbury went to the Quaker's, bought fourteen pounds of tea (on which the profit was large), and crossed over to Kinahan's, where he asked for a supply of sugar, on which the profits are or were nominal. While Kinahan was having the sugar weighed, Nott's porter entered the shop with the large parcel of tea for Lord Norbury. "Leave it there, on the counter," said my Lord. Then, turning to Kinahan who was dismayed at seeing one of his oldest and best customers a purchaser at his rival's, Norbury said, "I suppose, Mr. Kinahan, that *you* sell a great deal of sugar—by *Nott selling tea*."—Some thirty-five years ago, a lusty negro wench, who was called "The Hottentot Venus," was publicly exhibited in Ireland, on account of the remarkable size of her "Western Settlements." "I wonder," said Bushe, "whether she really was a Queen in her own country—as she boasts." Norbury answered, "No doubt: an *ebony ruler*, of course."—M.

by his slow and even gait, and his systematic and regulated gesture, Judge Mayne had contrived, when at the bar, to impose himself as a great lawyer on the public. When he was made a judge, upon the day on which he for the first time took his seat, Mr Keller, one of his contemporaries, and a bitter wag, came into court, and seeing him enthroned in his dignity, with his scarlet robes about him, leaned over the bar bench, and, after musing for some time, while he stretched out his shrewd sardonic face, muttered to himself, "Well, Mayne, there you are!—there you have been raised by your gravity, while my levity still sinks me here."

This pragmatical personage, who was considered deep, while he was only dark and muddy, was fixed, as if for the purposes of contrast, beside Lord Norbury, but so far from diminishing the effect of his judicial drolleries, the vapid melancholy of the one brought the vivacity of his companion into stronger light. In truth, the solemnity of Judge Mayne was nearly as comical as Lord Norbury's humor; and when, seeing a man enter the court who had forgotten to uncover, Judge Mayne rose and said, "I see you standing there like a wild beast, with your hat on,"—the pomp of utterance, and the measured dignity with which this splendid figure in Irish oratory was enunciated, excited nearly as much merriment as the purposed jokes and the ostentatious merriment of the chief of the court.

Nothing, not even Lord Norbury, could induce his brother judge to smile. His features seemed to have some inherent and natural incompatibility with laughter, which the Momus of the bench could not remove. While peals rang upon peals of merriment, and men were obliged to hold their sides, lest they should burst with excess of ridicule, Judge Mayne stood silent, starch, and composed, and never allowed his muscles of rusty iron to give way in any unmeet and extra-judicial relaxation. This union of the Allegro and Penseroso was invaluable to the seekers of fun in the Common Pleas, and it was with regret that the merry public were informed that Judge Mayne had been advised by his physicians to retire from the bench and take up his residence in France. He went, I understand, to Paris, where he used occasionally to walk, in the brilliant afternoons of that enchanting climate, in the garden of the Tuileries, and, Scott's Quentin Durward being then in vogue, Judge Mayne was taken for the spectre of Trois Echelles

The place of Judge Mayne was latterly supplied by a very able man and an excellent lawyer, Mr. Justice Johnson; and then a scene of a different character, but still exceedingly amusing, was afforded. Lord Norbury was now most unhappily situated, for he had Judge Fletcher upon one hand and Judge Johnson upon the other. The former was a man of an uncommonly vigorous and brawny mind, with a rude but powerful grasp of thought, and with considerable acquirements, both in literature and in his profession. He was destitute of all elegance, either mental or external, but made up for the deficiency by the massive and robust character of his understanding. He had been a devoted Whig at the bar, and hated Lord Norbury for his politics, while he held his intellect in contempt. Dissimulation was not among his attributes; and, as his indifferent health produced a great infirmity of temper (for he was the converse of what a Frenchman defines as a happy man, and had a bad stomach and a good heart), he was at no pains in concealing his disrelish for his brother on the bench. Judge Johnson, who occupied the seat on Lord Norbury's left hand, completed his misfortunes in juxtaposition. There is nothing whatever about Judge Johnson to be laughed at, although his bursts of temperament may sometimes prevoke a smile; but, in adding to Lord Norbury's calamities, he augmented the diversions of the court. He was less habitually atrabilious than Judge Fletcher,* whose characteristic was moroseness

* In the rampant times of "Protestant Ascendency in Church and State," when the government policy was to report Ireland in a state of insurrectionary feeling, and within a hair's-breadth of actual rebellions (so as to justify coercive Acts of Parliament, with which to keep the people quiet), Judge Fletcher gave immense offence to the ruling powers by his charges to Grand Juries, on Circuit, in which he always stated, that if they were rightly governed the Irish would be as well conducted as any people on earth. He used to tell the country-gentlemen, too, that whenever a county, or a district, became disturbed, the great probability was that the landlords' oppressions (though middlemen) or neglect of duty caused the evil. — M.

rather than irritability, but he had an honest vehemence and impetuosity about him, which, whenever his sense of propriety was violated, he could not restrain.

When the Chief-Justice, who was thus disastrously placed, was giving judgment (if the *olla-podrida* which he served up for the general entertainment can be so called), the spectacle derived from the aspect of his brother-judges furnished a vast accession of amusement. Judge Fletcher, indignant at all the absurdity which was thrown up by Lord Norbury, and which bespattered the bench, began expressing his disgust by the character of bilious severity which spread over his countenance, of which the main characteristic was a fierce sourness and a scornful discontent. Judge Johnson, on the other hand, endeavored to conceal his anger, and, placing his elbows on the bench, and thrusting his clinched hands upon his mouth, tried to stifle the indignation, with which, however, it was obvious that he was beginning to tumefy. After a little while, a growl was heard from Judge Fletcher, while Judge Johnson responded with a groan. But, undeterred by any such gentle admonition, their incomparable brother, with a desperate intrepidity, held on his way.

Judge Fletcher had a habit, when exceedingly displeased, of rocking himself in his seat; and, as he was of a considerable bulk, his swinging, which was known to be an intimation of his augmenting anger, was familiar to the bar. As Lord Norbury advanced, the oscillations, accompanied with a deeper growling, described a greater segment of a circle, and shook the whole bench; while Judge Johnson, with his shaggy brows bent and contracted over his face, and with his eyes flashing with passion, used, with an occasional exclamation of mingled indignation and disgust, to turn himself violently round. Still, on Lord Norbury went; until at length, Judge Fletcher, by his pendulous vibrations, came into actual collision with him upon one side, and Judge Johnson, by his averted shrug, hit him on the shoulder upon the other; when, awakened by the simultaneous shock, his Lordship gave a start, and, looking round the bar, who were roaring with laughter at the whole proceeding, discharged two or three puffs; and, felicitating his brothers on their urbanity and good manners, in revenge for their contumelious estimate of his talents, generally called on the tipstaff to bring him a judicial convenience, and, turning to the wall of the court, retaliated from the bench for the aspersions which they had cast upon him. From one of these two formidable commentators he was latterly relieved, and although Judge Johnson remained beside him, still, in the absence of Judge Fletcher as an auxiliary, he became latterly somewhat mitigated; while Judge Moore, during the Chief-Justice's legal expositions, did no more than intimate his feelings by a look of good-natured commiseration; and Judge Torrens* turned a polite and fastidious smile, full of the gracefulness of the Horse-Guards, upon his noble and learned brother.

Such was Lord Norbury as a Judge. It remains to say a few words of him as a politician. It is almost unnecessary to state that, with such intellectual endowments, he did not coincide with Grattan, and Curran, and Plunket, and Bushe, in the views which were taken by those inferior persons of the interest of their country, but that he agreed in principle and in feeling with Doctor Duigenan, Mr. Dawson, and Sir George Hill,†

* James Torrens, senior puisne judge of the Common Pleas in Ireland, is brother to the late Sir Henry Torrens, who accompanied "The Duke" (then Sir Arthur Wellesley), to Portugal, acted as his Military Secretary, finally (in 1820) became an Adjutant-General of the British army, was the intimate confidant of the Duke of York, and died in 1828.—This relationship, backed by his own reputation as a lawyer, obtained Mr. Torrens' advancement to the bench.—M.

† Sir George Hill and Mr. George Robert Dawson were the Protestant Ascendency members for the city of Londonderry. The name of the former will be recollected, not for any merits of him who bore it, but in connection with the arrest of Tone. In September, 1798, Tone, then holding a military commission under the French Directory, went to make a descent upon Ireland, with three thousand men, and a small naval force under Admiral Bompert. The expedition was met by a British squadron under Admiral Warren. A battle ensued, and, after a gallant combat of six hours' duration, the French were defeated. Tone, who had commanded a battery on board the Admiral's ship, was among the captured officers. He was not recognised—perhaps some who knew him generously avoided doing so. It was suspected that he was of the party. Sir George Hill, his fellow-student at Trinity college, *volunteered* to identify him. While the prisoners were breakfasting with the Earl of Cavan, they were disturbed by Hill and a party of police-officers. Stepping up to Tone, he

and the rest of the illustrious statesmen by whom the cause of Ascendency has been so firmly and so appropriately supported. Lord Norbury was an excellent and uniform Protestant. This was always well known in Ireland, but, his buffoonery having swollen up and concealed the other traits of his character, little notice was taken of his personal predilections.

It was, indeed, his habit to deliver orations to the grand-jury upon the church and state in the home circuit; and in reference to I. K. L.* he often poured out a tirade against "Moll Doyle," one of the wild personifications of agrarian insurrection in the south of Ireland; but, however indecorous these allusions were deemed in a Chief-Justice, the people were so much accustomed to laugh at his Lordship, that even where there was good cause for remonstrance, they could not be prevailed on to regard anything he did in a serious way. As *carte blanche* is given to Grimaldi,† the public allowed Lord Norbury an unlimited license; and in law, politics, and religion, never placed any restraint upon him. At length, however, an

said, "Mr. Tone, I am *very happy* to see you." With much composure Tone replied that he was happy to see Sir George, and politely inquired after Lady Hill. Tone was taken into another room, ironed, sent off to Dublin, tried by court-martial, and sentenced to death, which he anticipated by suicide.—George Robert Dawson, married to Sir Robert Peel's sister, held office under the Duke of Wellington's Administration, and had long been a decided opponent of the Catholic Claims. In 1828, at a Corporation dinner, in Londonderry, he ventured to hint that it might be better to settle the Catholic question, by fair concession, than hazard civil war by continuing to oppose it. This, at such a meeting, was received with groans and hisses. The Orange press denounced Dawson as a traitor—but more rational politicians felt that a Government official would never have uttered such words, except with some knowledge of a coming change of measures, and this was confirmed by Dawson's continuing in office. It was seen that something was in agitation, and that Dawson's speech was a *feeler*. A few months after this, Catholic Emancipation was granted.—Mr. Dawson, who is an excellent man of business, uniting talent with industry, and conscientious principle with both, is now Deputy-Chairman of the Commissioners of Customs, in England.—M.

* The late Dr. Doyle, Catholic Bishop of Kildare and Leighlin.—M.

† Joseph Grimaldi, born in 1779, and deceased in 1837, was noted and poppular, in London, for forty years, as an unrivalled pantomimic clown at the theatres. His biographer speaks of a "rich and (paradoxical as the term may seem) *intellectual* buffoonery, peculiarly his own—portraying to the life all that is grotesque in manners, or droll in action."—M.

event occurred which awakened the general notice; and, as there was another and a very obnoxious individual concerned, excited among the Roman Catholics universal indignation.

Lord Norbury has been always remarkable for his frugality. He was in the habit of stuffing papers into the old chairs in his study, in order to supply the deficiency of horse-hair which the incumbency of eighty years had produced in their bottoms. At last, however, they became, even with the aid of this occasional supplement, unfit for use, and were sent by his Lordship to a shop in which old furniture was advertised to be bought and sold. An individual of the name of Monaghan got one of these chairs into his possession, and, finding it stuffed with papers, drew them out. He had been a clerk in an attorney's office, and knew Mr. Saurin's handwriting. He perceived, by the superscription of a letter, that it was written by the Attorney-General, and on opening it he found the following words addressed to a Chief-Justice, and a going Judge of assize, by the principal law-officer of the Crown:—

"DUBLIN CASTLE, *August* 9.

"I transcribe for you a very sensible part of Lord Ross's* letter to me. 'As, Lord Norbury goes our circuit, and as he is personally acquainted with the

---

* Lord Ross, who advises Mr. Saurin to adopt the course which he so faithfully pursued, was once Sir Laurence Parsons, and was in the habit of speaking in the Irish House of Commons in favor of emancipation. He was not only an orator, but a poet. In the appendix to the first volume of "Wolfe Tone's Memoirs," a poem is inserted, which would have entitled him to the place of Laureate to the United Irishmen. The following are the opening lines:—

"How long, O Slavery! shall thine iron mace
Wave o'er this isle, and crouch its abject race?
Full many a dastard century we've bent
Beneath thy terrors, wretched and content.

"What though with haughty arrogance of pride
England shall o'er this long-duped country stride,
And lay on stripe on stripe, and shame on shame,
And brand to all eternity its name:

"'Tis right, well done, bear all and more, I say,
Nay, ten times more, and then for more still pray!
What state in something would not foremost be?
She strives for fame, thou for servility."

[The present Earl of Rosse, born in 1800, confers a lustre on the title far greater than what he derives from it. His successful devotion to the physical

gentlemen of our county, a hint to him may be of use. He is in the habit of talking individually to them in his chamber at Phillipstown; and if he were to impress on them the consequence of the measure, viz., that however they may think otherwise, the Catholics would, in spite of them, elect Catholic members (if such were eligible), that the Catholic members would then have the nomination of sheriffs, and in many instances, perhaps of the judges; and the Protestants would be put in the back-ground, as the Protestants were formerly; I think he would bring the effect of the measure home to themselves, and satisfy them that they could scarcely submit to live in the country if it were passed.' So far Lord Ross. But what he suggests in another part of his letter, that 'if Protestant gentlemen, who have votes and influence and interest, would give these venal members to understand that if they will purchase Catholic votes by betraying their country and its constitution, they shall infallibly lose theirs; it would alter their conduct, though it could neither make them honest or respectable. If you will *judiciously administer* [*!!*] *a little of this medicine* to the King's County, and other members of Parliament, that may fall in your way, you will deserve well. Many thanks for your letter, and its good intelligence from Maryborough. Jebb is a most valuable fellow, and of the sort that is most wanted.'

"Affectionately and truly yours,

"WILLIAM SAURIN."

When this letter was first disclosed, it was vehemently asserted by Mr. Saurin's friends, that a man of his fame and constitutional principles could not have written it, and they alleged that it was a mere fabrication; but afterward, when the handwriting was perceived to be indisputable, and the author of the letter did not dare to deny its authenticity, Mr. Peel, and the other advocates of Mr. Saurin, contented themselves with exclaiming against the mere impropriety of its production. From this ground of imputation they were, however, effectually driven by Mr. Brougham,† when he called to the Minister's recollection, and especially to that of the Secretary of the Home Department, whom it chiefly concerned, the foul

sciences, especially to optics and astronomy, has given him high place among the knowledge-seekers of the age. In 1849, Lord Rosse was elected President of the Royal Society of England.—M.

† Mr. Brougham laid a trap for Mr. Peel. The writer of this article was told, upon good authority, that he introduced Mr. Saurin's letter into the debate, in order to allure Mr. Peel into a censure of the use which had been made of it. The latter fell into the snare, and the moment he began to inveigh against the production of the letter, Mr. Brougham, who had been intently and impatiently watching him, slapped his knee, and cried, "I have him!"

means adopted to get at evidence against the Queen.* Since that time we have heard no more of the violation of all good feeling in the Catholics, when they availed themselves of a document in the handwriting of an Attorney-General, in order to establish the fact which had been frequently insisted on, that poison had been poured into the highest sources of justice.

The moral indignation of Protestants has subsided, but they have not recovered from their astonishment, that a man so cautious and deliberate as William Saurin, should have put himself in the power of such a person as Lord Norbury, and intrusted him with a communication, which has eventually proved so fatal to himself. He must have known the habits of the man, and it is difficult to conceive how he could look upon the alliance of so singular an individual as of importance to his party, or regard him as likely to produce any impression upon the grand juries to which his loyal exhortations were to be addressed.

The discovery of this letter has been of great prejudice to Mr. Saurin, as it renders it impossible to promote him, with any sort of decency, after such a proceeding; but it was of use to Lord Norbury. When his incompetence in his office was mentioned in Parliament, the Orange faction considered

* The manner which the evidence against Queen Caroline, consort of George IV., was got up by the British Government was illegal. The scale of payment was in a manner regulated by the extent of the evidence given! The more damning the testimony, the greater the reward.—There always has been a popular belief in England (though the fact was denied, as if on authority, by Fox, in Parliament), that George IV. was married, previous to his union with Caroline of Brunswick, to Mrs. Fitzherbert—the lady described as "fat, fair, and forty," when he first met her. It was on this marriage, and the subsequent royal repudiation of the lady, that Moore wrote the Irish Melody, "When first I met thee, warm and young," which Byron was fond of chanting, in his solitary hours at Venice, where (to use his own words) "like a hunted stag, he had taken to the waters, and there stood at bay."—Queen Caroline had her joke on the *liaison* or marriage (whichever it might be) with Mrs. Fitzherbert, and said, in 1820, "I never was guilty of adultery but once—and that was with Mrs. Fitzherbert's husband!" Another of her hits was her saying, when asked, on her return to England, where she intended to stop in London, "I think I shall take a *chop* at the *King's Head*."—M.

themselves bound by that principle of fidelity to each other, by which, to do them justice, they are characterized to support a very zealous, if not a very respectable partisan; and accordingly Mr. Goulburn, with the effrontery which distinguishes him, pronounced a panegyric upon his judicial excellences, and stated (to the great and just indignation of the other judges of the Common Pleas) that in a difficult and complicated case he had evinced more knowledge and astuteness than any of them. To this encomium, Mr. Peel, with all his manliness, and although he values himself on his reformation of the abuses of justice, gave his sanction. Lord Norbury, finding himself sustained by his party in the House of Commons, turned a deaf ear to all private solicitations, of which his resignation was the object.*

At length Mr. O'Connell presented a petition for his removal, setting forth, among other grounds, that he had fallen asleep during the trial of a murder case, and was unable to give any account of the evidence, when called on for his notes by the Lord Lieutenant. Mr. Scarlett,† to whom the petition was

* When it was determined to give Lord Norbury a hint that it was time to retire, the task — which was one of delicacy, if not of peril — was confided to William Gregory, then under-secretary for Ireland. Norbury got scent of the object of his visit, and, the moment he appeared, locked the door, with a confidential and grave air, and said, "You are one of my best and oldest friends. I was just writing for you to come here, when I heard your voice. I am told that I am to be insulted — that they mean to ask me to resign. The mock-monarch in Phœnix Park is irresponsible, but the hack that he sends shall be his proxy. I'll have his life, or he'll have mine — ay, if he were my brother. My old friend Gregory, you will stand by me? Here are the hair-triggers." Here he opened his pistol-case. "Here they are, as ready now as when they blazed at Fitzgerald, and almost frightened Napper Tandy out of his skin. Stay and dine with me, and we'll talk it over."—Peaceable Mr. Gregory declined the invitation, but did *not* perform his mission. That, however, was done by letter from Peel, who was then Home Secretary. The rest of the story, as to the forced resignation, is exactly as Mr. Sheil tells it. Norbury made good terms — two steps in the peerage (he was raised from the dignity of Baron to that of Viscount and Earl), and a pension of four thousand pounds a year.— M.

† James Scarlett, afterward Lord Abinger, was more distinguished as an advocate than a judge. Born in Jamaica, in 1769 (his brother was Chief-Justice of the island), Mr. Scarlett was called to the English Bar, in 1791, closely and patiently studied the law (chiefly making himself acquainted with the mod-

intrusted, did not move upon it, in consequence of a personal assurance from Mr. Peel, that he would do everything in his power to induce him, of his own accord, to retire. For although Mr. Peel ostensibly defended him as a friend and partisan, yet he was, in reality, ashamed of such an incubus upon the bench. Lord Norbury at last went so far as to intimate that he would consult his friends on the subject, and required a reasonable time to do so, which was accordingly granted. After the lapse of a month, Mr. Goulburn called again to know the result of his deliberations, when his lordship stated that Lord Combermere was his most particular friend, and that he had written to him at Calcutta. Mr. Goulburn, finding himself thus evaded, and being conscious that he was as well qualified at eighty-six as he had ever been (for no increased hallucination is perceptible about him), was a good deal at a loss what to do. But suddenly Mr. Canning became lord of the ascendant; and Lord Norbury, who never wanted sagacity, feeling that under the new system he could not expect the support of ministers, wisely came into terms; and having stipulated for an earldom, as a consideration, resigned in favor of Lord Plun-

ern reports), chose the northern circuit, and became distinguished, almost from starting, for his knowledge of law and his dexterous examination of witnesses. In 1816, he was made King's Counsel, and entered Parliament, as a Whig, in 1818. He was not a good debater and did not shine as a senator. His votes were on the liberal side, and he supported the attempts of Romilly and Macintosh to ameliorate the Draconian severity of the criminal code. Under Canning's administration, in 1827, Mr. Scarlett was made Solicitor-General and knighted. He retained office under the Wellington Cabinet—changing his political opinions, much to the damage of his popularity. When Catholic Emancipation was granted, in 1829, he succeeded to the office of Attorney-General, vacated by Sir Charles Wetherell, who was hostile to the measure, and earned additional unpopularity by a crusade against the press. For this, he was introduced into Bulwer's *Paul Clifford*, as "Scarlett Jem, good at a press." When his old friends, the Whigs, came into office in 1830, they cashiered their quondam ally. But, in 1834, under Peel's premiership, Sir James Scarlett was made Chief-Baron of the Exchequer, and raised to the peerage. Latterly, ill health made his temper irritable. He had to preside, in 1841, at the trial of certain Chartists charged with sedition, and exhibited such an angry partisan feeling against them as to cause much public disapprobation, and some parliamentary censure. He died, in 1844, in his seventy-fifth year.—M.

ket, who, like an unskilful aëronaut, has made a bad descent into the Common Pleas.*

Thus had this man, without talent, or knowledge, or anything to recommend him, beyond his personal and animal spirit, to the favor of government, raised himself to a high station on the bench, which he enjoyed for seven-and-twenty years; and now, laden with wealth, effects his retreat through a loftier grade in the peerage. He has accumulated an immense fortune, partly from the lucrative offices of which he was so long in the enjoyment, and partly through his rigid economy. I ought not, however, to omit that, parsimonious as his habits are, still they do not prevent him from exercising the best kind of charity, for he is an excellent landlord. In his dealings with his inferiors, too (I gladly avail myself of the opportunity of bestowing on him such praise as he deserves), he is kind and considerate; and toward his domestics is a gentle and forbearing master. In his deportment to the Bar, too, he was undeviatingly polite, and never forgot that he was himself a member of the profession, on which the recollection of every judge should forbid him to trample. In private society, he is a most agreeable, although a very grotesque companion.

He is not wholly destitute of literature; having a great

* John Toler, who died Earl and Baron Norbury and Viscount Glandine (having also obtained a distinct peerage for his wife), was born in 1745, and was the son of a country gentleman in Tipperary. He was called to the Irish bar in 1770; entered Parliament in 1776; obtained a silk gown in 1781; was made Solicitor-General in 1789; succeeded Wolfe as Attorney-General, in 1798, was made Chief-Justice of the Common Pleas in 1800, being created Baron Norbury; retired in 1827, bargaining for two steps in the peerage, and a pension of four thousand pounds sterling a year; and died in July, 1831, aged eighty-six. Perhaps no one ever wore the ermine so wholly unqualified for its dignity and responsibility, as Lord Norbury. So cruel, that he was called "the hanging judge;" so indecorous, that he would jest, even at the expense of the wretch he was dooming to the gallows; so callous, that public reprobation never galled him; so partial, that power, however unjust, might count upon his assistance; so bad a lawyer, that the merest tyro in the profession had often to set him right. Truly was it said, when he died, "Mercy droops not beside his tomb; nor will justice, eloquence, or learning, stretch themselves within it." In a word, among bad men, at a time when oppression and injustice prevailed, one of the very worst was this wicked judge, Lord Norbury.—M.

memory, he is fond of repeating passages from the older poets, which he recites with propriety and force. Of modern authors he is wholly ignorant, nor is a new book to be found in his library. His study presents, indeed, a curious spectacle. In the centre of the room lies a heap of old papers, covered with dust, mingled with political pamphlets, written some forty years ago, together with an odd volume of the "Irish Parliamentary Debates," recording the speeches of Mr. Sergeant Toler. On the shelves, which are half empty, and exhibit a most "beggarly account," there are some forty moth-eaten law-books; and by their side appear odd volumes of "Peregrine Pickle," and "Roderick Random," with the "Newgate Calendar," complete. A couple of wornout saddles, with rusty stirrups, hang from the top of one of the bookcases, which are enveloped with cobwebs; and a long line of veteran boots of mouldy leather are arrayed on the opposite side of the room. King William's picture stands over the chimney-piece, with prints of Eclipse and other celebrated racers, from which his lordship's politics, and other predilections, may be collected.

He was a remarkably good horseman, and even now always appears well mounted in the streets. A servant, dressed in an ancient livery, rides close beside him; and by his very proximity and care, assists a certain association with loneliness which has begun to attend him. He has, in truth, assumed of late a very dreary and desolate aspect. When he rode to court, as he did every day while a judge, he exhibited, for his time of life, great alacrity and spirit; and as he passed by Mr. Joy, whom he looked upon as his probable successor, putting spurs to his horse, he cantered rapidly along. But now he is without occupation or pursuit, and looks alone in the world. His gayety is gone, and when he stops an old acquaintance in the street to inquire how the world wags, his voice and manner exhibit a certain wandering and oblivion, while his face seems at once dull, melancholy, and abstracted.

Sometimes he rides beyond Dublin, and is to be met in lonely and unfrequented roads, looking as if he was musing over mournful recollections, or approaching to a suspension of all thought. Not many days ago, on my return to town from a short excursion in the country, as the evening drew on, I saw him riding near a cemetery, while the chill breezes of October were beginning to grow bitter, and the leaves were falling rapidly from the old and withered trees in the adjoining churchyard. The wind had an additional bleakness as it blew over the residences of the dead; and although it imparted to his red and manly cheeks a stronger flush, still, as it stirred his gray locks, it seemed with its wintry murmurs to whisper to the old man a funeral admonition. He appeared, as he urged on his horse and tried to hurry from so dismal a scene, to shrink and huddle himself from the blast. In anticipation of an event, which can not be remote (while I forgot all his political errors, and only remembered how often he had beguiled a tedious hour, and set the Four Courts in a roar), I could not help muttering, as I passed him, with some feeling of regret, "Alas, poor Yorick!"

CLONMEL ASSIZES.

The delineation of the leading members of the Irish bar is not the only object of these sketches. It is my purpose to describe the striking scenes, and to record the remarkable incidents, which fall within my own forensic observation. That these incidents and scenes should take place in our courts of justice, affords a sufficient justification for making the "Sketches of the Irish Bar" the medium of their narration. I might also suggest that the character of the bar itself is more or less influenced by the nature of the business in which it is engaged. The mind of any man who habitually attends the assizes of Clonmel carries deep, and not perhaps the most useful, impressions away from it. How often have I reproached myself with having joined in the boisterous merriment which either the jests of counsel or the droll perjuries of the witnesses have produced during the trial of a capital offence! How often have I seen the bench, the jury, the bar, and the galleries, of an Irish court of justice, in a roar of tumultuous laughter, while I beheld in the dock the wild and haggard face of a wretch who, placed on the verge of eternity, seemed to be surveying the gulf on the brink of which he stood, and presented, in his ghastly aspect and motionless demeanor, a reproof of the spirit of hilarity with which he was to be sent before his God!

It is not that there is any kind of cruelty intermixed with this tendency to mirth; but that the perpetual recurrence of incidents of the most awful character divests them of the power of producing effect, and that they—

"Whose fell of hair
Would at a dismal treatise rouse and stir
As life were in 't"—

acquire such a familiarity with direness, that they become not only insensible to the dreadful nature of the spectacles which are presented, but scarcely conscious of them. But it is not merely because the bar itself is under the operation of the incidents which furnish the materials of their professional occupation that I have selected the last assizes at Clonmel as the subject of this article. The extensive circulation of this periodical work affords the opportunity of putting the English public in possession of many illustrative facts; and in narrating the events which attended the murder of Daniel Mara, and the trial of his assassins, I propose to myself the useful end of fixing the general attention upon a state of things which ought to lead all wise and good men to the consideration of the only effectual means by which the evils which result from the moral condition of the country may be remedied.*

In the month of April, 1827, a gentleman of the name of Chadwick was murdered in the open day, at a place called Rath Cannon, in the immediate vicinity of the old Abbey of Holycross. Mr. Chadwick was the member of an influential family, and was employed as land-agent in collecting their rents. The person who fills this office in England is called "a steward;" but in Ireland it is designated by the more honorable name of a land-agency. The discharge of the duties of this situation must be always more or less obnoxious. In times of public distress, the landlord, who is himself urged by his own creditors, urges his agent on, and the latter inflicts upon the tenants the necessities of his employer.

I have heard that Mr. Chadwick was not peculiarly rigorous in the exaction of rent, but he was singularly injudicious in his demeanor toward the lower orders. He believed that they detested him; and, possessing personal courage, bade them defiance. He was not a man of a bad heart; but was despotic and contumelious in his manners to those whose hatred he returned with contempt. It is said that he used to stand among a body of the peasantry, and, observing that his corpulency was on the increase, was accustomed to exclaim, "I think I am fattening upon your curses!" In answer to these taunts,

* This sketch was published in July, 1828.—M.

the peasants who surrounded him, and who were well habituated to the concealment of their fierce and terrible passions, affected to laugh, and said that "his honor was mighty pleasant; and sure his honor, God bless him, was always fond of his joke!" But while they indulged in the sycophancy under which they are wont to smother their sanguinary detestations, they were lying in wait for the occasion of revenge. Perhaps, however, they would not have proceeded to the extremities to which they had recourse, but for a determination evinced by Mr. Chadwick to take effectual means for keeping them in awe. He set about building a police-barrack at Rath Cannon. It was resolved that Mr. Chadwick should die.

This decision was not the result of individual vengeance. The wide confederacy into which the lower orders are organized in Tipperary held council upon him, and the village areopagus pronounced his sentence. It remained to find an executioner.

Patrick Grace, who was almost a boy, but was distinguished by various feats of guilty courage, offered himself as a volunteer in what was regarded by him as an honorable cause. He had set up in the county as a sort of knight-errant against landlords; and, in the spirit of a barbarous chivalry, proffered his gratuitous services wherever what he conceived to be a wrong was to be redressed. He proceeded to Rath Cannon; and, without adopting any sort of precaution, and while the public road was traversed by numerous passengers, in the broad daylight, and just beside the barrack, in the construction of which Mr. Chadwick was engaged, shot that unfortunate gentleman, who fell instantly dead.

This dreadful crime produced a great sensation, not only in the county where it was perpetrated, but through the whole of Ireland. When it was announced in Dublin, it created a sort of dismay, as it evinced the spirit of atrocious intrepidity to which the peasantry had been roused. It was justly accounted, by those who looked upon this savage assassination with most horror, as furnishing evidence of the moral condition of the people, and as intimating the consequences which might be anticipated from the ferocity of the peasantry, if ever they should be let loose. Patrick Grace calculated on impunity; but his confidence in the power and terrors of the confederacy with which he was associated was mistaken. A brave, and a religious man, whose name was Philip Mara, was present at the murder. He was standing beside his employer, Mr. Chadwick, and saw Grace put him deliberately to death. Grace was well aware that Mara had seen him, but did not believe that he would dare to give evidence against him. It is probable, too, that he conjectured that Mara coincided with him in his ethics of assassination, and applauded the proceeding. Mara, however, who was a moral and virtuous man, was horror-struck by what he had beheld; and, under the influence of conscientious feelings, gave immediate information to a magistrate. Patrick Grace was arrested, and tried at the summer assizes of 1827.

I was not present at his trial, but have heard from good authority that he displayed a fearless demeanor; and that when he was convicted upon the evidence of Philip Mara, he declared that before a year should go by he should have vengeance in the grave. He was ordered to be executed near the spot where his misdeed had been perpetrated. This was a signal mistake, and produced an effect exactly the reverse of what was contemplated. The lower orders looked upon him as a martyr; and his deportment, personal beauty, and undaunted courage, rendered him an object of deep interest and sympathy upon the scaffold. He was attended by a body of troops to the old Abbey of Holycross, where not less than fifteen thousand people assembled to behold him.

The site of the execution rendered the spectacle a most striking one. The Abbey of Holycross is the finest and most venerable monastic ruin in Ireland. Most travellers turn from their way to survey it, and leave it with a deep impression of its solemnity and grandeur. A vast multitude was assembled round the scaffold. The prisoner was brought forward in the midst of the profound silence of the people. He ascended and surveyed them; and looked upon the ruins of the edifice which had once been dedicated to the worship of his religion, and to the sepulchres of the dead which were strewed among its aisles, and had been for ages as he was in a few minutes about to be. It was not known whether he would call for vengeance from his survivors, or for mercy from Heaven. His kindred, his close friends, his early companions, all that he loved, and all to whom he was dear, were around him, and nothing, except a universal sob from his female relatives, disturbed the awful taciturnity that prevailed. At the side of Patrick Grace stood the priest — the mild admonitor of the heart, the soother of affliction, and the preceptor of forgiveness — who attended him in the last office of humanity, and who proved by the result how well he had performed it.

To the disappointment of the people, Patrick Grace expressed himself profoundly contrite; and, although he evinced no fear of death, at the instance of the Roman Catholic clergyman who attended him, implored the people to take warning by his example. In a few moments after, he left existence. But the effect of his execution will be estimated by this remarkable incident. His gloves were handed by one of his relations to an old man of the name of John Russel, as a keepsake. Russel drew them on, and declared at the same time that he should wear them "till Paddy Grace was revenged;" and revenged he soon afterward was, within the time which he had himself prescribed for retribution, and in a manner which is as much calculated to excite astonishment at the strangeness, as detestation for the atrocity of the crime, of which I proceed to narrate the details.

Philip Mara was removed by Government from the country. It was perfectly obvious that, if he had continued to sojourn in Tipperary, his life would have been taken speedily, and at all hazards, away. It was decided that all his kindred should be exterminated. He had three brothers; and the bare consanguinity with a traitor (for his crime was treason) was regarded as a sufficient offence to justify their immolation. If they could not procure his own blood for the purposes of sacrifice, it was however something to make libation of that which flowed from the same source. The crimes of the Irish are derived from the same origin as their virtues. They have powerful domestic attachments. Their love and devotion to their kindred instruct them in the worst expedients of atrocity. Knowing the affection which Mara had for his brothers, they found the way to his heart in the kindest instincts of humanity; and, from the consciousness of the pain which the murder of "his mother's children" would inflict, determined that he should endure it.

It must be owned that there is a dreadful policy in this system. The Government may withdraw their witnesses from the country, and afford them protection; but their wives, their offspring, their parents, their brothers, sisters, nay their remotest relatives, can not be secure, and the vengeance of the ferocious peasantry, if defrauded of its more immediate and natural object, will satiate itself with some other victim. It was in conformity with these atrocious principles of revenge that the murder of the brothers of Philip Mara was resolved upon. Strange to tell, the whole body of the peasantry in the neighborhood of Rath Cannon, and far beyond it, entered into a league, for the perpetration of this abominable crime; and while the individuals who were marked out for massacre were unconscious of what was going forward, scarcely a man, woman, or child, looked them in the face who did not know that they were marked out for death.

They were masons by trade, and were employed in building the barrack at Rath Cannon, on the spot where Chadwick had been assassinated, and where the funeral of Patrick Grace (for so his execution was called) had been performed. The peasantry looked in all probability with an evil eye upon every man who had put his hand to this obnoxious work; but their main object was the extermination of Philip Mara's brothers. They were three in number—Daniel, Laurence, and Timothy. On the first of October they were at work, with an apprentice in the mason trade, at the barrack at Rath Cannon. The name of this apprentice was Hickey. In the evening, about five o'clock, they left off their work, and were returning homeward, when eight men with arms rushed upon them. They were fired at; but the firearms of the assassins were in such bad condition, that the discharge of their rude musketry had no effect. Laurence, Timothy, and the apprentice, fled in different directions, and escaped. Daniel Mara lost his presence of mind, and instead of taking the same route as the others, ran into the house of a poor widow. He was pursued by the murderers, one of whom got in by a small window, while the others burst through the door, and with circumstances of great savageness put him to death.

The intelligence of this event produced a still greater sensation than the murder of Chadwick; and was as much the subject of comment as some great political incident, fraught with national consequences, in the metropolis. The Government lost no time in issuing proclamations, offering a reward of two thousand pounds sterling for information which should bring the assassins to justice. The magnitude of the sum induced the hope that its temptation would be found irresistible to poverty and destitution so great as that which prevails among the class of ordinary malefactors. It was well known that hundreds had cognizance of the offence; and it was concluded that, among so numerous a body, the tender of so large a reward could not fail to offer an effectual allurement. Weeks, however, passed over without the communication of intelligence of any kind. Several persons were arrested on suspicion, but were afterward discharged, as no more than mere conjecture could be adduced against them.

Mr. Doherty, the Solicitor-General, proceeded to the county of Tipperary, in order to investigate the transaction; but for a considerable time all his scrutiny was without avail. At length, however, an individual of the name of Thomas Fitzgerald was committed to jail upon a charge of highway robbery, and, in order to save his life, furnished evidence upon which the Government was enabled to pierce into the mysteries of delinquency. The moment Fitzgerald unsealed his lips, a numerous horde of malefactors were taken up, and further revealments were made under the influence which the love of life, and not of money, exercised over their minds. The assizes came on; and on Monday, the 31st of March [1828], Patrick Lacy and John Walsh were placed at the bar, and to the indictment for the murder of Daniel Mara pleaded not guilty.

The Court presented a very imposing spectacle. The whole

body of the gentry of Tipperary were assembled in order to witness a trial on which the security of life and property was to depend. The box which is devoted to the grand-jury was thronged with the aristocracy of the county, who manifested an anxiety far stronger than the trial of an ordinary culprit is accustomed to produce. An immense crowd of the peasantry was gathered round the dock. All appeared to feel a deep interest in what was to take place, but it was easy to perceive in the diversity of solicitude which was expressed upon their faces, the degrees of sympathy which connected them with the prisoners at the bar. The more immediate kindred of the malefactors were distinguishable, by their profound but still emotion, from those who were engaged in the same extensive organization, and were actuated by a selfish sense that their personal interests were at stake, without having their more tender affections involved in the result.

But besides the relatives and confederates of the prisoners, there was a third class among the spectators, in which another shade of sympathy was observable. These were the mass of the peasantry, who had no direct concern with the transaction, but whose principles and habits made them well-wishers to the men who had put their lives in peril for what was regarded as the common cause. Through the crowd were dispersed a number of policemen, whose green regimentals, high caps, and glittering bayonets, made them conspicuous, and brought them into contrast with the peasants by whom they were surrounded. On the table stood the governor of the jail, with his ponderous keys, which designated his office, and presented to the mind associations which aided the effect of the scene.

Mr. Justice Moore appeared in his red robes lined with black, and intimated by his aspect that he anticipated the discharge of a dreadful duty. Beside him was placed the Earl of Kingston,* who had come from the neighboring county of Cork to

* Mr. Sheil's description of the late Earl of Kingston is very accurate, but words can not paint the brutality of this man's appearance. When I was a lad, I often saw him, as he was Chairman of the Magistrates at the Sessions, in Fermoy, where I was educated—one schoolmate being Francis Hincks, now of Canada, and the schoolmaster being Dr. Hincks, his father. The Earl

witness the trial, and whose great possessions gave him a peculiar concern in tracing to their sources the disturbances which had already a formidable character, and intimated still more

of Kingston was an immense man, bulky and burly, with his features almost hidden in a mass of dark whiskers, and his deep-set eyes glaring beneath shaggy, black eyebrows, and a forehead "villanous low." His voice, that all might be *en suite*, was at once deep and loud. I never saw a man who had a more brutal appearance. He took large quantities of snuff, which he carried loose in a waistcoat-pocket lined with tin, and his method was to take small handfuls of it, throw part of it up into his immense nostrils, and fling away the remainder over his left shoulder—the consequence of which was, that nobody who knew him would sit upon that side. When he was a young man, he held a commission in the North Cork Militia—a corps of Orangemen, who committed fearful barbarities in the fatal 1798, and used to amuse themselves, when they did shoot or bayonet a suspected "rebel," with setting fire to his house, filling a brown paper cone with hot pitch, thrusting it upon his shorn head, and enjoying the "fun" of seeing him writhe under the torture, and laughing at him as the hot fluid ran down his face and breast. The "rebels" made a prisoner of Lord Kingston, and his life was very much in danger—for he was well known, and much hated. They employed him, however, to make terms for them with the Royalists, and he was allowed to depart, on his solemn promise to perform their wish. The moment he reached his friends, he made use of the information as to the strength of the "rebels," which he had picked up, while a captive, utterly betrayed the trust reposed in him, and broke his plighted word of honor, by setting on his soldiers to massacre the trusting foe. The populace, who recollected this, constantly predicted a violent death to this man brute. They rejoiced when the news reached them, in October, 1839, that the Earl of Kingston, after some years' dreadful sufferings, had miserably died, in London, of *morbus pediculosus*—the dreadful disease by which King Herod perished in his pride. He erected the Castle of Mitchelstown as a residence; and I recollect that the men, who quarried the limestone of which it is built, were paid only eight cents a day for twelve hours' work. A very different man was his eldest son, the Viscount Kingsborough, author of that magnificent work, "The Antiquities of Mexico." Born in 1795, he represented his native county (Cork), in the Parliament of 1820–'26. Thenceforth, he devoted himself to literary and antiquarian researches. In 1831, was published his great work on Mexico, in six folio volumes, got up at a cost of many thousand pounds. The illustrations consisted of fac-simile engravings from drawings and MSS., in the royal libraries of Paris, Dresden, and Berlin; the imperial library of Vienna; the library of the Vatican; the Borgean Museum; the library of the Institute at Bologna; the collections of Laud and Selden in the Bodleian, at Oxford. Four copies of this work—the largest ever published by an author, on his own account—were printed upon vellum; of these he presented one to the Bodleian library, and another to the British Museum. The price of an ordinary copy was a hundred and eighty guineas. The work

terrible results. His dark and massive countenance, with a shaggy and wild profusion of hair, his bold, imperious lip, and large and deeply-set eye, and his huge and vigorous frame, rendered him a remarkable object, without reference to his high rank and station, and to the political part which he had played in circumstances of which it is not impossible that he may witness, although he should desire to avert, the return.

The prisoners at the bar stood composed and firm. Lacy, the youngest, was dressed with extreme care and neatness. He was a tall, handsome young man, with a soft and healthful color, and a bright and tranquil eye. I was struck by the unusual whiteness of his hands, which were loosely attached to each other. Walsh, his fellow-prisoner and his brother in crime, was a stout, short, and square-built man, with a sturdy look, in which there was more fierceness than in Lacy's countenance; yet the latter was a far more guilty malefactor, and had been engaged in numerous achievements of the same kind, whereas Walsh bore an excellent reputation, and obtained from his landlord, Mr. Creagh, the highest testimony to his character.

The Solicitor-General, Mr. Doherty, rose to state the case. He appeared more deeply impressed than I have ever seen any public officer, with the responsibility which had devolved upon him; and, by his solemn and emphatic manner, rendered a narration, which was pregnant with awful facts, so impressive, that, during a speech of several hours' continuance, he kept attention upon the watch, and scarcely a noise was heard, except when some piece of evidence was announced which surprised the prisoners, and made them give a slight start, in which their astonishment and alarm at the extent of the information of the Government were expressed.*

can not be obtained now, it is so scarce, but a copy is in the Astor Library, New York.—Viscount Kingsborough was unfortunately induced to become security for debts incurred by his father, and that worthy actually allowed him to become an inmate of the Sheriff's Prison, in Dublin, where he died, of typhus fever, on the 27th of February, 1837, aged forty-two.—M.

* The speech of Mr. Doherty was highly eloquent. He took occasion to describe the general condition of the county in language equally simple, powerful, and true. To the causes of that condition he did not advert, for it did

They preserved their composure while Mr. Doherty was detailing the evidence of Fitzgerald, for they well knew that he had become what is technically called "a stag," and turned informer. Neither were they greatly moved at learning that another traitor of the name of Ryan was to be produced, for rumors had gone abroad that he was to corroborate Fitzgerald. They were well aware that the jury would require more evidence than the coincidence of swearing between two accomplices could supply. It is, indeed, held that one accomplice can sustain another for the purposes of conviction, and that their concurrence is sufficient to warrant a verdict of guilty; still juries are in the habit of demanding some better foundation for their findings, and, before they take life away, exact a confirmation from some pure and unquestionable source.

The counsel for the prisoners participated with them in the belief that the Crown would not be able to produce any witnesses except accomplices, and listened, therefore, to the details of the murder of Daniel Mara, however minute, without much apprehension for their clients, until Mr. Doherty, turning toward the dock, and lifting up and shaking his hand, pronounced the name of "Kate Costello." It smote the prisoners with dismay! At the time, however, that Mr. Doherty made

not fall within his official province to do so; but he has since, in the House of Commons, pointed out what he conceived to be the real sources of these deplorable evils. I regret that Mr. Doherty did not take the pains to publish his speeches at Clonmel. Justice has not been done to the diction in the newspapers in which they were reported. The publication of those speeches in an authentic form would not only evince the talents of the able advocate by whom they were delivered, but would also have the effect of showing, in a striking view, the unfairness of not allowing the counsel for the prisoners to speak, while the Crown enlists all the power of rhetoric against them. The fault is not with Mr. Doherty, but in the system. "Aperi os tuum muto, et vindica inopem," is written in golden letters in the Court. The law, instead of vindicating the poor man, shuts his counsel's mouth. I have seen many cases where a powerful speech might have saved a prisoner's life. A good appeal to the Jury would have preserved two of the men who were convicted of the murder of Barry, at Clonmel. It is said that Judges would not have time to go through the trials, if counsel for the prisoners were allowed to speak. In other words, they would be delayed from their vacation villas upon circuit. What an excuse! [The law has been changed since this was written, and counsel are allowed **to** *all* prisoners. — M.]

this announcement, he was himself uncertain, I believe, whether Kate Costello would consent to give the necessary evidence; and there was reason to calculate upon her reluctance to make any disclosure by which the lives of "her people," as the lower orders call their kindred, should be affected.

The statement of Mr. Doherty, which was afterward fully made out in proof, showed that a wide conspiracy had been framed in order to murder Philip Mara's brothers. Fitzgerald and Lacy, who did not reside in the neighborhood of Rath Cannon, were sent for by the relatives of Patrick Grace, as it was well known that they were ready for the undertaking of "the job." They received their instructions, and were joined by other assassins. The band proceeded to Rath Cannon, in order to execute their purpose, but an accident prevented their victims from coming to the place where they were expected, and the assassination was, in consequence, adjourned for another week. In the interval, however, they did not relent; but, on the contrary, a new supply of murderers was collected, and on Sunday, the 30th day of September [1828], the day preceding the murder, they met again in the house of a farmer, of the name of Jack Keogh, who lived beside the barrack where the Maras were at work. Here they were attended by Kate Costello, the fatal witness, by whom their destiny was to be sealed.

On the morning of Monday, the 1st of October, they proceeded to an elevation called "The Grove," a hill covered with trees, in which arms had been deposited. This hill overlooked the barrack where the Maras were at work. A party of conspirators joined the chief assassins on this spot, and Kate Costello, a servant and near relative of the Keoghs (who were engaged in the murder), again attended them. She brought them food and spirits. From this ambush they remained watching their prey until five o'clock in the afternoon, when it was announced that the Maras were coming down from the scaffolding on which they were raising the barrack. It appeared that some murderers did not know the persons whose lives they were to take away, and that their dress was mentioned as the means of recognition. They advanced to the number of eight, and, as I have already intimated, succeeded in slaying one only of the three brothers.

But the most illustrative incident in the whole transaction was not what took place at the murder, but a circumstance which immediately succeeded it. The assassins, with their hands red with the gore of man, proceeded to the house of a farmer in good circumstances, whose name was John Russel. He was a man of a decent aspect and demeanor, above the lower class of peasants in station and habits, was not destitute of education, spoke and reasoned well, and was accounted very orderly and well conducted. One would suppose that he would have closed his doors against the wretches who were still reeking with their crime. He gave them welcome, tendered them his hospitality, and provided them with food. In the room where they were received by this hoary delinquent, there were two individuals of a very different character and aspect from each other. The one was a girl, Mary Russel, the daughter of old Jack Russel, the proprietor of the house. She was young, and of an exceedingly interesting appearance; her manners were greatly superior to persons of her class, and she was delicate and gentle in her habitual conduct and demeanor. Near her there sat an old woman, in the most advanced stage of life, who was a kind of Elspeth among them, and from her age and relationship was an object of respect and regard. The moment the assassins entered, Mary Russel rushed up to them, and, with a vehement earnestness, exclaimed, "Did you do any good?" They stated in reply that one of the Maras was shot; when Peg Russel (the withered hag), who sat moping in the revery of old age, till her attention was aroused by the sanguinary intelligence, lifted her shrivelled hand, and cried out with a shrill and vehement bitterness, "You might as well not have killed any, since you did not kill them all!"

Strange and dreadful condition of Ireland! The witness to a murder denounces it. He flies the country. His brothers, for his crime, are doomed to die. The whole population confederate in their death. For weeks the conspiracy is planned, and no relenting spirit interposes in their slaughterous deliberations. The appointed day arrives, and the murder of an innocent man is effected, while the light is still shining, and with the eye of man, which is as little feared as that of God, upon them. The murderers leave the spot where their fellow-creature lies weltering; and, instead of being regarded as objects of execration and of horror, are chid by women for their remissness in the work of death, and for the scantiness of the blood which they had poured out! Thus it is that in this unfortunate country not only men are made barbarous, but women are unsexed, and filled—

——"from the crown to the toe, top-full
Of direst cruelty!"

These were the facts which Mr. Doherty stated, and they were established by the evidence. The first witness was Fitzgerald. When he was called, he did not appear on the instant, for he was kept in a room adjoining the Court, in order that he might not avail himself of the statement, and fit his evidence to it. His testimony was of such importance, and it was known that so much depended upon it, that his arrival was waited for with strong expectation; and, in the interval before his appearance on the table, the mind had leisure to form some conjectural picture of what he in all likelihood was. I imagined that he must be some fierce-looking, savage wretch, with baseness and perfidy, intermingled with atrocity, in his brow, and whose meanness would bespeak the informer, as his ferocity would proclaim the assassin. I was deceived.

His coming was announced—way was made for him—and I saw leap upon the table, with an air of easy indifference and manly familiarity, a tall, athletic young man, about two or three and twenty, with a countenance as intelligent in expression and symmetrical in feature, as his limbs were vigorous and well-proportioned. His head was perfectly shaped, and surmounted a neck of singular strength and breadth, which lay open and rose out of a chest of unusual massiveness and dilation. His eyes were of deep and brilliant black, full of fire and energy, intermixed with an expression of slyness and sagacity. They had a peculiarly-watchful look, and indicated a vehemence of character, checked and tempered by a cautious and observant spirit. The nose was well formed and deeply rooted, but rose at the end with some suddenness, which took off from the dignity of the countenance, but displayed considerable breadth about the nostrils, which were made to breathe fierceness and disdain. The mouth of the villain (for he was one of the first magnitude) was composed of thick but well-shaped lips, in which firmness and intrepidity were strongly marked; and, when opened, disclosed a range of teeth of the finest form and color. His hair was short and thick, but his cheek was so fresh and fair, that he scarcely seemed to have ever had any beard.

The fellow's dress was calculated to set off his figure. It left his breast almost bare, and, the knees of his breeches being open, a great part of his muscular legs appeared without covering, as his stockings did not reach to the knee. He was placed upon the chair appropriated to witnesses, and turned at once to the counsel for the Crown in order to narrate his own doings as well as those of his associates in depravity. I have never seen a cooler, more precise, methodical, and consistent witness.

He detailed every circumstance to the minutest point, which had happened during a month's time, with a wonderful accuracy. So far from manifesting any anxiety to conceal or to excuse his own guilt, he on the contrary set it forth in the blackest colors. He made himself a prominent actor in the business of blood. The life which he led was as singular as it was atrocious. He spent his time in committing outrages at night, and during the day in exacting homage from the peasantry, whom he had inspired with a deep dread of him. He walked through the county in arms, and compelled every peasant to give him bed and board wherever he appeared. In the caprices of his tyranny, he would make persons who chanced to pass him, kneel down and offer him reverence, while he presented his musket at their heads. Yet he was a favorite with the populace, who pardoned the outrages committed on themselves, on account of his readiness to avenge the affronts or the injuries *which they* suffered from others. Villain as the fellow was, it was not the reward which tempted him to betray his associates. Though two thousand pounds sterling had been offered by Government, he gave no information for several months; and when he did give it, it was to save his life, which he had forfeited by a highway robbery, for which he had been arrested. He seemed exceedingly anxious to impress upon the crowd that, though he was "a stag," it was not for gold that he had sold the cause. Life itself was the only bribe that could move his honor, and even the temptation which the instinctive passion for existence held out to him was for a long while resisted.

Mr. Hatchell cross-examined this formidable attestator with extraordinary skill and dexterity, but he was still unable to shake his evidence. It was perfectly consistent and compact, smooth and round, without any point of discrepancy on which the most dexterous practitioner could lay a strong hold. The most unfavorable circumstance to his cross-examiner was his openness and candor. He had an ingenuousness in his atrocity which defied all the ordinary expedients of counsel. Most informers allege that they are influenced by the pure love of justice to betray their accomplices. This statement goes to shake their credit, because they are manifestly perjured in the declaration. Fitzgerald, however, took a very different course. He disclaimed all interest in the cause of justice, and repeatedly stated that he would not have informed, except to rescue himself from the halter which was fastened round his neck. When he left the table, he impressed every man who heard him with a conviction of, not only his great criminality, but his extraordinary talents.

He was followed by another accomplice, of the name of Ryan, who was less remarkable than Fitzgerald, but whose statement was equally consistent, and its parts as adhesive to each other, as the more important informers. They had been left in separate jails, and had not had any communication, so that it could not be suggested that their evidence was the result of a comparison of notes, and of a conspiracy against the prisoners. This Ryan also alleged that he had informed merely to save his life.

These witnesses were succeeded by several, who deposed to

minute incidents which went to corroborate the informers; but notwithstanding that a strong case had been made out by the Crown, still the testimony of some untainted witness to the leading fact was requisite, and the counsel for the prosecution felt that on Kate Costello the conviction must still depend. She had not taken any participation in the murder. She could not be regarded as a member of the conspiracy; she was a servant in the house of old John Keogh, but not an agent in the business; and if she confirmed what the witnesses had deposed to, it was obvious that a conviction would ensue; while, upon the other hand, if she was not brought forward, the want of her testimony would produce a directly opposite result.

She was called, and a suspense far deeper than the expectation which had preceded the evidence of Fitzgerald was apparent in every face. She did not come, and was again summoned into court. Still Kate Costello did not appear. Repeated requisitions were sent by the Solicitor-General, but without effect. At length, every one began to conjecture that she would disappoint and foil the Crown, and the friends of the prisoners murmured that "Kate Costello would not turn against her people." An obvious feeling of satisfaction pervaded the crowd, and the prisoners exhibited a proportionate solicitude, in which hope seemed to predominate.

Suddenly, however, the chamber-door communicating with the room where the witnesses were kept was opened, and one of the most extraordinary figures that ever appeared in that strange theatre, an Irish court of justice, was produced. A withered, diminutive woman, who was unable to support herself, and whose feet gave way at every step, into which she was impelled by her attendants, was seen entering the court, and tottering toward the table. Her face was covered, and it was impossible, for some time after she had been placed on the table, to trace her features; but her hands, which were as white and clammy as a corpse's, and seemed to have undergone the first process of decomposition, shook and shuddered, and a thrill ran through the whole of her miserable and wornout frame. A few minutes elapsed before her veil was removed; and, when it was, the most ghastly face which I have ever observed was disclosed! Her eyes were quite closed, and the eyelids shrunken as if by the touch of death. The lips were like ashes, and remained open and without movement. Her breathing was scarcely perceptible, and, as her head lay on her shoulder, her long black hair fell dishevelled, and added to the general character of disordered horror which was expressed in her demeanor.

Now that she was produced, she seemed little calculated to be of any use. Mr. Doherty repeatedly addressed himself to her, and entreated her to answer. She seemed unconscious even of the sound of his voice. At length, however, with the aid of water, which was applied to her mouth, and thrown in repeated aspersions over her face, she was in some degree restored, and was able to breathe a few words. An interval of minutes elapsed between every question and answer. Her voice was so low as to be scarcely audible, and was rather an inarticulate whisper than the utterance of any connected sentence. She was, with a great deal to do, conducted by the examiner through some of the preliminary incidents, and at last was brought to the scene in the grove where the murderers were assembled.

It remained that she should recognise the prisoners. Unless this were done, nothing would have been accomplished. The rod with which culprits are identified was put into her hand, and she was desired to stand up, to turn to the dock, and to declare whether she saw in court any of the men whom she had seen in the grove on the day of the murder. For a considerable time she could not be got to rise from her seat; and when she did, and stood up after a great effort over herself, before she had turned round, but while the rod was trembling in her hand, another extraordinary incident took place.

Walsh, one of the prisoners at the bar, cried out with the most vehement gesture—"O God! you are going to murder me! I'll not stand here to be murdered, for I'm downright murdered, God help me!" This cry, uttered by a man almost frenzied with excitation, drew the attention of the whole court to the prisoner; and the Judge inquired of him of what he complained. Walsh then stated, with more composure, that it was unfair, while there was nobody in the dock but Lacy and himself, to desire Kate Costello to look at him, for that he was marked out to her where he stood. This was a very just observation, and Judge Moore immediately ordered that other prisoners should be brought from the jail into the dock, and that Walsh should be shown to Kate Costello in the midst of a crowd.

The jail was at a considerable distance, and a good deal of time was consumed in complying with the directions of the Judge. Kate Costello sank down again upon her chair; and, in the interval before the arrival of the other prisoners, we engaged in conjectures as to the likelihood of Walsh being identified. She had never seen him, except at the grove, and it was possible that she might not remember him. In that event his life was safe. At last the other prisoners were introduced into the dock. The sound of their fetters as they entered the court, and the grounding of the soldiers' muskets on the pavement, struck me.

It was now four o'clock in the morning; the candles were almost wasted to their sockets, and a dim and uncertain light was diffused through the court. Haggardness sat upon the spectators, and yet no weariness or exhaustion appeared. The frightful interest of the scene preserved the mind from fatigue. The dock was crowded with malefactors, and, brought as they were in order that guilt of all kinds should be confused and blended, they exhibited a most singular spectacle. This assemblage of human beings laden with chains was, perhaps, more melancholy from the contrast which they presented between their condition and their aspect. Even the pale light which glimmered through the court did not prevent their cheeks from looking ruddy and healthful. They had been awakened in their lonely cells in order to be produced, and, as they were not aware of the object of arraying them together, there was some surprise mixed with fear in their looks. I could not help whispering to myself as I surveyed them, "What a noble and fine race of men are here, and how much have they to answer for, who, by degrading, have demoralized such a people!"

The desire of Walsh having been complied with, the witness

was called upon a second time to place the rod upon his head. She rose again, and turned round, holding the fatal index in her hand. There was a deep silence through the court; the face of Walsh exhibited the most intense anxiety, as the eyes of Kate Costello rested upon the place where he stood. She appeared at first not to recognise him, and the rod hung loosely in her hand. I thought, as I saw her eyes traversing the assemblage of malefactors, that she either did not know him, or would affect not to remember him. At last, however, she raised the rod, and stretched it forth; but, before it was laid on the devoted head, a female voice exclaimed, "Oh, Kate!" This cry, which issued from the crowd, and was probably the exclamation of some relative of the Keoghs, whose destiny depended on that of Walsh, thrilled the witness to the core. She felt the adjuration in the very recesses of her being.

After a shudder, she collected herself again, and advanced again toward the dock. She raised the rod a second time, and, having laid it on the head of Walsh, who gave himself up as lost the moment it touched him, she sank back into her chair. The feeling which had filled the heart of every spectator here found a vent, and a deep murmur was heard through the whole court, mingled with sounds of stifled execration from the mass of the people in the background. Lacy also was identified; and here it may be said that the trial closed. Walsh, who, while he entertained any hope, had been almost convulsed with agitation, resumed his original composure. He took no further interest in the proceeding, except when his landlord gave him a high character for integrity and good conduct; and this commendation he seemed rather to consider as a sort of bequest which he should leave to his kindred, than as the means of saving his life. It is almost unnecessary to add that the prisoners were found guilty.

Kate Costello, whose evidence was of such importance to the Crown, had acted as a species of menial in the house of old John Keogh, but was a near relation of her master. It is not uncommon among the lower orders to introduce some dependent relative into the family, who goes through offices of utility which are quite free from degradation, and is at the same time treated, to a great extent, as an equal. Kate Costello sat down with old Jack Keogh and his sons at their meals, and was accounted one of themselves. The most implicit trust was placed in her; and on one of the assassins observing that "Kate Costello could hang them all," another observed that "there was no fear of Kate." Nor would Kate ever have betrayed the men who had placed their confidence in her, from any mercenary motives. Fitzgerald had stated that she had been at "the Grove" in the morning of the day on which the murder was committed, and that she could confirm his testimony. She was in consequence arrested, and was told that she should be hanged unless she disclosed the truth. Terror extorted from her the revealments which were turned to such account. When examined as a witness on the trial of Lacy and Walsh, her agitation did not arise from any regard for them, but from her consciousness that if they were convicted her own relatives and benefactors must share in their fate.

The trial of Patrick and John Keogh came on upon Saturday, the 5th of April, some days after the conviction of Lacy and of Walsh, who had been executed in the interval. The trial of the Keoghs had been postponed at the instance of the prisoners, but it was understood that the Crown had no objection to the delay, as great difficulty was supposed to have arisen in persuading Kate Costello to give completion to the useful work in which she had been engaged. It was said that the friends of the Keoghs had got access to her, and that she had refused to come forward against "her people." It was also rumored that she had entertained an attachment for John Keogh, and although he had wronged her, and she had suffered severe detriment from their criminal connection, that she loved him still, and would not take his life away. There was, therefore, enough of doubt incidental to the trial of the Keoghs to give it the interest of uncertainty; and, however fatal the omen which the conviction of their brother-conspirators held out, still it was supposed that Kate Costello would recoil from her terrible task.

The court was as much crowded as it had been on the first trial, upon the morning on which the two Keoghs were put at the bar. They were more immediate agents in the assassination. It had been in a great measure planned, as well as executed by them; and there was a further circumstance of aggravation in their having been in habits of intimacy with the deceased. When placed at the bar, their appearance struck every spectator as in strange anomaly with their misdeeds. They both seemed to be farmers of the most respectable class. Patrick, the younger, was perfectly well clad. He had a blue coat and white waistcoat, of the best materials used by the peasantry: a black silk-handkerchief was carefully knotted on his neck. He was lower in stature and of less athletic proportions than his brother John, but had a more determined and resolute physiognomy. He looked alert, quick, and active. The other was of gigantic stature, and of immense width of shoulder and strength of limb. He rose beyond every man in court, and towered in the dock. His dress was not as neatly arranged as his brother's, and his neck was without covering, which served to exhibit the hugeness of his proportions. He looked in the vigor of powerful manhood. His face was ruddy and blooming, and was quite destitute of all darkness and malevolence of expression. There was perhaps too much fullness about the lips, and some traces of savageness as well as of voluptuousness might have been detected by a minute physiognomist in their exuberance; but the bright blue of his mild and intelligent eyes counterbalanced this evil indication.

The aspect of these two young men was greatly calculated to excite interest; but there was another object in court which was even more deserving of attention. On the left hand of his two sons, and just near the youngest of them, sat an old man, whose head was covered with a profusion of gray hairs, and who, although evidently greatly advanced in years, was of a hale and healthful aspect. I did not notice him at first, but in the course of the trial, the glare which his eye gradually acquired, and the passing of all color from his cheek, as the fate of his sons grew to certainty, drew my observation, and I learned on inquiry, what I had readily conjectured, that he was the father of the prisoners at the bar. He did not utter a word during the fifteen or sixteen hours that he remained in attendance upon the dreadful scene which was going on before him. The appearance of Kate Costello herself, whom he had fostered, fed, and cherished, scarcely seemed to move him from his terrible tranquillity.

She was, as on the former occasion, the pivot of the whole case. The anticipations that she would not give evidence "against her own flesh and blood" were wholly groundless, for on her second exhibition as a witness she enacted her part with much more firmness and determination. She had before kept her eyes almost closed, but she now opened and fixed them upon the counsel, and exhibited great quickness and shrewdness in their expression, and watched the cross-examination with great wariness and dexterity. I was greatly surprised at this change, and can only refer it to the spirit of determination which her passage of the first difficulty on the former trial had produced. The first step in blood had been taken, and she trod more firmly in taking the second. Whatever may have been the cause, she certainly exhibited little compunction in bringing her cousins to justice, and laid the rod on the head of her relative and supposed paramour without remorse.

At an early hour on Sunday morning the verdict of guilty was brought in. The prisoners at the bar received it without surprise, but turned deadly pale. The change in John Keogh was more manifest, as in the morning of Saturday he stood blooming with health at the bar, and was now as white as a shroud. The Judge told them that as it was the morning of Easter Sunday (which is commemorative of the resurrection of the dead), he should not then pronounce sentence upon them. They cried out, "A long day, a long day, my Lord!" and at the same time begged that their bodies might be given to their father. This prayer was uttered with a sound resembling the wail of an Irish funeral, and accompanied with a most pathetic gesture. They both swung themselves with a sort of oscillation up and down, with their heads thrown back, striking their hands, with the fingers half closed, against their breasts, in the manner which Roman Catholics use in saying "*The Confiteor.*" The reference which they made to their father drew my attention to the miserable old man. Two persons, friends of his, had attended him in court; and when his sons, after having been found guilty, were about to be removed, he was lifted on the table, on which he was with difficulty sustained, and was brought near to the dock. He wanted to embrace John Keogh, and stretched out his arms toward him. The latter, whose manliness now forsook him, leaned over the iron spikes to his full length, got the old man into his bosom, and, while his tears ran down his face, pressed him long and closely to his heart. They were at length separated, and the sons were removed to the cells appointed for the condemned.

The Judge left the bench, and the court was gradually cleared. Still the father of the prisoners remained between his two attendants almost insensible. He was almost the last to depart. I followed him out. It was a dark and stormy night. The wind beat full against the miserable wretch, and made him totter as he went along. His attendants were addressing to him some words of consolation connected with religion (for these people are, with all their crimes, not destitute of religious impressions), but the old man only answered them with his moans. He said nothing articulate, but during all the way to the obscure cellar into which they led him, continued moaning as he went. It was not, I trust, a mere love of excitement, which arises from the contemplation of scenes in which the passions are brought out, that made me watch this scene of human misery. I may say, without affectation, that I was (as who would not have been?) profoundly moved by what I saw; and when I beheld this forlorn and desolate man descend into his wretched abode, which was lighted by a feeble candle, and saw him fall upon his knees in helplessness, while his attendants gave way to sorrow, I could not restrain my own tears.

The scenes of misery did not stop here. Old John Russel pleaded guilty. He had two sons, lads of fifteen or sixteen, and, in the hope of saving them, acknowledged his crime at the bar. "Let them," he said, in the jail where I saw him—"let them put me on the trap if they like, but let them spare the boys."

But I shall not proceed further in the detail of these dreadful incidents. There were many other trials at the assizes, in which terrible disclosures of barbarity took place. For three weeks the two Judges were unremittingly employed in trying cases of dreadful atrocity, and in almost every instance the perpetrators of crimes the most detestable were persons whose general moral conduct stood in a wonderful contrast with their isolated acts of depravity. Almost every offence was connected with the great agrarian organization which prevails through the country.

It must be acknowledged that, terrible as the misdeeds of the Tipperary peasantry must upon all hands be admitted to be, yet, in general, there was none of the meanness and turpitude observable in their enormities which characterize the crimes that are disclosed at an English assize. There were scarcely any examples of murder committed for mere gain. It seemed to be a point of honor with the malefactors to take blood, and to spurn at money. Almost every offence was committed in carrying a system into effect, and the victims who were sacrificed were considered by their immolators as offered up upon a justifiable principle of necessary extermination. These are assuredly important facts, and, after having contemplated these moral phenomena, it becomes a duty to inquire into the causes from which these marvellous atrocities derive their origin.

But before I proceed to suggest what I conceive to be the sources of a condition so disastrous, it is not inappropriate to inquire how long the lower orders in Ireland have been habituated to these terrible practices, and to look back to the period at which they may be considered to have had their origin. If these crimes were of a novel character, and had a recent existence, that circumstance would afford strong grounds for concluding that temporary expedients, and the vigorous administration of the law applied to the suppression of local and ephemeral disturbances, would be of avail. But if we find that it is not now, or within these few years, that these symptoms of demoralization have appeared, it is then reasonable to conclude that there must be some essential vice, some radical imperfection in the general system by which the country is governed, and it is necessary to ascertain what the extent and root of the evil is, before any effectual remedy can be discovered for its cure.

This is a subject of paramount interest, and its importance will justify the writer of this article, after a detail of the extraordinary incidents which he has narrated, in taking a rapid retrospect of antecedent events, of which recent transactions may be reasonably accounted the perpetuation. In doing so, some coincidence may be found with what the writer may have observed elsewhere, but the fear of incurring the imputation of either tediousness or self-citation shall not deter him from references to what he conceives to be of great and momentous materiality.

The first and leading feature in the disturbances and atrocities of Tipperary is, that they are of an old date, and have been for much more than half a century of uninterrupted continuance. Arthur Young* travelled in Ireland in the years 1776, 1777, and 1778. His excellent book is entitled "A Tour in Ireland, with General Observations on the Present State of that Kingdom." Although the professed object of Arthur Young in visiting Ireland was to ascertain the condition of its agriculture, and a great portion of his work turns upon that subject, yet he has also investigated its political condition, and pointed out what he conceived to be the chief evils by which the country was afflicted, and the mode of removing them. He adverts particularly to the state of the peasantry in the south

* Arthur Young was one of the very few men who studied Agriculture, *as a science*, in the eighteenth century. That he might master it, he traversed the British islands, and extended his observations over France, Italy, and Spain. He was a great experimentalist. He published the Farmer's Calendar and the Annals of Agriculture, both of which were very popular, and among his contributors was George III., who aspired to be considered a country gentleman, by virtue of having a farm of his own, at Windsor. When Sir John Sinclair got the Government to establish the Board of Agriculture, he obtained the secretaryship for Mr. Young, who retained it until his death, in 1820. His Agricultural tours in England, Ireland, and France, were full of information, carefully collected and impartially communicated. His statements respecting the fallen condition of Ireland, and the causes of her decadence, were startling—because, from the writer's character, their truth was undoubted.—M.

of Ireland, and it is well worthy of remark that the outrages which are now in daily commission were of exactly the same character as the atrocities which were perpetrated by the Whiteboys (as the insurgents were called) in 1760.

"The Whiteboys," says Arthur Young, in page 75 of the quarto edition, "began in Tipperary. It was a common practice with them to go in parties about the country, swearing many to be true to them, and forcing them to join by menaces, which they very often carried into execution. At last they set up to be general redressers of grievances—punished all obnoxious persons who advanced the value of lands, or held farms over their head; and, having taken the administration of justice into their own hands, were not very exact in the distribution of it. They forced masters to release apprentices; carried off the daughters of rich farmers—ravished them into marriages; they levied sums of money on the middling and lower farmers, in order to support their cause, in defending prosecutions against them; and many of them subsisted without work, supported by these prosecutions. Sometimes they committed considerable robberies, breaking into houses and taking money under pretence of redressing grievances. In the course of these outrages they burnt several houses, and destroyed the whole substance of those obnoxious to them. The barbarities they committed were shocking. One of their usual punishments, and by no means the most severe, was taking people out of their beds, carrying them naked in winter on horseback for some distance, and burying them up to their chin in a hole with briers, not forgetting to cut off one of their ears." Arthur Young goes on to say that the Government had not succeeded in discovering any radical cure.

It will scarcely be disputed that the Whiteboyism of 1760 corresponds with that of 1828; and if, when Arthur Young wrote his valuable book, the Government had not discovered any "radical cure," it will scarcely be suggested that any remedy has since that time been devised. From the period at which these outrages commenced, the evil has continued in a rapidly-progressive augmentation. Every expedient which legislative ingenuity could invent has been tried. All that the terrors of the law could accomplish has been put into experiment without avail. Special commissioners and special delegations of counsel have been almost annually despatched into the disturbed districts, and crime appears to have only undergone a pruning, while its roots remained untouched.

Mr. Doherty is not the first Solicitor-General of great abilities who has been despatched by Government for the purpose of awing the peasantry into their duty. The present Chief-Justice of the King's Bench [Bushe], upon filling Mr. Doherty's office, was sent upon the same painful errand, and, after having been equally successful in procuring the conviction of malefactors, and brandished the naked sword of justice with as puissant an arm, new atrocities have almost immediately afterward broken forth, and furnished new occasions for the exercise of his commanding eloquence.

It is reasonable to presume that the recent executions at Clonmel will not be attended with any more permanently useful consequences; and symptoms are already beginning to reappear, which, independently of the admonitions of experience, may well induce an apprehension that, before much time shall go by, the law-officers of the Crown will have to go through the same terrible routine of prosecution. It is said, indeed, by many sanguine speculators on the public peace, that now, indeed, something effectual has been done, and that the jail and the gibbet there have given a lesson that will not be speedily forgotten. How often has the same thing been said when the scaffold was strewed with the same heaps of the dead! How often have the prophets of tranquillity been falsified by the event! If the crimes which, ever since the year 1760, have been uninterruptedly committed, and have followed in such a rapid and tumultuous succession, had been of only occasional occurrence, it would be reasonable to conclude that the terrors of the law could repress them.

But it is manifest that the system of atrocity does not depend upon causes merely ephemeral, and can not therefore be under the operation of temporary checks. We have not merely witnessed sudden inundations which, after a rapid desolation, have suddenly subsided: we behold a stream as deep as it is dark, which indicates, by its continuous current, that it is derived from an unfailing fountain, and which, however augmented by the contribution of other springs of bitterness, must be indebted for its main supply to some abundant and distant source. Where, then, is the well-head to be found? Where are we to seek for the origin of evils, which are of such a character that they carry with them the clearest evidence that their causes must be as enduring as themselves? It may at first view, and to any man who is not well acquainted with the moral feelings and habits of the great body of the population of Ireland, seem a paradoxical proposition that the laws which affect the Roman Catholics furnish a clew by which, however complicated the mazes may be which constitute the labyrinth of calamity, it will not be difficult to trace our way.

It may be asked, with a great appearance of plausibility (and indeed it is often inquired), what possible effect the exclusion of a few Roman Catholic gentlemen from Parliament, and of still fewer Roman Catholic barristers from the bench, can produce in deteriorating the moral habits of the people? This, however, is not the true view of the matter. The exclusion of Roman Catholics from office is one of the results of the penal code, but it is a sophism to suggest that it is the sum total of the law itself, and that the whole of it might be resolved into that single proposition. The just mode of presenting the question would be this: "What effect does the penal code produce by separating the higher and the lower orders from each other?"

Before I suggest any reasons of my own, it may be judicious to refer to the same writer, from whom I have extracted a description of the state of the peasantry, with which its present condition singularly corresponds. The authority of Arthur Young is of great value, because his opinions were not in the least degree influenced by those passions which are almost inseparable from every native of Ireland. He was an Englishman—had no share in the factious animosities by which this country is divided—he had a cool, deliberate, and scientific mind—was a sober thinker, and a deep scrutinizer into the frame and constitution of society, and was entirely free from all tendency to extravagance in speculation, either political or religious. Arthur Young's book consists of two parts. In the first he gives a minute account of what he saw in Ireland, and in the second, under a series of chapters, one of which is appropriately entitled "Oppression," he states what he conceives to be the causes of the lamentable condition of the people. Having prefixed this title of "oppression" to the 29th page of the second part of his book, he says: "The landlord of an Irish estate inhabited by Roman Catholics, is a sort of despot, who yields obedience in whatever concerns the poor to no law but his own will. To discover what the liberty of a people is, we must live among them, and not look for it in the statutes of the realm: the language of written law may be that of liberty, but the situation of the poor may speak no language but that of slavery. There is too much of this contradiction in Ireland; a long series of oppression, aided by many very ill-judged laws, has brought landlords into a habit of exerting a very lofty superiority, and their vassals into that of a most unlimited submission: speaking a language that is despised, professing a religion that is abhorred, and being disarmed, the poor find themselves, in many cases, slaves, even in the bosom of written liberty! . . . The abominable distinction of religion, united with the oppressive conduct of the little country-gentlemen, or rather vermin of the kingdom, who were never out of it, altogether bear still very heavy on the poor people, and subject them to situations more mortifying than we ever behold in England."

In the next page after these preliminary observations, this able writer (who said in vain fifty years ago what since that time so many eminent men have been in vain repeating) points out more immediately the causes of the crimes committed by the peasantry, which he distinctly refers to the distinctions of religion. "The proper distinction in all the discontents of the people is into Protestant and Catholic. The Whiteboys, being laboring Catholics, met with all those oppressions I have described, and would probably have continued in full submission, had not very severe treatment blown up the flame of resistance. The atrocious acts they were guilty of made them the objects of general indignation: acts were passed for their punishment, which seemed calculated for the meridian of Barbary. It is manifest that the gentlemen of Ireland never thought of a radical cure, from overlooking the real cause of the disease, which, in fact, lay in themselves, and not in the wretches they doomed to the gallows. Let them change their own conduct entirely, and the poor will not long riot. Treat them like men, who ought to be free as yourselves; put an end to that system of religious persecution which for seventy years has divided the kingdom against itself. In these two things lies the cure of insurrection—perform them completely, and you will have an affectionate poor, instead of oppressed and discontented vassals; a better treatment of the poor in Ireland is a very material point to the welfare of the whole British empire. Events may happen which may convince us fatally of this truth. If not, oppression would have broken all the spirit and resentment of men. By what policy the Government of England can, for so many years, have permitted such an absurd system to be matured in Ireland, is beyond the power of plain sense to discover."

Arthur Young may be wrong in his inference (I do not think that he is); but, be he right or wrong, I have succeeded in establishing that he, whose evidence was most dispassionate and impartial, referred the agrarian barbarities of the lower orders to the oppression of the Roman Catholics. But the passage which I have cited is not the strongest. The seventh section of his work is entitled "Religion." After saying that "the domineering aristocracy of five hundred thousand Protestants feel the sweets of having two millions of slaves" (the Roman Catholic body was then not one third of what the penal code has since made it), he observes: "The disturbances of the Whiteboys, which lasted ten years" (what would he now say of their duration?), "in spite of every exertion of legal power, were, in many circumstances, very remarkable, and in none more so than in the surprising intelligence among the insurgents, wherever found. It was universal, and almost instantaneous. The numerous bodies of them, at whatever distance from each other, seemed animated by one zeal, and not a single instance was known, in that long course of time, of a single individual betraying the cause. The severest threats and the most splendid promises of reward had no other effect than to draw closer the bonds which cemented a multitude to all appearance so desultory. It was then evident that the iron hand of oppression had been far enough from securing the obedience or crushing the spirit of the people; and all reflecting men, who consider the value of religious liberty, will wish it may never have that effect—will trust in the wisdom of Almighty God, for teaching man to respect even those prejudices of his brethren that are imbibed as sacred rights, even from earliest infancy; that, by dear-bought experience of the futility and ruin of the attempt, the persecuting spirit may cease, and toleration establish that harmony and security which, five-score years' experience has told us, is not to be purchased at the expense of humanity."

This is strong language, and was used by a man who had no connecting sympathy of interest, of religion, or of nationality, with Ireland. So unequivocal an opinion, expressed by a person of such authority, and whose credit is not affected by any imaginable circumstance, must be admitted to have great weight, even if there was a difficulty in perceiving the grounds on which that opinion rested. But there is little or none. The law divides the Protestant proprietor from the Catholic tiller of the soil, and generates a feeling of tyrannical domination in the one, and of hatred and distrust in the other. The Irish peasant is not divided from his landlord by the ordinary demarkations of society. Another barrier is erected, and, as if the poor and the rich were not already sufficiently separated, religion is raised as an additional boundary between them.

The operation of the feelings, which are the consequence of this division, is stronger in the county of Tipperary than elsewhere. It is a peculiarly Cromwellian district, or, in other words, the holy warriors of the Protector chose it as their land of peculiar promise, and selected it as a favorite object of confiscation. The lower orders have good memories. There is scarcely a peasant who, as he passes the road, will not point to the splendid mansions of the aristocracy, embowered in groves, or rising upon fertile elevations, and tell you the name of the pious corporal or the inspired sergeant from whom the present proprietors derive a title, which, even at this day, appears to be of a modern origin.

These reminiscences are of a most injurious tendency. But, after all, it is the system of religious separation which nurtures the passions of the peasantry with these pernicious recollections. They are not permitted to forget that Protestantism is stamped upon every institution in the country, and their own sunderance from the privileged class is perpetually brought to their minds. Judges, sheriffs, magistrates, Crown-counsel, law-officers—all are Protestant.* The very sight of a court of justice reminds them of the degradations attached to their religion, by presenting them with the ocular proof of the advantages and honors which belong to the legal creed. It is not, therefore, wonderful that they should feel themselves a branded caste; that they should have a consciousness that they belong to a debased and inferior community; and, having no confidence in the upper classes, and no reliance in the sectarian administration of the law, that they should establish a code of barbarous legislation among themselves, and have recourse to what Lord Bacon calls "the wild justice" of revenge. A change of system would not perhaps produce immediate effects upon the character of the people: but I believe that

* Having repeatedly mentioned "Protestant Ascendency," in these notes, it may not be improper to define what it was and what it meant. In an address from the Corporation of Dublin to the Protestants of Ireland, praying them to resist Catholic Emancipation, the following passage occurs: "Protestant Ascendency, which we have resolved with our lives and fortunes to maintain. And that no doubt may remain of what we understand by the words 'Protestant Ascendency, we have further resolved, that we consider the Protestant Ascendency to consist in—a Protestant King of Ireland—a Protestant Parliament—a Protestant hierarchy—Protestant Electors and Government—the benches of justice, the army, and the Revenue, through all their branches and details, Protestant—and this system supported by a connection with the Protestant Realm of Britain." Previous to this assertion of exclusive Protestant rights, the Lord Chancellor of Ireland had declared from the judgment-seat (in 1759) that "the laws did not presume a Papist to exist in the Kingdom, nor could they breathe without the connivance of government." Yet the Catholics, whose rights and very existence were legally ignored, were about seven times more numerous than the Protestants of Ireland.—M.

its results would be much more speedy than is generally imagined.

At all events, the experiment of conciliation is worth the trial. Every other expedient has been resorted to, and has wholly failed. It remains that the legislature, after exhausting all other means of tranquillizing Ireland, should, upon a mere chance of success, adopt the remedy which has at least the sanction of illustrious names for its recommendation. The union of the two great classes of the people in Ireland—in other words, the emancipation of the Roman Catholics—is in this view not only recommended by motives of policy, but of humanity; for who that has witnessed the scenes which I have (perhaps at too much length) detailed in these pages, can fail to feel that, if the demoralization of the people arises from bad government, the men who from feelings of partisanship persevere in that system of misrule, will have to render a terrible account?

THE CATHOLIC BAR.

"And ye shall walk in silk attire."—*Old Ballad.*

Upon the first day of last Michaelmas term [1826] eight gentlemen were called to the Bar, of whom four were Roman Catholics. This was a kind of event in the Hall of the Four Courts, and in the lack of any other matter of interest, such as the speech of a new Sergeant at a corporation dinner, which had by this time ceased to excite the comments of the attorneys, produced a species of excitation. There are two assortments of oaths for Catholics and Protestants upon their admission to the Bar. The latter still enter their protestations, in the face of Lord Manners and of Heaven, against the damnable idolatry of the Church of Rome. But when the more mitigated oath provided for the Roman Catholics happens to be rehearsed on the first day of term,* it is easy to perceive an expression of disrelish in the countenance of the court; and although it is impossible for Lord Manners to divest himself of that fine urbanity which belongs to his birth and rank, yet in the bow with which he receives the aspiring Papist, there are evident symptoms of constraint; and it is by a kind of effort even in his features that they are wrought into an elaborated smile.

It does not frequently happen that more than one or two Roman Catholics are called in any single term; and when

* This sketch was published in February, 1827, when Lord Manners was Chancellor.—Roman Catholics were not admitted to the Irish bar until 1798. —Among the earliest who availed themselves of this privilege, was Mr. O'Connell.—M.

Lord Manners heard four several shocks given to the Constitution, and the Roman Catholic qualification-oath coming again and again upon him, it is not wonderful that his composure should have been disturbed, and that the loyal part of the Bar should have caught the expression of dismay. Mr. Sergeant Lefroy, alarmed at the repeated omissions of those pious denunciations of the Virgin Mary, by which the laws and liberty of these countries are sustained, in the very act of putting a fee into his pocket, lifted up the whites of his eyes to Heaven: Mr. Devonshire Jackson let fall his mask, and determined on voting for Gerard Callaghan:* the Solicitor-General was observed to whisper Mr. Saurin, until the arrival of Mr. Plunket withdrew him from the ear of his former associate in office: to Mr. Saurin it was proposed by Barclay Scriven to petition Mr. Peel to appoint him Attorney-General in the island of Barbadoes; and it is rumored that another letter to my Lord Norbury has been discovered,† in which the writer protests his belief, that the Bar will soon be reduced to its condition in the reign of James the Second.

In the reign of James the Second, Roman Catholic barristers were raised to office; and, as the time appears to be at hand when they will be rendered eligible by law to hold places of distinction and of trust, it is worth our while to examine in what way they conducted themselves when, in the short interval of their political prosperity, Roman Catholics were invested with authority. Doctor King says, that "no sooner had the Papists got judges and juries that would believe them, but they began a trade of swearing and ripping up what they pretended their Protestant neighbors had said of King James, whilst Duke of York;" and proceeds to charge them with gross corruption in the administration of justice.

* Mr. Devonshire Jackson, a clever lawyer, very attenuated in person and intolerant in political polemics, is now one of the Judges of the Common Pleas in Ireland.—Mr. Gerard Callaghan, son of Daniel Callaghan, a rich victualler and contractor in Cork, was ineligible, as a Catholic, to sit in Parliament, so he changed his religion, and was elected for his native city. After Emancipation his brother Daniel was elected, without relinquishing his religious faith.—M.

† See the preceding sketch of Lord Norbury, in this volume.—M.

The Doctor was Archbishop of Dublin. He had originally been a sizar in the University; and having afterward obtained a fellowship, gradually raised himself, by dint of sycophancy and intrigue, to one of the richest sees in the richest establishment in the world.* Whether he exhibited all the arrogance of a Pontifical *parvenu;* whether he was at once a haughty priest and a consecrated jackanapes; whether he was a sophist in his creed, an equivocator in his statements, and a cobweb-weaver in his theology; whether he had a vain head, a niggard hand, and a false and servile heart, and betrayed the men who raised him, I have not been able to determine. He appears to have been an apostate in his politics.† His representation of the conduct of the Catholic judges in his time is not without some episcopal characteristics, and justifies what Leslie says of him:—"Though many things the archbishop says are true, yet he has hardly spoken a true word without a warp." The best and most incontrovertible evidence (that of Lord Clarendon, the Lord-Lieutenant, and a firm Protestant), could be adduced to show how widely the statements of Doctor King vary from the fact.

Lord Clarendon tells us that "when the Popish judges went to the assizes in the counties of Down and Londonderry, where many considerable persons were to be tried for words formerly spoken against King James, they took as much pains as it

* Dr. William King, born in 1650, was an Irishman educated at Trinity College, and for many years Archbishop of Dublin. It is worth mention, as showing how church patronage went in those days, and (it may be) how little they deserved promotion, that though, from 1609 to 1773, there were one hundred and eight appointments or translations to Irish sees, only twenty-three fellows of Trinity College (the only University in Ireland), were among the prize-holders. One of these was the illustrious James Usher, appointed Bishop of Meath in 1620 (a see now having Dr. Singer at its head), and Archbishop of Armagh in 1624. A celebrated wit, by the way, used to say that "Bishops," who are always removed merely to richer dioceses, "are the only things that do not suffer by *translation.*"—Archbishop King died in 1729.—M.

† Of these last sentences it might be said, addressing Dr. Magee, Archbishop of Dublin when they were written—

"Mutato nomine, de te fabula narratur."

Mr. Sheil appears to have a rooted antipathy to this divine, who was a liberal in his youth, but became intolerant in his later years.—M.

was possible to quiet the minds of the people wherever they went; and they took care to have all the juries mingled, half English and half Irish."—(State Letters, vol. i., p. 326.) "Judge Daly," he says, "one of the Popish judges, did, at the assizes of the county of Meath, enlarge much upon the unconscionableness of indicting men for words spoken so many years before; and thereupon the jurors, the major part of whom were Irish, acquitted them:" and he adds, that "Mr. Justice Nugent, another Popish judge, made the same declaration at Drogheda, where several persons were tried for words." Lord Clarendon further states, that he was in the habit of consulting Roman Catholics, who had been recently promoted, respecting the appointment of mayors, sheriffs, and common-council men. "I advise," he says, "with those who are best acquainted in these towns, particularly with Justice Daly, and others of the King's council of that persuasion; and the lists of names these men give me, are always equal, half English, half Irish, which, they say, is the best way to make them unite and live friendly together."—(State Letters, vol. ii., p. 319.)

In the first volume of the State Letters, p. 292, he says, "At the council-board, there was a complaint proved against a justice of the peace; and it is remarkable that several of our new Roman Catholic counsellors, though the justice was an Englishman and a Protestant, were for putting off the business; and particularly the three said Popish judges said, the gentleman would be more careful for the future." He adds, that "when the Popish judges were made privy-counsellors, they conducted themselves with singular modesty,"—a precedent which I have no doubt that Mr. Blake will follow, when he shall be elevated to the vice-regal cabinet.*

* Many a chance arrow hits the white; many a true word is spoken in jest; Mr. Sheil was an involuntary prophet. Anthony Richard Blake, who was Lord Wellesley's particular friend, was one of the earliest Catholic Privy Councillors in Ireland, after Emancipation. Born in 1786, he was called to the bar in 1813; was Chief-Remembrancer of Ireland from 1823 to 1842, when he resigned from ill-health; in 1844, was made a commissioner of charitable donations and bequests for Ireland; and died, in January, 1849, aged sixty-three.—M.

Of the Roman Catholics, who were promoted in the reign of James the Second, Sir Theobald Butler was by far the most distinguished. He was created Attorney-General, and discharged the duties of his office with perfect fairness and impartiality. This very able, and, as far as renown can be obtained in Ireland, this celebrated man was not only without an equal, but without a competitor in his profession. Although the reputation of a lawyer is almost of necessity evanescent, yet such was the impression produced by his extraordinary abilities, that his name is to this day familiarly referred to. This permanence in the national recollection is in a great measure to be attributed to the very important part which he took in politics, and especially in the negotiation of the treaty of Limerick. His high rank also, for he was a member of the great house of Ormond, added to his influence.

As far as I have been able to form an estimate of his intellectual qualities, from the speech which he delivered at the bar of the Irish House of Commons, he was more remarkable for strength, brevity, condensation, and great powers of argument, than for any extraordinary faculty of elocution. The speech to which I have adverted, has none of those embellishments of rhetoric, and those splendid vices in oratory, to which the school of Irish eloquence became subsequently addicted.* The whole of this oration is cast in a syllogistic mould, and exhibits too much logical apparatus. It was, I believe, the fashion of the time: still the vehemence of passion breaks through the artificial regularity of reasoning, and while he is proceeding with a series of propositions, systematically divided, the indignant emotions, which the injuries of his country could not fail to produce, burst repeatedly and abundantly out: in the midst of all the pedantic forms of scholastic disputation, Nature asserts her dominion; he gives a loose to anguish, and pours forth his heart.

Sir Theobald Butler had not only been among the besieged Catholics at Limerick, but was employed by his countrymen

* And of which Mr. Sheil's own oratory was a brilliant example; — so easy is it to perceive faults, and yet possess them — to approve of the "meliora," and yet have to add "sed inferiora sequor." — M.

to settle the articles of capitulation.* His name appears on the face of the treaty as one of the parties with whom, on behalf of the Irish, it was concluded. When in the year 1703, only twelve years after the articles had been signed, a bill (the first link of the penal code) was introduced into parliament, the effect of which was utterly to abrogate those articles, the eyes of the whole nation were turned upon the man who had been instrumental in effecting that great national arrangement. Independently of his great abilities as an advocate, he presented, in his own person, a more immediate and distinct perception of that injustice which was about to be exercised against the body, of which he was the ornament, and to which his eloquence now afforded their only refuge.

In a book entitled "An Account of the Debates on the Popery Laws," it is stated that the Papists of Ireland, observing that the House of Commons was preparing the heads of a bill to be transmitted to England to be drawn into an act to prevent the growth of Popery, and having in vain endeavored to put a stop to it there, at its remittance back to Ireland presented to the House of Commons a petition praying to be heard by their counsel against the bill, and to have a copy of the bill, and to have a reasonable time to speak to it before it passed, when it was ordered that they should be heard.

Upon Tuesday the 22d of February, 1703, Sir Theobald Butler appeared at the bar, and with the treaty of Limerick

* The defender of Limerick, when besieged by the army of William III., at the Revolution, was "the gallant Sarsfield"—so designated in the histories of the time. He was created Earl of Lucan, by James II., but the title was not legally recognised, for himself or his descendants, in Great Britain or Ireland. Limerick was surrendered to William, even while the Irish were within a few hours of assistance from France, upon conditions, which, if carried out by the English, would have secured equal civil rights and liberties to all of the Irish people, and bound Ireland to Great Britain by a stronger tie—that of justice rendered—than that of "allegiance." The treaty of Limerick, which terminated the Dutchman's contest for a throne, was basely violated by England, when penal laws against Catholics were enacted, instead of the promised justice. To this day, the very stone on which that Treaty was signed, is shown in Limerick, and one of O'Connell's most stirring speeches, during the "Monster Meetings" of 1843, was made within sight of this monument of Ireland's having trusted to the honor of England—and having been deceived.—M.

in his hand, requested, on behalf of the Irish Roman Catholics, to be heard. It must have been a very remarkable scene. Whether we consider the assembly to which the remonstrance was addressed, or the character and condition of the body on whose behalf it was spoken, whose leading nobles, and they were then numerous, stood beside their advocate at the bar of the House, we can not but feel our minds impressed with a vivid image of a most imposing, and in some particulars a very moving spectacle.

The first advocate of his time, who was himself a principal party in the cause which he came to plead, stood before a Protestant House of Commons; while below the bar were assembled about their counsel the heads of the Roman Catholic aristocracy. The latter constituted a much more extensive and differently-constituted class of men from those by whom they have been succeeded. They had been born to wealth and honor: they had been induced, by a sentiment of chivalrous devotion, to attach themselves to the fortunes of an unhappy prince. The source of their calamities was in a lofty sentiment. Almost all of them had been soldiers; scarce a man of them but had carried harness on his back. They were actuated by the high and gallant spirit which belongs to the profession of arms. On the banks of the Boyne, on the hill of Aughrim, and at the gates of Limerick, they had given evidences of valor, which, although unavailing, were not the less heroic. They had been worsted, indeed; but they had not been subdued: they had been accustomed to consider their privileges as secured by a great compact, and in substituting the honor of England for the bastions of Limerick, they looked upon their liberties as protected by still more impregnable muniments.

It is easy to imagine the dismay, the indignation, and the anguish, with which these gentlemen must have seen a statute in rapid progress through the legislature, which would not only have the effect of violating the treaty of Limerick, and reduce them to a state of utter servitude, but, by holding out the estate of the father as a premium for the apostacy of the child, would inculcate a revolt against the first instincts of nature, and the most sacred ordinances of God. Their advocate, at least, saw the penal code in this light. "Is not this," he exclaimed, "against the laws of God and man, against the rules of reason and justice; is not this the most effectual way in the world to make children become undutiful, and to bring the gray head of the parent to the grave with grief and tears?" In speaking thus, he did no more than give vent to the feelings which, being himself a father, he must have deeply experienced; and the heart of every parent whose cause he was pleading, must have been riven by their utterance.

If there was something imposing in the sight of so many of the old Catholic nobility of Ireland, of so many gallant soldiers, gathered round their counsel in a group of venerable figures (for most of those who had fought in the civil wars were now old), the assembly to which they were come to offer their remonstrances must have also presented a very striking spectacle. The Irish House of Commons represented a victorious and triumphant community. Pride, haughtiness, and disdain, the arrogance of conquest, the appetite of unsatisfied revenge, the consciousness of masterdom, and the determination to employ it, must have given this fierce and despotic convention a very marked character. Most of its members, as well as their Roman Catholic supplicants, had been soldiers; and to the gloom of Puritanism, to which they were still prone, they united a martial and overbearing sternness, and exhibited the flush of victory on their haughty and commanding aspect. To this day, there are some traces of lugubrious peculiarity in the descendants of the Cromwellian settlers in Ireland; at the period of which I speak, the children of the pious adventurers must have exhibited still deeper gloom of visage, and a darker severity of brow.

In addressing an assembly so constituted, and in surveying which an ordinary man would have quailed, Sir Theobald Butler had to perform a high and arduous duty. How must he have felt, when, advancing to the bar of the House, he threw his eyes around him, and beheld before him the lurid looks and baleful countenances of the Protestant conquerors of his country, and saw beside him the companions of his youth, the associates of his early life, many of them his own kindred, all of them his fellow-sufferers, clinging to him as to their only stay, and substituting his talents for the arms which he had persuaded them to lay down! The men whom he had seen working the cannon at the batteries of Limerick stood now, with no other safeguard but his eloquence, at the mercy of those whom they had fought in the breach and encountered in the field. An orator of antiquity mentions that he never rose to speak upon an important occasion without a tremor. When the advocate of a whole people rose in the deep hush of expectation, and in all that thrilling silence which awaits the first words of a great public speaker, how must his heart have throbbed!

Sir Theobald Butler's speech (I dwell thus long upon the subject, because the event which produced it has been attended with such important consequences) comprehends almost every reason which can be pressed against the enactment of the penal code, as a violation of public faith. He did not, however, confine himself to mere reasoning upon the subject, but made an attempt to touch the feelings of his Protestant auditors. He has drawn a strong and simple picture of the domestic effects of the penal code in the families of Roman Catholics. by transferring the estate of the father to his renegade son. "That the law should invest any man with the power of depriving his fellow-subject of his property would be a grievance. But my son—my child—the fruit of my body, whom I have nursed in my bosom, and loved more dearly than my life—to become my plunderer, to rob me of my estate, to take away my bread, to cut my throat—it is enough to make the most flinty heart bleed to think on it. For God's sake, gentlemen, make the case your own," &c.*

This adjuration exhibits no art of phrase, but it has nature, which, as was observed by Dryden of Otway's plays, is, after

* Extracts from Sir Theobald Butler's speech were given about a year ago in the *Etoile* newspaper, which in a series of articles on Ireland contributed to produce that calculation upon the feeling of the Roman Catholic body recently evinced in the debates of the French parliament. [The extracts referred to were supplied to *L'Etoile* by Mr. Sheil himself, with other articles (many of them from his own pen), which were translated into English, and published by the London press, as indicating *French* opinions on Irish subjects.—M.]

all, the greatest beauty. Those simple words, which contained so much truth, can not be read without emotion; but how far greater must have been their effect when uttered by a parent, who was lifting up his voice to protect the sanctuaries of nature against violation! In what tone must a father have exclaimed, "It would be hard from any man; but from my son, my child, the fruit of my body, whom I have nursed in my bosom!" Surely, in the utterance of this appeal—not by a mere mercenary artificer of passion, but by a man whom everybody knew to be speaking the truth, and whose trembling hands and quivering accents must have borne attestation to his emotions—the sternest and most resolved of his judges must have relented, and, like the evil spirit at the contemplation of all the misery he was about to inflict—

> "For a moment stood
> Divested of his malice."

And if the hearts of the Protestant confiscators were touched, did not the tears roll down the faces of the unfortunate Catholics who stood by—did they not turn to sob in the bosom of their children, and, clasping them in their arms, inquire, in the dumb eloquence of that parental embrace, "whether they would ever strike the poniard, with which the law was about to arm them, into their breasts?" Their advocate did not, however, merely appeal to the sensibilities of his auditors, but swept his hand over strings by which a still deeper vibration must have been produced.

He assumed a loftier and a bolder tone. He raised himself up to the full height of his mind, and, appealing to the principles of eternal truth and justice, denounced the vengeance of Heaven on those who should be so basely perfidious as to violate a great and sacred compact; and was sufficiently courageous to remind a Protestant House of Commons that the treaty of Limerick had been signed, "when the Catholics had swords in their hands." This was a stirring sentence, and sent many a heart-thrilling recollection into the hearts of those to whom it was addressed. The prince of the conquerors must have started, and the conquered must have looked upon hands in which there were swords no more. It is recorded of an ancient orator, that he exercised over the minds of his heroes an influence so powerful, that his description of a battle was interrupted by the exclamation of a soldier who had been present at the engagement, and whom the spell of eloquence had carried back to the field.

Even at this day, every reference to the siege of Limerick produces an extraordinary excitation in Roman Catholic assemblies; and if the descendants of those whose rights were secured by the treaty of Limerick, recur with indignation to the incidents of that celebrated siege, to what a point of excitation must the gallant cavaliers, by whom the advocate of the Irish nation was surrounded, have been wrought, when he, who was himself a party to that great national indenture, with that deep and solemn tone and that lofty gravity of demeanor for which he was remarkable, recalled the events in which almost every man who heard him bore a conspicuous part. It is in the remembrance of such scenes that memory may be justly called, "The actor of our passions o'er again." I do not think that I am guilty of any exaggeration, when I say that in appealing to the time when the Roman Catholics had arms in their hands, the advocate of their rights and the representative of their emotions must have brought back many a martial recollection to the clients in whose front he stood, and whose cause he was so emphatically pleading. The city, from which William at its first siege, with an army of thirty thousand men, had been driven back—the fortress, which art and nature had conspired to make strong, and which valor and constancy would have rendered impregnable—must have risen before them. All the glorious circumstance incidental to their former occupation must have returned. The shout of battle, the roar of the cannon, the bloody foss, the assault and the repulse, the devotion and abandonment, with which whole regiments rushed through the gates, and precipitated themselves into imaginary martyrdom—Sarsfield upon the battlements, the green flag floating from the citadel, and the cry of "Help from France!"—these must have been among the recollections which were awakened by their advocate, while he appealed to the time "when they had arms in their hands," and stood in the fire of their batteries, and not at the threshold of the House of Commons.

But, if the sentiment of martial pride was rekindled for an instant, how quickly it must have gone out, and how soon those emotions must have collapsed into despair. They must have known, for the countenances of their victors must have apprized them, that they had nothing to expect but servitude and all the shame that follows it; and then, indeed, they must have mourned over the day when, at the head of a powerful army, in a strong fortification, with several garrison-towns still in their possession, with a great mass of the population ready to rush again to the field, and with a French fleet freighted with arms and with troops in the Shannon, they had been induced, upon the faith of a solemn compact, to lay down their swords, and put their trust in the honor of the King and the integrity of his people. They must have cursed the day, when, instead of adding their bones to the remains of those who lay slaughtered in the trenches of Limerick, they survived to behold the Protestants of Ireland taking advantage of that fatal surrender, and in defiance of the most solemn compacts, in violation of a clear and indisputable treaty, not only excluding them from the honors and privileges of the state, but wresting their property from their hands, instituting a legalized banditti of "discoverers," exciting their children into an insurrection against human nature, converting filial ingratitude into a merit, and setting up parricide as a newly-invented virtue, in the infernal ethics of the law.

As Sir Theobald Butler had anticipated (for he intimates it in an involuntary expression of despondency), his arguments were of little avail, and he lived long enough to see the penal code carried to its atrocious perfection, and chain after chain thrown upon his country. He even survived an act of parliament by which Roman Catholics were excluded from the profession in which he had earned fortune and renown. It is a common notion that he changed his religion in order to avert the evils which he so powerfully described ; but I was informed by his grandson, Mr. Augustine Butler, that he died in the religion in which he had lived,* and that his great estates became in consequence equally divisible among his children.† He was interred in the church-yard of St. James's church, in Dublin, where a huge but rather uncouth monument has been raised to his memory. His epitaph differs from most obituary panegyrics, by the adherence of encomium to truth. It is inscribed under a rude and now mutilated bust, and runs as follows:—

Designatur hac effigie
Theobaldus e gente Butlera
Hibernus Jurisconsultus
Legum, Patriæ, nominis decus
Dignitate equestri donatus, non auctus
Causidicus
Argutus, concinnus, integer
Barbarie forensi, et vernacula disertus
Non partium studio
Non favoris aucupio
Non verborum lenocinio
Sed rerum pondere
Et ingenii vi insitâ
Et legum scientia penitiori
Pollens
Quem lingua solers, illibata fides
Comitate et sale multo condita gravitas
Quem vitæ tenor sincerus
Et recti custos animus
Legum recondita depromere sagax
Ad famæ fastigium evexere
Fortunæ etiam, ni religio obstaret, facile evexissent.
Obiit Septuagenarius XI Martii, 1720.

Notwithstanding the exclusion of Roman Catholics from the Bar, the expedient which was adopted for the purpose does not appear to have been found effectual. A certificate of

* Sir Theobold Butler died in March, 1720, aged seventy.—M.

† The anti-Catholic Penal code enacted, among many other things, that no Catholic heir could profit by primogeniture, but that the real estate was equally divisible among all the children, but that if he turned Protestant he would then have the whole estate, even in his father's lifetime: if a Protestant went over to the Church of Rome, or procured another to do so, it was high treason. A Catholic wife was allowed an increase of jointure, on becoming a Protestant. A priest who married a Catholic to a Protestant, was liable to be hanged.—M.

conformity was all that was required, and this certificate was so easily obtained, that the members of the obnoxious religion were still able to creep and steal into the profession. The letters of Primate Boulter,* who governed Ireland for a considerable time, and whose simple maxim it was to keep Ireland divided in order that her dependency might be secured, give us a very curious insight into the state of the Irish Bar in the year 1727. In a letter dated the 7th of March, 1727, he writes: "There is a bill gone over to regulate the admission of barrister, attorneys, six clerks, solicitors, sub-sheriffs, &c., which is of the last consequence to this kingdom. The practice of the law, from the top to the bottom, is at present mostly in the hands of new converts, who give no further security on this account than producing a certificate of their having received the sacrament in the Church of England or Ireland, which several of them, who were Papists in London, obtain in the road hither, and demand to be admitted barristers in virtue of it at their arrival, and several of them have *Popish wives*, and have masses said in their houses. Everybody here is sensible of the terrible effects of this growing evil, and both Lords and Commons are most eagerly desirous of this bill." (Boulter's Letters, vol. i., p. 179.)

The horror entertained by his Grace of Dublin for barristers, whose better halves were infected with Popery, appears ludicrous at this day. Doctor King considered the division of allegiance at the Bar, between the law and the fair sex, as highly dangerous to the security of the Established Church, and would have taken "*au pié de la lettre*" what Lord Chesterfield said of the beautiful Lady Palmer,† that she was the only "dangerous Papist" he had ever seen in Ireland.

* Hugh Boulter was Archbishop of Armagh, Primate of Ireland, and virtual Governor of the country, during the earlier period of the Hanoverian dynasty, and is chiefly remarkable for having established schools for the instruction of the Irish children; which seminaries were eventually perverted, by the Ascendency party, to purposes of proselytism.—Primate Boulter died in 1742.—M.

† The writer of this article was acquainted with Lady Palmer, when she was upward of one hundred years of age. The admiration which Lord Chesterfield is known to have entertained for this lady induced me to seek an introduction to her. Although rich, she occupied a small lodging in Henry street,

I know not, however, whether the feeling by which Doctor King was influenced, be wholly extinct. I do not mean to say that Lord Wellesley would object to a barrister on account of

where she lived secluded and alone. Over the chimney-piece of the front drawing-room was suspended the picture of her platonic idolater. It was a half-length portrait, and had, I believe, been given to her by the man of whose adoration she was virtuously vain. I was engaged in looking at this picture, while I waited on the day of my first introduction for this pristine beauty of the Irish court. While I gazed upon the picture of a man who united so many accomplishments of manner and of mind, and observed the fine intellectual smile, which the painter had succeeded in stealing upon animated canvass, I fell into a somewhat imaginative strain of thought, and asked myself what sort of woman "the dangerous Papist" must have been, in whom the master of the graces had found such enchanting peril. "What a charm," I said, "must she have possessed, upon whose face and form those bright eyes reposed in illuminated sweetness,—how soft and magical must have been the voice from whose whispers those lips have hung so often, what gracefulness of mind, what an easy dignity of deportment, what elegance of movement, what sweet vivacity of expression, how much polished gayety and bewitching sentiment must have been united!" I had formed to myself an ideal image of the young, the soft, the fresh, the beautiful, and tender girl, who had fascinated the magician of so many spells. The picture was almost complete. The Castle in all its quondam lustre rose before me, and I almost saw my Lord Chesterfield conducting Lady Palmer through the movements of a minuet, when the door was slowly opened, and in the midst of a volume of smoke, which, during my phantasmagoric imaginations, had not inappropriately filled the room, I beheld in her own proper person the being, in whose ideal creation I had indulged in a sort of Pygmalian dream. The opening of the door produced a rush of air, which caused the smoke to spread out in huge wreaths about her, and a weird and withered form stood in the midst of the dispersing vapor. She fixed upon me a wild and sorceress eye, the expression of which was aided by her attitude, her black attire, her elongated neck, her marked and strongly-moulded, but emaciated features. She leaned with her long arm and her withered hand of discolored parchment upon an ivory-headed cane, while she stretched forth her interrogating face, and with a smile, not free from ghastliness, inquired my name. I mentioned it, and her expression, as she had been informed that I was to visit her, immediately changed. After the ordinary formulas of civility, she placed herself in a huge chair, and entered at once into politics. She was a most vehement Catholic, and was just the sort of person that Sir Harcourt Lees would have ducked for a rebel and a witch. Lord Chesterfield and the Catholic question were the only subjects in which she seemed to take any interest. Upon the wrongs done to her country, she spoke not only with energy, but with eloquence, and with every pinch of snuff poured out a sentence of sedition. "Steth, sir, it is not to be borne," she used to exclaim, as she lifted her figure from the stoop of age, with her eyes flashing with fire, and struck her cane vio-

his "having a Popish wife, and mass said in his house; but it is observable that, of the three Catholic barristers who have been promoted under his Lordship's administration, by a strange matrimonial coincidence every one is married to a Protestant.

The bill sent over by Primate Boulter was carried, and Catholics were effectually excluded from the Bar. From 1725 to 1793 lawyers earnestly and strenuously professed the doctrines of the state; and although upon his death-bed many an orator of renown supplicated in a Connaught accent for a priest, yet his lady, whose gentility of religion was brought into some sort of question, and who would have considered it as utterly derogatory to set up a widow's cap to the memory of a relapsed papist, either drowned the agonies of conscience in the vehemence of her sorrows, or slapped the door in the face of the intrepid Jesuit, who had adventured upon the almost hopeless enterprise of saving the soul of the expiring counsellor. The Bar gradually assumed a decidedly Protestant character; and although an occasional Catholic practised as a conveyancer, yet none obtained any celebrity in the only department of the law from which Roman Catholics were not actually excluded. Indeed, they held so low a place, that it appears to have been a kind of disrepute to have had anything to do with them; and I remember to have read, in the cause of Simpson against Lord Mountmorris, the deposition of a witness, who stated as a ground for impeaching a deed, executed by the Earl of Anglesea, that it was drawn by a Papist. Roman Catholics were, at this period, excluded from the

lently to the ground. Wishing to turn the conversation to more interesting matter, I told her I was not surprised at Lord Chesterfield having called her a "dangerous Papist." I had touched a chord, which, though slackened, was not wholly unstrung. The patriot relapsed into the woman; and passing at once from her former look and attitude, she leaned back in her chair, and drawing her withered hands together, while her arms fell loosely and languidly before her, she looked up at the picture of Lord Chesterfield with a melancholy smile. "Ah!" she said —— But I have extended this notice beyond all reasonable compass. I think it right to add, after so much mention of Lady Palmer, that although she was vain of the admiration of Lord Chesterfield, she took care never to lose his esteem, and that her reputation was without a blemish.

English, as well as from the Irish Bar; but Booth, the great conveyancer, was a Roman Catholic, and, before the professors of his religion were admissible to the rank of counsel, Mr. Charles Butler, of Lincoln's Inn, had obtained great fame.

In the year 1793 the great act for the relief of the Roman Catholics was passed. It was a piece of niggard and preposterous legislation: all, or nothing, should have been conceded. The effect of a partial enfranchisement was to give the means of acquiring wealth, influence, intelligence, and power, and yet withhold the only legitimate means of employing them. The Roman Catholics were not admitted into, but brought within reach of the constitution. They were still placed beyond the state, and were furnished with a lever to shake it. They obtained that external *point d'appui* from which they have been enabled to exercise a disturbing power. The extension of the elective franchise to men, who were at the same time declared to be ineligible to parliament, and the admission of Catholics to the Bar while they were denied its honorable reward, are conspicuous instances of impolicy.

The late Mr. George Ponsonby* was strongly impressed with the imprudence of allowing Roman Catholics to enter the race of intelligence, and yet shut up the goal. He felt that the government were disciplining troops against themselves, and insisted on the absurdity of exciting ambition, and at the same time closing the avenues to its legitimate gratification. He saw that, so far from conciliating the Roman Catholic body by so imperfect and lame a measure of relief, their indignation would rather be provoked by what was refused, than their gratitude be awakened by what was granted: desire would be inflamed by an approach to its object, while it was denied its natural and tranquillizing enjoyment. Mr. Ponsonby's anticipations were well-founded, and are going through a rapid process of verification.

The first Roman Catholics who took advantage of the ennobling statute, were Mr. Donnellan, Mr. Mac Kenna, Mr. Lynch, and Mr. Bellew. Every one of those gentlemen (*quod*

* Lord Chanceller of Ireland under "All the Talents" Ministry of 1806–'7. A brief memoir of him occurs in the previous volume.—M.

nota, as Lord Coke says in his occasional intimations to Junior Bar) was provided for by Government. Mr. Donnellan obtained a place in the revenue; Mr. Mac Kenna wrote some very clever political tracts, and was silenced with a pension; Mr. Lynch married a widow with a pension, which was doubled after his marriage; and Mr. Bellew is in the receipt of six hundred pounds a year, paid to him quarterly at the Treasury. The latter gentleman is deserving of notice. Whether I consider him as an individual, as the representative of the old Catholic aristocracy at the Bar, as a politician, a religionist, or a pensioner, I look upon this able, upright, starch, solemn, didactic, pragmatical, inflexible, uncompromising, obstinate, pious, moral, good, benevolent, high-minded and exceedingly wrong-headed person, as in every way entitled to regard.

Mr. William Bellew is a member of one of the most distinguished Roman Catholic families in Ireland. There was formerly a peerage attached to his name, which was extinguished in an attainder. A baronetcy was retained. His father, Sir Patrick Bellew, was a man of a high spirit, distinguished for his munificence, and that species of disastrous hospitality, by which many a fine estate was so ingloriously dismembered. He constituted a sort of exception among the Catholic gentry; for at the time when that body sank under the weight of accumulated indignities, Sir Patrick Bellew exhibited a lofty sense of his personal importance, and was sufficiently bold to carry a sword. His property descended to his eldest son, Sir Edward Bellew.* Mr. William Bellew, the barrister, who was his second son, was sent to the Anglo-Saxon university of Douay, whence he returned with all the altitude of demeanor for which his father was remarkable, but with a profound veneration for all constituted authorities, of whatever nature, kind, or degree, and with abstract tendencies to political submission, which are by no means at variance with a man's interests in Ireland.

* Sir Edward Bellew, who died in 1827, was M. P. for, and Lord Lieutenant of, the County of Louth. He was succeeded by his son, the present Sir Patrick Bellew.—M.

He was one of the first Roman Catholics called to the Bar, and I have understood from some of his contemporaries, that, as he represented the Catholic gentry, and was considered to take a decided lead in their proceedings, in his first appearance in the Four Courts he attracted much notice. His general bearing produced a sort of awe; and it was obvious that, as Owen Glendower says, "he was not in the roll of common men." His lofty person, his stately walk, his perpendicular attitude, the rectilineal position of his head, his solemnity of gesture, the deep and meditative gravity of his expression, his sustained and measured utterance, the deliberation of his tones, his self-collectedness and concentration, and that condensed, but by no means arrogant or overweening, look of superiority by which he is characterized, fixed a universal gaze upon him; and from the contrast between him, and the rapid, bustling, and airy manner of most of his brethren, excited a general curiosity. Heedless of observation, and scarcely conscious of it, the forensic aristocrat passed through the throng of wondering spectators, and as Horatio says of the Royal Dane,

> "with solemn march
> Went slow and stately by them."

There was, indeed, something spectral in his aspect. The phantom of the old Catholic aristocracy seemed to have been evoked in his person, while the genius of Protestant ascendency shrunk before its majestic apparition. All idea of checking "the growth of Popery" vanished in an instant at his sight; the only man who could compete with him in longitude of dimensions being Mr. Mahaffy; but that gentleman's stupendous length sat uneasily upon him, whereas the soul of the lofty Papist seemed to inhabit every department of his frame, and would have disdained to occupy any other than its sublime and appropriate residence. High as his post and demeanor were, they were wholly free from affectation. With a great deal of pride, he manifested neither insolence nor conceit. He looked far more dignified than authoritative; and although a strong expression of austerity was inscribed upon his countenance, it was by no means heartless or even severe. If I were a painter and were employed to furnish illustrations of Ivanhoe, I do not think that I could find a more appropriate model than Mr. Bellew for the picture of Lucas Beaumanoir. His visage is inexorable without fierceness; and many a time hath he been observed fixing his immitigable eye upon a beauty in the dock at the assizes of Dundalk, with that expression with which the Grand Master is represented to have surveyed the unfortunate Jewess. His friend Mr. Mac Kenna used to observe, that "if William Bellew saw a man hanging from every lamp-post down Capel street, in his morning walk from Great Charles street to the Four Courts, the only question he would ask, would be whether they were hanged according to law?"

Mr. Bellew came with signal advantages to the Bar. He was closely connected with the oldest and most opulent Roman Catholic families, and was employed as their domestic counsel. Their wills, their purchases, and marriage articles were drawn under his inspection. It was, I have heard, not a little agreeable to behold Mr. Bellew going through a marriage settlement, where an ancient Catholic family was to be connected with an inferior caste. In Ireland, as well as in the sister-country, the pride of birth prevails among the Roman Catholic gentry beyond almost any other passion. As in England we find a universal diffusion of cousinship through the principal Catholic houses, so the ancient blood of the Catholics of the Pale has been, by a similar process of intermarriage, carried through an almost uniform circulation.

This pride of birth among the Catholic gentry, when excluded from political distinction, was perfectly natural. Having no field for the exercise of their talents, and without any prospect of obtaining an ascent in society through their own merits, they looked back to the achievements of their ancestors, and consoled themselves with the brilliant retrospect. While a young Irish Protestant threw himself into the field of politics, an Irish Catholic was left without the least scope for enterprise, and had scarce any resource, but to pace up and down the damp apartments of his family mansion, and to commune with the high-plumed warriors of the Pale, who frowned in mouldering paint before him. The young ladies too were instructed to look with emulation on the composed visages of their grand aunts, and to reverence the huge circumference of hoop in which their more sacred symmetries were encompassed and concealed.

For a considerable time, it was possible to maintain the dignity of the Roman Catholic families without any plebeian intercourse; but at last the pressure of mortgages and judgments became too great, and it was requisite to save the estate at the expense of the purity of its owner's blood. After a struggle and a sigh, the head of an old Catholic house resigned himself to the urgency of circumstances, and yielded to the necessity of intermingling the vulgar stream, which had crept through the grocers and manufacturers of the Liberty, with a current which, however pure, began to run low. A priest, a friend of the family—who, as matrimony is one of the seven sacraments, thinks himself in duty bound to promote so salubrious a rite, is consulted. He gives a couple of taps to his gold snuff-box, tenders a pinch to the old gentleman; protests that there are risks in celibacy—that it is needful to husband the constitution and the estate; and, observing that the young squire, though a little pale, is a pretty fellow, puts his finger to his nose, and hints at a young damsel in New-Row (a penitent of his reverence, and a mighty good kind of young woman, not long come from the Cork convent), with ruddy cheeks and vigorous arms, a robust waist and antigallican toes. The parties are brought together. The effect of juxtaposition is notorious—most of my readers know it by experience. The young gentleman stutters a compliment; the heart of the young lady and her wooden fan are in a flutter; the question is popped. The old people put their heads together. Consideration of the marriage, high blood, and equity of redemption, upon one side; and rude health and twenty thousand pounds on the other. The bargain is struck; and, to insure the hymeneal negotiation, nothing remains but that Counsellor Bellew should look over the settlements.

Accordingly a Galway attorney prepares the draft marriage settlement, with a skin for every thousand, and waits on Mr. Bellew. Laying thirty guineas on the tables, and thinking that upon the credit of such a fee he may presume to offer his opinion, he commences with an ejaculation on the fall of the good old families, until Mr. Bellew, after counting the money, casts a Caius Marius look upon him, and awes him into respect. He unrolls the volume of parchment, and the eye of the illustrious conveyancer glistens at the sight of the ancient and venerable name that stands at the head of the indenture. But, as he advances through the labyrinth of limitations, he grows alarmed and disturbed; and, on arriving at the words "on the body of the said Judy Mac Gilligan to be begotten," he drops his pen, and puts the settlement away, with something of the look of a Frenchman when he intimates his perception of an unusually bad smell. It is only after an interval of reflection, and when he has recalled the fiscal philosophy of Vespasian, that he is persuaded to resume his labors; but does not completely recover his tranquillity of mind until, turning the back of his brief, he marks that most harmonious of all monosyllables, "paid," at the foot of the consolatory stipend.

No man at the Bar is more exact, careful, technical, and expert, in conveyancing, than Mr. Bellew. He at one time monopolized the whole Catholic business.

Nor was it to the Roman Catholic body that his reputation as a lawyer was confined. He deservedly obtained a very high character with the whole public for the extent of his erudition, his familiar knowledge of equity and of the common law, the clearness of his statements, the ingenuity and astuteness of his reasoning, and for that species of calm and deliberative elocution which is of such importance in the Court of Chancery.* I look upon Mr. Bellew as a man who has most

* In a book like this, chiefly devoted to legal subjects, it can not be out of place to make a brief statement respecting the British Court of Chancery. Next below the House of Lords, before which come all final appeals — the Chancery Court has jurisdiction. Originally established to moderate the severity and rectify the errors of the other Courts, its proceedings are essentially in *equity*, though, at times, it can act in the capacity of a Court of *common law*, though it can not summon a jury or try facts. Its power has been immense since its establishment, the exact date of which is not known, though it is ascertained that this Court had a separate jurisdiction on the reign of Edward

grievously suffered by his exclusion from the inner bar, from which nothing but his religion could have kept him. It was in the Court of Chancery that his business lay almost entirely;

III., and is believed to have been derived from the rule of the Saxon monarchs, when a party who thought justice was not rendered to him could appeal to the King in Council, for his revision of the case, most of which appeals, as they grew numerous, were transferred to a subject "learned in the law"—usually an ecclesiastic, at that time. This Court (amid other means to defeat and punish fraud, oppression, breaches of trust, and every kind of injustice) can compel a defendant to discover facts which are against his own cause. But the great evil, arising from increase and accumulation of business as well as from the delays of judges, has been the dilatory nature, with the consequent expense of the proceedings requisite to obtain a decision. Under Lord Eldon, who was Lord Chancellor for five-and-twenty years, and who doubted upon the simplest points, though his judgments were excellent when given, the Court of Chancery became a crying evil instead of a substantial good. Expenses and delays ruined many wealthy persons who had come before this tribunal, and it caused many a broken heart, and ruined hope. In Lord Eldon's time, owing to the accumulation of business, the amount of property litigated in Chancery, was eleven million pounds sterling or fifty-five million dollars. When Brougham was in the House of Commons, he repeatedly and strongly contended for the necessity of a Reform in the Court of Chancery. In 1830, Brougham became Chancellor. "There is Brougham," said Sydney Smith, "sworn in as Chancellor at noon, and laying on the table of the Lords, at six o'clock the same day, a Bill for Chancery Reform." A great deal was attempted in this respect —but the Lord Chancellor, who is not only a judge, but also a political leader, as one of the Cabinet, besides having to sit as Speaker of the House of Lords, is unable to do everything, unless he had fifty hands and twice fifty heads. The separation of the judicial from political labors of the Chancery has been suggested, and will probably take place. Lord Brougham, during the four years he presided, disposed of nearly all the arrears of his predecessors, Eldon and Lyndhurst, and cleared off, by prompt adjudication, the cases which originated in his own time and were ripe for decision. His successors (Cottenham, Lyndhurst, and Truro), did not follow in his steps; ill-health, pre-occupation with other matters, and disinclination to labor prevented them. In 1852, during nine months of which Lord St. Leonards was Chancellor, he manifested a strong inclination to reform the Chancery system; his successor, Lord Cranworth, appears disposed to let matters rest as they are. But there is a vast improvement on the system as it was in Lord Eldon's doubtful era. In his time, and greatly against his consent, a Vice-Chancellor was appointed, to assist the Chancellor—there now are *three*, besides two Lord Justices of Appeal, while a great deal of equity business continues to be done by the Master of the Rolls. The delaying course of referring cases to the Masters in Chancery, for inquiry, is in course of change; the number of Masters is lessened, and on the judges themselves will principally rest the immediate inquiry into, and examination of

and in that Court, it is absolutely necessary to have a silk gown, in order to be listened to with ordinary attention. The reason is this: not that Lord Manners pays no respect to any individual who is not in silk attire, but because the multitude of King's Counsel, who precede a lawyer in a stuff gown, of necessity exhaust the subject, and leave him the lees and dregs of the case.*

Mr. Bellew has lived to see his inferiors in talent and in knowledge raised above his head, and it is now his doom, at the end of a cause, to send his arguments like spent shot, after the real contest has been decided, and the hot fire is over. His situation would be very different, indeed, if it were his office to state cases and open important motions, for which no man is more eminently qualified. The whole Bar feel that he labors under a great hardship in this particular, for which a pension of six hundred pounds sterling a-year affords a very inadequate compensation. Mr. Bellew's pension of six hundred pounds has effectually excluded him from all useful interference in Roman Catholic affairs; for, whenever he opposes a popular measure, it is sufficient to refer to his salary at the Castle, in order to excite the popular feeling against him. He has, however, upon this subject, been a good deal misrepresented, and it is only an act of justice to him to state the facts.

The Catholic aristocracy supported the Union. They were led astray by a promise from Lord Cornwallis, and by such an intimation from Pitt as induced him to resign.† I do not

facts. With such "aids and appliances to boot," it is natural to expect that in future, cases will not be before the Court for forty, thirty, or even twenty years: one case was actually undecided after it had been over a century in the Court.—M.

* At the Irish, as well as at the English bar, no counsel is allowed to go over the same line of argument taken by another. Therefore, pre-audience being the right of those who have patents of precedency, or wear the silk gown or the coif, the junior in a stuff gown usually finds the subject exhausted, by previous speakers, before he has an opportunity of speaking. Now and then, a junior makes a hit by coming out with points of law or quoting cases neglected by his seniors—but this is rare.—M.

† There is no doubt that Pitt, when he intrigued to effect the Union, promised that it should be followed by Catholic Emancipation. When he found that George III. would not allow him to fulfil this promise, Pitt at once re-

intend to discuss the merits of the question, but can readily conceive that many a good man might have advocated the measure, without earning for his motto, "*Vendidit hic auro patriam.*"* I am fully convinced, from what I know of the honorable cast of Mr. Bellew's mind, that he never did promote the measure from any sordid views to his own interest. Lord Castlereagh was well aware of the importance of securing the support of the leading Roman Catholic gentry, and the place of assistant-barrister was promised to Mr. Bellew. Whether the promise was made before or after the Union, I am not aware; nor is it of consequence excepting we adopt the scholastic distinction of Father Foigard; in his argumentative assault upon Cherry's virtue: "If it be before, it is a bribe; if it be after, it is only a gratification." At all events, I am convinced that Mr. Bellew did nothing at variance with honor and conscience from any mercenary consideration.

The place of assistant-barrister became vacant: Lord Castlereagh was reminded of his engagement, when, behold! a petition, signed by the magistrates of the county to which Mr. Bellew was about to be nominated, is presented to the Lord-Lieutenant, praying that a Roman Catholic should not be appointed to any judicial office, and intimating their determina-

signed—as it was made, with an impression on his mind, cunningly kept up by the King, that there would be no obstacle, on the part of Royalty, to admitting the Catholics within the pale of the Constitution.—Lord Cornwallis, mentioned in the text, was Lord Lieutenant of Ireland during the insurrection of 1798, and went as plenipotentiary to France, in 1801, in which capacity he signed the treaty of Amiens. His whole public course was distinguished. In 1770, he was one of the four young peers who joined Lord Camden in a protest against the taxation of America, which made Lord Mansfield sneeringly say, "Poor Camden! he could only get four boys to support him"—yet, as a military man, Lord Cornwallis had a command in the American war, where he concluded his operations by being out-generalled by Washington, to whom he surrendered himself and his army. In 1786, he went out to India, as Governor-General and commander-in-chief, where he distinguished himself against Tippoo Saib. On his return, he was made a Marquis, in 1792. He was again sent to India in 1804, where he died, in 1805, aged sixty-seven. He was popular in Ireland, as well as in India, having certainly exerted himself to check the inhumanity of the triumphant royalists. He had no genius, but a great deal of common sense—which is more rare and valuable.—M.

* He sold his country for gold.—M.

tion not to act with him. The government were a good deal embarrassed by this notification; and in order at once to fulfil the spirit of their contract, and not to give offence to the Protestant magistrates, a pension equivalent to the salary of a chairman was given to Mr. Bellew, and he was put in the enjoyment of the fruits of the office, without the labor of cultivation.*

That it was reprehensible to tax the people with an additional pension on the part of the Irish government, out of the miserable dread of irritating a few Protestant gentlemen, can not, I think, be questioned: and but few persons will be inclined to attach any great blame to Mr. Bellew for having accepted of this compensation. It would be very idle, however, to enter into any explanation upon these subjects with the Roman Catholic body, among whom the very name of pensioner, connected as it is with all sorts of back door and postern services at the Castle, carries a deep stigma. No matter how well Mr. Bellew may argue a point at a Catholic assembly; no matter how cogent and convincing his arguments may

* The County judges in Ireland, who virtually preside at Quarter Sessions, while they are supposed only to advise the justices of the peace who sit (ignorant of law) upon the Bench, are called Assistant-Barristers, an appellation which by no means indicates their position and duties. Richard Martin, formerly of the Irish and now of the English bar—a man of great legal acumen, clear and reasoning eloquence, ready wit, and vast personal weight—tells a good anecdote illustrative of this. Henry Deane Freeman, an eminent lawyer, was "Assistant Barrister" in one of the Connaught counties, and went the Munster-Circuit, as a practising lawyer. He was prosecuting a man accused of robbery, who produced as witness to his character, another worthy, instantly recognised by Mr. Freeman, as an old acquaintance. In cross-examination this man was asked, "Have not you stood in the dock, as a criminal?"—The witness sulkily replied, "What's that to you?"—Mr. Freeman; "You must answer me. Were not you tried in Galway for robbery?" Witness: "Well, if I was, I didn't do it."—Mr. Freeman: "Of course not—the number of innocent culprits is immense. Were not you convicted and sent to jail for six months?"—By this time, the witness had recognised his examiner, who, as Assistant-Barrister in Galway, had tried and sentenced him. Turning to the judge, with a side-long look of contempt at Mr. Freeman, he said, *sotto voce*, as if he were confidentially communicating valuable information, "My Lord! you must not mind what that fellow says. He's an imposter. He isn't a real barrister. He's only an *Au*-sistant Barrister, and not worth your notice."—M.

be in favor of a more calm and moderate tone of proceedings; the moment Mr. O'Connell lifts up his strong arm, and with an ejaculation of integrity "thanks his God that he is not a pensioner!" all the Douay syllogisms of Mr. Bellew vanish at the exclamation, and yells and shouts assail the retainer of government from every side. Had he the eloquence of Demosthenes, the clinking of the gold would be heard amid the thunder.

Yet I entertain no doubt that Mr. Bellew has not, in his political conduct, been actuated by any mean and dishonest motive. I utterly dissent from him in his views, principles, and opinions; but I believe that he is only acting in conformity with impressions received at a very early period, which his education and habits tended not a little to confirm. His first opinions were formed at a period when the Roman Catholic aristocracy was actuated by a spirit very different from that which it has lately evinced. Much condemnation has been attached to that body for their want of vigor in the conduct of Catholic affairs. But allowances ought to be made for them. The penal code had, after a few years, ground the gentry almost to powder. They lived in a state of equal terror and humiliation. From their infancy they were instructed to look upon every Protestant with alarm; for it was in the power of the meanest member of that privileged class to file a bill of discovery, and strip them of their estates. At their ordinary meals, they must have regarded their own children with awe, and felt that they were at their mercy.

Swift represents the whole body as little better than hewers of wood and drawers of water. The complication of indignities to which they were exposed must necessarily have generated bad moral influences; and accordingly we find in their petitions and remonstrances a tone of subserviency at which their descendants would blush. Even after the penal code was relaxed, and they were restored to the rank of citizens, they preserved the attitude of humility to which they had been accustomed; and when the load which they had carried so long was taken off, they retained a stoop. At length, however, they stand erect in their country; and, with very few exceptions, exhibit the same spirit as the great mass of the people.

Lord Fingall, though prevented by his health from taking an active part in public affairs, gives evidence of his assent to the bold and vigorous course of measures adopted by the body, of which he is the hereditary head, by the presence of his son. The latter, Lord Killeen, manifests as much energy and determination, as he does sound sense and admirable discretion.* Lord Gormanstown has thrown himself with enthusiasm into the national cause, and feels the injuries of his country with a deep and indignant sensibility;† and even Lord Kenmare, whose love of retirement excludes him from the bustle of public meetings, lends to the Catholic Association the authority of his name, and shows that the spirit of patriotism has penetrated the deep woods of Killarney, in which his lordship and his excellent lady (the sister of Mr. Wilmot Horton) are connubially embowered.‡ I should not omit to add,

* The late Earl of Fingall was the Catholic Peer who, at the Royal visit to Ireland in 1821, was made a Knight of St Patrick by George IV. In the poem called "The Irish Avatara," in ridicule of the servility of all ranks and creeds on this occasion, Byron asks

"Will thy yard of blue riband, poor Fingall, recall
The fetters from millions of Catholic limbs?"

The barony of Killeen dates as early as 1181. The Earldom was created in 1628, and Lord Fingall was made a peer of the United Kingdom in 1831. He died in July, 1826. His son, Lord Killeen, who is Lord Lieutenant of Meath, represented that county in 1831, and took a prominent part in politics, before the Catholic Relief Bill was passed, in 1829. He is a Privy Counsellor of Ireland.—M.

† An ancestor of Viscount Gormanstown sided with James II., in Ireland, and after his death William's government passed an outlawry against him for high treason. The title ceased to be legally recognised, but in August, 1800, on proceedings taken in the Court of King's Bench, by consent of the Crown, the outlawry was reversed, and Jenico Preston received a writ of summons as a peer, and is the twelfth Viscount. He took part with O'Connell in the agitation preceding Emancipation.—M.

‡ The ancestor of the Earl of Kenmare received a peerage from James II. which was not recognised, as it was conferred after that Monarch had lost the throne. In 1800, the Earldom was created anew. In 1841, Lord Kenmare was made a British peer. After Emancipation, he took little part in politics, but was a Catholic and a Whig. He died in the autumn of 1853. The Ken-

that Sir Edward Bellew and his son, who is a young man of very considerable abilities, and likely to make a distinguished figure, displayed during the late election for the county of Louth great public spirit, energy, and determination.

But amid this almost universal change in the general temperature of the country, amid this general ascent of the mercurial spirit of the people, Mr. William Bellew remains at zero. Not the smallest influence is perceptible in the cold rigidity of his opinions. True to the doctrine of non-resistance, he brings up in its support the whole barbarous array of syllogistic forms with which his recollections of Douay can supply him. It is in vain that the rapid progress of the Catholic cause is urged against him: you appeal in vain to the firmness, union, and organization of the people, which have been effected through the Catholic Association: the insurrection of the peasantry against their landlords, and the consequent sense of their own rights with which they have begun to be impressed, are treated with utter scorn by this able dialectician, who meets you at every step with his major drawn from religion, and his minor derived from passive obedience, and disperses your harangue with his peremptory conclusion. Nor is it to speculation that he confines his innate reverence for the powers that be; for after the dissolution of the old Roman Catholic Association by an act of Parliament, when an effort was making to raise another body out of its ruins, of his own accord Mr. Bellew gratuitously published a letter, in the public journals, to demonstrate to the Attorney-General that it would be legal to put it down. In this view Mr. Plunket does not appear to have concurred.

mare estates include some of the finest parts of Killarney scenery, and the Earl, who was not an absentee, was an excellent landlord.—Sir Robert Wilmot Horton, who assumed the latter name on marriage with an heiress—a very lovely woman, upon whom Lord Byron wrote the lines commencing

"She walks in beauty—like the light
Of cloudless climes and stormy skies,
And all that's best of dark and bright
Meet in her aspect and her eyes;"

was an earnest advocate for Emigration, went to Ceylon as Governor, and died in 1841.—M.

Notwithstanding the censure which I have intimated of Mr. Bellew's political tendencies and opinions, I repeat, and that sincerely and unaffectedly, that I entirely acquit him of all deliberate corruption. His private life gives an earnest of integrity which I can not question. It is, in all his individual relations in society, deserving of the most unqualified encomium. It would be a deviation from delicacy, even for the purposes of praise, to follow Mr. Bellew through the walks of private life. Suffice it to say, that a more generous, amiable, and tender-hearted man is not to be found in his profession, and underneath a frozen and somewhat rugged surface, a spring of deep and abundant goodness lives in his mind.

If in the hasty writing of the present sketch, I have allowed grotesque images in connection with Mr. Bellew to pass across my mind, I have "set down naught in malice;" and if I have ventured on a smile, that smile has not been sardonic. In addition to the other qualities of Mr. Bellew for which he merits high praise, I should not omit his sincere spirit of religion. He is one of those few who unite with the creed of the Pharisee the sensibilities of the Samaritan. Mr. Bellew is a devout and unostentatious Roman Catholic, deeply convinced of the truth of his religion, and most rigorous in the practice of its precepts. The only requisite which he wants to give him a complete title to spiritual perfection, is one in which some of his learned brethren are not deficient; and it can not be said that he "has given joy in heaven," upon the principle on which so many barristers have the opportunity of administering to the angelic transports. One of the results of his having been always equally moral and abstemious as at present is, that his dedication to religion attracts no notice. If another barrister receives the sacrament, it is bruited through town; and at all the Catholic parties, the ladies describe, with a pious minuteness, the collected aspect, the combined expression of penitence and humility, the clasped hands, and the uplifted eyes of the counsellors; while the devout Mr. Bellew, who goes through the same sacred exercise, passes without a comment.

In truth, I should not myself know that Mr. Bellew was a

man of such strong religious addictions, but for an incident which put me upon the inquiry. Upon Ash-Wednesday, it is the practice among pious Catholics to approach the altar; and while he repeats in a solemn tone, "Remember, man, that thou art dust," with the ashes which he carries in a vase the priest impresses the foreheads of those who kneel before him with the sign of the cross.

Some two or three years ago, I recollect the court was kept waiting for Mr. Bellew, and the Master of the Rolls began to manifest some unusual symptoms of impatience, when at last Mr. Bellew entered, having just come from his devotions; and such was his haste from chapel, that he had omitted to efface the "*memento mori*" from his brow. The countenance of this gentleman is in itself sufficiently full of melancholy reminiscences; but when the Master of the Rolls, raising his eyes from a notice which he was diligently perusing, looked him full in the face, he gave an involuntary start. The intimation of judicial astonishment directed the general attention to the advocate; and traced in broad sepulchral lines, formed of ashes of ebony in the very centre of Mr. Bellew's forehead, and surmounted by an ample and fully-powdered wig, the black and appalling emblem. The burning cross upon the forehead of the sorcerer, in "The Monk," could not have produced a more awful effect. The Six Clerks stood astonished; the Registrar was petrified; the whiskers of Mr. Daniel M'Kay, the Irish Vice-Chancellor, stood on end; and while Mr. Driscoll explained the matter to Mr. Sergeant Lefroy, Sir William M'Mahon with some abruptness of tone declared that he would not go beyond the motion.*

* Sir William M'Mahon, appointed Master of the Rolls in Ireland, through the influence of his brother, Sir John, Private Secretary to George IV. when Regent, was anything but a lawyer. Mr. Sheil's first wife was Miss O'Hallaron, niece to Sir William.—M.

MICHAEL O'LOGHLIN.

"COUNSELLOR O'LOGHLIN, my motion is on, in the Rolls!" "Oh, Counsellor, I'm ruined for the want of you in the Common Pleas!" "For God's sake, Counsellor, step up for a moment to Master Townsend's office!" "Counsellor, what *will* I do without you in the King's Bench!" "Counsellor O'Loghlin, Mr. O'Grady is carrying all before him in the Court of Exchequer!" Such were the simultaneous exclamations, which, upon entering the Hall of the Four Courts, at the beginning of last term, I heard from a crowd of attorneys, who surrounded a little gentleman, attired in a wig and gown, and were clamorously contending for his professional services, which they had respectively retained, and to which, from the strenuousness of their adjurations, they seemed to attach the utmost value.

Mr. O'Loghlin stood in some suspense in the midst of this riotous competition. While he was deliberating to which of the earnest applicants for his attendance he should addict himself, I had an opportunity to take notes of him. He had at first view a very juvenile aspect. His figure was light—his stature low, but his form compact, and symmetrically put together. His complexion was fresh and healthy, and intimated a wise acquaintance with the morning sun, more than a familiarity with the less salubrious glimmerings of the midnight lamp. His hair was of sanded hue, like that of his Danish forefathers, from whom his name, which in Gaelic signifies Denmark, as well as his physiognomy, intimates his descent. Although at first he appeared to have just passed the boundaries of boyhood, yet upon a closer inspection all symptoms of puerility disappeared. His head is large, and, from the breadth and altitude of the forehead, denotes a more than ordinary quantity of that valuable pulp, with the abundance of which the intellectual power is said to be in measure. His large eyes of deep blue, although not enlightend by the flashings of constitutional vivacity, carry a more professional expression, and bespeak caution, sagacity, and slyness, while his mouth exhibits a steadfast kindliness of nature, and a tranquillity of temper, mixed with some love of ridicule, and, although perfectly free from malevolence, a lurking tendency to derision.* An enormous bag, pregnant with briefs, was thrown over his shoulder. To this prodigious wallet of litigation on his back, his person presented a curious contrast.

At the moment I surveyed him, he was surrounded by an aggregate meeting of attorneys, each of whom claimed a title paramount to "the Counsellor," and vehemently enforced their respective rights to his exclusive appropriation. He seemed to be at a loss to determine to which of these amiable expostulators his predilections ought to be given. I thought that he chiefly hesitated between Mr. Richard Scott, the protector

* Mr. O'Loghlin's appearance was very distinguished. He had clear blue eyes, which almost seemed to smile, if I may so express it. His light hair curled closely and crisply on a head which was beautifully set upon his shoulders. His figure was compact and light, and, as much as any one whom I recollect on the Munster Circuit, his neatness of attire evidenced that he cultivated the graces. In those days, barristers wore neither wigs nor gowns in the Assize Courts, on circuit, and thus every one could notice their "human face divine," without the professional accompaniments which so much change its expression. Mr. O'Connell very frequently wore a green sporting jacket, in the Assize Court—but his usual attire was the "customary suit of solemn black." He was careful, and rather felicitous, in the tie of his white cravat, but, when he warmed in a speech, he used to seize this article of his dress and pull it on one side or the other, occasionally varying the action, by twitching his black wig from right to left, and back again, as if to adjust it properly on his head.—Mr. Wolfe, who subsequently became Chief Baron of the Exchequer, presented a marked contrast to O'Loghlin and O'Connell. He was careless in his attire, wore his garments as if he never had consulted a mirror, and had a habit of thrusting his long hands through his dark hair. He was tall in stature, awkward and angular in his movements, and swarthy in complexion. His voice, like that of most Irish barristers, was clear and strong; his utterance good; and his occasional emphacising very effective with juries.—M.

of the subject in Ennis, and Mr. Edward Hickman, the patron of the crown, upon the Connaught circuit. Ned, a loyalist of the brightest water, had hold of him by one shoulder, while Dick, a patriot of the first magnitude, laid his grasp upon the other. Between their rival attractions, Mr. O'Loghlin stood with a look, which, so far from intimating that either of "the two charmers" should be away, expressed regret at his inability to apportion himself between these fascinating disputants for his favors. Mr. Scott, whose countenance was inflamed with anxiety for the numerous clients, exhibited great vehemence and emotion. His meteoric hair stood up, his quick and eager eye was on fire, the indentations upon his forehead were filled with perspiration, and the whole of his strongly Celtic visage was moved by that honorable earnestness, which arises from a solicitude for the interest of those who intrust their fortunes to his care. Ned Hickman, whose countenance never relinquishes the expression of mixed finesse and drollery for which it is remarkable, excepting when it is laid down for an air of profound reverence for the Attorney-General, was amusingly opposed to Mr. Scott; for Ned holds all emotion to be vulgar, and, on account of its gentility, hath addicted himself to self-control.

Mr. O'Loghlin, as I have intimated, seemed for some time to waver between them, but at length Mr. Hickman, by virtue of a whisper, accompanied by a look of official sagacity (for he is one of the crown solicitors), prevailed, and was carrying Mr. O'Loghlin off in triumph, when a deep and rumbling sound was heard to issue from the Court of Exchequer, and shortly after, there was seen descending its steps, a form of prodigious altitude and dimensions, in whose masses of corpulency, which were piled up to an amazing height, I recognised no less eminent a person than Bumbo Green.* He came like an ambula-

* The individual known as "Bumbo" Green, was well known, in the Irish law-Courts, some five-and-twenty years ago. I saw him once — and to see was to remember. He was an attorney in good practice; hailing, I believe, from the west of Ireland. He knew the private affairs of three fourths of the estated gentlemen in the counties of Galway and Clare, and no lawsuit of any importance was entered into, in that part of the world, without Mr. Green being em-

tory hill. This enormous heap of animation approached to put in his claim to Mr. O'Loghlin. Bumbo had an action, which was to be tried before Chief Baron O'Grady against the proprietor of the mail-coach to Ennis, for not having provided a vehicle large enough to contain him. Mr. O'Loghlin was to state his case. Bumbo had espied the capture which Ned Hickman had made of his favorite counsel. It was easy to perceive, from the expression of resolute severity which sat upon his vast and angry visage, that he was determined not to acquiesce in this unwarrantable proceeding. As he advanced, Ned Hickman stood appalled, and, conscious of the futility of remonstrance, let loose the hold which he had upon the Counsellor, while the latter, with that involuntary and somewhat reluctant, but inevitable submission, which is instinctively paid to great by little men, obeyed the nod of his enormous employer, and, with the homage which the Attorney-General for Lilliput might be supposed to entertain for a solicitor from Brobdignag, passively yielded to the do-

ployed, on one side or the other. He was "a noticeable man" (to use Coleridge's phrase)—but chiefly on account of his immense size. The great Daniel Lambert died before my time, so that I can not personally compare him with Bumbo Green;—I suspect that in corporeal extent there could not have been much difference. Mr. Green was the biggest man I ever saw. He was tall, but, from his obesity, appeared below the ordinary stature. He had a smiling, winning manner, and was liked, for his good temper and fun, by every one. To see him attempt to sit down on the attorney's narrow bench was ludicrous in the extreme. What is called "the small of the back" he was not possessor of, and therefore to rest upon a narrow seat was as hopeless a task for him, as it would have been for a cherub—but from quite a different cause, "Bumbo" Green having a redundancy of what cherubs are so deficient in, that it is evident they never can *sit* for their portraits! Bumbo Green flourished in the ante-railway era, and, on a journey, had to occupy and pay for two seats in the stage-coach. On one occasion, he ordered his servant to take two seats for him in the mail-coach from Ennis to Dublin. The man executed the command, but, being a rather green hand, only a few days in Green's employment, committed a trifling mistake. When Bumbo Green went to the coach-office, he found all the inside seats occupied, except one. His servant not knowing his habit, had taken the seats—one outside, and the other within!—Bumbo Green, like nearly all very stout men whom I have ever known, was fond of dancing, and danced lightly too. He had a great many good qualities, and the perpetual sunshine of good temper gleamed brightly over them all.—M.

minion, and followed into the Exchequer the gigantic waddle of Bumbo Green.

But a truce to merriment. The merits of Mr. O'Loghlin, with whom I open this continuation of the Sketches of the Catholic Bar, are of a character which demand a serious and most respectful consideration. He is not of considerable standing, and yet is in the receipt of an immense income, which the most jealous of his competitors will not venture to insinuate that he does not deserve. He is in the utmost demand in the Hall of the Four Courts, and is among the very best of the commodities which are to be had in that staple of the mind. He is admitted, upon all hands, to be an excellent lawyer, and a master of the practice of the courts, which is of far greater importance than the black and recondite erudition, to which so many barristers exclusively devote so many years of unavailing labor. The questions to which deep learning is applicable are of frequent occurrence, while points connected with the course and forms of legal proceedings arise every day, and afford to a barrister, who has made them his study, an opportunity of rendering himself greatly serviceable to his clients. It is not by displays of research upon isolated occasions, that a valuable and money-making reputation is to be established. "Practice," as it is technically called, is the alchemy of the Bar. When it is once ascertained that a lawyer is master of it, he becomes the main resource of attorneys, who depend upon him for their guidance through the mazes of every intricate and complicated case. Mr. O'Loghlin has Tidd at his fingers' ends, and is, besides, minutely acquainted with that unwritten and traditional practice which governs Irish justice; and which, not having been committed to books, is acquired by an unremitting attention to what is going on in court.*

* Mention has been made, in a previous note, of the rates of payment to the judges, varying from eight hundred to one thousand pounds sterling a year (the salaries of Irish Assistant-Barristers, Scottish Sheriffs, and English County Court Judges), to ten thousand pounds sterling per annum, the amount fixed, by Act of Parliament, as the Lord-Chancellor's official income. Those who are accustomed to the present very small remuneration allowed to the occupants of judicial seats in the United States may consider the British payment

It is not to be considered, from the praise bestowed upon Mr. O'Loghlin in this most useful department of his profession, that he does not possess other and very superior qualifications.

as extravagant—especially, as the offices (with the exception of the Chancellorship, which is political as well as legal) are held for life, or during good behavior, which is the same. Added to this is the system of granting pensions or retiring allowances to the judges—amounting to nearly two thirds of their annual salaries—after fifteen years' service or in the event of earlier retirement from ill health. The British plan is based upon a very broad principle—namely, that of tempting the very best lawyers to become judges, by making it worth their while to surrender the great incomes which they can earn at the bar. In Great Britain and Ireland, a lawyer in full practice may earn from three thousand to twelve thousand pounds sterling per annum—some have obtained more. To tempt any of these men, in the prime of life and the fullness of profitable labor, to assume the ermine of the judge instead of the gown of the barrister, there are three or four conjunct inducements. There is a permanent station of honorable rank secured to him who becomes a judge. There is a certain income, which, though far lower than he may have previously earned, is obtained in comparative ease and repose. There is the removal of all doubt as to the future—for a failure of health may assail the most active lawyer, and speedily incapacitate him from future exertion, whereas, when a judge, he may retire after a certain length of public service, provided for, during the residue of life, by the bountiful gratitude of the public, which also provides for his future, in case of his health breaking up. On the bench, it is true, a lawyer does not wholly enjoy "otium cum dignitate,"—for the judge, if he do his duty, has no sinecure. But he is removed from the cares, the bustle, the struggles, which are inseparable from the active life of a busy lawyer, and which form the wear and tear of his mind, and he assumes a position of dignified and honorable labor, in the discharge of duties more important than those of an advocate, while they are of a different and less mind-oppressing order. A seat upon the judicial bench, therefore, is the object of a British lawyer's honorable ambition, for which he strives and competes—not by linking himself with any political party, not by descending to canvassing or solicitation, but by knowledge of the laws, by industry, and by unimpeachable conduct. These judicial appointments are virtually held for life, because the becoming entitled to a pension after fifteen years' service, does not necessarily cause a judge to retire at the expiration of that period. For the most part, we find the judges continuing in office to the end. Of late years there have been only two retirements—Erskine (son of the Chancellor) from ill health, and, more recently, Patteson, from deafness. It is to the credit of George III. (who had the good sense, amid much obtuseness, sometimes to take advice) to commence his reign, in 1760, by recommending Parliament to enact that the judges should not be removable, as before, by the demise of the Sovereign cancelling their Commissions. It had been the custom to issue new Commissions, in such cases, and then a judge who had rendered himself obnoxious by independence, might be displaced, as

He is familiar with every branch of the law, and has his knowledge always at command. There are many whose learning lies in their minds, like treasure in rusty coffers which it is a toil to open, or masses of bullion in the vaults of the Bank of Ireland, unfit for the purposes of exchange, and difficult to be put into circulation. Mr. O'Loghlin bears his wealth about him—he can immediately apply it—and carries his faculties like coined money, "*in numerato habet.*" He is not a maker of sentences, and does not impress his phrases on the memory of his hearers; but he has what is far better than what is vulgarly designated as eloquence. He is perfectly fluent, easy, and natural. His thoughts run in a smooth and clear current, and his diction is their appropriate channel. His perceptions are exceedingly quick, and his utterance is, therefore, occasionally rapid; but, although he speaks at times with velocity, he never does so with precipitation. He is extremely brief, and indulges in no useless amplification.

matter of routine, on the accession of a new sovereign. The result has been that, since this independence has thus been established, we have had some remarkable instances where a judge has acted directly in opposition to the desires and interests of the Government. For example, Lord Camden (when Chief Justice of the Common Pleas, in 1763) decided that the Secretary of State had acted illegally, in arresting John Wilkes, on a general warrant—which ought not to be issued except in the urgent case of high treason. So, a few years ago, Lord Chief Justice Denman's denial, as a constitutional lawyer (*in re* Stockdale *v.* Howard) that either House of Parliament had a right to publish libels, as part of their proceedings, and to authorize their public sale. In England, there are few instances of a judge soiling his ermine by truckling to Power. I recollect only two instances in my own time. Once, on the trial of William Hone for publishing parodies on parts of the Bible (his real offence being that he had ridiculed the Prince Regent) when Lord Ellenborough actually *desired* the jury to bring in a verdict of guilty, which they declined doing. The other, during the trial of the Chartist rioters, when Lord Abinger, who tried the case, acted more like the prosecuting counsel than the judge, and roundly abused the prisoners on account of their politics. But in Ireland, where there are corrupt sheriffs and packed juries, partisan judges have not been so rare. That class did not cease with Lord Norbury: it still exists. In questions between man and man, the bulk of the Irish judges have shown praiseworthy impartiality. When it was the Government against the subject, the case sometimes became different. The State Trials of 1844 and 1848, were conducted in a manner which reminded us of 1798, and which would have almost driven England into insurrection, had it occurred there.—M.

There is not the smallest trace of affectation in anything which he either does or says; and it is surprising with what little appearance of exertion he brings all the powers of his mind into play. His points are put with so much brevity, simplicity, and clearness, that he has, of necessity, become a great favorite with the Judges, who give him a willing audience, because he is sure to be pertinent and short; and having said all that is fitting to be said, and no more, has immediately done. He is listened to the more readily, because he is apparently frank and artless; but he merely puts on a show of candor, for few possess more suppleness and craft.

No man adapts himself with more felicity to the humors and the predispositions of the judges whom he addresses. Take, for example, the Exchequer, where, both on the law and equity sides of the court, he is in immense business. He appeals to the powerful understanding, and sheer common-sense, of Standish O'Grady,* in whom Rhadamanthus and Sancho

* Of Standish O'Grady, Chief-Baron of the Irish Exchequer, from 1803 to 1831, a notice has already been given (vol i., p. 135), but an anecdote can scarcely be out of place here. He had a caustic wit, which was the more keen because ever unobtrusive. The quiet manner in which the Chief-Baron would insult a man, barbed the shaft. For example, a certain Mr. Burke Bethell was at the Irish bar. He had ability, learning, eloquence, and industry, but was one of the men who appeared as if born under an evil star, and never could get on. It was stated, and believed, that he took business at any rate — that is, he would initial a brief marked two, five, or ten guineas, as if he had received that amount (for without such proof of payment the taxing-master would strike the item out of the attorney's bill of costs), and accept a fourth of the nominal sum. This had reached the ears of O'Grady, who had never known the want of money, and had a lofty idea of what is called "the dignity of the profession." On one occasion, Burke Bethell had the luck, by some accident, to receive a brief in some small case in which the Crown was seeking penalties, under the Excise laws, from some fiscal delinquent. The Court of Exchequer was the tribunal before which the case was to be tried, Bethell, determined to cut a figure, had somewhat Adonized his attire, and presented himself before the Chief-Baron, who, affecting not to recognise him (wearing the unusual disguise of a clean shirt), surveyed him through his eye-glass, and, stooping down, asked who the gentleman was — with an air like that which Brummell must have worn when he asked his companion, who stopped to speak to George IV., "Who is your fat friend?" — Bethel, with an air of great importance, thus commenced: "My Lord, on this occasion, I have the honor to appear for the Crown." The Chief-Baron, interrupting him, in his

Panza seem combined. He hits the metaphysical propensities of Baron Smith,* with a distinction, in which it would

blandest manner, and with his sweetest smile, interjected, "And, sometimes, I believe, Mr. Bethell, *for the half-crown!*" — On the subject of taking less than the regulation fee or *honorarium*, I recollect an illustration or two. Fitzgibbon, father of Lord-Chancellor Clare, was a lawyer in good practice, and very fond of money. A client once brought him a brief and fee, that he might personally apologize for the smallness of the latter. Fitzgibbon, muttering that they should have intermediately reached him through the hands of an attorney, took both — but looked most gloomily on the very limited amount of the fee. The client sorrowfully admitted the cause for discontent, but added, that it was "all he had in the world." — "Well, then," said Fitzgibbon, "as that's the case, and you have no more, why, I must — *take it.*" Which he did, no doubt. — To match this, there is an anecdote of a certain Mr. Sergeant Cockle, of the English bar, who was accused of the grave offence of having taken a half fee, and even of having accepted part of the money in the copper coin of the realm. The charge duly came before the bar-mess for adjudication, and was fully sustained by evidence. In defence, Cockle briefly said: "It is quite true that I took half a guinea, where the fee should have been a guinea, and that it was made up of a crown-piece, four shillings, two sixpences, and sixpence in copper." There was a great sensation on this confession of the charge. But Cockle went on: "But, gentlemen, before I took the money, I ascertained it was the last farthing the poor devil had, and I appeal to the honorable profession, whether, under such circumstances, taking his last penny from him, I was not quite justified, and have maintained the character of the bar?" It was unanimously agreed that he had done all that a lawyer could do, in such a case, and, honorably acquitting Cockle, the bar-mess inflicted the fine of a basket of claret upon his accuser — the grand rule at all mess-trials being that somebody must be mulcted in the generous juice of the grape! — How different is this merely professional acquisitiveness from the generous feeling of the sailor at Gibraltar, during the early and warlike years of the present century. Landing at "the Rock," with his comrades, all agreed, having plenty of money, that it would be suitable and creditable for each to purchase a gold-laced cocked-hat. On reassembling at night, one man had a silver-laced hat and was immediately denounced (with a promise of early *cobbing*, when they were on board) as a shabby fellow. His protest had all the energy of truth. "Messmates," said he, "I scorn the charge. When I went to the man who sells the gold-lacers, I found that he had not one left. So, I took this silver-lacer, but paid him for it *all as one as if 'twere gold.*" Of course, Jack was honorably acquitted. — M.

* Sir William Cusack Smith, one of the Barons of the Exchequer in Ireland, was a remarkable man. He was born in January, 1766, and died in August, 1836, in his seventy-first year. His father, Sir Michael Smith, was a great lawyer, and finally became Master of the Rolls. The younger Smith studied at Oxford, and there obtained the friendship of Edmund Burke, at whose

have puzzled St. Thomas Aquinas, without the aid of inspiration, to detect a difference: when every other argument has failed with Baron M'Cleland, he tips him the wink, and point-

country-house, in a neighboring county, he passed all his leisure. In 1788, he was called to the Irish bar, and soon after became Doctor of Civil Law, to qualify him for practice in the Ecclesiastical Courts. In 1795, Mr. William Smith was made king's counsel, and entered Parliament in the same year. He strenuously supported the Union, not only by his votes and speeches, but as a pamphleteer. In 1800, he was made Solicitor-General, and in 1802, when his father, who then was a *puisne* Baron of the Exchequer, was raised to the higher dignity of Master of the Rolls (the second equity Judge in Ireland, and not removable as the Chancellor is, on a change of ministry), the younger Smith succeeded him. In 1808, by his father's death, he succeeded to the baronetcy. Sir William Smith, who had studied in the school of Burke, was what is called "an old whig," and strongly advocated the justice and policy of Catholic Emancipation. When this was granted, and the Repeal agitation followed, Sir William Smith denounced it as impolitic, ungrateful, and illegal. Up to that time, he had been in high favor with the Catholic leaders. But, in February, 1834, Mr. O'Connell moved that the House of Commons should appoint a Committee to inquire into Sir William Smith's judicial conduct — mainly complaining that, in his charges to grand-juries at the Assizes, he largely introduced political subjects, and that his habits were singularly at variance with what ought to be the habits of a judge. It was stated by Mr. O'Connell (and not denied) that Baron Smith commonly came into the Court about half-past twelve at noon — that he thus delayed the despatch of business — that, at Armagh, he had tried fourteen prisoners between six o'clock in the evening and six in the morning — that one of these trials had actually commenced long after midnight, and that his whole course was irregular. This *primâ-facie* case against Baron Smith was so strong, that (the whig ministry siding with Mr. O'Connell) the motion for inquiry was carried by a majority of 167 to 74. A week after, however, Mr. Peel and his party reopened the question, defended Baron Smith, accused O'Connell of personal and vindictive motives, and proposed that the vote for inquiry be rescinded — which was done, by a majority of 165 to 159. There is no doubt that Baron Smith's habits had latterly become very eccentric. As a judge he was impartial, and was humane even to a fault. He had a horror of sentencing a culprit to death, and "leant to mercy's side" on the trial of all capital offences. He was attached to letters, and published several pamphlets, chiefly on politics, which are forgotten. He also was author of an examination of the Hohenloe miracles. The only work by which he is likely to be remembered as an author, is a singular production called "Metaphysical Rambles." — His second son, Thomas Berry Cusack Smith, Attorney-General under the Peel administration, conducted the O'Connell State Trials in 1844. He is now (1854) Master of the Rolls, as his grandfather was, and completes the singular instance of three out of one family having successively worn the ermine. — M.

ing with his thumb to the opposite attorney, suggests the merits of the client, by a pantomimic reference to those of his representative; and with the same spirit of exquisite adaptation, plunges into the darkest abysses of black-letter erudition with Baron Pennefather, and provokes his Lordship into a citation from the Year-books (which excruciates the ears of Mr. Furlong) in Tipperary French.

Mr. O'Loghlin is a native of Clare.* I had at first, and before I had made more minute inquiries, conjectured, from the omega in his name, that he must be lineally descended from some of the ancient monarchs of Ireland, or be at least collaterally connected with one of the Phenician dynasties. Upon investigation, however, I discovered that "the big O," the celebrated object of royal antipathy, was but a modern annexation; and that, as I have already intimated, Mr. O'Loghlin

* The late Sir Michael O'Loghlin, it is scarcely too much to say, was one of the best judges that Ireland ever possessed. Able, acute, clear-headed, and thoroughly just, he towered above his fellows. He was born in October, 1789, and though he had immense practice at the bar, was excluded by his religion (he was a Catholic) from obtaining professional preferment as early as he deserved it. When the liberals came into power, after the granting of Emancipation, his talents obtained due recognition. He was made third Sergeant in 1831; second Sergeant in 1832; Solicitor-General in 1834; Attorney-General in 1835; and was made one of the Barons of the Exchequer in 1836—being, I think, the first Catholic judge for one hundred and fifty years. On the Bench he maintained and, if possible, increased the reputation he had won at the bar. All parties and all creeds honored and respected the upright judge, and the urbane and accomplished gentleman. There was a general feeling of gratification, at the bar, and among the public, when, in 1837, he was raised to the dignity of Master of the Rolls. In this capacity, he showed the great grasp of his mind, for, though his bar-practice had chiefly been at *common law*, his decisions in *equity* were irrefragable. In 1838, he was created a Baronet. Sir Michael O'Loghlin died, September, 1842, aged fifty-three. The legal profession of Ireland, who knew his value, raised a large sum for the purpose of erecting a monument to perpetuate their sense of his worth. It has been erected, and consists of his statue, by M'Dowall (an Irish artist), which is appropriately placed in the Hall of the Four Courts, Dublin—the only other statue in that suitable situation being one of Justice, toward which it looks.—Sir Coleman O'Loghlin, educated at London University, and called to the Irish bar in 1840, is eldest son of the late Master of the Rolls, and has already obtained a high reputation. He was employed for the defence, in the State Trials of 1844 and 1848, and acquitted himself with great distinction.—M.

is of a Danish origin. It has often been observed that the face of some remote progenitor reappears, after the lapse of centuries, in his progeny; and in walking through the halls of ancient families, it is surprising sometimes to see, in the little boy who whips his top beside you, a transcript of some old warrior who frowns in armor on the mouldering canvass above your head. There is preserved among the O'Loghlins a picture of their ancestor. He was a captain in the Danish navy. The likeness of this able cruiser off the Irish coast to the Counsellor is wonderful. He was a small, square, compact, and active little fellow, with great shrewdness and intelligence of expression. Domestic tradition has preserved some traits of his character, which show that the mind, as well as the face, can be preserved during ages of unimpaired transmission to the last. He was remarkable for his skill as a navigator. Not a pilot in all Denmark worked a ship better. He sent his light and quick-sailing galley through the most intricate quicksands. His coolness and self-possession never deserted him, and in the worst weather he was sure to get into port. He generally kept close to the shore, and seldom sailed upon desperate adventures. Remarkable for his talent in surprising the enemy, and stealing into their creeks and harbors, he would unexpectedly assail them, and carry some rich prize away. The descendant of this eminent cruiser works a cause upon the same principles as his ancestor commanded a ship. He holds the helm with a steady and skilful hand, and shifts his sails with the nicest adaptation to every veering circumstance that occurs in his course. Sometimes, indeed, he goes very close to the wind, but never misses stays. I scarcely ever saw him aground. He hits his adversary between wind and water, and, when he lies most secure, sails into his anchorage, boards, and cuts him out. It is not, therefore, to be wondered at, that he is in as great practice in the Hall as his forefather was upon the ocean, of whom it is recorded that he—

> "Pursued o'er the high seas, his watery journey,
> And merely practised as a sea-attorney."

FRANCIS BLACKBURNE.

I AM one of those whose political information is derived from a perusal of "The Weekly Register,"* through the ample columns of which I disport myself upon Saturday evening, and refresh myself with news much older than the beverage with which I raise my spirit to the proper pitch of patriotism, in order to wash down the eloquence of the Catholic Association. While others busy themselves in political anticipations, and leave Time panting and toiling after them, I follow him at a distance, and am contented if, upon the eve of the Sabbath, I can collect enough of news to join in the discussions of divers Popish counsellors, who assemble at half past one o'clock to offer their devotions to "our Lady of Carmel," under the auspices of Mr. L'Estrange, in the avenues of Clarendon-street Chapel. In this sacred spot, just after benediction, one may observe a certain convocation of politic lawyers with huge prayer-books, bound in green morocco, under their arms. After years of hebdomadal employment, the golden pages of these holy volumes look as bright and fresh as when they issued from the burnishing hands of the bookseller to Maynooth College, and bear evidence of the care which the pious

* A newspaper of great influence in those days (1827) and for twenty years after. It sided with Mr. O'Connell through the great struggle for Emancipation, and the various efforts to obtain Repeal, by means of a Parliamentary enactment. When Mr. Duffy, in *The Nation*, and Mr. John Mitchel, in *The United Irishman*, advocated the bolder policy of force (argument having wholly failed) the *Weekly Register*, which was opposed to physical force, fell to the ground.—M.

votaries of Themis have taken not to profane them with too frequent an application of their forensic fingers.

But this is parenthetically observed—I was going on to say, that I merely prepared myself upon Saturday evening to talk over the memory of Lord Wellesley with Mr. Farrel; the lamentable increase of crime upon the Munster circuit with Mr. Wolfe;* sacerdotal riots at Birr, and the validity of excommunication with Mr. Cruise; and the recollections of Wolfe Tone† with Mr. Sheil. Such being my indifference to political events, it not unfrequently happens that a great incident takes place of which I do not hear until after its more immediate effects upon the public mind have subsided—until after Mr. O'Connell has ordered a gown of Irish silk in the Liberty; Mr. Sergeant Lefroy has sought the consolations of religion

* Stephen Wolfe, a good lawyer and a liberal man, obtained neither notice nor preferment from the anti-liberal Governments preceding the grant of Emancipation. In 1834, he was made third Sergeant: Solicitor-General in 1836, Attorney-General in 1837, and Chief Baron of the Exchequer in 1838, on the death of Joy. Mr. Wolfe earnestly pressed the Government to appoint Mr. Pennefather, as fittest for this post, and that he (Wolfe) should merely take the puisne judgeship to be vacated by the promotion of Pennefather. But the Government, whose politics differed very much from those of Mr. Pennefather, declared that, under no circumstances, would they consider his claims; whereupon Mr. Wolfe was appointed Chief Baron. He died, June, 1840.—M.

† Theobold Wolfe Tone, actual founder of the "Society of United Irishmen," was born in 1763; called to the bar in due course; published a pamphlet against British mis-government in 1790; and founded the above society in 1793. From that time,

"Per varios casus, per tot discrimina rerum,"

Tone devoted himself to negotiations with the French Government to send men and arms to win back "Ireland for the Irish." One such expedition, under General Hoche, actually sailed, but a hurricane dispersed the fleet (consisting of 17 sail of the line, 13 frigates, &c., with 14,000 soldiers, and 40,000 stand of arms, besides artillery) before it could reach Bantry Bay, in the south of Ireland, and the French Government declined sending another large expedition. A petty armament was despatched, but beaten in a contest with an overpowering British fleet. Tone, who had fought bravely, was captured, tried by a Court Martial, and sentenced to be hanged, which he evaded by suicide. On the publication of Tone's autobiography, seven-and-twenty years after his death, Sheil attempted "to point a [political] moral" from it, in one of his Catholic Association Speeches, and was prosecuted for it by Mr. Plunket, then Attorney-General, but never brought to trial.—M.

in the College chapel, and Mr. Sergeant Blackburne, the subject of the present article, has bitten his nails to the roots for having, in a moment of weakness, yielded to the solicitations of Master Ellis, and allowed himself to be debauched so far from his characteristic prudence as to sign the anti-Catholic petition.

I have mentioned this habit of mine in order to account for my surprise at the strange appearance which was exhibited not very long ago by the Hall of the Four Courts, when I was struck by the sudden change of aspect and of manner which several individuals had, in the course of a few hours, undergone. Had I been acquainted with the news which had that morning arrived in Dublin, I should not have wondered at the transformation of the loyal portion of the bar; but I should have been prepared for something extraordinary, for, in my way to the Hall, I observed Mr. Secretary O'Gorman coming down Mass-lane, and just as he turned the corner, Mr. Peter Fitzgibbon Henchey (although Mr. Saurin and the Chancellor happened at the moment to be passing!) gave a look of unqualified recognition to the great plenipotentiary, which was returned with an air of official affability which became so eminent a functionary as Mr. O'Gorman.

The appearance of the latter gentleman, indeed, was sufficient to intimate that some momentous incident had taken place. Upon occasions of great importance, Mr. O'Gorman puts on a pair of white silk stockings, striped with black, such as he observed to be worn by Lord Grey, when the Secretary attended the Catholic Deputation.* The hosiery of the ultra-patriot Earl struck the fancy of Mr. O'Gorman, and ever since, upon great occasions, I have observed a fac-simile of his Lordship's stockings distended upon the herculean symmetries of the Irish orator; and it must be owned that, being a little spattered, and not much the better for the wear, they are not a little emblematic of some part of Lord Grey's recent

* The descent upon England, of O'Connell, Sheil, and others forming "The Catholic Deputation," in the spring of 1825, is the subject of one of the following Sketches — certainly inferior to none in personal, as well as in political interest. O'Gorman was secretary to the Irish Catholics.— M.

parliamentary conduct.* The conjecture which I had formed from the Catholic Secretary's inferior habiliments was confirmed by the cognizance which was taken of him by Mr. Henchey, who, although his ancestors were deprived of their estates in the county of Clare for their creed, is now a devout adherent to the Chancellor's religion.

Mr. Henchey has three manners of recognition. If he walk to court, and meet a junior counsel, who has held a brief with him in the matter of Lord French a bankrupt, this gentleman, who has inherited his prenomen from Lord Clare, gives a nod of rather equivocal intimacy, in which the consciousness of his own consequence is not altogether merged. If Mr. Henchey has started on horseback from his splendid residence in Merrion-square (which was once the town mansion of Lord Wicklow), with a servant riding in gorgeous livery on a prancing palfrey behind him, he throws a casual look upon his pedestrian brethren, and following those canons of conduct, which Malvolio lays down for himself upon his anticipated elevation, "quenches his familiar smile with an austere regard of control." But when Peter Fitzgibbon Henchey, one of his Majesty's counsel at law, seats himself in his carriage, and rolls in all the pomp of legal state along the rattling pavement of Nassau street, he would be a bold man indeed, unless placed in immediate vicinage to the bench, who, by any intrusive salutation, should attempt to disturb Peter's meditations on his own dignity, and seek to attract an eye, that, bordered with deeply-pursed and half-closed lids, seems to be abstracted from all external objects, and to have fixed itself in an inward contemplation of the importance of the eminent person in whose solemn and mysterious visage it is awfully and profoundly set. Recollecting the habits of Mr. Henchey, when I observed a person hitherto so conspicuous for his loyalty, according to the sense attached by Lord Manners to the word, even in the presence of the Chancellor, leaning from the window of his carriage, and suddenly recovering his natural faculty of telescopic vision, waving his hand to the Secretary of all the Cath-

* The late Lord Grey's determined and personal opposition to Canning, the liberal Premier, in 1827.—M.

olics of Ireland (Mr. Henchey's nearest relatives inclusive), I concluded that something marvellous must have happened.

I entered the Hall of the Four Courts, and found in the looks of Barclay Scriven, who was sitting on the basement of one of the pillars, a farther ground for surmise. A few days before he was in the height of hilarity, when Master Ellis was putting the anti-Catholic Petition into circulation, with the assistance of a young gentleman, whose aunt *ex-parte paternâ* is the abbess of a convent. But now Barclay Scriven would have furnished Cruikshank with a model for a burlesque of Ugolino. He formed a strong contrast with Sergeant Goold, whom I observed tripping it on a toe (which, although no longer light, is still fantastic), with a renovation of his former alacrity, around the Hall. He has been lately looking a little autumnal, and has fallen into the sear, the yellow leaf. He is no longer what he was, when he danced a pas-seul in the vagaries of his youth at Fishamble street; for although he retains his gracefulness of attitude, he has sustained some diminution of agility, and is no longer so well qualified to dispute the palm with the "god of dance" upon the stage. But now his vivacity seemed to be in a great measure restored. He looked as if he had been newly boiled in Medea's caldron, or had received from Mr. Godwin a recipe for everlasting youth, and had started back some twenty years to life again.* I was de-

* William Godwin's striking romance of "St. Leon" (the interest of which turns on the hero having obtained the *elixir vitæ*, which was to give perpetual youth, and become master of the art of transmuting the meaner metals into gold), will be recollected, by posterity, when his "Political Justice" is forgotten. That work, the boldest piece of republicanism ever published in England, made Godwin a marked man during the greater part of his life — long after he had laid politics aside. He published "St. Leon," in 1799, and wrote several other works of fiction. He died in April, 1836, aged eighty, and for the last five years of his life, had a competency from a small sinecure place to which Lord Grey's Reform Administration had appointed him.— Mary Wolstoncroft who wrote the once famous "Vindication of the Rights of Women," was his wife (she had previously lived with him, "on principle," as his mistress), and died in giving birth to a daughter, who is known in the world of letters, as the wife of Percy Bysshe Shelley, the poet (who was drowned, July, 1822), and was herself a distinguished writer, as her "Frankenstein" shows :— she was born in 1797, and died in 1851.— M.

lighted at the favorable appearance in this able and honest man, who has been uniformly faithful to his country, and never sacrificed his principles to his interests by the abandonment of a cause in which he enlisted in the enthusiasm of his youth, and has since adhered to with a constancy which no temptation could ever disturb.

The next individual of note whom I observed was Mr. Sergeant Lefroy. His eyes were fixed on the ground. This was not unnatural, nor inconsistent with the angelic nature, for we are told by Milton, that there was a spirit

> "Whose looks and thoughts were always downward bent;"

and who was occupied in admiring

> "The riches of Heaven's pavement, trodden gold."

The way to Heaven, if we may form a conjecture from the lives of the devout, would appear to be composed of the same materials as its pavement. I at first thought the Sergeant was engaged in his usual celestial occupation; but looking more attentively, I observed that the gloom of worldly solicitude was mixed with the consciousness of his being in the enjoyment of those rewards of piety which are promised, in the Old Testament, to the servants of the Lord. I thought the pious jurisconsult looked deeply melancholy; perhaps I was mistaken, and he was only revolving a point of casuistry for the approaching college election, and preparing to demonstrate the proposition which he afterward broached, that "no man at an election is bound by a promise to a candidate, where the safety of religion is at stake."

I had scarcely passed this eminent theologian, when I saw Judge Moore* entering the Court of Common Pleas, and, observing in that truly liberal and patriotic judge (who has approved himself on the bench the foe to faction, consistent with the principles which rendered him, in the worst times, the dauntless friend of Ireland and of Henry Grattan), a joyous and unaccustomed spirit, I concluded that something fortunate for his country had taken place.

This impression was strengthened when I noticed Peter

* This is not the present Justice Richard Moore, of the Queen's Bench.—M.

Burrowes, as he came in an opposite direction into the Hall, with that aspect of heart-contentedness which he is sure to manifest whenever the interests of Ireland are likely to be promoted. Availing myself of some acquaintance with this veteran in the cause of Whiggism, I advanced toward him, and inquired whether some extraordinary news had not arrived. Mr. Burrowes is a remarkably absent man, and not having heard my question, stood in revery beside me, muttering an occasional word or two, when I repeated my interrogatory.* He was

* Peter Burrowes was born in 1753 and died in 1843, having reached the age of ninety, retaining his mental faculties to the close. In 1774, he entered college, and won a scholarship, by sound and varied learning, in 1777. He was a frequent speaker in the Historical Society, where his good sense and sound information were highly estimated. He was of a sluggish temperament, a heavy manner, and an ungainly person — but independence was to be achieved, and he was assiduous and persevering. In 1785, he was called to the Irish bar, and obtained his first honors in 1791, as counsel for Sir Lawrence Parsons (afterward Earl of Rosse and father of the astronomer and present President of the Royal Society of London), who had been a candidate for the representation of the University and had been defeated, it was averred, by Provost Hutchinson unduly using his influence for his own son. Continuing to win reputation at the bar, Burrowes did not receive a silk gown, owing to an impression on the part of Government that he was friendly to the United Irishmen — an impression which was not hastily removed. He finally obtained the honor and was one of fourteen King's Counsel who signed a public protest, in December, 1799, against the proposed Union. He sat in the last session of the Irish Parliament. In 1806, he received the lucrative appointment of Counsel to the Commissioners of Customs, but had to resign it, when "All the Talents" quitted office. His future course was one of hard labor, for his strong liberal opinions excluded him from preferment at the hands of a Tory Ministry. In 1822, when Plunket was made Attorney-General, he had Burrowes made Commissioner of the Insolvent Debtors' Court, the large salary of which set him at ease for the rest of his life. He eventually retired on a pension of sixteen hundred pounds sterling a year. He was convivial and witty in private: earnest rather than eloquent at the bar. Yet, some of his touches were good. In one case, where a man, who had been flogged nearly to death in 1798, brought an action against the High Sheriff who ordered the torture to be inflicted, when the jury laughed at a jest arising out of the cruel details, Burrowes indignantly exclaimed, "Ay, gentlemen, *you* may laugh, but my client *was writhing*."— In the case of a young lady who had suffered the worst wrong, in 1798, from a troop of brutal yeomanry, Burrowes thus described the victim's entry into Waterford: "The shades of evening fell, as this young creature, foot sore, and alone, entered with a palpitating heart, that greatest of wildernesses — a great city." This is simple and pathetic, as well as sublime in its simplicity.— His absence of mind has

awakened to a perception of the objects around him — a finely-illuminated smile succeeded the broad gaze of vacancy with which his eyes were at first fixed upon me, and he exclaimed, "Why is not Grattan alive to-day!"

I was about to ask for some more explicit information, when, fortunately, my friend Eccles Cuthbert came up, and having an equal talent and propensity for narration, put me, with great clearness and volubility, in possession of the news, and informed me of the revolution in the Cabinet. "In short," said Mr. Cuthbert (a phrase of which this excellent Whig is somewhat inappropriately fond)...But before Mr. Cuthbert had concluded a sentence which commenced with this intimation of brevity, Mr. Sergeant Blackburne walked by. The moment I saw him, I interrupted Mr. Cuthbert, and assured him that, "if I had entertained any skepticism with respect to his intelligence, the aspect of the Sergeant would set all my doubts at rest.

"Yea, this man's brow, like to a title-leaf,
Foretells the nature of a tragic volume."

The Sergeant was changed indeed. A little while before, when the party under whose banners he had enlisted himself, confidently anticipated the expulsion of Mr. Canning from the Cabinet, Mr. Sergeant Blackburne exhibited as much alertness as his grave and sedate nature permitted him to wear. His

been mentioned in a previous note. On a trial for murder, it was important to the prisoner that the bullet found in the wound should be produced. It was handed to Burrowes, who was occasionally taking a lozenge for a hoarseness. In the middle of his speech he paused, and suddenly exclaimed, "O Lord, I have swallowed the bullet by mistake."—He was found shaving opposite a wall on which there was no mirror. "Sir," said the servant, who was asked where it was, "my mistress had it removed six weeks ago!"—Plunket, once at a festive entertainment, said, "Although I am about proposing the health of Peter Burrowes, I am not inclined to conceal his faults, much less to describe him as faultless. I will not dwell upon his minor peccadilloes, but shall only allude to those by which he is continually offending. I know no man who has more to answer for. He has spent his life in doing acts of kindness to every human being but himself. He has been prodigal of his time, of his trouble, of his talents, of his money, to every human being who had or had not a claim, and this to the serious neglect of his own interests. In short," added Plunket, "I can only account for such an anomaly as this, by supposing him *utterly destitute of the instinct of selfishness*."—M.

habitual composure, and the sort of "wilful stillness" which he successfully entertains, had given way to an unaccustomed spirit, and it was manifest that all his thoughts had been put into an agreeable and pleasurable movement. He never wanted brilliancy of eye; but he had been used to subdue its expression with a certain solemnity of aspect, which made him look as if he were rehearsing the part of a judge, long before it should come to his turn to perform the part. Thus he had contrived to invest features, which, with the exception of his eyes, are rather of an ordinary cast, with an important soberness and an aspect of not undignified meditation. His figure, although below the common height, and of broad and quadrangular dimensions, was stiffened into a kind of stunted stateliness that gave him an imposing and somewhat authoritative deportment. His walk and gesture were always in measure with the march of his steady and uniform mind, which was never betrayed into any unseemly precipitation. Such was the ordinary man; but he was now entirely altered. The fire of his eye had gone out; his walk was loose, slouched, and irregular; restlessness and inquietude were apparent in the whole frame and body of the man, and dejection, mingled with the fretfulness of disappointment, spread over his countenance. He seemed to have been reduced an inch in elevation, and to have shrunk back from his artificial altitude into himself. How changed from him who not long before, amidst the orgies of the corporation, with his cup overflowing with claret, announced himself, amidst the acclamations of inebriated aldermen, to be the champion of the church and state! Peter Burrowes, who is full of the milk of human kindness, though it occasionally turns a little sour, fixed upon him his vast blue eyes, which would fitly provide a brace of Cyclops with the orbs of vision, and exclaimed, in his usual tone of rough and hoarse benevolence, "I pity Blackburne!"

The Sergeant's mistake in signing the anti-Catholic Petition might have excited the commiseration of Mr. Burrowes; but it produced in the public, on account of its imprudence, more surprise than sympathy. For my own part, I was not at all astonished at the last step taken by Mr. Blackburne, because it was in perfect consistency with the first which he adopted when he crossed the threshold of his profession.

He was called to the bar about the time that the celebrated John Philpot Curran was made Master of the Rolls.* A

* When the Whigs came into office, in 1806, on the death of Pitt, they appointed John Philpot Curran to the bench, as Master of the Rolls, which office he held until 1814, when he resigned, on a pension of three thousand pounds sterling, and resided from that time chiefly in London, where he died, in 1817, aged sixty-seven. He was by no means a good equity judge, and considered himself unfairly used by not being made Attorney-General, for which his familiarity with common law qualified him, and from which office (had his party remained in power, which was not the case), the natural transition would have been to the Queen's Bench, Common Pleas, or Exchequer, as Chief Judge. Curran, born in 1750, of poor parents in the County of Cork, was educated by a benevolent clergyman, named Boyce (ever let us record the names of good-doers) who strained his own limited means to send him to college and get him to the bar. Fortuneless, and nearly friendless, Curran's early struggle, ere he obtained law-practice, was bitter and painful. But his talents brought him on. He entered Parliament, and won repute there. He was the advocate of nearly all the persons charged with political offences, during the last eight years preceding the Union (which he opposed), and his forensic eloquence, on these occasions, excited general admiration. His fearlessness as an advocate injured him at the bar, for Lord-Chancellor Clare let it be seen that Mr. Curran and his arguments had no favor with *him*, but gave him immense popularity. His appeals to juries were powerful, beyond any conception which can be formed from his published, but uncorrected Speeches. In one case, where a clergyman named Massey sued the Marquis of Headford (an Irish peer, nearly, but not quite as wicked as his almost namesake, the English Marquis of Hertford) for seduction of his wife, Curran—who had himself sustained a similar wrong—pleaded so powerfully that the jury returned a verdict of Ten Thousand Pounds sterling against the "noble" Adulterer. Curran's conversational were equal to his oratorical powers. His *bon mots* are widely known. Byron, who only knew him in his later years, when the wine of life was on the lees, chronicled his impressions in his private journal: "His imagination is beyond human, and his humor (it is difficult to define what is wit) perfect. He has fifty faces, and twice as many voices, when he mimics. I never met his equal." Again:—"Curran, Curran's the man who struck me most. Such imagination! There never was anything like it." And, further on: "I have heard that man speak more poetry than I have ever seen written, though I saw him seldom, and but occasionally."—Curran was small in statue, swarthy in complexion, and with an Irish face, in which brilliant eyes redeemed everything. Phillips thus sketches him, in 1805, as he appeared in the Hall of the Four Courts: "Mark well that slight, short figure, with restless gait, and swaying motion, and speaking gesture—he with the uplifted face, protruded upper-lip, and eyes like liv-

meeting of the bar was held for the purpose of presenting to Mr. Curran a congratulatory address. When this assembly had been convened, and after some of the most eminent persons in the profession had delivered their opinions, a young gentleman drew upon himself the general attention by coming deliberately forward and opposing the motion to offer a tribute of respect to a man whose genius had reflected so much honor upon his country, and in whose speeches passages are to be found which rival the masterpieces of eloquence in ancient language. It would not have been extraordinary if some hoary pleader, actuated by political prejudices operating upon a naturally narrow mind, which had undergone still greater contraction in the inferior departments of the profession, had opposed the tribute which it was intended to offer to the most renowned advocate at the bar: but it excited no little surprise, that a man who was not old enough to have personally mingled in the ferocious contests of the civil war (during which Mr. Curran had displayed an intrepidity which excited the animosities of the successful party), and whose mind ought to have been susceptible of the impressions which the eloquence of Mr. Curran was so well calculated to produce upon the young and sensitive, should have tendered himself as a volunteer to the faction of which that great speaker was the antagonist, and had earned his best honors in their hate.

The boldness of this proceeding was quite sufficient to attract notice. Every eye was fixed upon this juvenile and unknown dissentient from the great body of the bar. They saw a formal and considerate-looking person, with a gravity far beyond his years, advance with perfect coolness and self-possession; and while they condemn the feelings by which he

ing diamonds."—Curran was fortunate in his biographers. The volume, by Mr. O'Regan, published soon after his death, is chiefly anecdotal. His son, William Henry Curran, wrote an excellent Memoir, in two volumes, long out of print, and Charles Phillips' "Recollections of Curran" (re-cast and much extended, in 1850), supplies a vast quantity of information about the man, his times, and his contemporaries.—The address from the bar, on his appointment as Master of the Rolls, mentioned by Mr. Sheil as opposed by Mr. Blackburne, was very brief, and while it congratulated him on his promotion, complimented him on the public grounds of his ability, independence, and integrity.—M.

was instigated, they could not but perceive that he had qualifications which were calculated to raise him to great eminence in his profession. His enunciation was perfect; every tone was mellow and musical, and the cadences marking his flowing and unelaborated sentences, manifested the finest sense of harmony, and a peculiarly rhythmical elocution. To those external qualities was added an easy, round, graceful, and unstudied gesture. Although he took the side upon which many angry and vindictive passions were marshalled, yet he betrayed none of the violence of political detestation. He was throughout calm, sober, and subdued, and displayed that clearness in statement, and that faculty for methodical exposition, which have since so much contributed to his great success in his profession. It was painful to see Mr. Blackburne, exhibiting at the same time so much ability, and so little sense of the transcendent merits of the celebrated person whose laurels he endeavored to blight. This step was the subject, I have heard, of general comment. It was considered a decided intimation of the course in politics which the young gentleman intended to take, and his promotion under a Tory ministry was generally anticipated. This precocious disposition to sustain the "ascendency," might, to use Rosalind's illustration, be compared to a medlar; and it might have been not unhappily said to Mr. Blackburne, by any lover of quotations, "you will be the earliest fruit in the country: for you'll be rotten, ere you be half ripe, and that's the right virtue of the medlar."

Mr. Blackburne, however, did not fulfil the anticipations which had been formed in his regard, notwithstanding this unequivocal intimation of his political predilections. He got rapidly into business, and wisely dedicated himself exclusively to it. In a short time his first exploit was forgotten; and as the Irish Catholics are disposed to consider all those who are not ostensibly against them, as with them, a notion crept gradually abroad that Mr. Blackburne had leanings to the liberal side. However, as he did not interfere, little was said with respect to his political opinions, and his efficiency in his profession caused both Catholic and Protestant solicitors to make large contributions to his bag. To his admirable manner he owes much of his reputation. He has a finer voice than any man at the bar, and has an ear so accurate, that the nicest analyzer of tones could not detect the least deviation from harmony in his utterance, which is so perfect, that Doctor Spray, of Christ church Cathedral [Dublin], who was master of the science, used to declare that he could set his intonations to music. The Sergeant himself is an excellent singer, and passionately fond of that accomplishment in others. It creates no little surprise among persons who are not aware of his being possessed of this talent, when, hearing on a sudden a peculiarly rich and sweet voice breathing in delightful tones one of Moore's enchanting melodies, they turn round, and find in the musician no other than the grave and solemn person, whom they may have seen in the morning engaged in a controversy respecting the form of a notice with his Honor the Master of the Rolls.

But it is not to manner that the merits of Mr. Blackburne are confined. Although I do not consider him as by any means so ingenious and astute as Mr. Pennefather, who unites almost every qualification which can be desired in an advocate, yet Mr. Blackburne is surpassed by no man at the bar in perspicuity; and while he renders subjects the most difficult and entangled, perfectly simple and clear, he, at the same time, avoids a defect sometimes incidental to the talent for exposition, and is by no means lengthy and prolix. It would be wonderful, if, with these faculties, he had not succeeded; and accordingly in a few years we find him in the foremost rank of the Chancery Bar. I have mentioned that he observed a systematic abstinence from all political discussion, in the interval which was employed in scaling the heights of his profession; but shortly after the arrival of Lord Wellesley as Lord-Lieutenant, the extension of the Insurrection Act over several of the southern counties, and the provision contained in that statute, that a barrister, holding the rank of King's counsel, should preside over the deliberations of the magistrates, brought Mr. Blackburne again upon the political stage. A most favorable opportunity of recommending himself to Government was presented by the refusal of Mr. Pennefather to undertake the ungracious office of putting this curfew law into execution; and Mr. Blackburne verified the maxim, that men are often more advantaged by the omissions of others, than by any desert of their own. Mr. Pennefather was pressed by Government to proceed to one of the disturbed districts, invested with Proconsular authority; but that gentleman, not liking the occupation, and being besides in bad health at the time, declined the honor intended to be conferred upon him. This refusal gave, I believe, some offence, and afforded an excuse for not promoting Mr. Pennefather to the place assigned to him by the unanimous suffrages of the profession.

An application was made to Mr. Blackburne to undertake the duties which had been declined by Mr. Pennefather, and the proposition was immediately acceded to. It were unjust not to state that, in this new employment Mr. Blackburne acquitted himself in such a way as to give satisfaction to the Government and to the public; for while he manifested a proper zeal in quelling insubordination, he restrained the ferocious passions of the exasperated gentry, and prevented this iron implement of oligarchical dominion from being converted into the means of gratifying individual animosities, and promoting the sordid or tyrannical views of every needy or vindictive justice of the peace.

It is said that Mr. Blackburne, not only by his conduct, but by his despatches to Lord Wellesley, raised himself not a little in the estimation of the Marquis, and the subsequent intercourse between them improved the impression which had been previously made. Lord Wellesley is fond of the echo of his own voice, which comes back to him in an important reverberation from the halls of the viceregal palace; and Mr. Blackburne, who, although a good speaker, has upon proper occasions a great talent for silence, and has a fine listening eye, in the audiences which he gave Lord Wellesley, afforded that distinguished nobleman the best proofs of attachment to his sovereign, as evinced by his admiration of his representative. Accordingly, when the office of Sergeant became vacant, while the Bar pointed to Mr. Pennefather as best entitled to promotion, the Government, at, it is believed, the instance of Lord

Wellesley, selected Mr. Blackburne. Although many regretted that Mr. Pennefather, whose manners render him as popular as his talents make him conspicuous, had been passed by, yet the appointment of Mr. Blackburne gave satisfaction, as he is indisputably a person of great merit, and has not yet completely enrolled himself under the banners of a faction. Mr. O'Connell, who carries about him the credulity of good-nature, believed that the new Sergeant was favorable to Emancipation, and announced his promotion as an auspicious circumstance; but those who remembered his first entrance upon the political theatre, did not permit themselves to be so readily led astray.

An event soon after occurred, which showed pretty clearly the bearings of Mr. Blackburne's inclinations. At a civic dinner, he delivered a speech, in which he intimated his strong Protestant predilections.* I do not, however, attribute this display of unanticipated loyalty to any ebullition of feeling upon the Sergeant's part. There can be no doubt that, previous to the recent resignation of Mr. Peel and the Protestant portion of the Cabinet, it was rumored, among the circles of their supporters in Ireland, that Mr. Canning would be ejected from power. This opinion gained ground every day, and grew

* The mild, temperate, and humane disposition of the Orange body may be surmised from the charter-toast of the association, drunk with great solemnity and joy, at civic feasts and on the first day of July (anniversary of the Battle of the Boyne) every man kneeling as he repeated the words—said to have been put together in 1689. The toast ran thus: "The glorious, pious, and immortal memory of the great and good King William, who saved us from pope and popery, brass money and wooden shoes. He that won't drink this toast, may the north wind blow him to the south, and a west wind blow him to the east; may he have a dark night, a lee shore, a rank storm, and a leaky vessel to carry him over the ferry to hell; may the devil jump down his throat with a red hot harrow, that every pin may tear out his inside; may he be jammed, rammed, and dammed into the great gun of Athlone, and fired off into the kitchen of hell, where the pope is roasting on a spit and the devil pelting him with cardinals!" The Catholics, and liberal Protestants who refused to drink this toast, which was a standing dish, late in the evening, after the dinners of Dublin and other Corporations, were incontinently declared, from such recusancy, to be "bad subjects." Not only ignorant yeomanry and country gentlemen, but nobles, prelates, and princes (for the Duke of Cumberland was Grand Master of the Orangemen!) used to drink this toast, and swear to stand by the order—when they were too far gone with drink to stand by anything else. —M.

into a sort of certainty, when the anti-Catholic Petition was presented for their signatures to the bar. The crisis of Sergeant Blackburne's fate had arrived. There is generally in the life of every man some one incident which is the hinge of his destiny, and the Sergeant had touched that cardinal point. By joining the Protestant party, he would have given himself, in the event of their success in the bold experiment which was then in contemplation, a strong title to their patronage, and might ultimately have attained the highest honors which it is in the power of Government to confer. He did not resist the allurements which were held out to him; and, giving way to those original propensities which he had manifested in the early period of his life, and acting partly upon calculation, in an unluckly hour he attached his name to Master Ellis's petition.

But for this injudicious step, it is likely that Sergeant Blackburne would be Solicitor, and in a short time Attorney-General, for Ireland. Upon the former office having become vacant, his friends strongly insisted upon his pretensions; but it was urged, and with great truth, that to promote a decided and avowed enemy to Emancipation, would be at variance with the principles on which Mr. Canning's administration was built, and would excite the indignation of the Catholic body, whose passions it was so much the interest of the new Ministry to assuage. The consequence was, that Mr. Sergeant Blackburne was put aside, and Mr. Doherty, who, besides being the friend and relative of the Prime Minister, is member for the city of Kilkenny, was named by the Cabinet as successor to Mr. Joy.

Sergeant Blackburne is an eminent lawyer;* and for calm

* The reputation of Mr. Sergeant Blackburne (and his strong political bias), caused him to be made Chief Justice of the Queen's Bench, in which capacity he presided over the trial of Mr. Smith O'Brien, for high treason, at Clonmel, in 1848. In 1852, when the Earl of Derby formed an administration, he raised Blackburne to the Chancellorship of Ireland, for which his former practice in Equity, with the inclination of his mind and the particular range of his legal acquirements, had well qualified him. As he was only nine months in that office, he had little opportunity of "making his mark" upon the public mind, but the clearness of his intellect, the extent of his knowledge, together with his patience and good temper (requirements so essential in a judge), impressed

discussion of questions of equity, exhibits in mind and manner a most happy aptitude: but he never enjoyed any very considerable reputation as a public speaker, and, in addressing a jury upon any topic of importance, as well as in the cross-examination of witnesses, being very inferior to Mr. Doherty, is by no means as well qualified as that gentleman to render the Crown efficient service. If any state-prosecutions should be instituted, the accused would find in Mr. Doherty a far more dangerous assistant of the Attorney-General than the learned Sergeant. Of the fitness of the latter of those two gentlemen for this important office, I had a recent occasion to form an accurate estimate.

The last assizes of Clonmel [1828] presented a dreadful miscellany of the most barbarous crimes, most of which were of an insurrectionary character, and required the exercise of the strongest powers of the law. There were not less than three hundred and eighty prisoners upon the calendar, from which Judge Burton seemed to recoil in dismay. The Government felt that it was necessary to do their utmost in order to repress so alarming a growth of crime; and with a view to the production of effect, and in order to give the administration of justice more impressiveness, deemed it advisable to send Mr. Sergeant Blackburne as special counsel for the Crown. He accordingly arrived in Clonmel at the commencement of the Assizes; and, as he enjoyed no ordinary reputation, his mission had the desired effect, by drawing the general attention to the cases which he conducted.

I felt a good deal of interest in some of the most important of the prosecutions, and had a particular opportunity of observing Mr. Blackburne. Upon the first day of his appearance he availed himself of the right of the Crown to address the jury (although that privilege is denied to the prisoner against whom a speech is directed!), in order to present a picture of the

the legal profession, who naturally can form the truest opinion on such a point, with respect and admiration. Mr. Blackburne was offered a peerage, on his appointment, but declined it. When the Derby Ministry broke up, Mr. Blackburne resigned office — taking the usual retiring pension of four thousand pounds sterling a year. He was succeeded, in December, 1852, by Mr. Maziere Brady, whom he had displaced nine months previously. — M.

general condition of the county. This was a noble opportunity for genuine eloquence. The best materials that can be well conceived for a powerful harangue were gathered together. The county was almost in a state of insurrection. Armed bands of peasants traversed the country in the open day, and put to death in the face of the sun whoever presumed to violate the code of regulations which they had arbitrarily imposed, under the authority of their invisible chieftain, Captain Rock. During the assizes themselves, two murders were committed, and Mr. Lanigan, the land-agent of Lord Landaff, was fired at by a party of forty men. The evils by which the county was actually afflicted were in themselves sufficiently alarming, without looking into ulterior results; but it was impossible not to reflect upon the consequences which might ensue from the political and moral state of a famished and ferocious population, provided with arms, regularly organized, and acting upon systematic principles of insubordination.

Independently of the general aspect of the county, which opened such a wide field to a powerful speaker, the individual case in which he addressed the jury was one of the most appalling that can be imagined, and attended with circumstances of strangeness as well as of atrocity, which furnished an occasion for the noblest oratory. Eighteen individuals had been burnt alive in one of the dark and lonely glens of the mountain of Slievenamaun, and the chief perpetrator of that terrible deed stood in all the ghastliness of guilt at the bar. The courthouse was filled to suffocation, by persons of all classes; and the vast assembly, together with the leading aristocracy of that opulent county, included in all likelihood some of the brother-incendiaries of the villain who was brought at last to a tardy justice. The deepest silence prevailed. The Judge himself, however, from his judicial experience disastrously familiar with scenes of this kind, seemed to be awe-struck by the consciousness of the important consequences of the trial, and weighed down by the magnitude of the crimes over the investigation of which he was condemned to preside. While the oath was administered to each of the jury, every eye was riveted upon the individual who held the sacred volume in his hand. While he pressed the word of God to his lips, his countenance was closely watched, and it was easy to perceive upon the faces of the twelve men, upon whose concurrent voices the life of their fellow-creature was to depend, a strong solicitude, amounting almost to an expression of fear, at the hazard which they were about to incur by a conviction.

It was under these circumstances, and in the midst of a solemn hush, that Mr. Sergeant Blackburne rose to address the court; and I do him no wrong in stating that he did not raise himself to the height of the great argument, nor did he even make an approach to its elevation. He stated a case fraught with incidents which were enough to make "the hair stir as life were in't," with a coolness and *sang-froid* which would have become the argument of a demurrer in the Rolls. He brought to a court of criminal justice the language, the gesture, and the intonations, to which he had been familiar in a court of equity; and, in my opinion, his having failed to produce a deep impression arose from the very qualities which render him an accomplished advocate in another branch of his profession.

It may perhaps be thought that, feeling the injustice done to the prisoner in cases of felony, by permitting the counsel for the Crown to inflame the passions of the jury, while the right of speech is denied to the defendant's advocate, Mr. Sergeant Blackburne benevolently abstained from eloquence, and from motives of commiseration hid his brilliant faculties under a merciful mediocrity and charitable commonplace. I am far from thinking him capable of using any undue efforts to procure the conviction of any individual of whose guilt he could entertain the slightest doubt: he is a man of unimpeached probity and honor; but, while I acquit him of any such sanguinary intent, it is due to frankness to add that he entered into a general view of the state of the county, and, by exciting the alarm of the jury, enforced the necessity of making an example, and of striking terror into the mind of the populace. Perhaps this course was unavoidable; for it is obvious that the exercise of this privilege by the counsel for the Crown must have the effect of heating the minds of the jurors, and of preparing them for the reception of the evidence, with that inevitable bias against the prisoner, arising from the predisposition to convict, which an appeal to their passions and an inculcation of the necessity of repressing insurrection can not fail to create. The humane and truly constitutional Judge [Burton] who presided in the criminal court at the last assizes of Clonmel, and who brought with him from England those habits of justice by which he is distinguished, was sensible of the disadvantage under which the prisoners labored, from the causes to which I have referred, and appeared to me to allude to Mr. Blackburne's speech, when he told the jury to discharge their minds of all considerations excepting the evidence immediately applicable to the specific case before them. I do not think that Mr. Sergeant Blackburne was much more successful in cross-examination, to which he is not accustomed, than in his oratorical displays; and it was the general impression of the bar that the Crown was indebted for the convictions which took place to the superior skill of Mr. Doherty, in breaking down, as it is technically called, the witnesses produced for the defendants.

In the course of the speeches delivered by Mr. Sergeant Blackburne, in the discharge of his functions as counsel for the Crown, after a general delineation of the character and habits of the county of Tipperary, he proceeded to state what he conceived to be the causes of the miserable condition of that populous and fertile district, and to point out a remedy for the evils by which it is oppressed. He stated that the frightful crimes which had been committed had their origin in the spirit of organization to which the peasantry were inveterately prone; and suggesting that the rigorous administration of justice was adequate to the cure of every evil, called upon the jury to apply, what his professional predilections, in conformity with the proverb, naturally induced him to consider of sovereign efficacy in removing all political distempers. There can be no doubt that the tendency of the people to enter into illegal combinations is among the ingredients of national calamity, but it is far more a consequence of remote influences than it is an essential and leading cause. Mr. Sergeant Blackburne, in endeavoring to discover the sources of that deep stream of bitterness, the wide and almost periodical inundation of whose waters has produced so rank a fertility of crime, must have made but little progress toward the fountain-head, and mistaken one of the branches of the river for its source.

The most remarkable of the many important cases in which Mr. Sergeant Blackburne acted as leading counsel for the Crown, was the trial of William Gorman, to which I have already referred, for "the burning of the Sheas." It is by that title that the terrible crime in which so many immolators and so many victims were involved, is habitually designated; and whenever a man expatiates upon the atrocities which disgrace the country, and upon the conflagrations by which its character is blackened, he refers, as to a leading illustration, to "the burning of the Sheas."

I shall not readily forget the impression which was produced upon me, on my first passing near the spot in which that dreadful incident took place, when some of its details were narrated by one of my fellow-travellers, in descending the narrow defile of Glenbower. The remains of the habitation in which eighteen human beings were committed together to the flames, are not visible from the road that winds at the foot of the mountain on which it was situated; but the dark and gloomy glen in which the deed was done, can be pierced by the eye, when the mists that hang upon the lofty ridge do not envelop it; and it is always with awe, which is not a little assisted by the loneliness and dreariness of the scene, that the traveller turns his eyes toward that dismal valley, to which his attention is directed by the habitual exclamation which I had never failed to hear: "There is the place where the Sheas were burnt!" I had an opportunity, in consequence of having attended two trials connected with that frightful event, of learning the circumstances by which it was attended; and as in these sketches I have not only endeavored to draw the portraits of individual barristers, but also to describe the character of their occupations as influenced by the nature of the cases in which they are engaged, an occasional account of the most important and striking of those cases falls within the scope of these essays, and at all events may not be unattended with interest to the reader. Passing, therefore, from the advocate to the prosecutions in which he was engaged, it will not be inappropriate that I should proceed to detail the incidents which attended "the burning of the Sheas."

Upon the morning of the 20th of November, 1821, the remains of the house of Patrick Shea, a respectable farmer, who held a considerable quantity of land at the foot of the mountain of Slievenamaun, exhibited an appalling spectacle. It had been consumed by fire on the preceding night; and a large concourse of people (the intelligence of the conflagration having been rapidly diffused through the neighboring glens) assembled to look upon the ruins. Of the thatched roof which had first received the fire, a few smoking rafters were all that remained. The walls had given way, and stood gaping in rents, through which, on approaching them, the eye caught a glimpse of the dreadful effects of the devouring element. The door was burnt to its hinges; and, on arriving at the threshold, as awful a scene offered itself to the spectator as is recorded in the annals of terror. The bodies of sixteen human beings of both sexes lay together in a mass of corpses. The door having been closed when the flames broke out, the inhabitants precipitated themselves toward it, and in all likelihood mutually counteracted their efforts to burst into the open air. The house being a small one, every individual in it had an opportunity of rushing toward the entrance, where they were gathered by hope, and perished in despair. Here they lay piled upon each other. Those who were uppermost were burnt to the bones, while the wretches who were stretched beneath them were partially consumed. One of the spectators, the uncle of a young woman, Catherine Mullaly, who perished in the flames, described the scene with a terrible particularity. With an expression of horror which six years had not effaced, he said, when examined as a witness, that the melted flesh ran from the heap of carcasses in black streams along the floor.

But terrible as this sight must have been, there was another still more appalling. The young woman, whom I have already mentioned, Catherine Mullaly, resided in the house, and had been not very long before married. She had advanced a considerable period in pregnancy, and her child, which was born in the flames in a premature labor, made the eighteenth victim. I shall never forget the answer given by her uncle at the trial, when he was asked how many had perished, he answered that there were seventeen; but that if the child that was dropped (that was his phrase) in the fire was counted, the whole would make eighteen. His unfortunate niece was delivered of her offspring in the midst of the flames. She was not found among the mass of carcasses at the door. There were sixteen wretches assembled there, but, on advancing farther into the house, in a corner of the room, lay the body of this unhappy young creature, and the condition in which her child was discovered accounted for her separation from the group of the dead. A tub of water lay on the ground beside her. In it she had placed the infant of which she had been just delivered while the fires were raging about her, in the hope of preserving it; and in preserving its limbs she had succeeded, for the body was perfect with the exception of the head, which was held above the water, and which was burned away. Near this tub she was found, with the skeleton of the arm with which she had held her child hanging over it! It will be supposed that the whole of this spectacle excited a feeling of dismay among the spectators; but they were actuated by a variety of sentiments. Most of them had learned caution and silence, which are among the characteristics of the Irish peasantry, and, whatever were their feelings, deemed it advisable to gaze on without a comment; and there were not wanting individuals who, folding their arms, and looking on the awful retribution, whispered sternly to each other that "William Gorman was at last revenged!"

When information of this dreadful event reached Dublin, it produced, as it was natural to expect, a very great sensation. It was at first believed that "the burning of the Sheas" was the result of that confederacy by which the peasantry had regulated the taking of lands; and that as the previous tenant, one William Gorman, had been ejected by the Sheas, against the will of the people, the house had been set on fire. But it was asked, "What object could there be in destroying so many individuals who were innocent of all crime, and were mere laborers and servants in the employment of the occupying farmer?" This reflection, and a wish to rescue the national character from the disgrace of so wanton an atrocity, gradually induced a surmise that the fire had been accidental; and this conjecture was confirmed by the fact that, notwithstanding a large reward had been offered for the discovery of the incendiaries, no information was given to the Government. At length, however, the fatal truth was disclosed, and it was ascertained that the conflagration was the result of a plot executed by a considerable band of men, and that the whole population in the neighborhood were well aware both of the project and of its execution. The first clew to this abominable transaction was given by a woman of the name of Mary Kelly.

This female had been a person of dissolute life, and had married a servant, who, having relinquished his employment, some time after his marriage, established, with the assistance of his wife, what is commenly called a *shebeen-house,* in the vicinity of the Sheas, at the foot of Slievenamaun. It was a kind of mountain-brothel, or rather combined the exercise of a variety of trades, which, in the subdivision of labor that takes place in towns, are generally practised apart. Her husband stated that he sold spirits without license; provided board and lodging to any passengers who thought it expedient to take up their abode with him; and that if a young man and woman had any wish to be left alone in his hospitable and accommodating mansion at a late hour at night, he and his wife did not think it genteel to meddle with their discourse. It will be thought singular that, in so wild and desolate a district, in the midst of solitary glens and moors, such conveniences should exist; but they are not unfrequent; and one often meets these traces of civilization in parts of the country which carry no other evidence of refinement!

Mary Kelly appears to have superintended and conducted this establishment; her husband merely giving it the sanction of wedlock, and joining in the licentious conviviality which took place under his auspices. But although his wife had, upon her own admission, been of profligate habits, until time had transmuted her, by the ordinary process, from a harlot to a procuress, yet she does not appear to have been utterly devoid of all virtuous sentiment; and, indeed, the scene which she had witnessed was of such a nature as to awaken any remnant of conscience, which often, in the midst of depravity, is found to linger behind.

A peasant of the name of William Gorman, at whose trial Sergeant Blackburne conducted the prosecution, had originally held the house where the Sheas resided. He was their under-tenant, and held the lowest place in those numerous gradations of tenure into which almost every field is divided and subdivided; for the Sheas were not middle-men in the strict sense of the word, but stood themselves at a great distance from the head-proprietor of the estate, although they were the immediate landlords of Gorman. The more remote the head-landlord, the heavier the weight with which oppression falls on the occupier of the soil. The owner of the fee presses his lessee; the latter comes down upon the tenant, who derives from him, who, in his turn, crushes his own immediate serf; and if, which often happens in this long concatenation of vassalage, there are many other interventions of estate, the occupier of the soil is in proportion made to suffer; and is, to use the expression of Lord Clare, "ground to powder," in this complicated system of exaction! William Gorman was dealt with most severely. He was distrained, sued in the superior courts, processed by civil bill—in short, the whole machinery of the law was put into action against him. Driven from his home, deprived of his few fields, without covert or shelter, he made an appeal to the league of peasants with whom he was associated; and, as the Sheas had infringed upon their statutes, it was determined that they should die, and that an exemplary and appalling vengeance should be taken of them.

I saw William Gorman at the bar of the court in which he was condemned. He heard the whole detail of the atrocities of which he had been the primary agent. He was evidently most solicitous for the preservation of life; yet the expression of anxiety which disturbed his ghastly features occasionally gave way to the exulting consciousness of his revenge; and, as he heard the narration of his own delinquencies, so far from intimating contrition or remorse, a savage joy flashed over his face; his eyes were lighted up with a fire as lurid as that which he had kindled in the habitation of his enemies; his hand, which had previously quivered, and manifested, in the irregular movement of his fingers, the workings of deep anxiety, became, for a moment, clinched; and when the groans of his victims were described, his white teeth, which were unusually prominent, were bared to the gums; and, though he had drained the cup of vengeance to the dregs, still he seemed to smack his lips, and to lick the blood with which his injuries had been redressed!

This man had the vindictive feelings of a savage; but, while his barbarities admit of no sort of extenuation, they still were not without a motive. His co-partners in villany, however, who arranged and conducted the enterprise, had no instigation of personal vengeance, toward the oppressors of William Gorman. At their head was a bold and sagacious ruffian, whose name was Maher. It was determined that their plot should be carried into execution on Monday, the 20th of November. On the preceding Saturday, Maher went to Mary Kelly's house, and retired to a recess in it, where he employed himself in melting lead, and fusing it into balls. He was supposed to be a paramour of Mary Kelly (though she strenuously denied it), and she was certainly familiar with him. She had heard (indeed, it was known through the whole of that wild vicinage) that it was intended to inflict summary justice upon the Sheas; and being well aware that Maher was likely to dip his hands in any bloody business which was to go on, and observing his occupation, which he did not seek to hide from her, she taxed him with his "slaughterous thoughts," and having some good instincts left, begged him not to take life away. Maher answered with equivocation.

During this colloquy, Catherine Mullaly, a cousin of Mary Kelly, came into the house. Maher was well acquainted with her, and had the rude gallantry which is common among the Irish peasantry. She resided as a servant with the Sheas. Maher believed that there were arms in the Sheas' possession, and knew that there were a number of persons living in the house, with a view to their defence. The extent, however, of their means of self-protection the murderers had not ascertained, and it was important to learn the fact, in order that they might adapt to circumstances their mode of attack. It is probable, that, if there had been no weapons in the house, the conspirators would have burst open the door, dragged the Sheas out, and put them to death, and would have spared the more unoffending victims: but having discovered that there were firearms in abundance, they considered the burning of the house as a measure of self-defence, independently of the impression which a massacre upon a large scale would be likely to produce. Maher, therefore, sought to ascertain the state of defence from Catherine Mullaly, and entered into conversation with her in the tone of mixed joke and gibe, of which the lower orders, who delight in repartee, are exceedingly fond. The young woman was pleased with his attentions, and in the innocence of her heart, not having any suspicion of his intent, gradually disclosed to him that there was a quantity of arms in the house. Maher, on her departure, put on her cloak, and bade her farewell in the tone of friendship. Mary Kelly, who knew him well, and guessed at his object, the moment Catherine Mullaly was gone (for she did not dare to speak in her presence) implored Maher, whatever he might intend, not to harm Catherine Mullaly.

She extorted a promise from him to that effect, on which she relied for the moment, and they separated; Maher with his balls, and Mary Kelly with the undertaking for the life of Catherine Mullaly, in which she placed so mistaken a confidence. After some reflection, however, her alarm for the safety of her relative, to whom she was much attached, revived, and during the next day her suspicions were increased by the notes of preparation which she observed between Maher and his confederates. However, she did not venture to speak; for, to use her own phrase, "a word would have been as much as her life was worth;" still a terrible inquietude preyed upon her, and, as if actuated by some mysterious impulse, upon Monday night, when her husband, to whom she never communicated her apprehensions, was asleep, she silently rose from bed, and having huddled on his coat, left her cabin, though it was near midnight, and advanced cautiously and slowly along the hedges, until she made her way to near Maher's house. She stopped, and heard the voices of men engaged in discussion, which lasted some time; at length the door opened—she hid herself behind some brambles, and bending down, in order to avoid detection, which would have been death, she marked the murderers as they came forth. They issued from Maher's house in arms, and walked in a sort of array, advancing in file. Eight of them she knew; and, as she alleged, distinctly recognised them by their voices and looks. One of them carried two pieces of turf, lighted at the extremities, and kept the fire alive with his breath.

They passed her without observation, and proceeded upon their dreadful destination. Trembling and terror-struck, but still impelled to pursue them, she followed on from hedge to hedge, until they got beyond her; and perceiving that they proceeded toward the house of the Sheas, she stopped at a spot from which the house was visible, and by which the murderers, after executing their diabolical purpose, afterward returned. Here she remained in terrible anticipation, and her conjecture was speedily verified. A fire suddenly appeared in the roof of Shea's house; the wind high, it rose rapidly into a flame, and the whole was speedily in a blaze. It cast round the rocky glen a frightful splendor, and furnished, in its extensive diffusion of light, the means of beholding all that took place close to the burning cottage, in which shrieks and cries for mercy began to be heard. The murderers had secured the door; and having prevented all possibility of escape, stood in groups about the house, and gazed on the progress of the conflagration. So far from being moved to pity, they answered the invocations of their victims with yells of ferocious laughter. They set up a war-whoop of exultation, and, in token of triumph, discharged their guns and blunderbusses to celebrate their achievement. There was an occasional pause in their shouts: nothing then was heard but the crackling of the flames, that shed far and wide their desolate illumination; and the spectatress of this dreadful scene, though at some distance from it, declared that, in the temporary abatement of the wind, and the cessation of its gusts, she could at intervals hear the deep groans of the dying, and the gulps of agony with which their tortures were concluding.

But the fiends by whom these infernal fires were kindled, soon reiterated their cries of exultation, and discharged their guns again. The report of their firearms, which was taken up by the echoes of the mountain, produced a result which they had not anticipated. On the opposite side of a hill which adjoined the house, there resided a man of the name of Philip Dillon, who was a friend of the Sheas. Hearing the discharge of guns, and suspecting what had taken place, he summoned as many as he could gather together, and proceeded at their head across the hill, in order, if possible, to save the Sheas. They advanced toward the house, but arrived too late: neither had they courage to attack the murderers, who at once drew up before the flames to meet them. Philip Dillon, indeed, defied them to come on, but they declined his challenge, and waited his attack, which, as his numbers were inferior, he thought it prudent not to make. Both parties stood looking at each other, and in the meanwhile the house continued to blaze. The groans were heard for a little time, until they grew fainter and fainter; and at length all was silent.

Although the arrival of Philip Dillon did not contribute to save any of the sufferers, still it was the means of convicting William Gorman, by affording a corroboration to the testimony of Mary Kelly. John Butler, a boy, who was in the employment of Philip Dillon, and accompanied him to the burning house, was the brother of one of the servants of the Sheas. Notwithstanding he could not give any assistance to his brother, yet his anxiety to discover the murderers induced him to approach nearer than his companions to the flames, when, by the fire which they had kindled, Butler had an opportunity of identifying William Gorman, against whom he gave his testimony, and thus sustained the evidence of Mary Kelly.

All was now over—the roof had fallen in, and the ruins of the cottage were become a sepulchre. Gorman and Maher, with their associates, left the scene of their atrocities, and returned by the same path by which they had arrived. Another eye, however, besides that of God, was upon them. They passed a second time near the place where Mary Kelly lay concealed; again she cowered at their approach; and, as they went by, had a second opportunity of identifying them. Here a circumstance took place which is, perhaps, more utterly detestable than any other which I have yet recorded. The conversation of the murderers turned upon the doings of the night, and William Gorman amused the party by mimicking the groans of the dying, and mocking the agonies which he had inflicted.

The morning now began to break, and Mary Kelly, haggard, affrighted, and laden with the dreadful knowledge of what had taken place, returned to her home. Well aware, however, of the consequences of any disclosure, she did not utter a syllable to her husband, or to her son, upon the subject; and although examined next day before a magistrate, who conjectured, from the ill-fame of her house, that she must have had some cognizance of what had taken place, she declared herself to be innocent of all knowledge. John Butler, too, who had witnessed the death of his brother, immediately proceeded to the house of his mother, Alicia Butler, an old woman, who was produced as a witness for the crown; he awoke her from sleep, and told her that her son had been burned alive. Her maternal feelings burst into an exclamation of horror upon first hearing this dreadful intelligence; but, instead of immediately proceeding to a magistrate, she enjoined her son not to speak on the subject, lest she herself, and all her family, should suffer the same fate.

For sixteen months, no information whatever was communicated to Government. Mary Kelly was still silent, and did not dare to reproach Maher with the murder of Catherine Mullaly, for whose life she had made a stipulation. She did not even venture to look in the face of the murderer, although, when he visited at her house, which he continued to do, she could not help shuddering at his presence. Still the deeds which she had seen were inlaid and burned in dreadful colors in her mind. The recollection of the frightful spectacle never left her. She became almost incapable of sleep; and, haunted by images of horror, used in the dead of night to rise from her bed, and wander over the lonely glen in which she had seen such sights; and although one would have supposed that she would have instinctively fled from the spot, she felt herself drawn by a kind of attraction to the ruins of Shea's habitation, where she was accustomed to remain till the morning broke, and then return wild and wan to her home. She stated, when examined in private previous to the trial in which she gave her evidence, that she was pursued by the spectre of her unfortunate kinswoman, and that whenever she lay down in her bed, she thought of the "burning," and felt as if Catherine Mullaly was lying beside her, holding her child, "as black, as a coal, in her arms." At length her conscience got the better of her apprehensions, and in confession she revealed her secret to a priest, who prevailed upon her to give information, which, after a struggle, she communicated to Captain Despard, a justice of the peace for the county of Tipperary.

Such were the incidents which accompanied the perpetration of a crime, than which it is difficult to imagine one more enormous. To do the people justice, immediately after the conviction and execution of William Gorman, they appeared to feel the greatest horror at his guilt; and of that sentiment a Roman Catholic assembly, held during the assizes, afforded a strong proof. The assizes had gathered an immense concourse of the lower orders from all parts of the country, and Mr. Sheil, conceiving that a favorable opportunity had presented itself for giving a salutary admonition to the people, and believing that his advice would be fully as likely to produce an impression as the Protestant declamation of Mr. Sergeant Blackburne, used his influence in procuring a public meeting to be summoned. A vast multitude thronged to the place of assembly; and I am bestowing no sort of encomium upon Mr. Sheil, when I say that his speech produced a great deal of effect upon the peasantry, for the bare statement of the facts which appeared in evidence in the course of the assizes, would have been sufficient to awaken deep emotions wherever the instincts of humanity were not utterly extinguished. As

Mr. Sheil's address contained a summary of the principal cases in which Sergeant Blackburne was engaged, and he dwelt especially upon that of Matthew Hogan, which was attended by many afflicting circumstances, I shall close this article by a citation from the concluding passages of that gentleman's speech. "The recollection," he continued, "of what I have seen and heard during the present assizes, is enough to freeze the blood. Well might Judge Burton, who is a good and tender-hearted man—well might he say, with tears in his eyes, that he had not in the course of his judicial experience beheld so frightful a mass of enormities as the calendar presented. How deep a stain have those misdeeds left upon the character of your county, and what efforts should not be made by every man of ordinary humanity, to arrest the progress of villany, which is rolling in a torrent of blood, and bearing down all the restraints of law, morality, and religion, before it. Look, for example, at the murder of the Sheas, and tell me if there be anything in the records of horror by which that accursed deed has been excelled! The unborn child, the little innocent who had never lifted its innocent hands, or breathed the air of heaven—the little child in its mother's womb . . . I do not wonder that the tears which flow down the cheeks of many a rude face about me should bear attestation to your horror of that detestable atrocity. But I am wrong in saying that the child who perished in the flames was not born. Its mother was delivered in the midst of the flames. Merciful God? Born in fire! Sent into the world in the midst of a furnace! transferred from the womb to the flames that raged round the agonies of an expiring mother! There are other mothers who hear me. This vast assembly contains women, doomed by the primeval malediction to the groans of childbirth, which can not be suppressed on the bed of down, into which the rack of maternal agony still finds its way. But say, you who know it best, you who are of the same sex as Catherine Mullaly, what must have been the throes with which she brought forth her unfortunate offspring, and felt her infant consumed by the fires with which she was surrounded! We can but lift up our hands to the God of justice, and ask him why has he invested us with the same forms as the demons who perpetrated that unexampled murder! And why did they commit it?—by virtue of a horrible league by which they were associated together, not only against their enemy, but against human nature and the God who made it!—for they were bound together—they were sworn in the name of their Creator, and they invoked Heaven to sanctify a deed which they were confederated to perpetrate by a sacrament of Hell. Although accompanied by circumstances of inferior terror, the recent assassination of Barry belongs to the same class of guilt. A body of men at the close of day enter a peaceful habitation, on the Sabbath, and regardless of the cry of a frantic woman, who, grasping one of the murderers, desired him 'to think of God, and of the blessed night, and to spare the father of her eight children!' dragged him forth, and when he, 'offered to give up the ground tilled and untilled if they gave him his life,' answered him with a yell of ferocious irony, and telling him 'he should have ground enough,' plunged their bayonets into his heart! An awful spectacle was presented on the trial of the wretched men who were convicted of the assassination. At one extremity of the bar there stood a boy, with a blooming face and with down on his cheek, and at the other an old man in the close of life, with a wild haggard look, a deeply-furrowed countenance, and a head covered with hoary and dishevelled hair. In describing the frightful scene it is consoling to find that you share with me in the unqualified detestation which I have expressed; and, indeed, I am convinced that it is unnecessary to address to you any observation on the subject.

"But, my good friends, I must call your attention to another trial, I mean that of the Hogans, which affords a melancholy lesson. That trial was connected with the insane practice which exists among you, of avenging the accidental affronts offered to individuals, by enlisting whole clans in the quarrel and waging an actual war, which is carried on by sanguinary battles. I am very far from saying that the deaths which occur in these barbarous feuds are to be compared with the guilt of preconcerted assassination, but that they are accom panied with deep criminality there can be no question: the system, too, which produces them, is as much marked with absurdity as it is deserving of condemnation. In this county, if a man chances to receive a blow, instead of going to a magistrate to swear informations, he lodges a complaint with his clan, which enters into a compact to avenge the insult—a reaction is produced, and an equally extensive confederacy is formed on the other side. All this results from an indisposition to resort to the law for protection; for among you it is a point of honor to avoid magistrates, and to reject all the legitimate means provided for your redress. The battle fought between the Hickeys and the Hogans, in which not less than five hundred men were engaged, presents in a strong light the consequences of this most strange and preposterous system. Some of the Hickey party were slain in the field, and four of the Hogans were tried for their murder:—they were found guilty of manslaughter—three of them are married and have families, and from their wives and children are condemned to separate for ever. In my mind, these unhappy men have been doomed to a fate still more disastrous than those who have perished on the scaffold. In the calamity which has befallen Matthew Hogan every man in court felt a sympathy. With the exception of his having made himself a party in the cause of his clan, he has always conducted himself with propriety. His landlord felt for him not only an interest, but a strong regard, and exerted himself to the utmost in his behalf. He never took a part in deeds of nocturnal villany. He does not bear the dagger and the torch; honest, industrious, and of a mild and kindly nature, he enjoyed the good will of every man who was acquainted with him. His circumstances in the world were not only comparatively good, but, when taken in reference to his condition in society, were almost opulent; and he rather resembled an English yeoman than an Irish peasant. His appearance at the bar was in a high degree moving and impressive—tall, athletic, and even noble in his stature, with a face finely formed, and wholly free from any ferocity of expression, he attracted every eye, and excited, even among his prosecutors, a feeling of commiseration. He formed a remarkable contrast with the ordinary class of culprits who are arraigned in our public tribunals. So far from having guilt and depravity stamped with want upon him, the prevailing character of his countenance was indication of gentleness and humanity. This man was convicted of manslaughter; and when he heard the sentence of transportation for life, all color fled from his cheek, his lips became dry and ashy, his hand shook, and his eyes were the more painful to look at from their being incapable of tears. Most of you consider transportation a light evil, and so it is, to those who have no ties to fasten them to their country. I can well imagine that a deportation from this island, which, for most of its inhabitants is a miserable one, is to many a change greatly for the better. Although it is to a certain extent, painful to be torn from the place with which our first recollections are associated, and the Irish people have strong local attachments, and are fond of the place of their birth, and of their fathers' graves—yet the fine sky, the genial climate, and the deep and abundant soil of New Holland, afford many compensations. But there can be none for Matthew Hogan:—He is in the prime of life, was a prosperous farmer:—he has a young and amiable wife, who has borne him children; but, alas!

> "'Nor wife, nor children, more shall he behold,
> Nor friends, nor sacred home.'

He must leave his country for ever—he must part from all that he loves, and from all by whom he is beloved, and his heart will burst in the separation. On Monday next he will see his family for the last time. What a victim do you behold, in that unfortunate man, of the spirit of turbulence which rages among you! Matthew Hogan will feel his misfortune with more deep intensity, because he is naturally a sensitive and susceptible man. He was proved to have saved the life of one of his antagonists in the very hottest fury of the combat, from motives of generous commiseration. One of his own kindred, in speaking to me of his fate, said, 'he would feel it the more, because' (to use the poor man's vernacular pronunciation) 'he was so *tinder*.' This unhappy sensibility will produce a more painful laceration of the heart than others would experience, when he bids his infants and their mother farewell for ever. The prison of this town will present on Monday next a very afflicting spectacle. Before he ascends the vehicle which is to convey him for transportation, to Cork, he will be allowed to take leave of his family. His wife will cling with a breaking heart to his bosom; and while her arms are folded round his neck, while she sobs in the agony of a virtuous anguish on his breast, his children, who used to climb his knees in playful emulation for his caresses, his little orphans, for they are doomed to orphanage in their father's lifetime——— I will not go on with this distressing picture: your own emotions (for there are many fathers and husbands here) will complete it. But the sufferings of poor Hogan will not end at the threshold of his prison:—He will be conveyed in a vessel, freighted with affliction, across the ocean, and will be set on the lonely and distant land, from which he will return no more. Others, who will have accompanied him, will soon forget their country, and devote themselves to those useful and active pursuits for which the colony affords a field, and which will render them happier, by making them better men. But the thoughts of home will still press upon the mind of Matthew Hogan, and adhere with a deadly tenacity to his heart. He will mope about, in the vacant heedlessness of deep and settled sorrow; he will have no incentive to exertion, for he will have bidden farewell to hope. The instruments of labor will hang idly in his hands; he will go through his task without a consciousness of what he is doing: or if he thinks at all while he turns up the earth, he will think of the little garden beside his native cottage, which it was more a delight than a toil to till. Thus his day will go by, and at its close his only consolation will be to stand on the seashore, and fixing his eyes in that direction in which he will have been taught that his country lies—if not in the language, he will at least exclaim in the sentiments which have been so simply and so pathetically expressed in the Song of Exile:—

"'Erin, my country! though sad and forsaken,
In dreams I revisit thy sea-beaten shore;
But, alas! in a far foreign land I awaken,
And sigh for the friends that can meet me no more.'"

CONFESSIONS OF A JUNIOR BARRISTER.*

My father was agent to an extensive absentee property in the south of Ireland. He was a Protestant, and respectably connected. It was even understood in the country that a kind of Irish relationship existed between him and the distant proprietor whose rents he collected. Of this, however, I have some doubts; for, generally speaking, our aristocracy are extremely averse to trusting their money in the hands of a poor relation. Besides this, I was more than once invited to dine with a leading member of the family when I was at the Temple, which would hardly have been the case, had he suspected on my part any dormant claim of kindred. Being an eldest son, I was destined from my birth for the Bar. This, about thirty years ago, was almost a matter of course with our secondary gentry. Among such persons it was, at that time, an object of great ambition to have "a young counsellor" in the family. In itself it was a respectable thing—for, who could tell what the "young counsellor" might not one day be? Then it kept off vexatious claims, and produced a general

* This amusing sketch, of which it may be said, "*Se non è vero, è ben trovato*," was prefaced with the following notice:—"Mr. Editor: The author of the Irish Bar Sketches seems of late to have suspended his labors: and should he resume them, I question whether it forms any part of his plan to take up the subject upon which I now propose to trouble the public. I trust, therefore, that he will not consider it an act of undue interference with his exclusive rights, if, pending his present silence, I solicit the attention of your readers to the following sketch of myself. It may be vanity on my part, but it does strike my humble judgment that the details I am about to submit, and I shall be candid even against myself, have an interest of their own, which will excuse their publication."—The suspension spoken of here was imaginary, as one of the Sketches had appeared in May, and this was published in July, 1825.—M.

interested civility in the neighborhood, under the expectation that, whenever any little point of law might arise, the young counsellor's opinion might be had for nothing. Times have somewhat changed in this respect. Yet, to this day, the young counsellor who passes the law-vacations among his country friends finds (at least I have found it so) that the old feeling of reverence for the name is not yet extinct, and that his *dicta* upon the law of trespass and distress for rent are generally deferred to in his own county, unless when it happens to be the assizes'-time.

I passed through my school and college studies with great *éclat*. At the latter place, particularly toward the close of the course, I dedicated myself to all sorts of composition. I was also a constant speaker in the Historical Society, where I discovered, with no slight satisfaction, that popular eloquence was decidedly my forte. In the cultivation of this noble art, I adhered to no settled plan. Sometimes, in imitation of the ancients, I composed my address with great care, and delivered it from memory: at others, I trusted for words (for I am naturally fluent) to the occasion; but, whether my speech was extemporaneous or prepared, I always spoke on the side of freedom. At this period, and for the two or three years that followed, my mind was filled with almost inconceivable enthusiasm for my future profession. I was about to enter it (I can call my own conscience to witness) from no sordid motives. As to money matters, I was independent; for my father, who was now no more, had left me a profit-rent of three hundred pounds a-year.

No; but I had formed to my youthful fancy an idea of the honors and duties of an advocate's career, founded upon the purest models of ancient and modern times. I pictured to myself the glorious occasions it would present of redressing private wrongs, of exposing and confounding the artful machinations of injustice; and should the political condition of my country require it, as in all probability it would, of emulating the illustrious men whose eloquence and courage had so often shielded the intended victim against the unconstitutional aggressions of the state. It was with these views, and not from a love of "paltry gold," that I was ambitious to assume the robe. With the confidence of youth, and of a temperament not prone to despair, I felt an instinctive conviction that I was not assuming a task above my strength; but, notwithstanding my reliance upon my natural powers, I was indefatigable in aiding them, by exercise and study, against the occasions that were to render me famous in my generation. Deferring for the present (I was now at the Temple)* a regular course of legal reading, I applied myself with great ardor to the acquirement of general knowledge. To enlarge my views, I went through the standard works on the theory of government and legislation. To familiarize my understanding with subtle disquisitions, I plunged into metaphysics; for, as Ben Jonson somewhere says, "he that can not contract the sight of his mind, as well as dilate and disperse it, wanteth a great faculty;" and, lest an exclusive adherence to such pursuits should have the effect of damping my popular sympathies, I duly relieved them by the most celebrated productions of imagination in prose and verse. Oratory was, of course, not neglected. I plied at Cicero and Demosthenes. I devoured every treatise on the art of rhetoric that fell in my way. When alone in my lodgings, I declaimed to myself so often and so loudly, that my landlady and her daughters, who sometimes listened through the keyhole, suspected, as I afterward discovered, that I had lost my wits; but, as I paid my bills regularly and appeared tolerably rational in other matters, they thought it most prudent to connive at my extravagances. During the last winter of my stay at the Temple, I took an active part, as Gale Jones,† to his cost, sometimes found, in the debates of

* Irish barristers are compelled to "study" at the Temple, or some other Inn of Court, in London, besides eating half their term dinners at the Queen's Inn, Dublin. If an Irish barrister wish to practise at the English bar, he must first pass two years at a London Inn of Court, and pay the heavy stamp-duties and other charges—though he had already paid them in Dublin.—M.

‡ John Gale Jones was a notoriety—in his way. He was born in 1771, and before he had reached the years of manhood, had declared himself enamored of French republican principles. Thence, until his death, in 1838, he was one of the boldest, ablest, and most constant speakers at political meetings in London. In 1810, he had arraigned the House of Commons at the bar of public

the British Forum, which had just been opened for the final settlement of all disputed points in politics and morals.

Such were the views and qualifications with which I came to the Irish Bar. It may appear somewhat singular, but so it was, that previous to the day of my call, I was never inside an Irish Court of Justice. When at the Temple, I had occasionally attended the proceedings at Westminster Hall, where a common topic of remark among my fellow-students was the vast superiority of our Bar in grace of manner and classical propriety of diction. I had, therefore, no sooner received the congratulations of my friends on my admission, than I turned into one of the Courts to enjoy a first specimen of the forensic oratory of which I had heard so much. A young barrister of about twelve years' standing was on his legs, and vehemently appealing to the court in the following words: "Your Lordships perceive that we stand here as our grandmother's administratrix *de bonis non;* and really, my Lords, it does humbly strike me that it would be a monstrous thing to say that a party can now come in, in the very teeth of an Act of Parliament, and actually turn us round under color of hanging us up on the foot of a contract made behind our backs." The Court

opinion, and the Commons, instigated by the Government, committed him to Newgate, where he remained until the prorogation of Parliament, when he was liberated as a matter of course—neither branch of the Legislature having the power of awarding imprisonment beyond its own Session. He was tried, at Warwick, for sedition, and acquitted through the efforts of his counsel, Sir Samuel Romilly. I heard him speak in 1830, when he was sixty years' old, and even then, though his health was rather broken, he displayed much of the boldness, fluency, and eloquence, which had distinguished him in his prime. At the time I heard him, and until his death, his chief means of subsistence were what he obtained by speaking for payment in the political and other discussions which took place at the Rotunda in Blackfriars Road, the Cicernian Coffee House, and other debating societies in London. I remember that on one occasion, when I had ventured to present some matters of fact and figures of arithmetic against his beautiful flowers of rhetoric, Gale Jones condescended to admit that he had been mistaken, and to invite me from the body of the Rotunda, where I sat, as a spectator, to the platform where he and the other orators were placed. On my declining the invitation (thinking that the "post of honor is the private station," in such cases), he requested that I would drink his health, and sent round his own particular "pewter pot," out of which he begged that I would make the friendly libation!—M admitted that the force of the observation was unanswerable, and granted his motion with costs. On inquiry, I found that the counsel was among the most rising men of the Junior Bar.

For the first three or four years, little worth recording occurred. I continued my former studies, read, but without much care, a few elementary law-books, picked up a stray scrap of technical learning in the courts and the hall, and was now and then employed by the young attorneys from my own county as conducting counsel in a motion of course. At the outset I was rather mortified at the scantiness of my business, for I had calculated upon starting into immediate notice; but being easy in my circumstances, and finding so many others equally unemployed, I ceased to be impatient. With regard to my fame, however, it was otherwise. I had brought a fair stock of general reputation for ability and acquirement to the bar; but, having done nothing to increase it, I perceived, or fancied I perceived, that the estimation I had been held in was rapidly subsiding. This I could not endure; and as no widows or orphans seemed disposed to claim my protection, I determined upon giving the public a first proof of my powers as the advocate of a still nobler cause. An aggregate meeting of the Catholics of Ireland was announced, and I prepared a speech to be delivered on their behalf. I communicated my design to no one, not even to O'Connell, who had often urged me to declare myself; but, on the appointed day, I attended at the place of meeting, Clarendon-street Chapel.

The spectacle was imposing. Upon a platform erected before the altar, stood O'Connell and his staff. The chair which they surrounded had just been taken by the venerable Lord Fingal, whose presence alone would have conferred dignity upon any assembly. The galleries were thronged with Catholic beauties, looking so softly patriotic, that even Lord Liverpool would have forgiven in them the sin of a divided allegiance. The floor of the chapel was filled almost to suffocation with a miscellaneous populace, breathing from their looks a deep sense of rights withheld, and standing on tiptoe and with ears erect to catch the sounds of comfort or hope which their leaders had to administer. Finding it impracticable to force my way toward the chair, I was obliged to ascend and occupy a place in the gallery. I must confess that I was not sorry for the disappointment; for, in the first feeling of awe which the scene inspired, I found that my oratorical courage, which, like natural courage, "comes and goes," was rapidly "oozing out;"—but, as the business and the passions of the day proceeded—as the fire of national emotion lighted every eye, and exploded in simultaneous volleys of applause—all my apprehensions for myself were forgotten. Every fresh round of huzzas that rent the roof rekindled my ambition. I became impatient to be fanned, for my own sake, by the beautiful white handkerchiefs that waved around me, and stirred my blood like the visionary flags of the fabled Houris inviting the Mohammedan warrior to danger and to glory.

O'Connell, who was speaking, spied me in the gallery. He perceived at once that I had a weight of oratory pressing upon my mind, and good-naturedly resolved to quicken the delivery. Without naming me, he made an appeal to me under the character of "a liberal and enlightened young Protestant," which I well understood. This was conclusive, and he had no sooner sat down than I was on my legs. The sensation my unexpected appearance created was immense. I had scarcely said "My Lord, I rise," when I was stopped short by cheers that lasted for some minutes. It was really delicious music, and was repeated at the close of almost every sentence of my speech. I shall not dwell upon the speech itself, as most of my readers must remember it, for it appeared the next day in the Dublin Journals (the best report was in the Freeman), and was copied into all the London opposition papers except the Times. It is enough to say that the effect was, on the whole, tremendous.

As soon as I had concluded, a special messenger was despatched to conduct me to the platform. On my arrival there, I was covered with praises and congratulations. O'Connell was the warmest in the expression of his admiration: yet I thought I could read in his eyes that there predominated over that feeling the secret triumph of the partisan, at having contributed to bring over a young deserter from the enemy's camp. However, he took care that I should not go without my reward. He moved a special resolution of thanks "to his illustrious young friend," whom he described as "one of those rare and felicitous combinations of human excellence, in which the spirit of a Washington is embodied with the genius of a Grattan." These were his very words, but my modesty was in no way pained at them, for I believed every syllable to be literally true.

I went home in a glorious intoxication of spirits. My success had surpassed my most sanguine expectations. I had now established a character for public speaking, which, independently of the general fame that would ensue, must inevitably lead to my retainer in every important case where the passions were to be moved, and, whenever the Whigs should come in, to a seat in the British Senate.

* * * * * * * *

After a restless night—in which however, when I did sleep, I contrived to dream, at one time that I was at the head of my profession, at another that I was on the opposition-side of the House of Commons redressing Irish grievances—I sallied forth to the Courts to enjoy the impression which my display of the day before must have made there. On my way, my ears were regaled by the cries of the news-hawkers, announcing that the morning papers contained "Young Counsellor ——'s grand and elegant speech."—"This," thought I, "is genuine fame," and I pushed on with a quickened pace toward the Hall.

On my entrance, the first person that caught my eye was my friend and fellow-student, Dick ——. We had been intimate at College, and inseparable at the Temple. Our tastes and tempers had been alike, and our political opinions the same, except that he sometimes went far beyond me in his abstract enthusiasm for the rights of man. I was surprised—for our eyes met—that he did not rush to tender me his greetings. However, I went up to him, and held out my hand in the usual cordial way. He took it, but in a very unusual way. The friendly pressure was no longer there. His countenance, which heretofore had glowed with warmth at my approach, was still and chilling. He made no allusion to my speech, but looking round as if fearful of being observed, and muttering something about its being "Equity-day in the Exchequer," moved away. This was a modification of "genuine fame" for which I was quite unprepared. In my present elevation of spirits, however, I was rather perplexed than offended at the occurrence. I was willing to suspect that my friend must have found himself suddenly indisposed, or that, in spite of his better feelings, an access of involuntary envy might have overpowered him; or perhaps, poor fellow, some painful subject of a private nature might be pressing upon his mind, so as to cause this strange revolution in his manner. At the time I never adverted to the rumor that there was shortly to be a vacancy for a commissionership of bankrupts, nor had I been aware that his name as a candidate stood first on the Chancellor's list. He was appointed to the place a few days after, and the mystery of his coldness was explained.

Yet, I must do him the justice to say that he had no sooner attained his object than he showed symptoms of remorse for having shaken me off. He praised my speech, in a confidential way, to a mutual friend, and I forgave him—for one gets tired of being indignant—and to this day we converse with our old familiarity upon all subjects except the abstract rights of man. In the course of the morning I received many similar manifestations of homage to my genius from others of my Protestant colleagues. The young, who up to that time had sought my society, now brushed by me as if there was infection in my touch. The seniors, some of whom had occasionally condescended to take my arm in the Hall, and treat me to prosing details of their adventures at the Temple, held themselves suddenly aloof, and, if our glances encountered, petrified me with looks of established order. In whatever direction I cast my eyes, I met signs of anger or estrangement, or, what was still less welcome, of pure commiseration.

Such were the first fruits of my "grand and elegant speech," which had combined (O'Connell, may Heaven forgive you!) "the spirit of a Washington with the genius of a Grattan."

I must, however, in fairness state that I was not utterly "left alone in my glory." The Catholics certainly crowded round me and extolled me to the skies. One eulogized my simile of the eagle; another swore that the Corporation would never recover from the last hit I gave them; a third that my fortune at the Bar was made. I was invited to all their dinner-parties, and as far as "lots" of white soup and Spanish flummery went, had unquestionably no cause to complain. The attorneys, in both public and private, were loudest in their admiration of my rare qualifications for success in my profession; but, though they took every occasion, for weeks and months after, to recur to the splendor of my eloquence, it still somehow happened that not one of them sent me a guinea.

I was beginning to charge the whole body with ingratitude, when I was agreeably induced to change my opinion, at least for a while. One of the most rising among them was an old schoolfellow of mine, named Shanahan. He might have been of infinite service to me, but he had never employed me, even in the most trivial matter. We were still, however, on terms of, to me rather unpleasant familiarity; for he affected in his language and manners a certain waggish slang, from which my classical sensibilities revolted. One day, as I was going my usual rounds in the Hall, Shanahan, who held a bundle of briefs under his arm, came up and drew me aside toward one of the recesses. "Ned, my boy," said he, for that was his customary style of addressing me, "I just want to tell you that I have a sporting record now at issue, and which I'm to bring down to ——— for trial at the next assizes. It's an action against a magistrate, and a Bible-distributer into the bargain, for the seduction of a farmer's daughter. You are to be in it—I have taken care of that—and I just want to know if you'd like to state the case, for, if you do, it can be managed." My heart palpitated with gratitude, but it would have been unprofessional to give it utterance; so I simply expressed my readiness to undertake the office. "Consider yourself, then, retained as stating counsel," said he, but without handing me any fee. "All you want is an opportunity of showing what you can do with a jury, and never was there a finer one than this. It was just such another that first brought that lad there into notice," pointing to one of the sergeants that rustled by us. "You shall have your instructions in full time to be prepared. Only hit the Bible-boy in the way I know you can, and your name will be up on the circuit."

The next day Shanahan called me aside again. In the interval, I had composed a striking exordium and peroration, with several powerful passages of general application, to be interspersed according as the facts should turn out, through the body of the statement. "Ned," said the attorney to me, as soon as we had reached a part of the Hall where there was no risk of being overheard, "I now want to consult you upon"—here he rather hesitated—"in fact, upon a little case of my own." After a short pause he proceeded: "You know a young lady from your county, Miss Dickson?"—"Harriet Dickson?"—"The very one."—"Intimately well; she's now in town with her cousins in Harcourt street: I see her almost every day."—"She has a very pretty property too, they say, under her father's will—a lease for lives renewable for ever."—"So I have always understood."—"In fact, Ned," he continued, looking somewhat foolish, and in a tone half slang, half sentiment, "I am rather inclined to think—as at present advised—that she has partly gained my affections. Come, come, my boy, no laughing; upon my faith and soul, I'm serious—and what's more, I have reason to think that she'll have no objection to my telling her so: but, with those devils of cousins at her elbow, there's no getting her into a corner with one's self for an instant; so, what I want you to do for me, Ned, is this—just to throw your eye over a wide-line copy of a little notice to that effect I have been thinking of serving her with." Here he extracted from a mass of law-documents a paper endorsed, "Draft letter to Miss D——," and folded up and tied with red tape like the rest. The matter corresponded with the exterior. I contrived, but not without an effort, to preserve my countenance as I perused this singular production, in which sighs and vows were embodied in the language of an affidavit to hold to bail. Amid the manifold vagaries of Cupid, it was the first time I had seen him exchanging his ordinary dart for an Attorney's office-pen. When I came to the end, he asked if I thought it might be improved. I candidly answered that it would, in my opinion, admit of change and correction. "Then," said he, "I shall be eternally obliged if you'll just do the needful with it. You perceive that I have not been too explicit, for, between ourselves, I have one or two points to ascertain about the state of the property before I think it prudent to commit myself on paper. It would never do, you know, to be brought into court for a breach of promise of marriage; so you'll keep this in view, and before you begin, just cast a glance over the Statute of Frauds." Before I could answer, he was called away to attend a motion.

The office thus flung upon me was not of the most dignified kind, but the seduction-case was too valuable to be risked; so pitting my ambition against my pride, I found the latter soon give way; and on the following day I presented the lover with a declaratory effusion at once so glowing and so cautious, so impassioned as to matters of sentiment, but withal so guarded in point of law, that he did not hesitate to pronounce it a masterpiece of literary composition and forensic skill. He overwhelmed me with thanks, and went home to copy and despatch it. I now come to the most whimsical part of the transaction. With Miss Dickson, as I had stated to her admirer, I was extremely intimate. We had known each other from childhood, and conversed with the familiarity rather of cousins than mere acquaintances. When she was in town, I saw her almost daily, talked to her of myself and my prospects, lectured her on her love of dress, and in return was always at her command for any small service of gallantry or friendship that she might require. The next time I called, I could perceive that I was unusually welcome. Her cousins were with her, but they quickly retired and left us together. As soon as we were alone, Harriet announced to me "that she had a favor — a very great one indeed — to ask of me." She proceeded, and with infinite command of countenance. "There was a friend of hers — one for whom she was deeply interested — in fact it was — but no — she must not betray a secret—and this friend had the day before received a letter containing something like, but still not exactly a proposition of—in short, of a most interesting nature; and her friend was terribly perplexed how to reply to it, for she was very young and inexperienced, and all that; and she had tried two or three times and had failed; and then she had consulted her (Harriet), and she (Harriet) had also been puzzled, for the letter in question was in fact, as far as it was intelligible, so uncommonly well written, both in style and in sentiment, that her friend was, of course, particularly anxious to send a suitable reply—and this was Harriet's own feeling, and she had therefore taken a copy of it (omitting names) for the purpose of showing it to me, and getting me—I was so qualified, and so clever at my pen, and all that sort of thing—just to undertake, if I only *would*, to throw upon paper just the kind of sketch of the kind of answer that ought to be returned."

The preface over, she opened her reticule and handed me a copy of my own composition. I would have declined the task, but every excuse I suggested was overruled. The principal objection—my previous retainer on the other side—I could not in honor reveal; and I was accordingly installed in the rather ludicrous office of conducting counsel to both parties in the suit. I shall not weary the reader with a technical detail of the pleadings, all of which I drew. They proceeded, if I remember right, as far as a *sur-rebutter*—rather an unusual thing in modern practice. Each of the parties throughout the correspondence was charmed with the elegance and correctness of the other's style. Shanahan frequently observed to me, "What a singular thing it was that Miss Dickson was so much cleverer at her pen than her tongue;" and once upon handing me a letter, of which the eloquence was perhaps a little too masculine, he protested "that he was almost afraid to go farther in the business, for he suspected that a girl who could express herself so powerfully on paper would, one day or other, prove too much for him when she became his wife." But, to conclude, Shanahan obtained the lady, and the lease for lives renewable for ever. The seduction case (as I afterward discovered) had been compromised the day before he offered me the statement; and from that day to this, though his business increased with his marriage, he never sent me a single brief.*

Finding that nothing was to be got by making public speeches, or writing love-letters for attorneys, and having now idled away some valuable years, I began to think of attending sedulously to my profession; and, with a view to the regulation of my exertions, lost no opportunity of inquiring into the nature of the particular qualifications by which the men whom I saw eminent or rising around me had originally outstripped their competitors. In the course of these inquiries, I discovered that there was a newly-invented method of getting rapidly into business, of which I had never heard before. The secret was communicated to me by a friend, a king's counsel, who is no longer at the Irish Bar. When I asked him for his opinion as to the course of study and conduct most advisable to be pursued, and at the same time sketched the general plan which had presented itself to me, "Has it never struck you," said he, "since you have walked this Hall, that there is a shorter and a far more certain road to professional success?" I professed my ignorance of the particular method to which he alluded. "It requires," he continued, "some peculiar qualifications: have you an ear for music?"—Surprised at the question, I answered that I had. "And a good voice?"—"A tolerable one."—"Then, my advice to you is, to take a few lessons in psalm-singing; attend the Bethesda regularly; take a part in the anthem, and the louder the better; turn up as much of the white of your eyes as possible—and in less than six months you'll find business pouring in upon you. You smile, I see, at this advice; but I have never known the plan to fail, except where the party has sung incurably out of tune. Don't you perceive that we are once more becoming an Island of Saints, and that half the business of these Courts passes through their hands? When I came to the bar, a man's suc-

* This attorney's non-committal caution reminds me of another of the craft, who challenged a man to fight a duel with him, and fixed the meeting, "in the Phœnix Park, adjacent unto the city of Dublin, and in that part of it entitled 'The Fifteen Acres'—be the same more or less."—M.

cess depended upon his exertions during the six working-days of the week; but now, he that has the dexterity to turn the Sabbath to account is the surest to prosper: and

"'Why should not piety be made,
As well as equity, a trade,
And men get money by devotion
As well as making of a motion?'"

These hints, though thrown out with an air of jest, made some impression on me; but after reflecting for some time upon the subject, and taking an impartial view of my powers in that way, I despaired of having hypocrisy enough for the speculation, so I gave it up. Nothing therefore remaining, but a more direct and laborious scheme, I now planned a course of study in which I made a solemn vow to myself to persevere. Besides attending the courts and taking notes of the proceedings, I studied at home, at an average of eight hours a-day. I never looked into any but a law-book. Even a newspaper I seldom took up. Every thing that could touch my feelings or my imagination I excluded from my thoughts, as inimical to the habits of mind I now was anxious to acquire. My circle of private acquaintances was extensive, but I manfully resisted every invitation to their houses. I had assigned myself a daily task to perform, and to perform it I was determined. I persevered for two years with exemplary courage. Neither the constant, unvarying, unrewarded labors of the day, nor the cheerless solitude of the evenings, could induce me to relax my efforts.

I was not, however, insensible to the disheartening change, both physical and moral, that was going on within me. All the generous emotions of my youth, my sympathies with the rights and interests of the human race, my taste for letters, even my social sensibilities, were perceptibly wasting away from want of exercise, and from the hostile influence of an exclusive and chilling occupation. It fared still worse with my health: I lost my appetite and rest, and of course my strength; a deadly pallor overcast my features; black circles formed round my eyes; my cheeks sank in; the tones of my voice became feeble and melancholy; the slightest exercise exhausted me almost to fainting; at night I was tortured by headaches, palpitations, and frightful dreams; my waking reflections were equally harassing. I now deplored the sinister ambition that had propelled me into a scene for which, in spite of all my self-love, I began to suspect that I was utterly unfitted. I recalled the bright prospects under which I had entered life, and passed in review the various modes in which I might have turned my resources to honorable and profitable account. The contrast was fraught with anguish and mortification.

As I daily returned from the Courts, scarcely able to drag my wearied limbs along, but still attempting to look as alert and cheerful as if my success was certain, I frequently came across some of my college contemporaries. Such meetings always gave me pain. Some of them were rising in the army, others in the church; others, by a well-timed exercise of their talents, were acquiring a fair portion of pecuniary competence and literary fame. They all seemed happy and thriving, contented with themselves and with all around them; while here was I, wearing myself down to a phantom in a dreary and profitless pursuit, the best years of my youth already gone, absolutely gone for nothing, and the prospect overshadowed by a deeper gloom with every step that I advanced. The friends whom I thus met inquired with good-nature after my concerns; but I had no longer the heart to talk of myself. I broke abruptly from them, and hurried home to picture to my now morbid imagination the forlorn condition of the evening of life to a briefless barrister. How often, at this period, I regretted that I had not chosen the English Bar, as I had more than once been advised. There, if I had not prospered, my want of success would have been comparatively unobserved. In London I should, at the worst, have enjoyed the immunities of obscurity; but here my failure would be exposed to the most humiliating publicity. Here I was to be doomed, day after day and year after year, to exhibit myself in places of public resort, and advertise, in my own person, the disappointment of all my hopes.

These gloomy reflections were occasionally relieved by

others of a more soothing and philosophic cast. The catastrophe, at the prospect of which I shuddered, it was still in my own power to avert. The sufferings that I endured were, after all, the factitious growth of an unwise ambition. I was still young and independent, and might, by one manly effort, sever myself for ever from the spell that bound me; I might transport myself to some distant scene, and find in tranquillity and letters an asylum from the feverish cares that now bore me down. The thought was full of comfort, and I loved to return to it. I reviewed the different countries in which such a resting-place might best be found, and was not long in making a selection. Switzerland, with her lakes and hills, and moral and poetic associations, rose before me: there inhabiting a delightful cottage on the margin of one of her lakes, and emancipated from the conventional inquietudes that now oppressed me, I should find my health and my healthy sympathies revive.

In my present frame of mind, the charms of such a philosophic retreat were irresistible. I determined to bid an eternal adieu to demurrers and special contracts, and had already fixed upon the time for executing my project, when an unexpected obstacle interposed. My sole means of support was the profit-rent, of which I have already spoken. The land, out of which it arose, lay in one of the insurrectionary districts; and a letter from my agent in the country announced that not a shilling of it could be collected. In the state of nervous exhaustion to which the "blue books" and the blue devils had reduced me, I had no strength to meet this unexpected blow. To the pangs of disappointed ambition were now added the horrors of sudden and hopeless poverty. I sank almost without a struggle, and becoming seriously indisposed, was confined to my bed for a week, and for more than a month to the house.

When I was able to crawl out, I moved mechanically toward the Courts. On entering the Hall, I met my friend, the king's counsel, who had formerly advised the Bethesda: he was struck by my altered appearance, inquired with much concern into the particulars of my recent illness, of which he had not heard before, and, urging the importance of change of air, insisted that I should accompany him to pass a short vacation then at hand at his country-house in the vicinity of Dublin. The day after my arrival there, I received a second letter from my agent, containing a remittance, and holding out more encouraging prospects for the future. After this I recovered wonderfully, both in health and in spirits. My mind, so agitated of late, was now, all at once, in a state of the most perfect tranquillity: from which I learned, for the first time, that there is nothing like the excitement of a good practical blow (provided you recover from it) for putting to flight a host of imaginary cares. I could moralize at some length on this subject, but I must hasten to a conclusion.

The day before our return to town, my friend had a party of Dublin acquaintances at his house: among the guests was the late Mr. D——, an old attorney in considerable business, and his daughter. In the evening, though it was summer-time, we had a dance. I led out Miss D——: I did so, I seriously declare, without the slightest view to the important consequences that ensued. After the dance, which (I remember it well) was to the favorite and far-famed "Leg-of-Mutton jig," I took my partner aside, in the usual way, to entertain her. I began by asking if "she was not fond of poetry?" She demanded "why I asked the question?" I said, "Because I thought I could perceive it in the expression of her eyes." She blushed, "protested I must be flattering her, but admitted that she was." I then asked "if she did not think the Corsair a charming poem?" She answered, "Oh, yes!"—"And would not *she* like to be living in one of the Grecian islands?"—"Oh, indeed she would."—"Looking upon the blue waters of the Archipelago and the setting sun, associated as they were with the rest."—"How delightful it would be!" exclaimed she. "And so *refreshing!*" said I. I thus continued till we were summoned to another set. She separated from me with reluctance, for I could see that she considered my conversation to be the sublimest thing that could be.

The effect of the impression I had made soon appeared. Two days after, I received a brief in rather an important case from her father's office. I acquitted myself so much to his satisfaction, that he sent me another, and another, and finally installed me as one of his standing counsel for the junior business of his office. The opportunities thus afforded me brought me by degrees into notice. In the course of time, general business began to drop in upon me, and has latterly been increasing into such a steady stream, that I am now inclined to look upon my final success as secure.

I have only to add, that the twelve years I have passed at the Irish Bar have worked a remarkable change in some of my early tastes and opinions. I no longer, for instance, trouble my head about immortal fame; and, such is the force of habit, have brought myself to look upon a neatly-folded brief, with a few crisp Bank-of-Ireland notes on the back of it, as, beyond all controversy, the most picturesque object upon which the human eye can alight.

LORD MANNERS.

On the 31st day of July, in the year of our Lord 1827, Lord Manners, the late Keeper of his Majesty's Irish Conscience, bade the Irish bar farewell.* The scene which took place upon that melancholy occasion deserves to be recorded. It being understood that an address of professional condolence on behalf of the more loyal portion of the bar was to be pronounced by that tender enunciator of pathetic sentiment, the Attorney-General, the Court of Chancery was crowded at an early hour. The members of the Beef-Steak Club, with countenances in which it was difficult to determine whether their grief at the anticipated "export" from Ireland, or the traces

* Lord Manners, was son of Lord George Manners, of the Ducal house of Rutland. He was born in 1756, was educated at Cambridge, where he obtained the honor of being fifth wrangler, and, having been called to the bar, in due time became Solicitor-General to the Prince of Wales, and one of his parliamentary adherents. In 1802, when made Solicitor-General to the king, he was knighted. In 1803 he was one of the official prosecutors of Colonel Despard, tried and executed for high treason. He was made one of the Barons of the Exchequer in 1805, and in 1807 was raised to the peerage, on being appointed Lord-Chancellor of Ireland, as successor to Mr. Ponsonby. On demanding the Seals, with all wonted formality, he discovered that he had accidentally left behind him the authority for assuming the new dignity! Lord Manners held the Irish Chancellorship for twenty years—until July, 1827, when he was recalled, and succeeded by Sir Anthony Hart. As an equity judge, he wanted capacity, and was further deficient, by being a decided political partisan. Many of his judgments were reversed by the House of Lords, and nothing but the fact that he was ultra-Protestant in his principles could have retained him, so long, in a position where the general opinion of the profession as to his conduct and qualifications was contemptuous in the extreme. He died in May, 1842, aged eighty-six.—M.

of their multitudinous convivialities, enjoyed a predominance, filled the galleries on either side. The junior aristocracy of the bar, for whom the circuits have few attractions, occupied the body of the court; while the multitude of King's counsel, in whom his Majesty scarcely finds a verification of the divine saying of Solomon, were arrayed along the benches, where it is their prerogative to sit, in the enjoyment of that leisure which the public so unfrequently disturb. The assembly looked exceedingly dejected and blank. A competition in sorrow appeared to have been got up between the rival admirers of his Lordship, the Pharisees of Leeson and the Sadducees of the Beef-Steak Club. "The Saints," however, from their habitual longitude of visage, and the natural alliance between their lugubrious devotion and despair, had a decided advantage over the statesmen of revelry and the legislators of song; and it was admitted on all hands that Mr. M'Kaskey should yield the palm of condolence to a certain pious Sergeant, into whom the whole spirit of the prophet Jeremy appeared to have been infused.

But the person most deserving of attention was Mr. Saurin. Lord Manners had been his intimate associate for twenty years. He had, upon his Lordship's first arrival in Ireland, pre-occupied his mind; he took advantage of his opportunities of access, and, having crept like an earwig into his audience, he at last effected a complete lodgment in his mind. Mr. Saurin established a masterdom over his faculties, and gave to all his passions the direction of his own. A very close intimacy grew up between them, which years of intercourse cemented into regard. They were seen every day walking together to the court, with that easy lounge which indicated the carelessness and equality of their friendship. In one instance only had Lord Manners been wanting in fidelity to his companion. He had been commissioned to inform him (at least he was himself six months before apprized of the intended movement) that Mr. Plunket would, in return for his services to the Administration, be raised to the office of Attorney-General for Ireland. Had Mr. Saurin been informed of this determination, he might have acted more wisely than he did, when, in a fit of what his advocates have been pleased to call magnanimity, but which was nothing else than a paroxysm of offended arrogance, he declined the Chief-Justiceship of the King's Bench! Lord Wellesley took him at his word, and gave him no opportunity to retrace his steps. He would not, at all events, have been taken unawares. Mr. Saurin is not conspicuous for his tendencies to forgiveness, but he pardoned the person in whose favor, of all others, a barrister should make an exception from his vindictive habits. Their intercourse was renewed; and whatever might have been the state of their hearts, their arms continued to be linked together. This intimacy was noted by the solicitors, and, although deprived of his official power, Mr. Saurin retained his business, and the importance which attends it.

The resignation, therefore, of Lord Manners,* to whose court his occupations were confined, was accounted a personal misfortune to himself. From the peculiar circumstances in which he was placed, he drew the general notice in the scene of separation, and was an object of interest to those who, without any political sympathy or aversion, are observers of feeling, and students of the human heart. In justice to him it should be stated that his bearing did not greatly deviate from his ordinary demeanor, and that he still looked the character which he had been for some time playing, if not with profit, yet not without applause, as the stoic of Orangeism, and the Cato of "a falling state." Not that he appeared altogether insensible, but, in his sympathies, his own calamities did not seem to have any very ostensible share: any expression of a melancholy

* He was succeeded by Sir Anthony Hart, born in 1759 at St Kitt's, in the West Indies. He was once a Unitarian preacher at Norwich; went to the English bar; practised in equity for many years, and with such success that he was then made Master of the Rolls, succeeded Sir John Leach as Vice-Chancellor of England, in April, 1827, and was then knighted. In Ireland he gave much satisfaction, by reason of the soundness and impartiality of his judgments. He literally had no politics, and prided himself on being a lawyer and nothing else — in strong contrast to his predecessor, who was a political partisan and not much of a lawyer. He retired from office, at the close of 1830, when the Grey Ministry appointed Plunket to succeed him, and died December, 1831, aged seventy-two. — M.

kind, that was perceivable through his dark and Huguenot complexion, seemed to arise more immediately from the pains of friendship than from any sentiment in more direct connection with himself.

I can not avoid thinking, however, that his mind must have been full of scorpion recollections: there was, at least, one incident which must have deeply stung him. Had the address to Lord Manners been pronounced by Mr. Plunket, Mr. Saurin might have been reconciled to the representation of the bar, in the person of a man who had long approved himself his superior. But to see his own proselyte holding the place to which he had acquired a sort of prescriptive right, and to witness in Henry Joy the Attorney-General to a Whig Administration, while he was himself without distinction or office, was, I am sure, a source of corrosive feelings, and must have pained him to the core.

It would, however, have been a misfortune for the lovers of ridicule, if any man except Mr. Joy had pronounced the address which was delivered to the departing Chancellor. He is a great master of mockery, and looks a realization of Goethe's Mephistophiles. So strong is his addiction to that species of satire which is contained in exaggerated praise, that he scarcely ever resorts to any other species of vituperation. Nature has been singularly favorable to him. His short and upturned nose is admirably calculated to toss his sarcasms off; his piercing and peering eyes gleam and flash in the voluptuousness of malice, and exhibit the keen delight with which he revels in ridicule and luxuriates in derision. His chin is protruded, like that of the Cynic listening to St. Paul, in Raphael's Cartoon. His muscles are full of flexibility, and are capable of adapting themselves to every modification of irony. They have the advantage, too, of being covered with a skin that dimples into sneers with a plastic facility, and looks like a manuscript of Juvenal found in the ashy libraries of Herculaneum. In this eminent advocate, such an assemblage of physiognomical qualifications for irony are united, as I scarcely think the countenance of any orator in the ancient city of Sardos could have presented. His face was an admirable commentary on the enormity of the encomium which he was deputed to offer.

The "Evening Mail,"* indeed, the official organ of the Orange faction in Ireland, gives a somewhat different account of this amusing exhibition. "Every sound," says that graphic journalist, "was hushed, while the Attorney-General, with a tremulous voice, but with a feeling and emphasis which showed that the sentiments expressed came directly from his heart," and so forth. Then follows the address. I forbear from setting forth the whole of it, but select a single sentence: "We," said Mr. Joy, "can not but admire that distinguished ability, that strict impartiality, and that unremitting assiduity, with which you have discharged the various duties of your office." The delivery of this sentence was a masterpiece of sarcastic recitation; and, to any person who desired to become a proficient in the art of sneering, of which Mr. Joy is so renowned a professor, afforded an invaluable model.

Cicero, in his oratorical treatise, has given an analysis of the manner in which certain fine fragments of eloquence have been delivered; and for the benefit of the students of irony, it may not be improper to enter with some minuteness into a detail of the varieties of excellence with which Mr. Joy pronounced this flagitious piece of panegyric. With this view, I shall take each limb of the sentence apart. —"We can not but admire:"—In uttering these words, he gave his head that slight shake, with which he generally announces that he is about to let loose some formidable sarcasm. He paused at the

* The *Dublin Evening Mail*, long the leading ultra-Tory and ultra-Protestant newspaper in Ireland, was commenced in the heat of the agitation on the Catholic question, and obtained immediate notoriety and influence, by means of the talent and vigor with which it was conducted, and its boldness in personality. Curiously enough, the proprietors (brothers, named Sheehan), had been Catholics, and the violence of their Protestantism was greater (on that account?—for who so violent as a renegade?) than if they had been born to it. During the Session of Parliament, Remmy Sheehan resided in London, very much in the confidence of the leaders of the Tory party, and his correspondence in the *Evening Mail* often anticipated even the leading London papers in political information. The *Mail* still flourishes—but Remmy Sheehan is no more. It was said that he returned to the Catholic faith, before he died.—M.

same time, as if he felt a qualm of conscience at what he was about to speak, and experienced a momentary commiseration for the victim of his cruel commendations. This feeling of compassion, however, only lasted for an instant, and he assumed the aspect that became the utterance of the vituperative adulation which he had undertaken to inflict. "We can not but admire the distinguished ability:"—At the word "ability" it was easy to perceive that he could with difficulty restrain his sense of extravagance from breaking into laughter. However, he did succeed in keeping down the spirit of ridicule within the just boundaries of derision. At the same time he conveyed to his auditors (the Chancellor excepted) the whole train of thought that was passing in his mind; and by the magic of his countenance recalled a series of amusing recollections. It was impossible to look at him without remembering the exhibitions which for twenty years had made the administration of justice in the Irish Court of Chancery the subject of Lord Redesdale's laughter, and of John Lord Eldon's tears. He spoke it with such a force of mockery, that he at once brought to the mind of the spectators that spirit of ignorant self-sufficiency, and presumptuous precipitation, with which Lord Manners discharged the business of his court. A hundred cases seemed to rise in his face. Stackpoole and Stackpoole appeared in the curl of his lip; Blake and Foster quivered in the movement of his nostrils; Brossley against the Corporation of Dublin appeared in his twinkling eyes; and "reversal" seemed to be written in large characters between his brows.*

The next sarcasm which this unmerciful adulator proceeded to apply, turned on his lordship's selection of magistrates. At

* All these were important cases, which Lord Manners decided one way, while the House of Lords, assisted by the judges of England, on appeal, decided that he was wholly and almost flagrantly in error.—It would have been difficult, I suspect, to have found a worse equity judge than Lord Manners. Some time after his death, while I was going over these Sketches with Mr. Sheil, I asked his opinion of Lord Manners. His reply was emphatic enough:—"Go out into the street—pick up the first man in a decent coat, who is able to give correct replies to any three ordinary questions you may put to him—put that man on the Lord-Chancellor's seat, in Dublin, and he *must* make a better judge than Lord Manners was."—M.

the utterance of "strict impartiality," the smile of Mr. Joy gleamed with a still yellower lustre over his features, and he threw his countenance into so expressive a grimace, that the whole loyal, but pauper magistracy of Ireland was brought at once to my view. I beheld a long array of insolvent justices with their arms out at the elbows, who had been honored, by virtue of their Protestantism, with his Majesty's commission of the peace.*

I did not think it possible for the powers of irony to go beyond this last achievement of the Attorney-General, until he came to talk of his lordship's unremitting assiduity. It was well known to every man at the Bar, that Lord Manners abhorred his occupations. He trembled at an enthymem, he sunk under a sorites, and was gored by the horns of a dilem-

* It may be scarcely worth mention — but I may as well state that, when I lived in Ireland (five-and-twenty years ago: *eheu fugaces anni!*) I had frequent occasion to notice that the Catholics preferred going before a Protestant magistrate, even though a justice of their own persuasion might be nearer their vicinity. When I was a boy, I passed much of my time at the house of my uncle, the late John Shelton, of Rossmore, in my native county of Limerick, and I noticed that the peasantry always brought their complaints before him in preference to a Catholic Justice of the Peace who lived on the other side of the mountain, and nearer to their homes. Their complaint was that their own magistrate "was too severe, entirely, upon them." So, a few years after, when I was at school, at Fermoy, in the county of Cork, there was an excellent man, and a Catholic (Thomas Dennehy, of Belleview), who was a magistrate. He lived near Carrigaline, and between Glandalane and Fermoy, but the peasantry and the small farmers always passed him by, and went before George Walker, a Protestant magistrate. I ascertained the cause — the Catholic Justices, who were "few and far between," were so much exposed to, and afraid of, censure, that they usually inclined a trifle toward a Protestant complainant or defendant — for fear that they should be suspected of partiality toward persons of their own creed. — Perhaps I should apologize for thus bringing my own experiences into this note; but, when I resided, as a child, with my uncle, the magistrate, in the county of Limerick, I was usually thrust into the library, on wet days, being accused (very unjustly, of course) of being "a troublesome lad." This library consisted exclusively of a complete set of Walker's Hibernian Magazine, recording Irish history during the time of the Union, as well as many years preceding and following it, and the repeated perusal of these magazines made me so familiar with Irish matters that I recollect nearly all they told me — which may account for the particular and distinctive details which I have put into these notes. — M.

ma. His irritability in court was the subject of universal complaint. He seemed to labor under an incapacity of fixing his attention for any continuity of time to any given matter of meditation; and by his wriggling in his seat during the admirable arguments of Mr. Pennefather, and his averted eye, and the puffing of his cheeks, exhibited his strong distaste for reasoning, and the horror which he entertained for all inductive thought. It was in frosty weather that his excitability and fretfulness of temperament were particularly conspicuous. He was fond of shooting, and if he was detained by a long argument beyond the usual period which he allowed to the hearing of causes, about Christmas, he broke out into fits and starts of ludicrous irritation. Mr. Plunket used to say that whenever Lord Manners heard the name of Mr. Hitchcock (a gentleman of the Irish Bar of considerable talents) his lordship used to start, as if it were "Hish! Cock!" that had struck his ear. The memory of the Attorney-General, in complimenting him on his "unremitting assiduity," was, I am sure, carried back to those scenes of judicial impatience, in which, when the mercury stood at the freezing point, his lordship's intolerance of all argument was exemplified. The look with which Mr. Joy executed the recitation of this portion of his address, was, if possible, a higher feat. It was the *chef-d'œuvre* of mockery, and masterpiece of derision. His eyes, his brows, his nose and chin.—But I will not undertake to describe him —enough to say, that such was the potency of his sarcasm, that I was transported in fancy to the Duke of Leinster's demesne at Carton, where his lordship used to shoot, and I beheld him amid those brambles of which he was much fonder than the thorny quicksets of the law, with his chancellor hat, a green jacket, a scarlet waistcoat, silk breeches, and long black gaiters, which constituted his usual sporting attire.

I was, however, recalled from this excursion of the imagination, by the farewell address of his lordship to the Bar. The Attorney-General had concluded, and Lord Manners rose to bid it a long adieu. It did him great credit that he did not follow the example of Lord Redesdale, who wept and whimpered upon his taking leave of Ireland and ten thousand a year.

Lord Manners had the materials of consolation in his pocket, having received about two hundred thousand pounds of the public money, for "the distinguished ability, the strict impartiality, and unremitting assiduity," of which Mr. Joy had performed the panegyric. So far from indulging in any lachrymatory mood, his lordship proved himself a partisan to the last, by giving vent to his factious antipathies against the Solicitor-General. He had strenuously resisted the nomination of Mr. Doherty to the office, for which his talents as a speaker, both in Parliament and at the Bar, had eminently qualified him. There was not an individual of the profession, who did not feel convinced that Lord Manners was actuated by an hostility arising from political motives, founded upon Mr. Doherty's support of Catholic Emancipation.

Nearly the last sentence in his address is copied from the Evening Mail. "If," said his lordship, "I have disappointed or delayed the expectations of any gentleman of the Bar, I lament it. I can assure you, gentlemen, I have not been actuated by a personal motive, or hostile feeling against him, but by a sense of duty imposed on me, in the situation in which I am placed to protect the fair claims of the Bar, by resisting, to the utmost of my power, the interference of parliamentary or political interest in the advancements in the law." It is obvious that under the veil of affected regret which Lord Manners states himself to have felt at having, with a view to the promotion of Sergeant Lefroy, opposed the wishes of Mr. Canning and the directions of the Cabinet, there lurks in the intimation that his lordship had opposed the interference of parliamentary and political interest, a reflection upon Mr. Doherty, of which good feeling, as well as a sense of justice, should have forbidden the expression. This Parthian arrow should not have been discharged at such a moment. It was not a time for the indulgence of acrimonious feelings.

But, independently of the factious rancor which is conveyed in this reference to Mr. Doherty, it is surprising that such a want of ordinary discretion should have been manifested by an individual who was himself so obnoxious to the unkind observation with which, at parting, he wantonly aspersed the advancement of a member of the bar. Lord Manners had objected to Mr. Doherty upon the ground of his juniority. He was not, himself, of as long standing at the English Bar when he was created Solicitor-General. Mr. Doherty was at the head of his circuit, where he had evinced as high qualifications as a speaker as any gentleman in the whole profession. Lord Manners was unemployed at the bar, except when he got a brief from his brother-in-law, a solicitor of Lincoln's Inn. Lord Manners' objection to the exercise of parliamentary or political interest seems to be equally strange. What but the power of the house of Rutland could ever have raised a man of his feeble understanding and slight acquirements to the office of Lord Chancellor of Ireland, to the discharge of whose duties he was so utterly incompetent, that his able and erudite successor can scarcely refrain from expressing astonishment at the spirit of blunder in which almost every one of Lord Manners's orders, which came before him for revision, is conceived?

After Lord Manners had delivered his valedictory commemoration of his own deserts, he proceeded to his house in Stephen's Green,* for the purpose of receiving a deputation from the Corporation of Dublin, between whom and his Lordship twenty years of devoted adherence to the cause of loyal monopoly had established a profound sympathy. The Corpora-

* Stephen's Green is a square in Dublin, an Irish mile in circumference, if you walk round it by the houses: an English mile, if you measure by the circumference of the area within surrounded by iron railings. I should mention that *Irish* longitudinal exceed *English* miles, in the proportion of 11 of the former, to 14 of the latter.— Miss Edgeworth told a story of a traveller who complained to a Paddy, of the narrowness of the roads. "True enough," said Pat, "but what you lose in the *breadth*, you gain in the *length*." In my time the roads were excellent and not deficient in width. The system of Macadamization, as it is barbarously called, was practised on the Irish turnpike roads a hundred years before a "canny Scot" filched it, from Ireland, and made a fortune out of, and won a title from, John Bull, by passing it off as his own discovery. In 1847, under the Labor Expenditure system, some of the finest roads in Ireland were torn up, under the idea of improving them, and, the funds failing, before the "improvements" commenced, the poor roads were left in the ruined condition to which they had been reduced!— M.

tion of Dublin, it must be on all hands admitted, were under extraordinary obligations to Lord Manners: a deficiency in their accounts to the amount of upward of forty thousand pounds had been the subject of a bill in Chancery, at the suit of Mr. Brossley, who, at the instance of the Chamber of Commerce, had taken proceedings in order to compel them to disgorge the produce of their systematic extortion from the citizens of Dublin. To the astonishment of the whole Bar, Lord Manners refused all relief. I well remember the indignation of Mr. Plunket, when the Chancellor pronounced his decree. He shook his hand in mingled scorn for his intellect, and anger at the everlasting effrontery of the decision. The decree has been since opprobriously reversed in the House of Lords.

But the Corporation were grateful for the manifestations of his Lordship's good-will; and accordingly on the day of his departure, and after he had taken his farewell of the bar, the Lord-Mayor, the sheriffs, and Sir Abraham Bradley King, together with a train of civic baronets and knights, with whom his Majesty has repaired the exhausted aristocracy of Ireland, waited upon Lord Manners. The following is an extract from their address, taken from the faithful record, from which a relation has been already made: "We are not insensible that by your undeviating loyalty to your Sovereign, and attachment to the true and genuine principles of an unrivalled Constitution in Church and State, you have been exposed to the malignant attacks of base and dastardly demagogues, upheld by the vile vituperations of a licentious press."

The Evening Mail proceeds to state, that after the Town-Clerk had concluded (for it seems that a Lord-Mayor does not enjoy the advantages of Dogberry, and that reading and writing do not come to him by nature), his Lordship placed his hand upon his heart, and read the following answer: "After a residence of upward of twenty years in your capital, where my conduct in public and private life must be well known to you, this mark of approbation from the highly-respectable and loyal Corporation of the City of Dublin can not fail to be extremely gratifying to me: I receive it with pleasure, and shall remember it with gratitude. If I have any claim to be distinguished by you, it must arise from my having anxiously confined myself to the judicial duties of my office, and carefully abstained, as far as was consistent with the trust reposed in me, *from interfering in party or political topics.* This line of conduct has justified me in the consideration of your constitutional body, and may, in some degree, have entitled me to those expressions of kindness and good opinion which accompany your address, and for which I return you my warmest acknowledgments. I do assure you, my Lord-Mayor and gentlemen, I shall always feel a strong interest in the prosperity of your Corporation, and a grateful sense of the obligations I owe to Ireland."

The Evening Mail mentions that the Chancellor then handed the address to the Lord-Mayor; but it omits to record that the worthy functionary stood before the Chancellor in a state of cataleptic astonishment. The whole of his attendants, from the High-Sheriffs down to the Rev. Tighe Gregory, and Mr. David M'Cleary, the oratorical tailor, who cut out Sir Abraham Bradley's surtout, participated in the feeling of the Lord-Mayor, and stood with their eyes fixed upon the Chancellor, like the statues of amazement in all its different forms.*

The assurance given by his Lordship that he had never interfered in politics, struck them into stupefaction. Lord Manners was at a loss to account for this phenomenon, and vainly endeavored to rouse the Lord-Mayor from the influences of wonder to a consciousness of external objects. He placed the address in his hand, but it dropped out of it. He

* Sir A. B. King, Dr. Gregory, and Davy M'Cleary, were members of the Corporation of Dublin, in those days, and (as such) violent partisans and politicians. King was Stationer to the Crown, and the Grey Ministry broke his patent, thereby annulling the lucrative appointment. King, nearly ruined, and half heart-broken, went to O'Connell, against whom he had been making speeches for twenty years, and placed himself and his case in the hands of his old opponent. O'Connell devoted himself to the matter, obtained a pension of twelve hundred pounds sterling, for King, as compensation, and the Orangeman's death-bed words were of gratitude to O'Connell. M'Cleary is also dead. Gregory got a rich living in Ireland, and expecting no more gain by politics, is now a rational man.— M.

adopted various other expedients, but in vain. At length, however, he bethought himself of an artifice, which was attended with instantaneous success; and, as the Evening Mail has it, "invited the Lord Mayor and Corporation to partake of a collation prepared for them." The doors of an adjoining room were thrown open, and the moment the enchanting spectacle which was presented by a splendid banquet was disclosed, at the sight of "cold meats, fowls, turkeys" (they are thus enumerated in the gazette of loyalty), the effect was sudden and complete; they recovered at once from the petrifying power of astonishment, and precipitated themselves upon the viands which were prepared for them, with a voracity which well became "the ancient, loyal," hungry, and bankrupt Corporation of Dublin.*

* It was for calling it "a *beggarly* Corporation," in 1815, that Mr D'Esterre challenged Mr. O'Connell—which ended in his own death.—M.

THE MANNERS TESTIMONIAL.

Certain of the bar, consisting, to a great extent, of the eternal perambulators of the Hall, have recently subscribed for a piece of plate, which is to be called "The Manners Testimonial, or Forensic Souvenir." It was originally intended to throw the contributions of the profession into a silver cup, wherewith his Lordship might deeply drink to the memory of King William and to the oblivion of himself; but it was discovered that this ingenious idea had been forestalled by the Corporation, and it was determined, after mature consultation, to present the late Chancellor with a massive salver, upon which the principal incidents of his life should be represented. For the purpose of completing the commemorative donation, it became necessary to impose a new rate upon the loyalty of the bar. To this proposition the Commissioners of Bankrupts, notwithstanding their obligations to his Lordship, were at first strenuously opposed, not a single docket having been lately struck: but upon the change of Ministry, a rumor having gone abroad that Lord Manners was to return to administer justice, as he always did, indifferently in Ireland, the prudential objections of the judicial dignitaries of the Royal Exchange were laid aside. A sufficient fund has been collected, after a good deal of application to the political virtue and individual gratitude of the friends and admirers of Lord Manners, and a very fine piece of plate has been produced. It is not as yet quite finished; but, through the interest of Sergeant Lefroy with the pious silversmith to whom it has been intrusted, I have succeeded in obtaining an inspection. The salver contains, in exquisite relief, a record of the chief adventures of his Lordship's judicial and political life, together with an exemplification of the most characteristic traits of his character. If a contemporaneous commentary were not published, the figures which are introduced into this memorial of legal sensibility might hereafter afford as much matter for skeptical speculation as the celebrated shield in "*Martinus Scriblerus.*" With a view, therefore, to assist the curiosity of future antiquarians, some account of "The Manners Testimonial, or Forensic Souvenir," will be briefly given.

Upon the border, the busts of the most celebrated members of the bar, who have been most conspicuous in "getting the thing up," are admirably embossed. Mr. Whyte occupies, of necessity, a very considerable space in this part of the testimonial. A good deal of dead silver has been employed in doing him justice. Exactly opposite to Mr. Whyte, Mr. Peter Fitzgibbon Henchey appears with that look of egregious dignity which is peculiar to him. I am, however, inclined to think that the artist did not seize him at the most felicitous moment, for there is a touch of sadness in his importance. Perhaps the funds had sustained some sudden declination at the time; and the battle of Navarino has left its traces on his brow: or, peradventure (and that were the more amiable hypothesis), Mr. Henchey has discovered in Sir Anthony Hart a lamentable inferiority to his discriminating predecessor, and an unconstitutional disposition to lend an equal attention to the Catholics of the outer and to the Protestants of the inner bar. The rest of the heads that form a border to the testimonial are very exactly copied from most of the King's counsel, whom Lord Manners left as an appropriate deposite behind him. I do not know why Mr. Perrin and Mr. Richard Moore have been omitted.

But it is upon the reliefs in the body of the salver that the greatest skill has been displayed both in execution and in design. A series of beautiful biographical illustrations has been introduced, in the first of which Lord Manners appears, at the English bar, with an empty bag. In the background, the Minister is perceived eying him from a distance; while the Duke of Portland, who seems to be engaged in earnest discourse with the official detector of latent desert, points with one hand to the House of Commons, and with the other to the Bench.

In the next scene his Lordship is represented, in the enactment of the part of Baron Manners at the Assizes of Lancaster, trying the case of Weld *v.* Hornby (reported in 7 East 195), when his Lordship delivered an illegal but constitutional charge against the Jesuits of Stonyhurst. The case involved the right of the Jesuits to fish in the river Ribble, and it is surprising what an early zeal in the cause of Protestantism was displayed by the puisne Baron, who was afterward intrusted with the selection of impartial magistrates in Ireland. In the execution of this relief, great ingenuity has been evinced. I can not, however, say that the workmanship has surpassed the materials. The courthouse is filled with Jesuits. They are without their caps and gowns, which at Stonyhurst they did not presume to wear, although at Clongowes Wood, under Mr. O'Connell's advice, and the Solicitor-General's opinion, the body-guard of the Pope appear in full regimentals. Notwithstanding the want of the insignia of Loyolism, it is easy, from the expression of their faces, to detect the disciples of Ignatius. I recognise the deeply-furrowed face of Mr. Plowden,* in which time never could succeed in impairing the powerful St. Omer's physiognomy, for which he was remarkable. The likeness is so faithful, that I am disposed to think that Mr. Cruize, who sprang out of the hot-bed of orthodoxy, must have supplied the artist with a sketch of his old confessor. The very able chairman of the county of Clare, together with Mr. Nicholas Ball, who is rising so rapidly to the first eminence at the bar, are represented among a group of boys in the gallery of the courthouse. I think that I can also discover, in an acrimonious-looking urchin, who is taking down a note of Baron Manners' charge, the face of Mr. Sheil. The Judge is in the act of addressing the jury, with strong indications of loyal excitement, over

* The late Francis Plowden was an Irish barrister, author of a History of Ireland, popular in his day. He wrote two or three other books, chiefly on legal subjects. He was sued for a libel in his History, and cast in five thousand pounds sterling damages, rather than pay which, he retired to France, where he died, in 1829, at an advanced age.— M.

the bench in which he presides. The artist has engraven the significant motto, "*Qualis ab incepto.*" In the perspective there is a representation of the English Court of King's Bench, with Lord Ellenborough laughing grimly at the misdirections of the learned Judge, whose verdict he is in the act of ignominiously setting aside. Some of Lord Manners's friends objected to the record of this early incident in his judicial story; but it was answered that the illegality of his opinions was more than counterbalanced by his zeal for the constitution, and that the evidence of his inveterate Protestantism should be preserved at the expense of his legal reputation. It was besides observed, and with reason, that however his judgment might be obscured by his emotions, yet the purity of his intentions could not be brought into question.

After this specimen of his feats upon the English Bench, the records of his Irish Chancellorship appear. He is represented, on his arrival in Ireland, with Mr. Saurin bidding him welcome. An earwig is seen creeping into his ear. This is followed by Lord Manners presiding in court: Mr. O'Connell is addressing him, while his Lordship's eye is averted, and his cheeks are filled with the materials of a puff, which the learned Lord is preparing to discharge. The crier of the court is seen lighting the fire in the gallery, and throwing Vesey Junior and the Statutes into the flames. Various views of impatient adjudication occupy this part of the testimonial. The spirit of judicial hurry, for which his Lordship was remarkable, may at first view appear to be objectionable. But it must be remembered that, however the suitors may suffer, the counsel are gainers by the precipitation of a Judge. At present, for example, Sir Anthony Hart insists that due consideration shall be given to every cause of a difficult nature. The consequence is, that where twelve were heard, but not listened to, in a single day by Lord Manners, the present Chancellor bestows an equal time to a single cause. It is true that the parties are satisfied by his decision, and the occupation of Lord Redesdale in the House of Lords seems likely to be gone; but the counsel's fees are in proportion diminished; the crisp paper of the Bank of Ireland is no longer seen in such rapid circulation through the inner bar; and Sergeant Lefroy having stated his case in the morning, has leisure during the rest of the day to devote himself to less sublunary pursuits, and may exclaim with Hamlet, "For my own poor part, I will go pray."

I do not think it necessary to go through the whole of the reliefs which are intended to illustrate Lord Manners's judicial excellences. Dow's parliamentary cases contain an ample commentary on his faculties. One scene, however, in the testimonial, relating to this portion of his Lordship's character, is deserving of mention. I allude to the case of "Pims, minors." Lord Manners decided, without principle or precedent, that the infant daughters of a Catholic mother should be removed from her society on account of her profession of the illegal religion. The artist has chosen the separation of Mrs. Pim and of her family for the manifestation of his pathetic powers. Lord Manners surveys the spectacle of domestic anguish with a calm philosophy, in the expression of which it was no doubt intended to intimate that his high sense of public duty subdued in his Lordship's mind those infirmities to which, wherever the interests of Protestantism were concerned, he was never known, although in many respects a kind and amiable man, to give way.

He is next represented in his capacity of Superintendent of the Magistracy of Ireland, and in the act of refusing the commission of the peace to Sir Patrick Bellew, a Roman Catholic baronet of ancient family, and of considerable fortune; while the description of individuals whom he considered entitled to that important trust is illustrated by a group of pauper justices in the county of Waterford, who are seen in the background. One would at first take them to be a corps of the Mendicity Association; but the commission of the peace, which is seen sticking out of the rents of their ragged pockets, indicates their office; while the lilies that hang from their tattered shirts are beautifully emblematic of their constitutional qualifications.

His Lordship next appears as a member of the House of Lords. He is seen addressing his brother-peers on the trial of the Queen, when he called the consort of a King, and the childless mother of a buried Princess, "this woman!" The feeling of astonishment and disgust which pervades the House is well rendered. Even Lord Lauderdale himself looks surprised.

Some traits of his Lordship's domestic history succeed. He is represented as reading Fox's Martyrs to the Honorable Miss Butler, and reclaiming her from the errors of Popery—a temple of Hymen is seen in the distance.

His Lordship is afterward introduced at dinner. The object of this relief is to intimate his familiar cast of religious opinions. He was known to have as great a horror of a thirteenth at table as the Chief-Baron has of a thirteenth juror. The artist represents his Lordship surrounded by the ominous number, in a state of pious dismay.

This dinner-scene is followed in natural succession by a sermon at the Asylum in Leeson street. But there is nothing very remarkable in it, except the looks of profound reverence with which "the Saints" alternately direct their attention to the pulpit, which is occupied by Mr. Daly, and the pew in which the Chancellor is engaged in his devotions. I should not, however, omit to mention that the face of a Magdalen, peeping through the bars of the adjoining receptacle of repentant loveliness, at Mr. James Smith Scott, is beautifully finished, and that the mingled expression of reproach and of tenderness with which she regards him is admirably rendered.

But I find that I am dwelling with too minute an accuracy upon details; and while I am endeavoring to obviate by anticipation any doubts which may occur hereafter to the learned, who shall survey "The Manners Testimonial," I forget that I run the risk of wearying my readers of the present generation. I must, therefore, pass by many of the features of this beautiful piece of art, and leave them to puzzle posterity.

There is, however, one scene of splendid conviviality, on which I can not refrain from saying a word or two. I allude to the magnificent relief in the centre, which represents a meeting, at Morisson's Tavern, of the Beefsteak Club. Lord Rathdown, better known as Lord Monk, presides over the Bacchanalian confraternity. This is a wonderful likeness. The exact look has been preserved, which enabled him to play to admiration in the private theatricals at Kilkenny, at which his

Lordship's name appeared among the *dramatis personæ* in the following felicitous announcement: "Doodle, a foolish lord, Lord Monk." The noble Earl is represented in that felicitous moment when he gave as a toast, "The Pope in the pillory," with certain additional aspirations, which it is not necessary to record. The whole assembly of sympathizing compotators stand with uplifted glasses, replenished to the brim. The Irish Chancellor is seen at the right hand of the noble and intellectual chairman, in the usual "hip, hip, huzza" attitude. A ring, given him by the King during his visit in Ireland, sparkles on his finger, and he tramples the King's parting letter* under his feet.

* In this missive, written by Lord Sidmouth, as Home Secretary, in the name of George IV., it was strongly recommended that party squabbles should cease and liberality of thought and action be exercised in future.—M.

THE CATHOLIC DEPUTATION.

The Roman Catholic Association having resolved to petition the House of Commons against the Bill which was in progress for their suppression [in 1825], requested Mr. O'Connell and Mr. Sheil to attend at the bar of the house, and prayed that those gentlemen should be heard as counsel on behalf of the body in whose proceedings they had taken so active a participation.* They appeared to undertake the office with reluc-

* It may be necessary to preface this sketch with a rapid view of the position and prospects of the Catholic question at this time. In 1823, the Catholic Association was formed, and was in active operation during 1824. One result was that it literally put down the spirit of insurrection which had crowded the prison with inmates, and the gallows and the hulks with victims. It raised large sums, by means of small but numerous contributions to a fund called "The Catholic Rent." The Government, angry and jealous that the Association had restored that comparative tranquillity in Ireland which its own harsh rule had been unable to do, resolved that "it must be put down:"—and more particularly, as the general proceedings of this body were made very closely to resemble those of the Parliament in London. Accordingly, when the Session commenced, on February 3, 1825, the Ministerial document called "The speech from the Throne," suggested the suppression of the Association; and Mr. Goulburn, who was Irish Secretary, obtained leave to bring in a Bill for that purpose, on that day week. When intelligence of this reached Dublin, the Catholic Association resolved that a Deputation should be sent to London to watch over and take care of the interests of the Catholics. Messrs. O'Connell and Sheil were specially intrusted with this duty—all the Catholic Peers were declared members of the Deputation, which farther included as many members of the Association as chose to swell the cavalcade. Mr. Goulburn's bill was introduced. On February 17, 1825, Mr. Brougham presented a petition from the Catholics of Ireland, against a measure which so vitally threatened their interests, and moved that they be heard at the bar of the house, by themselves or their counsel, in opposition to the Act. This motion was keenly debated (as is described by Mr. Sheil in the text) and rejected by 222 to 189

tance. It involved a great personal sacrifice upon the part of Mr. O'Connell; and, independently of any immediate loss in his profession, Mr. Shiel could not fail to perceive that it must prejudice him in some degree as a barrister, to turn aside from the beaten track of his profession, in the pursuit of a brilliant but somewhat illusory object. It was, however, next to impossible to disobey the injunction of a whole people — they accepted of this honorable trust. At the same time that counsel were appointed, it was determined that other gentlemen should attend the debates of the House of Commons in the character of deputies, and should constitute a sort of embassy to the English people.

The plan of its constitution was a little fantastic. Any person who deemed it either pleasurable or expedient to attach himself to this delegation was declared to be a member, and, in consequence, a number of individuals enrolled themselves as volunteers in the national service. I united myself to these political missionaries, not from any hope that I should succeed in detaching Lord Eldon from the church, or in banishing the fear of Oxford from the eyes of Mr. Peel,* but from a natural curiosity to observe the scenes of interest and novelty, into which, from my representative character, I thought it not improbable that I should be introduced. I set out in quest of

votes. The Association-suppression bill passed rapidly through the Commons: reached the Lords, on the first, and received the Royal Assent on the ninth of March, 1825. Almost as a matter of course, and as if to fulfil O'Connell's boast that he "could drive a coach-and-four through any Act of Parliament," a new Catholic Association immediately sprung up out of the ashes of the old.— M.

* Peel was educated at Harrow, where Byron was his schoolmate. Thence he went to Oxford University, where he graduated with the highest honors, rarely conferred upon one person, though his successor Mr. Gladstone also won them. He took what is called "double-first" honors—i. e. in classics and science. When Abbott, the Speaker, was raised to the peerage in 1817, Peel was elected to succeed him as member for his Alma Mater, and retained this distinction (which, on account of his support of Catholic Emancipation, Canning had vainly sighed for, as he confessed, at the close), until 1829, when, ceasing to be Peel the intolerant, he rendered justice to the Catholics, and was defeated, on a contest for the seat for the University, by Sir. R. H. Inglis, a man of small ability but extensive illiberality. In 1825, as an Anti-Catholic, Peel was popular at Oxford.— M.

political adventure, and determined to commit to a sort of journal whatever should strike me to be deserving of note. Upon my return to Ireland, I sent to certain of my friends some extracts from the diary which I had kept, in conformity with this resolution. They told me that I had heard and seen much of what was not destitute of interest, and, at their suggestion, I have wrought the observations, which were loosely thrown together, into a more regular shape; although they will, I fear, carry with them an evidence of the haste and heedlessness with which they were originally set down.

The party of deputies to which I had annexed myself travelled in a barouche belonging to Mr. O'Connell, of which he was kind enough to offer us the use. I fancy that we made rather a singular appearance, for the eyes of every passenger were fixed upon us as we passed; and at Coventry (a spot sacred to curiosity), the mistress of the inn where we stopped to change horses, asked me, with a mixture of inquisitiveness and wonder, and after many apologies for the liberty she took in putting the interrogatory, "who the gentlemen were?" I contented myself with telling her that we were Irish. "Parliament folk, I suppose?" to which, with a little mental reservation, I nodded assent.

Mr. O'Connell, as usual, attracted the larger portion of the public gaze. He was seated on the box of the barouche, with a huge cloak folded about him, which seemed to be a revival of the famous Irish mantle; though far be it from me to insinuate that it was ever dedicated to some of the purposes to which it is suggested, by Spenser, that the national garment was devoted. His tall and ample figure enveloped in the trappings that fell widely round him, and his open and manly physiognomy, rendered him a very conspicuous object, from the elevated station which he occupied. Wherever we stopped, he called with an earnest and sonorous tone for a newspaper, being naturally solicitous to learn whether he should be heard at the bar of the house; and, in invoking "mine host," for the parliamentary debates, he employed a cadence and gesture which carried along with them the unequivocal intimations of his country.

Nothing deserving of mention occurred until we had reached Wolverhampton. We arrived at that town about eight o'clock in the morning, with keener appetites than befitted the season of abstinence [Lent], during which we were condemned to travel. The table was strewed with a tantalizing profusion of the choicest fare. Every eye was fixed upon an unhallowed round of beef, which seemed to have been deposited in the centre of the breakfast-room with a view to "lead us into temptation," when Mr. O'Connell exclaimed, "Recollect that you are within sacred precincts. The conqueror of Sturges, and the terror of the Vetoists, has made Wolverhampton holy." This admonition saved us on the verge of the precipice—we thought that we beheld the pastoral staff of the famous Doctor raised up between us and the forbidden feast, and turned slowly and reluctantly from its unavailing contemplation to the lenten mediocrity of dry toast and creamless tea. We had finished our repast, when it was suggested that we ought to pay Doctor Milner* a visit before we proceeded upon our journey. This proposition was adopted with alacrity, and we went forth in a body in quest of that energetic divine. We experienced some little difficulty in discovering his abode, and received most evangelical looks and ambiguous answers to our inquiries. A damsel of thirty, with a physiognomy which was at once comely and demure, replied to us at first with a mixture of affected ignorance and ostentatious disdain;

* At this time (1825), Dr. John Milner, the eminent Catholic controversialist, was seventy-three years old; he died in 1826.—Born in 1752, he completed his education at Douay, in France, was ordained a priest in 1777, and was stationed, two years after, at Winchester, where there were several French prisoners who were Catholics. In 1782, he published a funeral discourse on the death of Bishop Challoner, and became a voluminous writer. His learning, research, and skill, as an Antiquarian, were displayed in his History of the Antiquities of Winchester, and other works of merit. In his limited History he offended the prejudices of Dr. Sturges, a prebendary of the Cathedral, who assailed him in a History of Popery, to which the reply was Milner's well-known Letters to a Prebendary, in which he boldly and ably defended the Papal Church. He had a somewhat angry discussion, also, with Charles Butler, the Catholic barrister, on ecclesiastical points. In 1803, Dr. Milner was appointed Vicar-Apostolic in the Midland District of England, and removed to Wolverhampton—he was now Bishop of Castabala, *in partibus*. In 1818,

until Sir Thomas Esmonde,* who is "a marvellous proper" man in every sense of the word, whether it be taken in its physical or moral meaning, addressed the fair votary of Wesley with a sort of chuck-under-the-chin manner (as Leigh Hunt would call it), and, bringing a more benign and feminine smile upon a face which had been over-spiritualized by some potent teacher of the word, induced the mitigated methodist to reply, "If you had asked me for the Popish priest, instead of the Catholic bishop, I should have told you that he lived yonder," pointing to a large but desolate-looking mansion before us.

We proceeded, according to her directions, to Dr. Milner's residence. It had an ample but dreary front. The windows were dingy and covered with cobwebs, and the grass before the door seemed to illustrate the Irish imprecation. It is separated from the street by a high railing of rusty metal, at which we rang several times without receiving any response. It was suggested to us, that if we tried the kitchen-door, we should probably get in. We accordingly turned into a lane, leading to the postern-gate, which was opened by an old and feeble, but very venerable gentleman, in whom I slowly recognised the active and vigorous prelate whom I had seen some years ago in the hottest onset of the Veto warfare in Ireland. His figure had nothing of the Becket port which formerly belonged to it. A gentle languor sat upon a face which I had seen full of fire and expression; his eye was almost hid under the relaxed and dropping eyelid, and his voice was querulous, undecided, and weak. He did not recollect Mr. O'Connell, and appeared at a loss to conjecture our purpose. "We have come to pay you a visit, my lord," said Mr. O'Connell. The interpellation was pregnant with our religion; "my lord," uttered with a vernacular richness of intonation, gave him an

he published his "End of Religious Controversy," one of the ablest defences of the points in the Catholic faith, to which Protestants most commonly object. Bishop Milner was an amiable and pious man, and much beloved in the district over which he had ecclesiastical rule.—M.

* Sir Thomas Esmonde was an Irish Catholic baronet, who took a lively interest and an active part in Catholic politics, before the passing of the Relief Bill, in 1829.—M.

assurance that we were from "the Island of Saints," and on the right road to heaven.*

He asked us, with easy urbanity, to walk in. We found that he had been sitting at his kitchen-fire, with a small cup of chocolate, and a little bread, which made up his simple and apostolic breakfast. There was an English neatness and brightness in everything about us, which was not out of keeping with the cold but polished civility of our reception.

The Doctor was, for a little while, somewhat hallucinated, and still seemed to wonder at our coming. There was an awkward pause. At length Mr. O'Connell put him "*au fait.*" He told him who he was, and that he and his colleagues were going to London to plead the cause of their holy religion. The name of the counsellor did not give the Doctor as electric a shock as I had expected: he merely said that we did him very great honor, and wished us every success. He requested us to walk up stairs, and welcomed us with much courtesy, but little warmth. Time had been busy with him. His faculties were not much impaired, but his emotions were gone. His ideas ran clearly enough, but his blood had ceased to flow. We sat down in his library. The conversation hung fire. The inflammable materials of which his mind was originally composed, were damped by age. O'Connell primed him two or three times, and yet he did not for a long while fairly go off.

I resolved to try an expedient by way of experiment upon episcopal nature, and, being well aware of his feuds with Mr. Charles Butler† (the great lawyer and profound theologian of

* In the mediæval ages, when the rest of Europe was much obscured by ignorance, learning was largely cultivated in Ireland, which, from the large number of eminent and pious ecclesiastics which she then produced, was called "The Island of Saints."—M.

† Charles Butler, born in 1750, did not die until 1832. He was a Catholic who had closely studied the law, and, as a conveyancer, was held in high repute. He was an accomplished scholar. His "Notes to Coke upon Littleton" are prized by black-letter lawyers, and his "Reminiscences" are full of political, literary, and personal information. The rest of his works, which were numerous, were chiefly ecclesiastical, with, now and then, a political pamphlet. His Lives of the Saints, Historical Account of the Laws against the Roman Catholics, and his Book of the Catholic Church, excited great interest when they appeared, and still rank as standard works.—M.

Lincoln's Inn), asked him, with much innocence of manner, though I confess with some malice of intent, "whether he had lately heard from his old friend Charles Butler?" The name was talismanic—the resurrection of the Doctor's passions was instantaneous and complete. His face became bright, his form quickened and alert, and his eye was lighted up with true scholastic ecstasy. He seemed ready to enter once more into the rugged field of controversy, in which he had won so many laurels, and to be prepared to "fight his battles o'er again." To do him justice, he said nothing of his ancient antagonist in polemics which a bishop and a divine ought not to say: he, on the contrary, mentioned that a reconciliation had taken place. I could, however, perceive that the junction of their minds was not perfectly smooth, and saw the marks of the cement which had "soldered up the rift." The *odium theologicum* has been neutralized by an infusion of Christianity, but some traces of its original acidity could not fail to remain. He spoke of Mr. Butler as a man of great learning and talents; and I should mention parenthetically that I afterward heard the latter express himself of Doctor Milner as a person of vast erudition, and who reflected honor, by the purity of his life, and the extent of his endowments, upon the body to which he belonged. The impulse given to his mind by the mention of his achievements in controversy, extended itself to other topics. Cobbett had done, said Doctor Milner, service to Ireland, and to its religion, by addressing himself to the common sense of the English people, and trying to purge them of their misconceptions respecting the belief of a great majority of the Christian world.*

The Doctor spoke with a good deal of energy of the contests

* Cobbett's "History of the Protestant Reformation," had an immense sale in Great Britain and Ireland, was repeatedly and largely reprinted in America, and was translated into several European languages. It is full of interest—partly arising from the number and variety of its episodes on the popular topics of the day, and partly from the manner in which the writer showed up and condemned the spoliation of the Anglican Church, by Henry VIII., when he thought that "Gospel truth first beamed from Bullen's eyes." It was a singular book, at all events, for a Protestant (which Cobbett professed to be) to have written.—M.

which had been carried on between the clergy and the itinerant missionaries of the Bible Society in Ireland, and congratulated Mr. O'Connell and Mr. Sheil on their exertions in Cork, from which the systematic counteraction of the new apostles had originated.* Mr. O'Connell expressed his obligations upon this occasion to Doctor Milner's celebrated, and, let me add, admirable work, which has been so felicitously entitled "The End of Religious Controversy."—"Oh!" said the Doctor, "I am growing old, or I should write a supplement to that book." After some further desultory conversation, we took our leave. Doctor Milner, who had been aroused into his former energy, thanked us with simple and unaffected cordiality for our visit. He conducted us to the gate before his mansion (in which I should observe that neither luxury nor want appear), with his white head uncovered, and, with the venerable grace of age and piety, bade us farewell.

We proceeded upon our journey. No incident occurred deserving of mention, unless a change in our feelings deserves the name. The moment we entered England, I perceived that the sense of our own national importance had sustained some diminution, and that, however slowly and reluctantly we acknowledged it to ourselves, the contemplation of the opulence which surrounded us, and in which we saw the results and evidences of British power and greatness, impressed upon every one of us the consciousness of our provincial inferiority, and the conviction that it is only from an intimate alliance with Great Britain, or rather a complete amalgamation with her immense dominion, that any permanent prosperity can be reasonably expected to be derived. In the sudden transition from the scenes of misery and sorrow to which we are habituated

* In 1824, when the Protestant Reformation Society held a public meeting at Cork, a great deal of good and earnest abuse was poured out, by the clerical speakers, against the Catholics and the Pope. O'Connell, Sheil, and other Catholics, interrupted the proceedings, demanding to be heard, on the principle of fair play, in defence of their religion. This having been conceded, they delivered some very admirable polemical harangues, which the Reformation party did not even attempt to answer. It was considered, therefore, that the Catholic party, who remained masters of the field, had triumphed in the contest.—M.

in Ireland to the splendid spectacle of English wealth and civilization, the humiliating contrast between the two islands presses itself upon every ordinary observer. It is at all times remarkable. Compared to her proud and pampered sister, clothed as she is in purple and in gold, Ireland, with all her natural endowments, at best appears but a squalid and emaciated beauty. I have never failed to be struck and pained by this unfortunate disparity; but upon the present occasion the objects of our mission, and the peculiarly national capacity in which we were placed in relation to England, naturally drew our meditation to the surpassing glory of the people of whom we had come to solicit redress.

An occasional visit to England has a very salutary effect. It operates as a complete sedative to the ardor of the political passions. It should be prescribed as a part of the antiphlogistic regimen. The persons who take an active part in the impassioned deliberations of the Irish people are apt to be carried away by the strength of the popular feelings which they contribute to create. Having heated the public mind into an ardent mass of emotion, they are themselves under the influence of its intensity. This result is natural and just: but among the consequences (most of which are beneficial) which have arisen from the habitual excitation, and to which the Catholics have reasonably attributed much of their inchoate success, they have forgotten the effect upon themselves, and have omitted to observe in their own minds a disposition to exaggerate the magnitude of the means by which their ends are to be accomplished. In declaiming upon the immense population of Ireland, they insensibly put out of account the power of that nation from whom relief is demanded, and who are grown old in the habit of domination, which of all habits it is most difficult to resign.

A man like Mr. O'Connell who, by the force of his natural eloquence produces a great emotion in the midst of an enthusiastic assembly of ardent and high-blooded men — who is hailed by the community, of which he is the leading member, as their chief and champion — who is greeted with popular benedictions as he passes — whose name resounds in every alley, and "stands rubric" on every wall—can with difficulty resist the intoxicating influence of so many exciting causes, and becomes a sort of political opium-eater, who must be torn from these seductive indulgences, in order to reduce him into perfect soundness and soberness of thought. His deputation to England produced an almost immediate effect upon him. As we advanced, the din of popular assemblies became more faint: the voice of the multitude was scarcely heard in the distance, and at last died away. He seemed half English at Shrewsbury, and was nearly Saxonized when we entered the murky magnificence of Warwickshire. As we surveyed the volcanic region of manufactures and saw a thousand Etnas vomiting their eternal fires, the recollections of Erin passed away from his mind, and the smoky glories of Skifton* and Wolverhampton took possession of his soul. The feeling which attended our progress through England was not a little increased by our approach to its huge metropolis. The waste of wealth around us, the procession of ponderous vehicles that choked the public roads, the rapid and continuous sweep of carriages, the succession of luxurious and brilliant towns, the crowd of splendid villas, which Cowper has assimilated to the beads upon the neck of an Asiatic Queen, and the vast and dusky mass of bituminous

* Shifnal is the name of the place. It is situated between the busy little town of Wellington, in Shropshire, and the important borough of Wolverhampton, in Staffordshire. Shifnal is only important as being the centre of a great iron and coal district. Travellers to and from Ireland, viâ Holyhead, in the old time of mail-coaches, used to be startled, on a dark night, in rapidly passing over miles upon miles of a road, through a country, where, all around far as the eye could take in at one view, immense furnaces flung a lurid light through the gloom—which seemed all the gloomier by contrast—and hundreds of men flitted to and fro, feeding these furnaces with coal or throwing in heaps of the limestone used to flux the liquid iron as it was separated from the ore by heat. The sulphurous smell, from the immense quantity of coal thus consumed, is so unpleasant and unwholesome, that, rather than inhale it,

"The boldest held their breath,
For a time."

The railway from Wolverhampton to Shrewsbury passes through the Shifnal district—but travelling at forty miles an hour allows not much more than a few minutes' glance at the fiery furnaces I speak of. This is the scene of one of the most touching adventures of Dickens' Little Nelly.—M.

vapor which crowns the great city with an everlasting cloud, intimated our approach to the modern Babylon.

Upon any ordinary occasion I should not, I believe, have experienced any strong sensation on entering London. What is commonly called "coming up to town," is not a very sublime or moving incident. I honestly confess that I have upon a fine summer morning stood on Westminster Bridge, upon my return from the brilliant inanities of Vauxhall, and looked upon London with a very drowsy sympathy in the meditative enthusiasm which breathes through Wordsworth's admirable sonnet. But upon the occasion which I am describing, it needed little of the spirit of political romance to receive a deep and stirring impulse, as we advanced to the great metropolis of the British empire, and heard the rolling of the great tide—the murmurs, if I may so say, of the vast sea of wealth before us. The power of England was at this moment presented to us in a more distinct and definite shape, and we were more immediately led, as we entered London, to bring the two countries into comparison. This, we exclaimed, is London, and the recollection of our own Eblana* was manifest in the sigh with which the truism was spoken: yet the reflection upon our inferiority was not unaccompanied by the consolatory anticipation that the time was not distant, when we should be permitted to participate in all the advantages of a real and consummated junction of the two countries, when the impediments to our national prosperity should be removed, and Ireland should receive the ample overflowings of that deep current of opulence which we saw almost bursting through its golden channels in the streets of the immense metropolis.

Immediately after our arrival, we were informed by the agent of the Roman Catholic Association in London, Mr. Æneas M'Donnel† (and who, in the discharge of the duties

* Eblana is the Latin name of Dublin, and that by which that city was designated in early law documents.—M.

† Æneas M'Donnel, who had been editor of the *Cork Mercantile Chronicle*, was a good speaker and clever writer, who soon transferred himself to Dublin. Taking an active part in Catholic politics, he was appointed salaried agent for the Irish Catholics, and sent to London. He performed his duty, with ability and zeal, until 1829, when Emancipation was granted. From that time, his

confided to him, has evinced great talents, judgment, and discretion), that Sir Francis Burdett* was desirous to see us as soon as possible. We accordingly proceeded to his house in St. James's Place, where we found the Member for Westminster living in all the blaze of aristocracy. I had often heard Sir Francis Burdett in popular assemblies, and had been greatly struck with his simple, easy, and unsophisticated eloquence :—I was extremely anxious to gain a nearer access to a person of so much celebrity, and to have an opportunity of observing the character and intellectual habits of a man who had given so

course was altered by his applying himself, in the *London Standard* and other ultra-Tory Journals, to constant abuse of Mr. O'Connell, on the plea that Irish agitation ought to have ceased when Emancipation was obtained. Mr. M'Donnell is still living, and resides in London.—Lord Norbury, who never could resist a joke, on seeing M'Donnell coming out of the house of Dr. Troy, the Catholic Archbishop of Dublin, exclaimed, "There is the pious Æneas returning from the sack of Troy!"—It is well that a pun need not involve a *fact*, as Dr. Troy, who was the reverse of Falstaff, eschewed sack and other wines—his limited resources being distributed among the needy. When he died, the sum of a guinea was all that was found in the purse of this primitive Archbishop.—M.

* Sir Francis Burdett, whose rank and great fortune entitled him to a place among the British Aristocracy, was a most violent democrat, from his starting into public, until the last seven years of his life. He derived his political bias from Horne Tooke, author of The Diversions of Purley. Born in 1770, he entered Parliament in 1796, and immediately opposed Pitt's Government. With little intermission, he had a seat in the House of Commons until his death in 1844. Constantly opposing every Tory Ministry, in 1810, Burdett having published a letter to his constituents, in which (in no very measured terms) he said, that the House of Commons had illegally exercised their power in committing Gales Jones to prison, the speaker issued his warrant to apprehend him and convey him to the Tower, for "gross breach of privilege." Burdett barricaded his house in London, prepared to resist, and would have been backed by the populace, who loved him. He was taken to the Tower, however, and confined there until the prorogation of Parliament. He constantly supported liberal measures, which made him a sort of Pariah among the noble and the wealthy, and subjected him to imprisonment and fine. He advocated Parliamentary Reform, and Catholic Emancipation—but, in 1837, "England's pride and Westminster's Glory," as he was fondly styled, picking a quarrel with O'Connell, went over to the Tory party, and continued with them ever after.—He married one of the daughters of Thomas Coutts, the rich London banker, and their daughter, Angela Burdett, was left all the Coutts' fortune, by the banker's second wife (Harriet Mellon, an actress), whose second husband was the Duke of St. Albans. —M.

much of its movement to the public mind. He was sitting in his study when we were introduced by Mr. M'Donnel. He received us without any of that *hauteur* which I have heard attributed to him, and for which his constitutional quiescence of manner is sometimes mistaken. We, who have the hot Celtic blood in our veins, and deal in hyperbole upon occasions which are not calculated to call up much emotion, are naturally surprised at what we conceive to be a want of ardor upon themes and incidents in which our own feelings are deeply and fervently engaged.

During my short residence in London, I constantly felt among the persons of high political influence to whom we approached, a calmness, which I should have taken for the stateliness of authority in individuals, but that I found it was much more national than personal, and was, in a great degree, a universal property of the political world. There was a great deal of simple dignity, which was entirely free from affectation in the address of Sir Francis Burdett. Having requested us to sit, which we did in a large circle (his first remark indeed was, that we were more numerous than he had expected), he came with an instantaneous directness to the point, and after a few words of course upon the honor conferred upon him by being intrusted with the Catholic question, entreated us with some strenuousness to substitute Mr. Plunket in his place; he protested his readiness to take any part in the debate which should be assigned him; but stated, that there was no man so capable, and certainly none more anxious than the Attorney-General for the promotion of our cause. But for the plain and honest manner in which this exhortation was given, I should have suspected that he was merely performing a part—but I have no doubt of the sincerity with which the recommendation was given.

He dwelt at length upon the great qualifications of Mr. Plunket as a parliamentary speaker, and pressed us to waive all sort of form with respect to himself, and put him at once aside for an abler advocate. We told him that it was out of our power to rescind the decision of an aggregate meeting. This he seemed to feel, and said that he should endeavor to discharge the trust as efficiently as he was able. His heart, he said, was in the question—he knew that there could not be peace in Ireland until it was adjusted; and for the country he professed great attachment. He loved the people of Ireland, and it was truly melancholy to see so noble a race deprived of the power of turning their great natural endowments to any useful account. These observations, which an Irishman would have delivered with great emphasis, were made by Sir Francis Burdett almost without a change of tone or look. He made no effort at strong expression. Everything was said with great gentleness, perspicuity, and candor. I thought, however, that he strangely hesitated for common words. His language was as plain as his dress,* which was extremely simple, and indicated the favorite pursuit of a man who is "mad at a foxchase, wise at a debate."

I watched his face while he spoke. His eyes are small and bright, but have no flash or splendor. They are illuminated by a serene and tranquil spirit: his forehead is high and finely arched, but narrow and contracted, and, although his face is lengthy, its features are minute and delicately chiselled off. His mouth is extremely small, and carries much suavity about it. I should have guessed him at once to be a man of rank, but should not have suspected his spirit to be a transmigration of Caius Gracchus. I should never have guessed that he was the man whose breath had raised so many waves upon the public mind, and aroused a storm which made the vessel creak. I saw no shadow of the "tower of Julius" in his pure and ruddy color, and should never have conjectured that he had inhaled the evaporations of its stagnant moat.† At the same time I should observe that, if there were no evidences of a daring or adventurous spirit about this champion of the people, there are in his demeanor and bearing many indications of calm resolve and imperturbable determination.

* Summer or winter, Burdett appeared in the House of Commons in one invariable costume—broad-brimmed hat, blue, brass-buttoned coat, drab breeches, and top-boots; the regular dress, in fact, of a country-gentleman fond of field-sports.—M.

† At present, the moat which surrounds the Tower of London, is a moat *minus* water.—M.

I was a good deal more occupied in watching this celebrated person than in observing my companions. Yet I at once perceived that we were too numerous and gregarious a body for a council of state, and was glad to find Mr. O'Connell take a decided, and what was considered by some to be, a dictatorial tone among us. I saw that unless some one individual assumed the authority of speaking and acting for the rest, we should, in all likelihood, be involved in those petty squabbles and miserable contentions of which Bonaparte speaks as characteristic of the Irish deputies who were sent to Paris to negotiate a revolution.* I was much pleased to find that Mr. O'Connell gave, even in this early communication, strong proof of that wise, temperate and conciliatory spirit, by which his conduct in London was distinguished, and by the manifestation of which he conferred incalculable service on his country.

After this interview with Sir Francis Burdett, the chief object of which, upon his part, was to sound our disposition to confide the conduct of our cause to the Irish Attorney-General [Plunket], we proceeded to the House of Commons, for the purpose of attending the debate upon the petition to be heard by counsel at the bar. We had already been informed by Sir Francis Burdett that it was very unlikely that the House would accede to the petition, and that Ministers had collected their forces to oppose it.† For the result we were therefore pre-

* Napoleon's opinion, as reported by O'Meara, is unequivocal: "If the Irish had sent over honest men to me, I would certainly have made an attempt upon Ireland. But I had no confidence in either the integrity or the talents of the Irish leaders that were in France. They could offer no plan, were divided in opinion, and continually quarrelling with each other."—M.

† Lord Liverpool was at the head of that Ministry; Eldon was Chancellor: Peel, Home Secretary, and Mr. Canning the only member of the Cabinet who supported Catholic Emancipation. The petition from the Catholics of Ireland was intrusted, not to Plunket, who had constantly and ably advocated their claims (and was now a little out of favor because, as Irish Attorney-General, he had supported the measure for putting down the Association), but to Burdett, who presented it, March 1, 1825, and then moved for a committee of Catholic inquiry. He was supported, among others, by Plunket, Canning, and Brougham, and strongly opposed by Peel:—but the motion was carried by 247 to 234 and the Bill eventually passed the Commons. But between the first and second readings, the Duke of York, next heir to the Throne, made a speech, on April

pared; but we were extremely anxious to hear a discussion, in which Mr. Brougham was expected to display his great powers, and in which the general demerits of the association would in all probability be brought by Ministers under review. The Speaker* had the goodness to direct that the Catholic deputies should be allowed to sit under the gallery during the discussions which appertained immediately to the object of their mission; and we were, in consequence, accommodated with places upon this vantage-ground, from which I had an opportunity of observing the orators of the night. We found a considerable array in the House, and attracted universal observation.

In the front of our body was Mr. O'Connell, upon whom every eye was fixed. He affected a perfect carelessness of manner; but it was easy to perceive that he was full of restlessness and inquietude under an icy surface. I saw the current eddying beneath. Next him was Mr. O'Gorman, who carried a most official look as secretary to the Catholics of all Ireland, and seemed to realize the *beau-ideal* of Irish self-possession. (I should observe, by-the-way, that Mr. O'Gorman

25, 1825, in which, after declaring his hostility to the Catholic claims, he publicly vowed never to abate it, and affirmed this declaration, as if on oath, by the concluding words—"So help me God." This manifesto led to the loss of the measure in the Lords. In Moore's emphatic poem, "The Irish Slave," written, in 1827, on the death of the Duke of York, he thus alluded to this vow:—

"He had pledged a hate unto me and mine,
He had left to the future nor hope nor choice,
But sealed that hate with a Name Divine,
And now he was dead, and—I *couldn't* rejoice."

The Duke's speech was delivered, it has always been believed, at the instigation of Lord Eldon.—M.

* The Speaker was Charles Manners Sutton, who held that office, by repeated re-elections, from 1817 until 1835, when he was opposed by Mr. James Abercrombie, a Whig lawyer (and steward, or sort of upper-servant to the Duke of Devonshire), and rejected by a majority of ten. The ground for this opposition and rejection was a surmise that Manners Sutton had taken an active part in forming the Peel Ministry, in December, 1834. He was finally created Viscount Canterbury. As Speaker, his urbanity of manners and impartiality of conduct were remembered, when too late, in contrast with his successor Abercrombie, who was bearish and partial.—M.

was of great use in London in controlling that spirit of disputation among the deputies to which Irishmen are habitually prone, and which it required the perfect good-humor and excellent disposition of the learned functionary to assuage.)

The House began to fill about eight o'clock. The aspect of the members was not in general very imposing. Few were in full dress, and there was little, in the general demeanor of the representatives of the people, which was calculated to raise them in my reverence. This absence, or rather studious neglect, of ceremony, is perhaps befitting an assembly of the "citizens and burgesses in Parliament assembled." I remarked that some of the members were distinguished for their spirit of locomotion. The description of "the Falmouth—the heavy Falmouth coach," given by a jocular Secretary of State,* had prepared me to expect in a noble Lord a more sedentary habit of body; but he displayed a perfect incapacity to stay still, and was perpetually traversing the House, as if he wished, by the levity of his trip and the jauntiness of his movements, to furnish a practical reputation of ministerial merriment.

After some matters of form had been disposed of, Mr. Brougham rose to move, on behalf of the Association, that counsel should be heard at the bar of the House.† I had seen

* One of Canning's elaborated and therefore rather dull jokes at Lord Nugent, who was stout in person, having gone over to assist the Spanish liberals, in 1822. Lord N., it seems, put himself into the Falmouth mail.—M.

† To do anything like justice to the cyclopædiac knowledge, stirring eloquence, scientific discoveries, literary productions, philosophic researches, and public services of Henry Brougham, the great law-reformer, would require the compass of a volume rather than the narrow limit of a note. In another and future publication, perhaps, I may be tempted to trace his course, and sketch his character.—Born in Edinburgh (No, 19 St. Andrew's Square), on September 19, 1779, he was called to the Scottish bar at an early age, and practised there until 1807, his friends and companions being Jeffrey, Cockburn, and others who have attained eminence. Appearing before the House of Lords, in the Roxburgh peerage case, he so much distinguished himself, that he was strongly urged to leave the Scotch for the English bar, which he did. Henceforth, his course was one of increasing distinction. In 1810, he entered Parliament, on the liberal side, and distinguished himself by speaking against the Orders in Council, which caused the last war between England and America. In 1820, as Attorney-General to Queen Caroline, he successfully defended her

Mr. Brougham several years before, and immediately observed a great improvement in his accomplishments as a public speaker. Nature has not, perhaps, been very favorable to this very eminent man in his merely physical configuration. His person is tall, but not compact or well put together. There is a looseness of limb about him, which takes away from that stability of attitude which indicates the fixedness of the mind. His chest is narrow — he wants that bulk which gives Plunket an Atlantean massiveness of form, mentioned by Milton as the property of a great statesman. The countenance of Mr. Brougham wants symmetry and refinement. His features are strong, but rather wide. He has a Caledonian prominence of bone. His complexion indicates his intellectual habits, and is "sicklied o'er by the pale cast of thought." It seems smoked by the midnight lamp. His eyes are deeply sunk, but full at once of intensity and meditation. His voice is good — it is clear, articulate, and has sufficient melody and depth. He has the power of raising it to a very high key, without harshness or discord, and when he becomes impassioned he is neither hoarse nor shrill.

Such is the outward man; and if he has defects, they are not so numerous or so glaring as those over which the greatest orator of antiquity obtained a victory. In his ideal picture of a public speaker, Homer represents the most accomplished artificer of words as a person with few if any personal attractions. The characteristics of Brougham's oratory are vigor and passion. He alternates with great felicity. He possesses in a high degree the art of easy transition from impetuosity to

in her trial before the House of Lords. In 1827, he liberally supported the Government of Canning, with whom he had a personal quarrel some years before. In 1830, he was made Lord-Chancellor, on Lord Grey coming into power, and created Baron Brougham and Vaux. He had strongly supported Catholic Emancipation, and he now battled, with immense force, against the Aristocracy, and won Parliamentary Reform for the People. He left office in November, 1834, when (at the instance of Queen Adelaide?) the Melbourne Ministry were suddenly dismissed by William IV.— He has not since taken office, but has carried out Law Reform, has been active in varied literary and political composition, has made important researches in science, and has devoted himself, in the Lords, to the hearing of appeals from the courts of law. He is now [1854] in his seventy-fifth year, hale in health and strong in mind.— M.

demonstration. His blood does not become so over-heated as to render it a matter of difficulty for him to return to the tone and language of familiar discourse—the prevalent tone and language of the House of Commons. A man who can not rise beyond it will never make a great figure; but whoever can not habitually employ it will be accounted a declaimer, and will fall out of parliamentary favor. Mr. Brougham's gesture is at once senatorial and forensic. He uses his arms like an orator, and his hands like a lawyer. He employs great sweep of action, and describes segments of circles in his impassioned movements: here he forgets his forensic habitudes: but when he is either sneering or sophisticating, he closes his hands together with a somewhat pragmatical air, or uniting the points of his forefingers, and, lifting them to a level with his chair, embodies in his attitude the minute spirit of *nisi prius*. If he did this and nothing else, he would hold no higher place than the eternal Mr. Wetherell in the House.* But what, taken apart, may appear an imperfection, brings out the nobler attributes of his mind, and, by the contrast which it presents, raises his better faculties into relief.

Of the variety, nay, vastness of his acquirements, it is unnecessary to say anything: he is a kind of ambulatory encyclopedia, and brings his learning to bear upon every topic on which he speaks. His diction is highly enriched, or, if I may so say, embossed with figures executed after the pure clas-

* Sir Charles Wetherell was made Solicitor-General in 1821. Born in 1770, he was called to the bar in 1794, and practised for some time at the common law bar, but settled down, finally, into immense practice in chancery. He entered Parliament in 1818, and his careless dress, eccentric manner, and extraordinary way of speaking made him more noted than eminent. In 1827, when Copley (now Lord Lyndhurst) was made Master of the Rolls, he was succeeded as Attorney-General by Wetherell, who resigned, in 1829, on the Catholic Relief Bill being brought in without consulting him, the first law officer of the Crown. He opposed Catholic Emancipation and Parliamentary Reform, and quitted Parliament when the latter measure was passed. In the autumn of 1831, when he was unpopular, as an anti-Reformer, he appeared at Bristol to hold the Sessions, as Recorder of that city. He was mobbed, narrowly escaping with his life, and Bristol was the scene of dreadful riots, burning, and other devastations for the following day and night. He was one of the best equity lawyers of his time. He died immensely rich, in 1846, aged seventy-six.—M.

sical model; yet there are not, perhaps, any isolated passages which are calculated to keep a permanent residence in the recollection of his hearers. He does not venture, like Plunket, into the loftiest regions of eloquence; he does not wing his flight among those towering elevations which are, perhaps, as barren as they are high; but he holds on with steady continuity in a very exalted course, and never goes out of sight. His bursts of honest vehemence, and indignant moral reprobation, are very fine. He furnished, upon the night on which I heard him, an admirable exemplification of this commanding power. I allude to his reply to Mr. Peel upon the charges made against Hamilton Rowan.*

The Secretary for the Home Department is said to have delivered, upon this occasion, one of the best speeches which he ever pronounced in parliament. I own that he greatly surpassed my expectations. I was prepared, from the perusal of his speeches, and the character which I had heard of him, for a display of frigid ingenuity, delivered with a dapper neatness and an ironical conceit. I heard the late Mr. Curran say that "Peel was a mere official Jack-an-apes," and had built my conceptions of him upon a phrase which, valueless as it may appear, remained in my memory. But I was disabused of this erroneous impression by his philippic against the Association.

* Peel was hurried, by the ardor of debate, when denouncing the Catholic Association, to accuse that body of having presented an address to Archibald Hamilton Rowan, "an attainted traitor." Mr. Rowan had been Secretary to the United Irishmen. In 1794, he was tried for libel, defended by Curran (in one of the most eloquent speeches ever made, even by him), convicted, fined, and imprisoned. While suffering this sentence, he ascertained that his complicity in the intended "rebellion" had been disclosed to the Executive, and then, as is subsequently told, he escaped to France, and thence to America, where he maintained himself by the labor of his head and hands. Lord Chancellor Clare secured his pardon, but did not live to see Rowan's return. In 1805, he came back to Ireland, was formally arraigned at the bar of justice, before Lord Clonmel, and pleaded the King's pardon, briefly but eloquently expressing his gratitude for the boon. He retired into the bosom of domestic life, living on his large fortune. When Peel went out of his way to assail him, Mr. Rowan, though then seventy-five years old, immediately went from Ireland to London, to call him to account, but Peel frankly withdrew the expressions, and they parted, with a mutual sense of "satisfaction," other than that sought by the veteran.—M.

I do not mean to say that Mr. Peel has not a good deal of elaborate self-sufficiency. He is perpetually indulging in encomiums upon his own manliness and candor—and certainly there is much frankness in his voice and bearing—but any man who observes the expedients with which he endeavors to effect his escape from the grasp of some powerful opponent, will be convinced that there is a good deal of lubricity about him. He constantly advances arguments of the fallacy of which he can not fail to be conscious, and which would be a burlesque upon reasoning if they were not uttered from the Treasury Bench.

As a speaker, he should not be placed near Brougham, or Canning, or Plunket, although he rises far beyond that mediocrity to which in Ireland we are in the habit of condemning him. His language is not powerful, but it is perfectly clear, and uniformly correct. I observed, indeed, that his sentences were much more compact and unbroken, and their several parts better linked together, than those of Mr. Brougham; but the one evolves his thoughts in a lengthened and winding chain, while the other (having a due fear of the parenthetical before his eyes) presents an obvious idea in a brief and simple form, and never ventures to frame any massive or extended series of phrase. His gesture is, generally speaking, exceedingly appropriate, and if I found any fault with it, I should censure it for its minute adherence to grace. His hands are remarkably white and well formed, and are exhibited with an ostentatious care. He stands erect, and, to use a technical expression employed by French dancers, "*a-plomb*." This firmness of attitude gives him that appearance of determination, which is wanting perhaps in Mr. Brougham.

I do not like his physiognomy as an orator. He has a handsome face, but it is suffused with a smile of sleek self-complacency, which it is impossible to witness without distaste. He has also a trick of closing his eyes, which may arise from their weakness, but which has something mental in its expression; and, however innocent he may be of all offensive purpose, is indicative of superciliousness and contempt. I doubt not he found it of use in Ireland among the menials of authority, and acquired this habit at the Castle. In one, the best passage in his speech, and I believe the best he ever uttered, he divested himself of those defects.

Upon the moral propriety of his attack upon Hamilton Rowan it is unnecessary to say anything. The misfortunes of that excellent gentleman ought not to have been pressed into the service. After every political convulsion, a Lethe should be permitted to flow upon the public mind, and a sin of thirty years' standing ought not only to be pardoned, but forgotten. Mr. Peel, however, could not resist the temptation of dragging upon the stage a man whose white hair should hide every imperfection upon his head. Laying aside all consideration of the generosity evinced by Mr. Peel in the selection of the topic, it must be acknowledged that he pronounced his invective with great and very successful force. He became heated with victory, and, cheered as he was repeatedly by his multitudinous partisans, turned suddenly toward the part of the house where the deputies were seated, and looking triumphantly at Mr. O'Connell, with whom he forgot for a moment that he had been once involved in a personal quarrel,* shook his hand with scornful exultation, and asked

* In 1815, the late Sir Robert Peel, then Secretary for Ireland, considered himself insulted by some expressions in a speech made by Mr. O'Connell, and challenged him. It was agreed that the duel should take place in France, whither Peel went, but, as O'Connell was in London, *en route* to the assigned battle-ground, the object of his journey transpired, the police interfered, he was bound over to keep the peace, and the duel was thus prevented. (The late Dr. England, Catholic Bishop of Charleston, S. C., who then resided at Cork, pointed out the conjunct sin and folly of duelling, when he next met O'Connell, and induced him to give a solemn promise that, under no circumstances would he again appeal to arms.) It was whispered, at the time, that O'Connell might have passed over to France, undetected, if he had not delayed in London, to receive news of the health of his wife, whom he had left very ill in Dublin. Another public character had declined a challenge at the same time, on the plea of his daughter's illness, and the two-fold occurrence elicited the following impromptu from Charles Kendal Bushe:—

"Two heroes of Erin, abhorrent of slaughter,
Improved on the Hebrew command—
One honored his wife and the other his daughter,
That 'their days might be long in the land.'"

In Willis's "Pencillings by the Way" (one of the most delightful books of trav-

whether the House required any better evidence than the address of the Association to "an attainted traitor." The phrase was well uttered, and the effect as a piece of oratory was great and powerful. But for the want of moral dignity, I should say that it was very finely executed.*

We hung down our heads for a moment and quailed, under the consciousness of defeat. But it was only temporary. Mr. Brougham was supplied with various facts of great importance on the instant, and inflicted upon Mr. Peel a terrible retribution. His reply to the minister was, I understand, as effective as his celebrated retort upon the Queen's letters. He showed that the Government had extended to Mr. Rowan conspicuous marks of favor, and reproached Mr. Peel with his want of nobleness in opening a wound which had been so long closed, and in turning the disasters of an honorable man into a rhetorical resource. He got hold of the good feeling of the House. Their virtuous emotions, and those high instincts which even the spirit of party can not entirely suppress, were at once marshalled upon his side. Conscious of his advantage, he rushed upon his antagonist and hurled him to the ground. He displayed upon this occasion the noblest qualities of his eloquence—fierce sarcasm, indignant remonstrance, exalted sentiment, and glowing elocution. He brought his erudition to

elled observation and personal gossip) a different version of this epigram is given, as related by Moore, not so neatly turned as the above. The O'Connell family were very angry with Moore for having repeated the lines; and Mrs. Fitzsimon, one of O'Connell's daughters, recorded her indignation in some powerful stanzas, written in the album of Samuel Lover, the Irish lyrist.—Bushe, the real delinquent, had a knack in this way. Once upon a time, the members of the Leinster bar were prevented, by a violent storm, from crossing a ferry at Ballinlaw. Mr. Cæsar Colclough, heedless of danger, flung his saddle-bags into the boat, and desired the man to row him over. Bushe thus caught him in an impromptu—

"While meaner souls the tempest keeps in awe,
Intrepid Cæsar, crossing Ballinlaw,
Shouts to the boatman, shivering in his rags,
'You carry Cæsar and his—*saddle-bags!*'"—M.

* I had intended to introduce a sketch of Mr. Rowan's character into this article, but found that I could not compress it within its appropriate limits. The reader will find it appended in a separate article.

his aid, and illustrated his defence by a quotation from Cicero, in which the Roman extenuates the faults of those who were engaged on Pompey's side. The passage was exceedingly apposite, but was delivered, perhaps, with too dolorous and lacrymatory a tone. A man should scarcely weep over a quotation. But altogether the reply was magnificent, and made the minister bite the dust.* With this comfortable reflection we left the house.

* The late Sir Robert Peel, born in 1788, was the son of a man who had become a millionaire, as an enterprising cotton-manufacturer. Educated for political life, young Peel entered Parliament in 1809 (having previously had the unusual distinction of winning a "double-first class" degree at Oxford), and soon was noticed as a well-informed and judicious speaker and worker. In 1810, he was made Colonial under-secretary, Percival being Premier. From 1812 to 1818, he was Chief-Secretary for Ireland. In 1822, he succeeded Addington (Lord Sidmouth) as Home Secretary, and, in that capacity, commenced the mitigation and consolidation of the criminal law. When Canning became Premier, in 1827, Peel and five other Cabinet ministers resigned. In 1828, when Wellington formed his ministry, Peel was his Home Secretary, and, as such, introduced and carried the Catholic Relief Bill in 1829, thereby incurring the enmity of the great Tory exclusionist party. From 1830 to 1834, Peel headed the opposition to Lord Grey's Reform Ministry, and was summoned from Italy, at the close of the latter year, to form a ministry which was broken up in April, 1835. The Whigs resumed office, and retained it until the summer of 1841, when Lord Melbourne had to relinquish his position as Premier, and Peel succeeded him, amid general hope, from public confidence in his administrative faculties, that he would extricate the country from the financial and other difficulties in which the Melbourne Cabinet had involved it. He imposed an Income and Property tax (the best, if fairly assessed), and in 1842, commenced his system of Free Trade, by sweeping away hundreds of imposts—most of them small, but all vexatious. In 1845, he announced Free Trade in Corn, to the joy of millions, who were led to expect more from it than they have yet received, and to the dismay and anger of the landlords and farmers, who had looked on Peel as their great bulwark. The Corn Laws were abolished in June, 1846, and, immediately after, the Whigs and the Protectionists uniting to oppose Peel, beat him on the Irish Coercion Bill, and forced him to retire. On June 29, 1846, he announced the dissolution of his ministry, in one of the ablest speeches he had ever delivered, and quitted office, the people's favorite. For the following four years, his influence in public affairs was immense. He was understood not to desire a return to office—but he wielded immense moral power. On June 29, 1850, he was thrown off his horse, while riding up Constitution Hill (London) and died from the effects of the fall on July 2, 1850, mourned by the nation. All felt his loss—from the sovereign to the peasant. From the time that he threw off the trammels of party, Peel was

It is not, of course, my intention to detail every circumstance of an interesting kind which occurred in the course of this political excursion. From a crowd of materials, I select what is most deserving of mention. I should not omit the mention of a dinner given to the deputies by Mr. Brougham. He invited us to his house upon the Saturday after our arrival, and gave the Irish embassy a very splendid entertainment. Some of the first men in England were of the party. There were four Dukes at table. I had never witnessed an assemblage of so much rank, and surveyed with intense curiosity the distinguished host and his illustrious guests. It is unnecessary to observe that Mr. Brougham went through the routine of convivial form with dignified facility and grace. It was to his mind that I directed my chief attention, with a view to compare him, in his hours of relaxation, with the men of eminence with whom I had conversed in my own country.

The first circumstance that struck me was the entire absence of effort, and the indifference about display. I perceived that he stretched his faculties out, after the exhaustion of professional and parliamentary labor, in a careless listlessness; and, if I may so say, threw his mind upon a couch. Curran, Grattan, and Bushe, were the best talkers I had ever witnessed. The first (and I heard a person make the same remark in London) was certainly the most eloquent man whose conversation I ever had an opportunity of enjoying. But his serious reflections bore the character of harangue, and his wit, with all its brilliancy, verged a little upon farce. He was so fond, indeed, of introducing dialogue into his stories, that at times his conversation assumed the aspect of a dramatic exhibition. There was, perhaps, too much tension of the intellect in those masterpieces of mirth and pathos, in which he appeared to be under the alternate influence of Momus and of Apollo. The conversation of Mr. Grattan was not of an after-dinner cast. You should have walked with him among the woods of Tinnahinch, and listened to his recol-

emphatically, the great English statesman of his time. Amid the absorbing cares of public life, he was the patron and friend of art, literature, and science, and those who devote their minds to these ennobling pursuits.—M.

lections of a better day by the sound of the lulling and romantic waters of those enchanting groves, in which, it is said, he studied the arts of elocution in his youth, and through which he delighted to wander in the illuminated sunset of his glorious age. It was necessary that his faculties should be thrown into a swing before they should come into full play. He poured out fine sentiments in glittering epigrams. His mind became antithetical from continued habit, but it was necessary that it should be thrown into excitement to bring it into action. It was in sketches of character that he excelled; but you should give him time and leisure for the completion of his miniatures. Bushe . . . . . . But I am deviating from my theme.

To return to Mr. Brougham, he is, perhaps, more negligent and heedless of what he says than any of these eminent persons to whom I have alluded, and flings his opinions into phrase without caring into what shape they may be moulded. I remember to have read an article in the Edinburgh Review, upon Curran's life, that eminent men in England never make any effort to shine in conversation; and I saw an illustration of the remark at Mr. Brougham's table. He did not tell a single story — except, indeed, that he mentioned a practical joke which had been played upon Joseph Hume,* who takes things "*au pic de la lettre*," by passing some strange, uncouth person upon him as Mr. O'Connell. The latter sat between the Dukes of Devonshire† and Leinster. It was the

* Joseph Hume, born in Scotland in 1777, obtained a large fortune by contracts in India, during the Mahratta war. He returned in 1808, and entered Parliament in 1812. With slight intermission, he has been in the Commons ever since, and, from his superior length of service as a member, is now entitled to the Nestorian title of "Father of the House." Mr. Hume's great merit is that he applied himself, session after session, to correct the extravagant expenditure of successive Governments. At first, he was a Tory, but, for the last five-and-thirty years, has been a Liberal — so much so, indeed, that, on one occasion, he stated in Parliament that "he would vote that black was white, if it would serve his party!" As a speaker, Mr. Hume is much below par; as a man of business, industrious and good tempered, he has no superior. — M.

† The Duke of Devonshire, one of the wealthiest peers in England, has very large estates in the South of Ireland, which are let at low rents, and well administered. He is now in his sixty-fourth year, and has retired from public

place of honor, and the learned gentleman filled it without airs or affectation. In all his intercourse with the great in London, I remarked that he comported himself in a manner perfectly becoming his character and station in his own country. I was glad to find that, unlike Sir Pertinax, "he could stand straight in the presence of a great man." The attention of the company was very much fixed upon him. But he spoke little. I remember Mr. Moore telling me an anecdote of Mrs. Siddons, which is not unillustrative of the scene. A large party were invited to meet her. She remained silent, as is her wont, and disappointed the expectations of the whole company, who watched for every syllable that should escape her lips. At length, however, being asked if she would have some Burton ale, she replied, with a sepulchral intonation, that "she liked ale vastly."* To this interesting remark the display of her intellectual powers was confined. I do not think that Mr. O'Connell, upon this occasion, gave utterance to any more profound or sagacious observation.

Nearly opposite to him sat Sir Francis Burdett and Mr. Lambton.† The latter seemed to me to watch Mr. O'Connell

life—which he never cared for. He was spoken of, repeatedly, as being about to accept the office of Lord Lieutenant of Ireland, but the only public situation, in which he appeared, was that of Ambassador to Russia, in 1826, at the coronation of the Emperor Nicholas. He is a well-known patron of the fine arts, and his collection of sculpture, paintings, and books, at one of his seats (Chatsworth, in Derbyshire), is world-famed. He strongly advocated Catholic Emancipation.—M.

* I remember mentioning this anecdote to the late Mr. Maturin, who said "The voice of Mrs. Siddons, like St. Paul's bell, should never toll except for the death of kings." [Lockhart's Life of Scott records an instance of this, at the table of the Ariosto of the North, where Mrs. Siddons, in an eminently tragic voice, thus addressed a servant: "I asked for water, boy—you've brought me beer."—M.]

† John George Lambton, born April, 1792, entered Parliament early, and always opposed the Tory party. Lord Grey was his father-in-law, but Lambton did not follow that haughty aristocrat's example as regards Canning, whose Ministry he supported. In 1828, he was created Baron Durham. In 1830, he became a member of Lord Grey's Ministry, and was understood to have proposed a much larger measure of Parliamentary Reform than Lord Grey would sanction. Lord Durham became leader of the movement party, and his assumption of the office of Premier was considered at hand. But Lord Grey

with a very unremitting vigilance. He hardly spoke himself. His air is foreign; he is full of intelligence, and looks like a picture, by Murillo, of a young Spanish Jesuit who has just completed his novitiate. At the other end of the table sat the celebrated Mr. Scarlett,* who is at English *nisi-prius facile princeps.* I thought I could perceive the wile of a lawyer in his watchful and searching eye—

> "He is a great observer, and he looks
> Quite through the thoughts of men."

His smile, too, was perhaps a little like that of Cassius. He said little—altogether, there was not as much alertness in the dialogue as in the champagne.

The Duke of Sussex seemed to me the only person who exhibited much hilarity of spirit. There is a good deal of buoyancy in the temperament of his Royal Highness. He speaks with great correctness and fluency; is perfectly kind and affable; and laughs with all his heart at his friend's jokes as well as at his own. If the Duke of Sussex were our Lord Lieutenant (as I hope he yet may be), he would put us into good humor with each other in a month.† I would substitute Ober-

quitted office in 1834, and, in the year after (to get him out of the way?) Lord Durham was sent to Russia as Ambassador, where he remained for two years. In 1838, he was sent to Canada, as Governor-General, with almost dictatorial powers, in the use of which he was not supported by the Melbourne Ministry in England, whereupon he returned home, the same year. He died, July, 1840. In debate he was a good speaker, but an air of *hauteur* dulled the effects of his most impassioned language.—M.

* Sir James Scarlett, then a whig, but afterward Attorney-General under the Wellington Administration. He eventually became Lord Abinger, and Chief Baron of the Exchequer.—M.

† Augustus Frederick, Duke of Sussex, was sixth son of George III., and much offended his father by contracting marriage, when a minor, with Lady Augusta Murray, daughter of a Scottish Earl. (One of the newspapers of the day stated, that "Lady Augusta soon became pregnant, and returned to England; the Duke of Sussex *did the same.*") This union, which took place in Italy, was confirmed, on their return to England, and two children were "the consekence of that manoover," to use the classic words of the elder Mr. Weller. One of these was the late Sir Augustus d'Este, who unsuccessfully sought the Dukedom on his father's death, the other (who, when I first saw her, in 1828, was one of the finest women in England) was Mademoiselle d'Este, who, in middle age, married Sir Thomas Wilde, created Lord Truro and Chancellor of

on's whistle for Alecto's horn.* I should like to hear the honest and cordial laugh of the Duke of Sussex at an aggregate levée of Catholics and Protestants at the Castle. I should like to hear the echoes of St. Patrick's Hall,† taking up the royal mirth in a long and loud reverberation. What might, peradventure, be an excess of vivacity in a gentleman, would be condescending pleasantry in a prince.

I understood, at Mr. Brougham's, that it was intended to give a public dinner to the Catholic deputies, at which the leading advocates of Emancipation were to be present. Much preparation was made for this festival of liberality, but it was afterward conceived that it would be more judicious upon the part of the friends of religious liberty not to provoke their antagonists into a reaction, which it was thought likely might be produced. The idea was abandoned; but, in order to give the deputies an opportunity of expressing their sentiments in public, the British Catholics held a general meeting at the Freemasons' Hall.

The Duke of Norfolk was in the chair.‡ The assembly was

England in 1850.—The Prince's marriage was dissolved by the Prerogative Court, and the union accordingly ended in separation. At the age of twenty-eight, Prince Augustus was created Duke of Sussex, with an allowance of twelve thousand pounds sterling a year, afterward raised to twenty thousand pounds sterling a year—which he always complained was too small! He sided with the Whig party—as much as a Prince could. He laid himself out for popularity, and, at public dinners and charitable meetings, was liberal in giving—his speeches. He had a fine library, and had accumulated a magnificent collection of Bibles, in various languages and of various editions. Some time before his death, he wedded the rich widow of a city knight, bearing the illustrious name of—Buggins! She has since been created Duchess of Inverness. Born January, 1773, the Duke of Sussex died April, 1843, aged seventy. His pompous manner would have disgusted the Irish in a week, if he had been sent to Dublin as their Viceroy.—M.

* In Wieland's Oberon, at the sound of a magic whistle, laughter is instantaneously produced; a merriment takes the place of strife.

† A spacious apartment in Dublin Castle, in which Royalty (personally or by proxy) holds levées and drawing-rooms, and where the Installation of Knights of St. Patrick generally takes place.—M.

‡ The Duke of Norfolk, in 1825, was a stout, red-faced gentleman, looking very like a London Alderman, accustomed to civic banquets. He was as plain in his manners as in his appearance. Indeed, it was reported that he had been

not as numerous as I had expected—it was in a great measure composed of Irish. Many persons were deterred from attending by the title of the meeting, which seemed to confine it to Roman Catholics. In consequence of the impression that Protestants were not invited to assist in these proceedings, few of the Parliamentary supporters of Emancipation attended. Mr. Coke, of Norfolk, who sat next to the chairman, was almost the only English Protestant of distinction whom I observed at the meeting.* I believe, however, that an anxiety to hear Mr. O'Connell, induced a great number of the literary men attached to the periodical and daily press to attend.

Mr. O'Connell appeared to me extremely solicitous about the impression which he should produce, and prepared and arranged his topics with unusual care. In public meetings in Ireland, he is so confident in his powers, that he gives himself little trouble in the selection of his materials, and generally trusts to his emotions for his harangues.† He is, on that account, oc-

known as "Mr. Howard," a wine-merchant, in one of the streets off the Strand, in London, before the death of "the dirty Duke," without legitimate male issue, drove "all the blood of all the Howards" up to fever-heat, in expectation of turning out next of kin. The Duke, with the uncleanly *soubriquet*, had turned Protestant, in order to sit in Parliament. The present Duke has also abjured the faith of his ancestors. The "dirty Duke" never underwent voluntary ablution, but, once or twice a week, when dead-drunk, was stripped, laid upon a table, soaped, scrubbed, and towelled, into a state of comparative cleanliness.—The Dukedom, conferred in 1483, is the oldest in England, and its owner is therefore Premier Duke. He is also Hereditary Earl-Marshal, and, as such, has the regulation of the coronation ceremonies, and attests the signature of the Sovereign to the documents wherein Peers, Peeresses, Privy Councillors, and others, are invited to participate in the pageant.—M.

* Thomas William Coke, of Holkham, in the county of Norfolk, was a descendant of Sir Edward Coke, the great lawyer, and will be chiefly remembered for the extent and success of his improvements in English agriculture, by which he raised the value of his estates from two thousand to twenty thousand pounds sterling a year. He was of the extreme liberal party, from whom he presented so many remonstrant addresses to George III., that his Majesty jocosely said, "Coke, if you bring me another of these, I'll certainly *knight* you"—a severe threat to a man who prided himself on his old family, had declined a baronetcy as too low, and claimed a dormant earldom. His friends the Whigs, with whom he had always voted, created him Earl of Leicester in 1837, when he was eighty-five years old. He died in June, 1842, aged ninety.—M.

† The character of O'Connell's eloquence has never been clearly indicated.

casionally desultory and irregular. But there is no man more capable of lucid exposition, when he previously deliberates upon the order in which he should array the topics upon which he intends to dwell. He undertook, on this occasion, the very laborious task of tracing the progress of the penal code, and epitomized in some measure the history of his country. For the first hour he was, perhaps, a little encumbered with small details; but when he advanced into the general consideration of the grievances under which the great body of the people are doomed to labor — when he painted the insolence of the dominant faction — when he showed the effects of the penal code brought to his own door — he seized with an absolute dominion upon the sympathies of his acclaiming auditors, and poured the full tide of his own emotions into their hearts. I did not greatly heed the results of Mr. O'Connell's oratory upon the great bulk of his audience. Many a big drop, compounded of heat and patriotism, of tears and of perspiration, stood upon the rude and honest faces that were cast in true Hibernian mould, and were raised toward the glory of Ireland with a mixed expression of wonder and of love. I was far more anxious to detect the feeling produced upon the literary and English portion of the audience. It was most favorable.

Mr. Charles Butler, near whom I happened to sit, and whom

Its leading feature was *intense earnestness.* Whatever his style, and it would vary a dozen times in the same speech, he always had a purpose. He was not a man to string words together into pretty sentences, as women string beads of coral, but he spoke with a will and with an aim. His Irish auditors expected to be amused as well as roused, and O'Connell entertained as well as excited them. He had dropped his plummet into the Irish heart, and sounded its remotest depths. He has been compared, at various times, to the great orators whom Ireland has produced; but he resembled none of them singly. He had less imagination than Curran, less philosophy than Burke, less wit than Canning, less rhetoric than Sheil, less classicality than Bushe, less eloquence than Plunket, less pathos than Grattan; but he had more power than any of them. His language was forcible, even when he was most playful. And, when addressing an Irish audience, he applied himself to charm them, there was such an alternation of style — now soaring to the loftiest, and now subsiding to the most familiar — that he carried all hearts with him, until the listeners seemed under the spell of an enchanter, moved to anger or to mirth even as he might desire. This was to be indeed a great orator, and this was O'Connell. — M.

I should be disposed to account a severe but excellent critic, was greatly struck. He several times expressed his admiration of the powers of the speaker. The applause of such a man is worth that of a "whole theatre of others." Mr. Coke, also, whose judgment is, I understand, held in very great estimation, and who has witnessed the noblest displays of Parliamentary eloquence, intimated an equally high opinion. Immediately under Mr. O'Connell there was an array, and a very formidable one, of the delegates from the press. They appeared to me to survey Mr. O'Connell with a good deal of supercilious distaste at the opening of his speech; and, although some among them persevered to the last in their intimations of national disrelish, and shrugged their shoulders at "Irish eloquence," the majority surrendered their prejudices to their good feelings, and ultimately concurred in the loud plaudits with which Mr. O'Connell concluded his oration. It occupied nearly three hours and a half.

Mr. O'Hanlon succeeded Mr. O'Connell. He spoke well, but the auditory were exhausted, and began to break up. Less attention was paid to Mr. O'Hanlon than he would have received at a more opportune moment. The excitation produced by Mr. O'Connell, the lateness of the hour, and the recollections of dinner, were potent impediments to rhetorical effect.

Mr. Sheil rose under similar disadvantages. He cast that sort of look about him which I have witnessed in an actor when he surveys an empty house. The echo produced by the diminution of the crowd drowned his voice, which, being naturally of a harsh quality, requires great management, and, in order to produce any oratorical impression, must be kept under the control of art. Mr. Sheil became disheartened, and lost his command over his throat. He grew loud and indistinct. He also fell into the mistake of laying aside his habitual cast of expression and of thought, and, in place of endeavoring to excite the feelings of his auditory, wearied them with a laborious detail of uninteresting facts. He failed to produce any considerable impression excepting at the close of his speech, in which, after dwelling upon the great actions which were achieved by the Catholic ancestors of some of the eminent men around him, he introduced Jean of Arc prophesying to Talbot the observation of his illustrious name, and the exclusion of his posterity from the councils of his country.*

I should not omit to mention the speech delivered by Lord Stourton at this meeting. It was easy to collect from his manner that he was not in the habit of addressing a large assembly, but the sentiments to which he gave utterance were high and manly, and becoming a British nobleman who had been spoliated of his rights. His language was not only elegant and refined, but adorned with imagery of an original cast, derived from those sciences with which his Lordship is said to be familiar.† Some of the deputies dined with him after the meeting. They were sumptuously entertained.

I had now become more habituated to the display of patrician magnificence in England, and saw the exhibition of its splendor without surprise. Yet I confess that at Norfolk-house, where the Duke did Mr. O'Connell, Lord Killeen, and others of our deputation, the honor to invite them, and, in compliment to our cause, brought together an assemblage of men of the highest rank and genius in England, I was dazzled with the splendor and gorgeousness of an entertainment to which I had seen no parallel. Norfolk-house is one of the finest in London. The interior, which is in the style prevalent about eighty years ago in England, realizes the notions which one forms of a palace. It was indeed occupied at one time by some members of the royal family; and the Duke told us that the late King [George III.] was born in the room in which we dined. We passed through a series of magnificent apartments, rich with crimson and fretted with gold. There was no glare of excessive light in this vast and seemingly endless mansion; and the massive lamps which were suspended from the embossed and gilded ceilings, diffused a shadowed illumination, and left the

* Mr. Sheil, whose speech at this meeting was a failure — the patience of his audience having been exhausted before he rose — adroitly attempts here to explain away the fact. From some cause or other, his voice, naturally shrill, almost wholly failed him, and his auditors were greatly disappointed. — M.

† The Lord Stourton here mentioned was the seventeenth Baron of that name, the peerage bearing date 1448. The family is Catholic. — M.

distance in the dusk. The transition to the great chamber where the company were assembled, and which was glowing with light, presented a brilliant and imposing contrast. Here we found the Duke of Norfolk, surrounded by persons of high distinction. Among the company were the Dukes of Sussex, Devonshire, and Leinster, Lord Grey, Lord Fitzwilliam, Lord Shrewsbury, Lord Donoughmore, Lord Stourton, Lord Clifford, Lord Nugent, Lord Arundel, Sir Francis Burdett, Mr. Butler, Mr. Abercrombie, Mr. Blunt, Mr. Denman, and other persons of eminence and fame.*

The Duke of Norfolk came forward to meet us, and gave us a cordial and cheerful welcome. This amiable nobleman is distinguished by the kindness and goodness of his manners, which bespeak an excellent and unassuming spirit, and through all the political intercourse which we had with him the great question, in which he feels so deep an interest, manifested a shrewd sound sense, and a high and intense anxiety for the success of the great cause of religious liberty, from which very beneficial results have already ensued. He has been very instrumental in effecting a junction between the English and Irish Roman Catholics, and has thus conferred a great service upon both. We were received by him with the most gracious and unaffected urbanity.

I was struck with the perfect freedom from authoritativeness which characterized most of the eminent men who were placed about me. There is among the petty aristocracy of Ireland

* Of these, Lords Grey, Shrewsbury, Donoughmore, Clifford, Arundel, Mr. Butler, and Mr. Blunt, have departed this life. Mr. Abercrombie, then a very obscure man (who worked himself up, from being the Duke of Devonshire's steward), used his employer's interest to get him made Chief Baron of the Exchequer in Scotland, at four thousand pounds sterling a year. It was so much a sinecure, that, in the thirty months he held it, he only tried four cases, thus receiving ten thousand pounds for doing nothing. The sinecure was abolished, and Abercrombie was compensated by a pension of two thousand pounds, which was suspended when he was made Speaker of the House of Commons in 1837 (salary six thousand pounds a year, and one thousand pounds more for a house), and, after two years' service, retired on a pension of four thousand pounds for his own life and that of his son, and a peerage as Baron Dumferline. What renders this more strange is, that this man had boorish manners, no learning, no eloquence, nothing but the Duke of Devonshire's patronage to push him on. — M.

infinitely more arrogance of port and look than I observed among the first men of the British empire. Certain of our colonial aristocracy are far more bloated and full-blown with a notion of their own importance. The reason is obvious. The former rest in security upon their unquestionable title to respect. Their dignity fits them like an accustomed garment. But men who are raised but to a small elevation, on which they hold a dubious ground, feel it necessary to impress their consequence upon others by an assumption of superiority which is always offensive, and generally absurd. Lord Fitzwilliam was the person with whom I was disposed to be most pleased. This venerable nobleman carries, with a gray head, a young and fresh heart. He may be called the old Adam of the political world; and England might well exclaim to her faithful servant, in the language of Orlando—

"Oh, good old man, how well in thee appears
The constant service of the antique world!
Thou art not for the fashion of these times,
When none will sweat but for promotion."

It is impossible to look upon this amiable and dignified patrician of the olden stamp, without a feeling of affectionate admiration for his pure and distinguished patriotism and the warm love of his country, which lives (if I may so say) under the ashes of age, and requires but to be stirred to emit the flashes of its former fire. The natural apathy incidental to his time of life, appears habitually to prevail over him; but speak to him of the great interests of the empire—speak to him of that measure which at an earlier period he was delegated by his sovereign to complete—speak to him of Ireland, and through the dimness that loads his eye, a sudden illumination will break forth. For Ireland he entertains a kind of paternal tenderness. He reverted with a Nestorian pride to the period of his own government; and mentioned that he had preserved the addresses which he had received from the Roman Catholic body as among the best memorials of his political life. That he should live long enough to see the emancipation of the Irish people, seemed to be the wish nearest to his heart. It does one good—it is useful in a moral point of view, to approach such a person as Lord Fitzwilliam, and to feel that there is in public men such a thing as a pure and disinterested anxiety for the benefit of mankind, and that the vows of all politicians are not, whatever we may be disposed to think, "as false as dicers' oaths."

In describing the impression produced upon me by Lord Fitzwilliam, I have mentioned the result of my observation at Mr. Ponsonby's, where the deputies afterward met him, as well as at Norfolk house. Lord Grey also dined at Mr. Ponsonby's, where I had a better opportunity of noting him.* He is some-

* Charles, Earl Grey, born in 1764, was M. P. for his native county of Northumberland, almost as soon as he attained his majority. He soon displayed ability, as a debater on the liberal side, and was associated with Burke, Sheridan, and others, as one of the managers of the impeachment of Warren Hastings. He went beyond Fox in his democratical opinions. On Pitt's death, in 1806, when "All the Talents" formed a Cabinet, of which Fox was the actual, while the Duke of Portland was the nominal head, Mr. Grey (who now bore the honorary title of Viscount Howick, his father having been made Earl Grey in 1802) took office as First Lord of the Admiralty. In October, 1806, Lord Howick succeeded Fox as Foreign Secretary, but the Ministry soon broke up, and, on the death of his father in 1807, he went to the Upper House, as Earl Grey, and warmly defended Queen Caroline in 1820. He remained out of office until November 1830, but on two or three occasions, when a Coalition ministry was talked of, there were negotiations (always ending in failure) to bring in Lord Grey. His personal pride intervened — as he wanted first place, or none. This, no doubt, made him strongly oppose Canning's Ministry, in 1827 — it was "most tolerable and not to be endured" that a mere commoner should be Prime Minister, while Earl Grey was ready and anxious for the office! At last, in 1830, he obtained the prize — because Parliamentary Reform was needed, and, as Mr. Grey, he had suggested a plan some five-and-thirty years before. After a great struggle, Reform was granted — more than Grey actually thought prudent to bestow (having such a horror of democratic inroads that he once publicly declared that "he would stand by his order") but less than his son-in-law, Lord Durham, thought was wise and just. In July, 1834, he resigned office, and took no further part in politics. He died, July, 1845, aged eighty-one. As Minister of the Crown, he had one overpowering fault, which Peel was eminently free from — that of nepotism. It really appeared as if the object of his taking office was to provide for his family, his connections, for every one named Grey. For this he was constantly baited by Cobbett, who published what he called "The Grey List," stating the various offices to which Grey had been appointed, giving the name of each official, and showing that they were the recipients of about one hundred and seventy thousand pounds sterling a year — all, but twenty thousand pounds sterling, being derived from

what silent and reserved. It is the fashion among Tories to account him contemptuous and haughty; but I can not coincide with them. He has, indeed, a lofty bearing, but it is not at all artificial. It is the aristocracy of virtue as well as rank. There is something uncompromising, and perhaps stern as well as inflexible in his aspect. Tall, erect, and collected in himself, he carries the evidences of moral and intellectual ascendency impressed upon him, and looks as if he knew himself to be, in the proudest sense which the poet has attached to the character, not only a great but an honest man. And why should he not look exactly what he is? Why should he not wrap himself in the consciousness of his political integrity, and seem to say, "*meâ virtute involvo,*" while so many others, who were once the companions of his journey, and who turned aside into a more luxuriant road, in taking a retrospect, as the close of life is drawing near, of the mazy course which they have trod, behold it winding through a rich and champagne country, and occasionally deviating into low but not unproductive declivities? This eminent man, in looking back from the point of moral elevation on which he stands, will trace his path in one direct and unbroken line—through a lofty region which has been barren of all but fame, and from which no allurement of ease, or of profusion, could ever induce him to depart.

Lord Grey has a touch of sadness upon him, which would look dissatisfaction to a placeman's eye; but there is nothing really morose or atrabilious in his expression. He has found that sorrow can unbar the palaces of the great, as well as unlatch the cottages of the lowly. His dear friend and near ally is gone—his party is almost broken.* He has survived

life appointments! The truth of these accusations was undeniable, and helped, no doubt, to account for Lord Grey's unpopularity after the Reform struggle was ended. He was an eloquent speaker—seldom warmed into passion or even into excitement, but fluent, correct, and sometimes rather forcible.—M.

* The allusion here appears to be to Fox, who, however, had died nearly nineteen years before. Charles James Fox, born in 1749, was the second son of the first Lord Holland, by whom he was educated for political life. At the age of nineteen, two years before the legal age, he was elected member of parliament. From 1770 to 1774, he was an advocate of the Ministry, and was

the death, and, let me add, the virtue of many illustrious men, and looks like the lonely column of the fabric which he sustained so nobly, and which has fallen at last around him. It is not wonderful that he should seem to stand in solitary loftiness, and that melancholy should have given a solemn tinge to his mind. He spoke of the measures intended to be made collateral to emancipation, and said,† * * * *

successively Lord of the Admiralty and of the Treasury. At the age of 24, the Ministry dismissed him—thereby converting a warm friend into a bitter opponent. He resisted the American war, and on Lord North's removal, obtained a seat in the Cabinet, as Secretary of State. The Rockingham Administration breaking up, on the death of its head, Lord Shelburne became Premier, and after some time, Fox coalesced with Lord North (his old antagonist); a measure which nearly ruined the popularity of both. Their India Bill led to their downfall, and the nomination of William Pitt, in his 25th year, as Premier. Fox espoused the leading principles of the French Revolution, which Pitt contended against, and this also led to a total rupture with Burke, long his friend, and to the erasure of his name, by the hand of the King himself, from the Roll of the Privy Council. When Pitt died, in 1806, Lord Grenville drew Fox from opposition, and made him Foreign Secretary. He did not long hold office, for which he had so long contended, but died in September, 1806. The eloquence of Fox was vehement rather than polished, but it was forcible and effective. In private life he was convivial, witty, and genial. He was somewhat of an historian, too, but spoke better than he wrote. He was addicted to gaming, and was a man of uncalculating and almost boundless extravagance. He was buried in Westminister Abbey, close to his great rival Pitt. Scott says

" Drop upon Fox's tomb a tear
'Twill trickle to his rival's bier."

Fox was the intimate friend of the Prince of Wales, afterward George IV., for many years, but the intimacy broke off after the marriage of the Prince.—M.

† This article, published May, 1825, broke off thus abruptly, with "(*The Conclusion in our next Number*)," holding out promise of some more of the personal and political gossip which attracted much attention at the time. The "conclusion" never appeared. Mr. Sheil told me that, though written, it was suppressed, at the strong desire of the late Lord Grey, one of the haughtiest aristocrats in England, at the time, who was alarmed at the idea of any of his table-talk being reported! I believe that, until now, the exact reason of this suppression, though suspected at the time, has not been stated on authority.—M.

ARCHIBALD HAMILTON ROWAN.

Of all the remarkable men I have met, Hamilton Rowan, I think, is the one whose external appearance most completely answers to the character of his mind, and the events of his life. The moment your eye has taken in the whole of his fine athletic configuration, you see at once that nature designed him to be a great massive engine of a popular cause. When he entered life, he might easily have taken his place as a leading member of the aristocracy of his country. He had high connections, a noble fortune, manners and accomplishments that would have graced a court—but his high and adventurous spirit could not have brooked the sedentary forms, and still less the despotic maxims, of an Irish state-career. He never could have endured to sit at a council-board, with his herculean limbs gathered under him, to deliberate upon the most expedient modes of trampling upon public rights. As a mere matter of animal propensity, his more natural vocation was to take the side of enterprise and danger—to mingle in the tumult of popular commotion, and leading on his band of citizen-soldiers "to the portals of the Castle, to call aloud in their name for the minister to come forth and resist at his peril the national cry for 'Universal Emancipation.'"* This was his election, and his conscience coincided with his impulses. He became, as might be expected, the idol of the populace, and, from the qualities which made him so, too formidable to the state to be tolerated. He was prosecuted and convicted, by a tribunal of very doubtful purity,† of feeling too ardently for the political degradation of Ireland.

* See his trial in Howell's State Trials, for 1794.

† See the motion for a new trial, and the documents there used.—Howell's State Trials.

Thus far Hamilton Rowan had acted upon the principles of an Irish reformer, and if he avowed them indiscreetly, or pushed them too far, he suffered for it. In his imprisonment, which he at least considered as oppression, he was provoked to listen to more dangerous doctrines. He committed himself in conferences with a spy who procured a ready access to his presence; and to avoid the consequences, effected his escape to a foreign land.

After several years passed in wandering and exile, the merits of his personal character prevailed against the remembrance of his political aberrations, and an act of royal clemency, generously conceded without any humiliating conditions, restored him once more to his country. There he has since resided, in the bosom of domestic quiet, and in the habitual exercise of every virtue that can ennoble private life. He has the satisfaction, too, in his old age, of finding that, in a public point of view, his debt of gratitude to the Crown has not been wholly unpaid. In his eldest son (Captain Hamilton, of the Cambrian frigate) he has given to the British navy one of its most gallant and distinguished commanders, and for whose sake alone every man of a generous spirit should abstain from gratuitous and cruel railings at the obsolete politics of the father.*

Hamilton Rowan's exterior is full of interest. Whether you meet him abroad or in a drawing-room, you are struck at once with his physical pre-eminence. Years have now rendered his frame less erect, but all the proportions of a noble model remain. In his youth he was remarkable for feats of strength and activity. The latter quality was put to no ordinary test, in a principal incident of his life, to which I shall presently refer. His face, both in feature and expression, is in strict accordance with the rest of his person. It has nothing denoting extraordinary comprehension, or subtlety of intellect; but in its masculine outline, which the workings of time have brought out into more prominent relief—in the high and bushy

* This son, who died before his venerable father, eminently distinguished himself in the contest for the independence of Greece, and his father never recovered his loss.—M.

brow—the unblenching eye—the compressed lips, and in the composed yet somewhat stern stability of expression that marks the whole, you find the symbols of high moral determination—of fidelity to principle—of self-reliance and self-oblivion, and above all of an uncompromising personal courage, that could front every form of danger face to face.*

The austerity of his countenance vanishes the moment he addresses you. His manners have all the fascination of the old school. Every tone of his voice is softened by an innate and undeviating courtesy that makes no distinctions of rank or sex. In the trivial details of common life, Hamilton Rowan is as gentle and complimentary to men as other men are in their intercourse with females. This suavity of demeanor is not the velvet of art; it is only one of the signs of a comprehensive philanthropy, which as habitually breaks out in acts of genuine sympathy and munificent relief, wherever a case of human suffering occurs within its range.

The circumstances of Hamilton Rowan's escape from imprisonment, as I once heard them minutely detailed, possessed all the interest of a romantic narrative. The following are such of the leading particulars as I can recall, to my recollection. Having discovered (on the 28th of April, 1794) the extent of the danger in which he was involved, he arranged a

* Archibald Hamilton Rowan, who must have been a giant in his prime, was one of the most remarkable men I ever saw. One might almost think he had been made for one purpose—*digito monstrari!* He was long past seventy when I saw him. In stature he was even as one of the sons of Anak. His strongly-marked features indicated firmness and benevolence. His eyes, dark and flashing, beneath shaggy brows. His port, lofty. His stride, large. His manners, of the old school of gentlest courtesy—but his frown, when offended or excited, positively frightening! Crowds used to watch for a sight of this fine "old Irish gentleman," as he came out of the club-house in Kildare street, bearing in his hand a mighty blackthorn (which might have served Hercules for a club), and escorted, on either side, by two immense Irish wolf-dogs, reported to be the very last of their race. Looking at him, and surveying the generation among whom he towered, like a forest-oak over a crowd of plantation shrubs, a contemplative man might sigh, and utter, "There were *Men*—in the days when he began to live." Mr. Rowan died in November, 1834, aged eighty-four. In his latter years he was much afflicted with deafness, and grief for his gallant son, Captain Hamilton, who died before him, had affected his strong and truly masculine mind.—M

plan of flight to be put into execution on the night of the 1st of May. He had the address to prevail on the jailer of Newgate, who knew nothing farther of his prisoner than that he was under sentence of confinement for a political libel, to accompany him at night to Mr. Rowan's own house.* They were received by Mrs. R., who had a supper prepared in the front room of the second floor. The supper over, the prisoner requested the jailer's permission to say a word or two in private to his wife in the adjoining room. The latter consented, on the condition of the door between the two rooms remaining open. He had so little suspicion of what was meditated, that instead of examining the state of this other room, he contented himself with shifting his chair at the supper-table so as to give him a view of the open doorway. In a few seconds his prisoner was beyond his reach, having descended by a single rope, which had been slung from the window of the back chamber.

In his stable he found a horse ready saddled, and a peasant's outside coat to disguise him.† With these he posted to the house of his attorney, Matthew Dowling, who was in the secret of his design, and had promised to contribute to its success by his counsel and assistance. Dowling was at home, but unfortunately his house was full of company. He came out to the street to Mr. Rowan, who personated the character of a country client, and hastily pointing out the great risk to be incurred from any attempt to give him refuge in his own house, directed him to proceed to the Rotunda (a public building in Sackville street, with an open space in front) and remain there until Dowling could despatch his guests, and come to him. Irish guests were in those days rather slow to separate from the bottle. For one hour and a half the fugitive had to wait, leading his horse up and down before the Rotunda, and tortured between fear and hope at the appearance of every person that approached. He has often represented this as the most trying moment of his life.

* In order, he pretended, to make out a deed, as fear had been expressed that such an instrument signed in prison would be invalid.—M.

† Rowan states, in his autobiography, by which I correct Mr. Sheil's narrative, that, when he was in his wife's room, he changed his dress of a herdsman.—M.

Dowling at length arrived, and after a short and anxious conference, advised him to mount his horse, and make for the country-house of their friend Mr. Sweetman, which was situate about four miles off, on the northern side of the bay of Dublin. This place he reached in safety, and found there the refuge and aid which he sought.* After a delay of two or three days Mr. Sweetman engaged three boatmen of the neighborhood to man his own pleasure-boat, and convey Hamilton Rowan to the coast of France. They put to sea at night; but a gale of wind coming on, they were compelled to put back, and take shelter under the lee of the Hill of Howth. While at anchor there on the following morning a small revenue-cruiser sailing by threw into the boat copies of the proclamations that had been issued, offering two thousand pounds sterling for the apprehension of Hamilton Rowan. The weather having moderated, the boat pushed out to sea again. They had reached the mid-channel, when a situation occurred almost equalling in dramatic interest the celebrated *Cæsarem vehis* of antiquity. It would certainly make a fine subject for a picture. As the boat careered along before a favorable wind, the exiled Irishman perceived the boatmen grouped apart, perusing one of the proclamations, and by their significant looks and gestures, discovering that they had recognised the identity of their passenger, with the printed description. "Your conjectures are right, my lads," said Rowan, "my life is in your hands—but you are Irishmen." They flung the proclamation overboard, and the boat continued her course.† On the third morn-

* The moment his escape from prison was known, parties of soldiers were sent in pursuit of him, in all directions, and in his place of concealment he could hear their measured tread.—M.

† It is now several years since the particulars of Mr. Rowan's escape were related to me by a friend, as they had been communicated to him by the principal actor himself; and my present recollection is that the above incident was not included. I have often heard it, as I have given it, from other sources. [What little money Rowan had with him, he divided equally among these noble men, to whose generosity and quick sense of honor he owed his life—for had he been recaptured, he would assuredly have been tried, and, if tried, convicted, as his co-conspirator Jackson was.—There is an anecdote connected with Jackson's not escaping which interests me much more than Rowan's escape. Jackson was an Irish clergyman sent over from France, in 1794, to as-

ing, a little after break of day, they arrived within view of St. Paul de Leon, a fortified town, on the coast of Bretagne. As the sun rose, it dispersed a dense fog that had prevailed overnight, and discovered a couple of miles behind them, moving along under easy sail, the British Channel fleet, through the thick of which their little boat had just shot unperceived.

The party, having landed, were arrested as spies, and cast into prison, but in a few days an order from the French government procured their liberation. Hamilton Rowan proceeded to Paris, from which, in a political convulsion that shortly ensued, it was his fate once more to seek for safety in flight. He escaped this time unaccompanied, in a wherry, which he rowed himself down the Seine. The banks were lined with military; but he answered their challenges with so much address, that he was allowed to pass on unmolested. Having reached a French port, he embarked for the United States of America, where, at length, he found a secure asylum.

Hamilton Rowan, though of Irish blood, was born and educated in England. In his youth he acquired a large property under the will of his maternal grandfather, Mr. Rowan, a barrister and lay-fellow of Trinity College, Dublin, who, in a kind of prophetic spirit, made it a condition of the bequest, "that his grandson should not come to Ireland until after he should be twenty-five years old."

certain whether if the Directory invaded Ireland, the mass of the people would receive the French. He communicated his business to an attorney in London, who sold him to Pitt, and was employed to follow Jackson to Ireland and watch him. After a time, the informer "gave tongue," and Jackson was arrested—he was subsequently tried (the first case of high treason in Ireland for more than a century), convicted, and brought up for judgment, but he evaded it, by taking poison, and died in the dock, his last words, which were addressed to Curran, being those of Pierre, "We have deceived the senate." When in prison, Jackson was visited by a friend who remained until late at night. Jackson went with him to the door where the jailer generally waited. They found the man asleep and the prison-keys by his side, on the ground. Jackson took them up, opened the prison-door, and was urged by his friend to escape. He hesitated for a moment—"No," said he, "I *could* do it, but what would the consequences be to this poor fellow, who has been so kind to me? Let me remain and meet my fate." He closed the door, turning from his friend and liberty, locked himself in, and resumed his place in the dungeon.—M.]

JOHN LESLIE FOSTER.

The first opportunity I had of closely observing the eminent statesman and celebrated legislator whose name is prefixed to this article, was afforded by the Louth election [1826]. Mr. Foster is so intimately connected with that remarkable event, that some account of the details which accompanied it will not be inappropriate. The standard of the Association had been raised in Waterford, and Villiers Stuart proclaimed himself the antagonist of the House of Curraghmore. All eyes were directed to the field in which the great contest was to be waged. Both the combatants brought hereditary rank and vast opulence as their allies, besides the auxiliary passions of the powerful parties to which they were respectively attached. There was, however, nothing surprising in the enterprise of Mr. Stuart. During his minority, the savings of his estate had accumulated to a very large sum, and he was possessed of the means of engaging in a bold political adventure, without running any risk of permanently injuring his fortune. It would have been far stranger if, with his large property and his enlightened opinions, he had allowed the Beresfords to maintain an undisputed masterdom in his county.

While the national attention was fixed upon the events which were taking place in Waterford, news arrived in Dublin which excited a far greater sensation than the contest between the two rival patricians of Dromona and Curraghmore; and it was announced that Mr. Alexander Dawson, a retired barrister with a small fortune, had started for Louth. In that county the Protestant gentry were regarded as omnipotent. For upward of half a century, the Jocelyns and the Fosters had returned two members to Parliament, and divided the county, like a family borough, between them. A strong and apparently indissoluble coalition had been effected between Lord Roden* and Lord Oriel; and it was supposed to be impossible to make any effectual opposition to the union of Orangeism and of Evangelism, which the wily veteran of Ascendency, and the frantic champion of the New Reformation, had effected.

To this combination of power Mr. Dawson had neither wealth nor connections to oppose. He had even intimated that he would not bear any portion of the expenses, and must be returned by popular contribution. The ordinary preparations had not been made, and it was only three days before the election commenced that his intention was declared. Leslie Foster affected to treat his pretensions with derision. He was to be seen among groups of sympathizing king's counsel, and assentating assistant-barristers, with his forefinger and thumb brought into syllogistic conjunction, demonstrating the utter absurdity of Alexander Dawson in attempting a contest. A profound seriousness habitually pervades the countenance of Mr. Foster, who, accustomed to the most abstruse meditations upon political economy, and conversant with the deepest mysteries of legislation, has seldom

* The Earl of Roden (who sits in the House of Lords as Baron Clanbrassill, in the peerage of the United Kingdom), is now, in 1854, in his sixty-sixth year. He was long notorious for his connection with the Orange faction, and has taken great interest in all attempts at changing Irish Catholics (when food is scarce) into nominal converts. When the potato crop turns out favorably, the "reformed" lapse into their ancient faith. It was believed that Lord Roden's great test of a "renewed spirit" was the partaking of meat, on a Friday—hence they were called "leg-of-mutton converts." However misplaced his political and polemical zeal, Lord Roden is a good landlord. He has a pension of twenty-seven hundred pounds sterling, for the abolished office of Auditor-General in Ireland.—His eldest son, Viscount Jocelyn, born in 1816, was military secretary to the Chinese Expedition, and is author of "Six Months in China." He afterward held office under Sir Robert Peel (from February, 1845, to July, 1846), as one of the Secretaries of the India Board. He is a moderate conservative, and a well-informed, unpresuming man. His wife, one of the handsomest women in the Court of Victoria (she is daughter of Lady Palmerston, by her first marriage) is a Lady of the Bedchamber to the Queen.—Viscount Jocelyn has a seat in the House of Commons, as member for Lynn Regis, in the county of Norfolk, for which borough he was first elected in 1842.—M.

been known to use the risible organs for the purposes for which they were originally intended. The notion of a contest in Louth, however, seemed to strike him as so exceedingly ludicrous and extravagant, that upon this occasion he broke through all the rules of solemnity by which his physiognomy is usually controlled. Still, he had left off laughing for such a length of time, that his smile sat uneasily and unnaturally upon him, and the muscles of merriment had become so rusty and so destitute of pliability, that they accommodated themselves slowly and ponderously to their functions; and many of his friends, observing these novel phenomena of mirth, exclaimed, "What can be the matter with Leslie Foster!" He, however, made ample compensation for this sudden and unmeet deviation from his habitual gravity, by the seriousness of his aspect, upon his appearance at the hustings of Dundalk. I proceeded there before the arrival of Mr. Foster.

From the brow of a hill which surmounts the town, when I was at a short distance from it, I saw a vast multitude descending with banners of green unfurled to the wind, and shouting as they moved along. I could not at first discern with distinctness the gentleman who was the immediate object of this wild ovation; but, on approaching and mixing with the dense mass of enthusiastic patriots myself, I saw, seated in an old gig, Mr. Alexander Dawson, the aspiring candidate who had presumed to enter the lists with the hereditary representatives of the County of Louth. He wore an old frock-coat covered with dust, and a broad-brimmed, weather-beaten hat, which surmounted a head that streamed with profuse perspiration; his face was ruddy with heat, but, notwithstanding the excitement of the scene, preserved its habitual character of sagacious quietism and tranquil intelligence. He did not seem to be (though placed in a most extraordinary and trying situation) at all conscious of the boldness of the enterprise in which he was embarked, and was perhaps the least moved of the multitude that were rushing rapidly on; while the people were hurraing about him, throwing their hats into the air, and catching them with a wild shriek and prance (a common denotement of joy among the lower Irish), he sat composedly in his old vehicle, and was busy in preserving order and regularity in the procession. There were some three or four ragged fiddlers before him, who played with all their might, and in notes of the harshest discord, a tune which they intended for the popular air of "Nancy Dawson," and which they selected for no other reason than that it was connected with his name. It was only at intervals that the hard and vigorous scraping of these village violins was distinctly audible; for the cries of "Down with Foster!" and "Dawson for ever!" resounded from every side in yells of vehement uproar, and monopolized the hearing faculties. A wonderful enthusiasm prevailed through this vast gathering; and in the faces of the fierce and athletic peasants who drew their favorite on, as they occasionally turned their heads back to look on him, and shouted in the retrospect, the strongest passions of mingled joy, ferocity, and determination, were expressed.

In a few minutes Mr. Dawson and his gig were drawn into the main street of Dundalk, and stopped at Magrath's hotel, which was the rendezvous of patriotism during the election. There the committee, which had been hastily gotten up, was collected, and welcomed Mr. Dawson on his arrival. He descended amid loud acclamations, and soon after appeared at a window in the tavern, whence he addressed the people. Several thousands were assembled, and in an instant deep silence was obtained. In a plain, brief, perfectly simple, and intelligible speech, Mr. Dawson told them that for their sake, and not to gratify his personal ambition, he was determined to oppose Mr. Foster and Mr. Fortescue, and to break the Oriel and the Roden yoke. His speech was received with the most rapturous plaudits, and it was manifest that, whatever might be the issue, a spirit had arisen among the people which portended far more than could have been originally calculated. While Mr. Dawson and others of the same party were addressing the people, the carriages of the leading gentry, drawn by four horses, were seen entering the town, but, in order to avoid the multitude, wheeled round through a street parallel to that in the opening of which the people were gathered. Astonishment and apprehension were visible in their faces.

They perceived already that a dreadful struggle was about to take place.

The wonted harangues having been delivered to the people, Mr. Dawson and his committee proceeded to the Court-house, which occupies one side of a square in the centre of the town. This building presents in its exterior a very beautiful object. It was erected under the immediate superintendence of Mr. Foster, who furnished the design, which he took from the Temple of Theseus; for Mr. Foster values himself upon a universality of acquisition, and is a sort of walking encyclopedia, or peripatetic repertory of all the arts and sciences, and is as profoundly skilled in architecture as he is in any of the crafts of the Custom-House or the mysteries of the Excise. Opening Stuart's Athens, he lighted on the Temple of Theseus, and selected it as a model for a Court-house at Dundalk; and, accordingly, the most beautiful and inconvenient temple in which the rites of justice have ever been performed has been produced under his architectural auspices.

In that part of this incongruous edifice which is allocated to the County business, the High-Sheriff assembled the freeholders to read the writ. On his left hand stood Mr. Leslie Foster. How changed from him who had, a few hours before, derided as impotent the efforts of the Roman Catholic body to push him from his stool in the legislature! His complexion is naturally pale, but it now became deadly-white. He surveyed the dense mass of the people with awe, and seemed to recoil from the groans and hootings with which he was clamorously assailed. When proposed as a candidate, he delivered a speech, in which he clumsily sought to reconcile his auditors to his resistance of their claims, and appeared to be aware of the wretchedness of the task which he had imposed upon himself. The only relief which he received was derived from the execration which the mention of Lord Roden and his party produced in the assembly; for, obnoxious as that nobleman is through the rest of Ireland, his fanaticism and narrow-heartedness have secured for him a more condensed and concentrated odium in the town of Dundalk. Mr. Dawson spoke with equal brevity and perspicuity, and made it his boast that he belonged to the middle classes, and was best calculated to represent their feelings and to do justice to their interests.

On the succeeding day the polling commenced with activity, Mr. Fortescue being sustained by the Roden influence and a large portion of the Protestant aristocracy; the rest of that body were the supporters of Mr. Foster; while Mr. Dawson relied upon a few Roman Catholics of fortune, and on the spirit of agrarian insurrection, which had broken out among the forty-shilling freeholders. For the first few days, Mr. Foster and Mr. Fortescue acted in conjunction, because they calculated that they should be able to throw Mr. Dawson out; but, after some demonstration of the power of the people, the agent for Mr. Fortescue (Mr. Johnson) broke off the coalition, and the three candidates rested upon their individual resources.

In this state of things, Mr. Sheil, who was counsel for Mr. Dawson, applied to Mr. Johnson, as agent for Mr. Fortescue, and offered to give him a certain number of votes, upon condition that Mr. Fortescue should co-operate with the popular party in throwing Mr. Foster out; but Mr. Johnson, confident at the time that Lord Roden's interest was paramount, declined to accede to a proposition which it is probable his employer would have regarded as unworthy of him. Mr. Fortescue was, however, outwitted by Leslie Foster; for the coalition of the first days threw so many additional votes into the scale, as enabled him, ultimately, though only by a very small majority, to defeat his incautious and unskilful auxiliary.

Some time elapsed before any decided demonstrations of superiority took place; and the exertions of all parties were prodigious. Emissaries were despatched night and day through every part of the county, and no means of persuasion were spared by the Catholic, or of terror by the Protestant faction, to bring the freeholders in. Priests and attorneys were seen scouring the country in all directions, and landlords and drivers, armed with warrants of distress, knocked at the door of every hovel. The spirit of exertion which animated the contending parties extended itself to the counsel, and Mr. North (the brother-in-law of Mr. Foster), Mr. Murray, who was employed by Mr. Fortescue, and Mr. Sheil, who acted for

Mr. Dawson, in the High Sheriff's booth, exhibited a zeal and alacrity which a mere professional sympathy with their clients could scarcely have supplied.

The Sheriff's booth was in a small room adjoining the County-court, and offered, through the iron bars of its single window on the ground-floor, a dismal spectacle. A wall, at the distance of about four feet from this window, rises to a considerable height, and forms a small quadrangular space, covered with rank grass and broken stones, in which the murderers at Wildgoose Lodge are buried. In intervals of leisure, the eyes of the persons, whose business it was to remain in this room, would involuntarily rest upon this spot, and the conversation turned from the subject of the election to the terrible atrocity of which that dreary piece of ground was the memorial. The meditations which it supplied were, however, of brief duration, for a question connected with a vote would arise to dissolve them.

As the election proceeded, the anxieties of Mr. Foster augmented. He seemed to lose all command and self-possession. He would rush into the Sheriff's booth with a precipitate vehemence, which was the more remarkable from the contrast which it formed with his usual systematic and well-ordered behavior. "Soldiers!" he would cry, "soldiers, Mr. High-Sheriff! I call upon you to bring out troops, to protect me and my supporters. My life is in peril — my brother has just been assailed — we shall be massacred, if you persevere in excluding troops from the town!" Such were the exclamations he would utter, under the influence of mingled anger and alarm; for I believe that his fears, though utterly unfounded, were sincere. To these appeals the friends of Mr. Dawson would oppose equally vehement adjurations. "What! call out troops! bayonet the people! No, Mr. Foster; the scenes of 1798 are not returned; the Sheriff will not be deluded by the phantoms which issue from your over-excited imagination, or accede to your sanguinary invocations."

The High-Sheriff was placed in a very embarrassing condition in the midst of this uproar of remonstrance. It was said that his leanings were personally favorable to Mr. Foster; but he is a brewer of the famous Castlebellingham ale, and the interests of his brewery being at variance with his political predilections (if he have any), he was kept in a state of painful hesitation, until Mr. Chaigneau, who acted with the utmost impartiality as Assessor, resolved his difficulties, by very properly stating, that when evidence of danger should be laid before the Sheriff upon oath, he would act upon it. The town remained perfectly peaceable. There were, indeed, loud cries and vehement shoutings, but no personal molestation was offered to anybody. A perpetual procession of fiddlers and fife-players moved through the streets, who played no other air than "Nancy Dawson" from morning until twelve at night.

At the head of this body of everlasting minstrels were two singular persons, who carried large banners of green silk, with national emblems and mottoes figured upon them. One of these strange individuals was a doctor—a large, bloated, plethoric mass of a man, dressed in old rusty black, covered with snuff, with a protuberant belly, and a short, waddling gait, which a quantity of matutinal potations had rendered exceedingly unsteady; while his countenance, composed of large blotches of orbicular red, with a pair of large glazed eyes, surmounted by white shaggy eyebrows, confirmed the conjectures which the irregularity of his movements suggested. The doctor carried the Dawson standard, having two or three stout fellows to co-operate in his sustainment. When he arrived at the end of the street, in turning round to direct the procession, of which he was the chief leader, the doctor would utter a loud but inarticulate shout, and return toward the courthouse; and when he had arrived there, he would again wheel about at the head of the multitude with a similar hurrah. Thus, he traversed, from morning till sunset, the principal street of the town, taking a glass of Irish restorative at brief intervals in these strange perambulations.

Next in command to the doctor was old Harry Mills, whose fame has since travelled across the Atlantic, and who has not only had his health drunk in America, but has received a subscription of twenty pounds from the New World. This peasant was among the most conspicuous figures at the Louth election. He had about four acres of land, for which he paid a high rent to his landlord; and although he completely depended on him, this "village Hampden," as he was called, withstood the petty despotism of Mr. Woulfe M'Neil, and voted in despite of him for Mr. Dawson. Harry Mills had gone through many a wild adventure. He had been concerned in the affair of 1798, and was obliged to fly the country; but, as he said himself, he had the consolation of seeing an Orangeman's house on fire upon the shore, as he was sailing in a fishing-boat from the port of Dundalk. "Please your honor," Harry used to say, "as I was leaving ould Ireland, I saw the flames blazing out of the Cromwellian's house; and many a time, when I was keeping watch on the coast of Guinea, I used to think of that same fire." Harry was obliged to turn seaman, and became a sailor in a slave-ship. He was taken by a French privateer; and I do not recollect exactly how he contrived, after years had passed, to get back to Ireland. His spirit slumbered within him until the Louth election, and then it broke forth, like the flame from the Orangeman's house, which had ministered with its flashes to his retrospective consolations. With that ocean-look and attitude which belong to all seafaring people, Harry blended the sly cunning and observant sagacity which characterize the Irish peasant, and offered, to a lover of the moral picturesque, one of the most striking objects at the Louth election. He marched, in company with the doctor, as second standard-bearer to Mr. Dawson, and was as unwearied as his brother patriot in this his new, and, if we could judge from his shouts and exclamations, his delightful vocation.

But in drawing the figures and detailing the incidents by which Mr. Foster was surrounded, I allow him, perhaps, to leave the foreground of the picture. As the election advanced, his fears augmented, and he presented new phenomena of terror. His opponents felt a malevolent pleasure in watching the torture which he was undergoing, and in observing the writhings of the mind, which were apparent in his demeanor and countenance. But Alexander Dawson had in a few days ceased to be the immediate object of his competition; for the latter having obtained a vast majority, his return was no longer matter of speculation, and the fiercest contest was carried on between the Roden and the Oriel candidates, who had originally entered in alliance into the field. Though they agreed in all political opinions, they afforded proof of the promptitude with which abstract questions are lost in individual interests. The Catholics had carried Mr. Dawson's election, and Mr. Foster and his friends used all their efforts to induce them to remain neutral; observing that Mr. Foster (which was a just remark) was not personally obnoxious, that he was a good landlord, and that Lord Roden's candidate was not only politically but fanatically opposed to them.

These arguments had their weight with the liberal party; although the more sagacious saw that it would be a consummation of their victory, if they could eject from the House of Commons an individual who had contributed some talent and a great deal of research and industry to the maintenance of his party. Still, the antipathy to Lord Roden prevailed: and the detestation in which his wild, lugubrious doctrines were held; the recollection of his having refused a small piece of ground to erect a more commodious house of Catholic worship; his penurious piety; his omission, with all his ostentatious Christianity, to subscribe to a single charitable institution at Dundalk; and other circumstances of a similar character—made the majority of the people rather inclined toward Leslie Foster than to the candidate by which the Roden interest was represented. Mr. Fortescue had now abundant reason to regret the fastidious spirit with which a tender of Catholic support had been originally rejected.

Almost all the county had been polled out, and then, but when it was too late, it was communicated to the Catholics, but not through the ostensible agent of Mr. Fortescue, that their assistance was necessary to throw Mr. Foster out. Had this application been made the day before, the Catholics, who were three hundred ahead of the Protestant candidates, might have interfered with effect. Their committee refused to act; but individuals took upon themselves to gather as many straggling freeholders as could be collected. It is a rule that, after a certain number of days, if twenty persons do not poll before six o'clock, the booth where this deficiency takes place shall close. Every booth, excepting one, was shut about four o'clock; and if the Roden party could contrive to poll twenty before six, they would have been entitled to hold the booth open. They calculated that on the next day they could bring in enough of voters to obtain a majority, with the aid of such of the Catholics as did not hate Lord Roden less, but dreaded Leslie Foster more, and on that principle were doing their utmost to throw him out of Parliament. About four o'clock, Leslie Foster had a majority of nine or ten, and I believe all his votes were exhausted. Some twelve or thirteen persons had polled in the booth in question; and if Mr. Fortescue could procure so many persons merely to poll, as would, with the votes already given, make up twenty, his object would have been secured. The issue of the contest, therefore, depended upon minutes.

The booth presented a most singular scene. It was crowded to excess, from the condensation of the public interests within its narrow limits. Scarcely space enough was left for the admission of the voters; and, indeed, it was the object of the Foster faction to retard and obstruct their arrival by every possible expedient. In order to consume time, fellows were put up on Mr. Foster's tallies who had no votes; and their rejection, and the clamor and confusion which it produced, served to consume the hour, of which every instant was of value. Mr. Fortescue's party still contrived to poll a few freeholders, who were supplied by the Catholics; and it was matter of great doubt whether the important and decisive number "twenty" could be produced. After five o'clock, the suspense of all parties became increased, and every eye was alternately turned to the spot where the freeholders were polled, and to the watches which were held in the hands of the spectators, and which indicated the progress of time to that point on which the issue was to hang. I never saw a deeper expression of solicitude. Mr. Fortescue himself was not there, as he was confined by the gout; but his partisans showed an anxiety as great as if personally engaged by individual interest in the event.

The friends of Mr. Foster, who were gathered round the Sheriff, manifested, if possible, a still greater intentness of expectation. George Pentland, who had been long solicitor to the customhouse, of which Mr. Foster was, since 1818, the counsel, acted as his agent, with an alacrity which inveterate habits of professional sympathy had naturally produced. Many reciprocal obligations had endeared the counsel and the attorney to each other; and it would be difficult, perhaps, to adjust the balance of gratitude, and to determine on which side the golden scale ought to incline. Certain it is that Mr. Pentland exhibited upon this occasion, for a gentleman who was alternately his patron and his *protegé*, the most ardent sympathy. During the earlier period of the election, George had preserved that spirit of coaxing good-humor, and of humbug urbanity, which belongs to the good old school of Irish pensioners and placemen. "Oh, my good friend," George used to say (laying his customhouse gripe upon your shoulder, and refusing you a permit to pass), "you little know Leslie Foster. Mind what I say, and I have an eye in my head, Leslie will be found voting for you yet—mind"—(and then he would let loose your shoulder, while he placed his forefinger on the tip of his nose, and winked sagaciously at you)—"mind what I say—but I say nothing—mum's the word!" But George laid aside all his intimations, whether verbal, physiognomical, ocular, or nasal, as the fatal hour of six drew on; and with eyes glaring with expectation, and his brows raised in Saxon arches on his forehead, he sat waiting the eventful instant. Near him stood Mr. North, whose naturally sweet and placid countenance, without exhibiting the fierceness of faction, assumed for a moment an aspect of acerbity, while his lips, that were as white as ashes, trembled and quivered in the expression of the few words to which he occasionally gave utterance.

But where was Leslie Foster all this time? This question, which the reader will probably ask, I put to myself; and, on turning my eyes round, I was at first at a loss to discover him. At length I observed a person sitting in a remote corner of the room, upon a chair which was thrown back in such a way that it was balanced on two legs, while the head of the somewhat round and squat gentleman by whom it was occupied leaned against the wall. His hat was drawn over his brows, and his eyes were closed. His cheeks, which seemed to have been originally full and plentiful, appeared to have suffered a cadaverous collapse. Thick drops of perspiration trickled down his visage, which he occasionally wiped away with an Orange handkerchief held in his right hand; while a watch, on which, however, he did not look, was in the other. I did not at first recognise this extraordinary figure; but upon a sudden it started up, and on the opening of the eyes, and the full disclosure of the countenance, I thought I could perceive some faint resemblance to Leslie Foster. He seemed, at first, to stand in an attitude of cataleptic horror; and when he recovered himself, he clasped his hands, and, unable to sustain his agony, rushed with a frantic speed out of the room. He had given everything up for lost; but he was mistaken. The twenty votes had not been made up. The clock struck six, and John Leslie Foster was saved from being buried by torchlight [as a suicide], under the new act of Parliament, in the churchyard of Dundalk.

Mr. Dawson and Mr. Foster were returned as duly elected. The latter did not attend at the hustings when the event of the election was proclaimed. He set off for Cullen, the seat of Lord Oriel, in that heaving and agitation of mind which the stormy passions leave behind, after the immediate occasion of their excitement has ceased to act. His flight was considered as most inglorious, and it was boasted by the Catholic orators that he did not dare to meet them. This was a great disappointment to Mr. Sheil and other dealers in harangue, who expected to show off at his expense. He very wisely effected his retreat to his uncle's (the late Lord Oriel's) residence, whose octogenarian philosophy did not prevent him from feeling a deep and corroding interest in the event. Had Mr. Foster remained sequestered in the beautiful woods which the Speaker of the Irish House of Commons lived to see rise about him, he would have acted wisely.* But, after a short interval, the

* When the Union was passed, John Foster was Speaker of the House of Commons. He was Mr. Leslie Foster's uncle, and was raised to the peerage,

public were astonished by a resentful lucubration from his pen, in which he vilified the proceedings of the Catholics, and inveighed with great virulence against the priests. If ever he stands for the county of Louth again, which is very improbable, this document will be brought in judgment against him.

He was guilty of another indiscretion, or rather a piece of bad taste, as it was far more deserving of laughter than of condemnation. Having fled from Dundalk, where Mr. Dawson was chaired, he caused himself to be put through a similar

by the title of Lord Oriel.—I have so repeatedly had occasion to refer to the creation of peers, that it may not be out of place to say something about the cost ("surget amari aliquid"), which is considerable and is defrayed by the person who receives the elevation, except when the dignity is conferred for public services, when the amount is paid out of the sum granted by Parliament for Civil Contingencies. In 1853, on the motion of Mr. Hume, who always desires to know how the public money is expended, a Parliamentary return was printed, of the persons to whom, and for what services, the sum of four hundred and twenty pounds sterling, charged in the Civil Contingencies for 1852, was paid, and the names of the several persons receiving the same for the patent creating General Lord Fitzroy Somerset a baron of the United Kingdom. He had been Military Secretary, for a long period, to the Duke of Wellington when Commander-in-chief, and, on the Duke's death, in September, 1852, was appointed Master-General of the Ordnance, and called to the Upper House as Baron Raglan. It appears, by the official return, that, in the expenses of his patent of nobility, the crown-office charges amounted to £390, 15*s.* 4*d.*; and the authority for the same is stated "ancient usages." Of that sum, £150, 2*s.* went to the Stamp-office; £104, 6*s.* 10*d.* to the royal household. Some of the items are curious. The payment to the Lord Chancellor, Great Seal fee, is £2, 6*s.* 8*d.*; the clerk of the Hanaper, has £24, 13*s.* 4*d.*; the deputy, £1, 1*s.*; the Lord-Chancellor's purse-bearer, has £5, 5*s.*; the porter to the Great Seal, £1, 1*s.*: gentlemen to ditto, £6; sealer, £1, 2*s.* 6*d.*; deputy ditto, 10*s.* 6*d.* Chuffwax, £1, 2*s.* 2*d.*; deputy ditto, 10*s.* 6*d.*; principal Usher of Scotland, £6, 13*s.* 6*d.*; Scotch heralds, £16; English ditto, £36; Earl-Marshal, £5; Garter-King-at-Arms, £20; and the gold-emblazoned skin and boxes to hold the patent and seal, cost £9. The Patent-office charges amounted to £29, 18*s.* 6*d.* By the Attorney-General, £20, for approving, settling, and signing the Queen's warrant for Her Majesty's signature, according to "ancient usage." By the clerk of the Patents, to the Attorney-General, £7, 7*s.* 6*d.*, by ancient usage, and £1, 10*s.* stamp duty on warrant. By the engrossing clerk, £1, 1*s.*, for engrossing the warrant and for parchment. In this manner £420 was expended in the creation of a baron of the United Kingdom. The higher the rank conferred, the heavier the charges. It is understood that the cost of a Duke's patent is nearly four thousand pounds sterling.—M.

honor in his uncle's demesne. All the vassals and retainers of Lord Oriel, who could be procured, were collected together, and Mr. Foster having been placed upon the shoulders of four stout Protestant tenants, was conveyed through the village of Cullen, amid the plaudits of the yeomanry, the hurrahs of the schoolmaster, the sexton, and the parish-clerk, and the acclamations of the police.

I have hitherto considered Mr. Foster as a candidate, and I should give an equally minute account of him as a member of Parliament, but that I have not had the same fortunate opportunities of observation. I do, indeed, remember an incident, which may be considered, to a certain extent, illustrative of his influence as a legislative speaker; and, in the lack of any other means of describing him, it may not be inappropriate to set it down.

I was under the gallery of the House of Commons during the debate on the Catholic question, in the year 1825. The House was exceedingly full. Mr. Foster rose to speak, and the effect of his appearance on his legs was truly wonderful. In an instant the House was cleared. The rush to the door leading to the tavern up stairs, where the members find a refuge from the soporific powers of their brother-legislators, was tremendous. I was myself swept away by the torrent, and carried from my place by the crowd, that fled from the solemn adjuration with which Mr. Foster commenced his oration. The single phrase "Mr. Speaker" was indeed uttered with such a tone as indicated the extent of the impending evil; and finding already the influence of drowsiness upon me, I followed the example which was given by the representatives of the people, who, whatever differences may have existed among them upon the mode of settling Ireland, appeared to coincide in their estimate of Mr. Foster's elocution. From the Treasury benches, the opposition and the neutral quarters of the House, a simultaneous concourse hurried up to Bellamy's, and left Mr. Foster in full possession of that solitude which he had thus instantaneously and miraculously produced.

I proceeded up stairs with some hundreds of honorable gentlemen. The scene which Bellamy's presents to a stranger is striking enough. Two smart girls, whose briskness and neat attire made up for their want of beauty, and for the invasions of time, of which their cheeks showed the traces, helped out tea in a room in the corridor. It was pleasant to observe the sons of Dukes and Marquises,* and the possessors of twenties and thirties of thousands a year, gathered round these damsels, and soliciting a cup of that beverage which it was their office to administer. These Bellamy bar-maids seemed so familiarized with their occupation, that they went through it with

* The sons of the nobility are eligible to sit in the House of Commons, though it is an anomaly for persons belonging to the Aristocracy, by feeling and interest, as well as by birth, to be nominal representatives of the People. Irish peers may also be members of the House of Commons — but not for an Irish county or borough. Thus Earl Annesley represents Great Grimsby, in Lincolnshire, and Viscount Palmerston is member for Tiverton, in Devonshire. The eldest sons of Dukes, Marquises, and Earls, bear, by courtesy, the second titles of their fathers. Thus the Duke of Leinster's eldest son is called Marquis of Kildare: the Marquis of Westminster's is Earl of Grosvenor: the Earl of Lichfield's is Viscount Anson. In some few cases, the holder of a peerage has not also received the rank immediately below his own. Thus, the Duke of Manchester's second title is only Viscount Mandeville. The issue of junior children of Dukes, Marquises, and Earls, have respectively the title of "Lord" or "Lady" prefixed to their name — so we have Lord John Russell, Lady Blanche Gower. The eldest son of a Viscount or a Baron is plainly "The Honorable"— thus, Viscount Strangford's eldest son is "The Honorable George Smythe," and his brothers and sisters would be entitled to the same prefix, which is confined only to the nobility — not even a Baronet being entitled to it. A member of Parliament, spoken of *in* Parliament as "the honorable member for so-and-so," has no distinctive appellation *out* of it. Therefore we have plain Mr. Cobden; but when a man is a Privy Councillor, he has a permanent title — such as "The Right Honorable Benjamin Disraeli." Every peer is "right honorable." Courtesy titles are not recognised by law. Thus, if the late Duke of Wellington's eldest son, or the Duke of Bedford's brother were to be named in the *London Gazette*, as having obtained any appointment, the description would be "the honorable Arthur Wellesley, commonly called Marquis of Douro," or "the honorable John Russell, commonly called Lord John Russell."— The House of Commons consists of 658 members, and I find, on carefully going over the list, that 228 of these belong to the nobility by birth or marriage. That is, more than one third of the representatives of the *Commons* of the United Kingdom actually are members of the *Aristocracy*, the natural opponents of popular privileges and rights. The eventual remedy will be, to effect a reform by which peers' sons shall be disqualified from sitting in the Commons House of Parliament.— M.

perfect nonchalance, and would occasionally turn with petulance, in which they asserted the superiority of their sex to rank and opulence, from the noble or wealthy suitors for a draught of tea, by whom they were surrounded. The unfortunate Irish members were treated with a peculiar disdain, and were reminded of their provinciality by the look of these Parliamentary Hebes, who treated them as mere colonial deputies should be received in the purlieus of the state.

I passed from these ante-chambers to the tavern, where I found a number of members assembled at dinner. Half an hour had passed away, toothpicks and claret were now beginning to appear, and the business of mastication being concluded, that of digestion had commenced, and many an honorable gentleman, I observed, who seemed to prove that he was born only to digest. At the end of a long corridor, which opened from the room where the diners were assembled, there stood a waiter whose office it was to inform any interrogator what gentleman was speaking below stairs. Nearly opposite the door sat two English county members. They had disposed of a bottle each, and, just as the last glass was emptied, one of them called out to the annunciator at the end of the passage for intelligence. "Mr. Foster on his legs!" was the formidable answer. "Waiter, bring another bottle!" was the immediate effect of this information, which was followed by a similar injunction from every table in the room. I perceived that Mr. Bellamy owed great obligations to Mr. Foster. But the latter did not limit himself to a second bottle; again and again the same question was asked, and again the same announcement returned—"Mr. Foster upon his legs!" The answer seemed to fasten men in inseparable adhesiveness to their seats. Thus two hours went by—when, at length, "Mr. Plunket on his legs," was heard from the end of the passage, and the whole convocation of compotators rose together and returned to the House.

Some estimate of the eloquence of Mr. Foster may be formed from this evidence of its effects. I am unable myself to supply, from personal observation, any better detail of it. But it is not necessary: Mr. Plunket, in a single phrase, has described his legislative faculties, and on the night of which I have been speaking remarked that "he had turned history into an old almanac." I should not omit to mention, in justice to Mr. Foster, that in converting the annals of mankind to this valuable purpose, he exhibits a wonderful diligence. His speeches are the result of great industry, and he takes care not to deliver himself of any crude, abortive notions, such as are thrown off in extempore debate; but, after allowing his meditations to mature in a due process of conception in his mind, brings them forth with a laborious effort, and presents his intellectual offspring to the House in the "swaddling" phraseology in which they are always carefully wrapped up.

It was, indeed, at one time believed and studiously propagated by his friends, that he did not prepare his orations, and that he poured out his useless erudition, and his mystical dogmas, without premeditation or research. That erroneous conjecture has been recently corrected; for, upon a late occasion, when the Chaplain of the House of Commons was reading prayers, at four o'clock, Mr. Foster, who appeared to those at a distance to be kneeling in a posture of profound Parliamentary piety, with his hands raised, as is the fashion with the devout, to his lips, was heard to mutter through his fingers: "Had it been my good fortune, Mr. Speaker, to have caught your eye at an earlier period of the debate, I should have gone more at length, than I now, at this late hour of the night, intend to do, into the details of a question, upon which the integrity of the constitution, the sacred privileges of the Protestants of Ireland, and the purity of the reformed religion, entirely depend." Mr. Richard Martin, the then member for Connamara, who happened to hear Mr. Foster, communicated this important discovery; and it is now well ascertained that Mr. Foster takes exceedingly great if not very meritorious pains at his oratorical laboratory, and passes many a midnight vigil in compounding those opiates with which, at the expense of his own slumbers, he lulls the House of Commons to repose.

Mr. Foster may be considered in the various phases of barrister, scholar, commissioner of education, and counsel to the commissioners of customs and excise.* As a member of the bar, he is not very remarkable. He is not in considerable business, which I am inclined to attribute to his dedication of himself to political pursuits; for he came to the profession under great advantages, having industry, a tenacious memory, and the patronage of the late Chief-Justice Downes. I think that he would have succeeded in the Court of Chancery, had he attended exclusively to the bar; for certainly he is not destitute of the powers of clear reasoning and perspicuous exposition. His great fault is, that he diffuses an air of importance over all that he says, looks, and does, which is not unfrequently in ludicrous contrast with the matter before him. Instead of speaking trippingly upon the tongue, he loads his utterance

* John Leslie Foster was grandson of Chief Baron Foster, son of Dr. Foster, Bishop of Clogher (who died in 1787), and nephew to John Foster, Speaker of the Irish House of Commons, who was raised to the peerage as Lord Oriel. Without doubt, Mr. Leslie Foster took double pains to become a lawyer, for though called to the Irish bar in 1803, he had previously been admitted, by the Society of Lincoln's Inn, in London, to the English bar also. In 1804, he published a book "On the Principles of Commercial Exchanges." He was industrious, besides being connected with the nobility by relationship and marriage, and got on in his profession. He was successively appointed Commissioner of Education (salary twelve hundred pounds sterling a year) and counsel to the Commissioners of Customs and Excise — the average annual income of which, from 1818, when he entered into the office, until 1828 (when he received as "compensation," two thousand pounds sterling for life) was three thousand seven hundred and thirty pounds sterling. Therefore these two appointments, the duties of which were neither onerous nor troublesome, gave him about five thousand pounds sterling a year, besides the collateral business coming to him, from the position he had thus obtained; whatever other phenomenon marked his birth, Leslie Foster did not come into the world with a wooden spoon in his mouth. His politics were intensely Tory, and recommended him to Trinity College, Dublin, as a "marvellous proper man" to represent its intolerance in Parliament. His maiden speech was delivered in April, 1812, in opposition to Grattan's motion against the Penal Laws, and he published it in a pamphlet. In Parliament, from first to last, he was consistent — in resisting liberal measures, no matter by whom introduced. In July, 1830, the Duke of Wellington made him one of the Barons of the Court of Exchequer in Ireland. He was a laborious judge, and little more can be said of him in that capacity. In 1842, he was transferred to the Court of Common Pleas. He went the summer Assize, in 1842, and dined, apparently in good health, with the Sheriff and Magistrates at Cavan, but was suddenly taken ill, had time to execute a codicil to his will, and expired, July 10, 1842. He died immensely rich.— M.

with an immense weight of intonation, and is not more ponderous and oracular in Parliament than at the bar. That gravity, which Rochefoucauld has so well called "a mystery of the body," pervades his gesture, and sits in eternal repose upon his countenance. He advances to his seat, at the inner bar, like a priest walking in a procession; he lays down his bag upon the green table as if he were depositing a treasure; he bows to the court like a mandarin before the Emperor of China; quotes Tidd's Practice as a Rabbi would read the Talmud; and opens the "Rules and Orders" as a sorcerer would unclasp a book of incantation.

The solemnity which distinguishes him in Court, attends him out of it. He traverses the Hall with a gait and aspect of mystical meditation; and when he has divested himself of his forensic habiliments, still takes care to retain his walk of egregious dignity upon his return to Merrion-square. Mr. Foster has ascertained, with exact precision, the distance from his house to the Hall of the Four Courts; and has counted the number of paces which it is requisite that he should perform, whether he should go through College Green or by any of the lanes at the back of Dublin Castle. Both these ways have their attractions. In the centre of College Green stands the statue of King William, on which Mr. Foster sometimes pauses to cast a look, in which, of late, some melancholy has been observed. The purlieus of the Castle are, however, his more favorite, and perhaps appropriate walks, especially since the order for Lord Anglesey's removal has arrived.* But, which-

* The Marquis of Anglesey, who was born in 1768, was eldest son of the late Earl of Uxbridge, and, after studying at Oxford, was appointed, in 1793, when Lord Paget, to the command of a regiment he had raised among his father's tenantry. He served with this corps, under the Duke of York, in Flanders, and again in the expedition to Holland, in 1799. He had risen to the rank of Major-General when he joined Sir John Moore's army in the Peninsula, and assisted in the retreat of Corunna, and the battle there, January 16, 1809, where Moore was killed. He was married, in 1795, to a daughter of the Earl of Jersey, by whom he had eight children, but, soon after his return from Portugal figured as defendant in a crim. con. suit, in which the plaintiff was Mr. Henry Wellesley (brother to "The Duke," and created Lord Cowley, in 1828), who obtained twenty thousand pounds sterling, damages. The result was a double divorce: Lady Paget from him (she afterward married the

ever route he adopts, he never deviates from that evenness and regularity of gait with which he originally enumerated the number of paces from his residence to the Hall.

I was a good deal at a loss to account for this peculiar demeanor, until I had heard that Mr. Foster had spent some time at Constantinople. He was introduced, upon one occasion, to the Grand Seignior (a scene which he describes with great particularity), and has ever since retained an expression of dignity, which it is supposed he copied from the Reis Effendi,

late Duke of Argyll), and Mr. Wellesley from his guilty wife, *née* Lady Charlotte Cadogan. Lord Paget married the frail fair, in 1810, and they had a large family; two of their sons are members of the British House of Commons now [1854].—The trial and its revelations, gave much unenviable notoriety to Lord Paget. He was alluded to by Byron, in the line,

"And, worse of all, a Paget for your wife.

and Moore (albeit *Little* of a moralist), thus had his fling in a didactic poem, called "The Skeptic, a philosophical satire:"—

"Paget, who sees, upon his pillow laid,
A face for which ten thousand pounds were paid,
Can tell how quick, before a jury, flies
The spell that mocked the warm seducer's eyes."

Many years subsequently, when he had become viceroy, the Irish ladies declined visiting his wife, and having caused the arrest of O'Connell, on a charge of seditious language, the orator, in another speech, said, "He has caused my wife to weep. Does he know the value of a *virtuous* woman's tear?" —In 1812, Lord Paget succeeded his father, as Earl of Uxbridge. He had a cavalry command at Waterloo, and having there lost a leg, was created Marquis of Anglesey. In 1820, he voted for the bill of pains and penalties against Queen Caroline. In February, 1828, "The Duke," who had just became Premier, sent him to Ireland, as Viceroy, and his conduct there was generally impartial. But in December, 1828, having received a letter from Dr. Curtis (the Catholic Primate), which the Duke of Wellington had written to him, suggesting that the Catholic claims be "buried in oblivion" for a time, Lord Anglesey wrote back an epistle, which was published, recommending the continued agitation of the question. This gave great offence to George IV., who had become tired of eternal discussions on Catholic wrongs, and the writer was recalled. Two months after, the final settlement of the question was recommended in the King's Speech, at the commencement of the Parliamentary Session. Soon after, he was again made Viceroy of Ireland, and so continued until September, 1833. But his latter reign was not popular. He has held other high offices, connected with the army, and is the senior Field Marshal in the British army. He is now (January, 1854) in his eighty-sixth year.—M.

if not from the Sultan himself. Hitherto the negotiations with the Porte have been unsuccessful. If Mr. Foster were sent out as our minister, such a sympathetic solemnity would take place between him and the Grand Vizier, that many difficulties would, it is likely, be got rid of; and he would, by his Asiatic diplomacy of countenance and his Oriental gravity of look, accomplish far more than Lord Strangford* was able to effect.

As a scholar, Mr. Leslie Foster is, beyond all doubt, a person of very various and minute erudition. In every drawing-room and at every dinner-table at which he appears, amazement is produced by the vastness of his knowledge; and undergraduates from the College, and young ladies whose stockings are but darned with blue silk, wonder that even a head of such great diameter should be capable of containing such enormous masses of the most recondite and diversified lore.† The President of the Royal Academy of Laputa, or the father of Martinus Scriblerus, could not have surpassed him in the character, the extent, and the application of his knowledge. No matter what topics may be presented in the trivialities of discourse, he avails himself of every opportunity to evacuate his erudition. He buries every petty subject under the enormity of his learning, and piles a mountain on every pigmy theme. If he finds a boy whipping a top, he stops to explain the principles upon which it is put into motion. He is versed in all points of science connected with the playing of marbles. Should a pair of bellows fall in his way, he enters into a dis-

* Viscount Strangford, in the Irish, and Baron Penshurst, in the British peerage, distinguished himself nearly half a century ago, as the translator of Camoens, the Portuguese poet. For this, he was duly niched and pedestaled by Byron, in "*English Bards and Scotch Reviewers.*" He was born in 1780, and is yet alive [1854]; he has been Ambassador to Turkey, Russia, &c.—His son, Mr. Smythe, formerly M. P. for Canterbury, has written some pretty verses, is a good speaker, and, when in Parliament, was a leader of the Young England party.—M.

† If the quantity of brains be estimated by the size of the skull, Mr. Leslie Foster ought to have been a very clever man. His head was large, out of all proportion, and had a curious oscillating motion, more peculiar than graceful —something like the vibration of a Chinese Mandarin's image in a grocer's window.—M.

sertation upon the structure of the human lungs; and applies to those domestic conveniences of which there is such a want in the modern Athens, his learning in hydraulics.* In short,

* Such another "Admirable Crichton" as this, was to be found, a few years ago, in the person of the late Egerton Smith, for many years editor of *The Liverpool Mercury*, in England. He commenced life as a spectacle-maker, but had small skill in that craft, and took to the press. He sprinkled his articles with Greek and Latin sentences, rarely applicable to the subject, and apparently taken, at hap-hazard from some Dictionary of Quotations. In a previous work of mine, his character is sketched in full, and I take leave to reproduce it here. —"He bore the rather uncommon patronymic of SMITH. In his newspaper he was chiefly distinguished by reason of the number of hobbies which he rode. His original occupation of optician gave him a certain mechanical facility in making toys—puzzles for the curious and the idle. Asserting that he was one of the best swimmers in the world, his delight was to exhibit himself in the Mersey, floundering like a porpoise, and confident that the feats of Leander and Byron were trifling in comparison with his own. Avowing the most philanthropic motives, he invented cork-jackets to prevent death by drowning, and —sold them at a large profit. He contended that the boomerang of New South Wales was a weapon worthy of being universally adopted in European warfare, aud spent a whole summer in throwing this projectile into the air, to ascertain its force, and perfect his own skill. But the triumph of his experiments and discoveries in science, and that on which he chiefly prided himself, was to show that a top (such as children of a lesser growth are accustomed to whip, in play), might be kept spinning for half an hour upon a china plate. During a series of years, he kept this subject before the public, in his newspaper, devoting columns to its elucidations, and adorning them with diagrams and woodcuts, showing the course of the spinning top, with portraits of that new instrument of science. In his newspaper, also, were given views of the cork-jackets, and sketches of the boomerang. There, too, were occasionally exhibited sketches of himself in the Mersey—floating, swimming, or trying to perform some such notable aquatic feat. For a long series of years—certainly exceeding thirty—half a column a week was dedicated, by this illustrious obscure, to himself, his notions, and his hobbies. So strongly did he exhibit the spirit of egotism in these articles, that it was frequently remarked, that his biography might easily be compiled from the personal references to himself and his movements in the "Notices to Correspondents." On one occasion he announced, that having charitably lent an old umbrella to a strange lady, in a shower of rain, she actually had the dishonesty not to return it, and during many successive weeks, he poured out lamentations on his loss, describing the aspect of the article, the attire of the non-returning borrower, and amusing the public with his griefs over the missing umbrella,

"'Like the lost Plëiad, seen no more below.'

Nor were his personal confidences limited to his newspaper. Thence they were transferred to a cheap literary weakling which he also published, and

he is omniscient; and if I were a believer in the transmigration of souls, I should be disposed to think that the spirit of the professor at Bruges, who challenged all mankind to dispute with him "*de omni scibili et de quolibet ente*," had reappeared in his person; though I hope that he would be less puzzled in solving the question of law proposed by Sir Thomas More to that celebrated scholar respecting a replevin.*

finally found a resting-place in a monthly octavo composed of the picked matter of his newspaper and periodical. Meddling with Cobbett, in an attempt at political discussion, he incurred the anger of that nervous writer, who forthwith registered him as 'Bot Smith,' by which appellation, constantly repeated by him of the Gridiron, he eventually became so well known, in and out of Liverpool, that it was taken to be his true name, and letters were frequently so addressed to him. In a word, his case affords a striking example of the very small degree of intelligence sufficient to establish a local reputation as a 'triton of the minnows.' In a metropolis such a person would have speedily found his level, beneath the feet of real merit. When he died, about the year 1841, his townsmen gave him the honor of a public funeral, and I have heard that they placed his statue in their Mechanics' Institute! As the palette of Wilkie was let into the pedestal of his statue in the National Gallery, in London, a spinning-top and china-plate should have been introduced into the Smith statue at Liverpool. When the Pickwick Papers introduced the clever and striking full-length of Mr. Pott, Editor of the Eatanswill Gazette, many persons in Liverpool fancied that independent of the name being suggestive of the *soubriquet* bestowed on him by Cobbett, the original could have been no other than their own philosopher of the spinning-top. The appearance—'a tall, thin man, with a sandy-colored head inclined to baldness, and a face in which solemn importance was blended, with a look of unfathomable profundity;' the invariable attire—'a long brown surtout, with a black cloth waistcoat, and drab trousers;' the constant reference in conversation, to articles which he had written in his newspaper on local politics, the interest of which, trifling at any time, had long since passed away; the ruling idea, that throughout the country in general, and in London in particular, there was an intense excitement caused by whatever *he* wrote; the constant and uncourteous abuse of all opposing journalists; and, to crown all, the triumphant boast that his critic had written on Chinese Metaphysics by reading in the Encyclopedia under C for China, and under M for Metaphysics, and 'had combined his information,'—if all these coincidences were accidental, then, at hap-hazard, did Mr. Dickens unconsciously exhibit a person and an idiosyncracy remarkably like those of Mr. Bot Smith."—M.

* Mr. Foster is deeply versed in Irish antiquities. He alleges that he discovered in the county of Kerry, a very singular building, which is called Staigne Fort. General Vallancey thought that it was a Phœnician theatre. I am not aware what conjecture Mr. Foster formed respecting it; probably he takes it

I pass, by a natural transition, from the vast acquirements of Mr. Foster, to that office which, from its connection with learning, it would appear at first view that he was admirably qualified to fill. He was, for a considerable period, a Commissioner of Education, with an enormous salary; and thus, with the sums which he has received as a Commissioner of Inquiry into the Courts of Justice, and his vast emoluments as counsel to the Commissioners of Customs and Excise, Mr. Foster has poured an immense quantity of the public money into his coffers. But, however the love of learning, and its unquestionable possession, might appear to render Mr. Foster an eligible person to investigate the progress of education, yet his predilections, both political and religious, were so strong, that the Roman Catholics considered the appointment of a person so legally orthodox, to report upon the state of their schools, as an injustice.

In order to give some aspect of fairness to this proceeding, and to create a counterpoise to his prejudices, the Government united with Mr. Foster, a gentleman in every way well adapted to encounter him, the Remembrancer of the Court of Exchequer, Mr. Blake. I believe that it was not anticipated that that gentleman would have approved himself so stout and

for an old conventicle, employed by the Irish Christians before Popery was in use. Mr. Bland, the writer of an essay in the Transactions of the Royal Irish Academy, makes the following observations upon Mr. Foster's claims to the discovery of this building: "About nine years back, Mr. Leslie Foster visited this country, and passed Staigne by unnoticed; but being prevailed on by me, he was reluctantly induced to return and see it. He afterward published, in some periodical work or newspaper, an account of it; and being ignorant, I suppose, of what I have stated, respecting Mr. Pelham's correspondence with General Vallancey, he considered himself the first discoverer of this ancient structure."—Vol. XIV. p. 22. [General Vallancey, who was born in 1721, and wrote much upon the Antiquities of Ireland, was not "a son of the sod." In his youth, when quartered in Ireland as an officer of engineers, he closely studied the language, antiquities, and topography of the island. He closely and scientifically surveyed it (for which Government gave him one thousand pounds sterling), and besides contributing to various periodicals, wrote a Grammar and Dictionary of the Irish language, "Collectanea de Rebus Hibernicis," &c. Finally, he attained the rank of General. The object of most of his Irish works was to show, I believe, that Ireland was peopled by the Phœnicians. When Vallancey died (in 1812), he was more than ninety years old.—M.]

uncompromising an asserter of the interests of his country and the honor of his religion. Mr. Foster had originally, from his previous habits of mystical research, and from his familiarity with the mysterious, great advantages over Mr. Blake, in examining the Catholic priesthood upon questions of dogmatic theology; but Mr. Blake, who has extraordinary powers of acquiring knowledge, and of fitting his mind to every intellectual occupation, resolved to make himself a match for this Aquinas of Protestantism, and threw himself off from the heights of the law into the deepest lore into which Mr. Foster had ever plunged. He rose from the dark bottoms of divinity as black and as begrimed with mysteries as his brother Commissioner; and, thus prepared, they set off upon their tour through the Catholic colleges of Ireland.

The object of Leslie Foster was to bring out whatever was unfavorable to the Irish priesthood; while Mr. Blake (himself a Roman Catholic) justly endeavored to rectify the misconstructions of his brother inquirer, and to present the doctrines of his religion, and the character of its ministers, in the least exceptionable form. When Mr. Foster got hold of a country priest, and put him to his shifts by some interrogatory touching the decrees of the earlier Councils, Mr. Blake would intervene, and rescue his fellow-Catholic from his embarrassments by suggesting a solution of the difficulty; and, without getting into it, helped him out of the deep quagmire of theology into which his examiner had led him. If Mr. Foster attempted to quote a passage from some moth eaten folio with any deviation from a just fidelity of citation, Mr. Blake would immediately detect him. Mr. Foster would rely upon the disputable ethics of some ancient Catholic schoolman; and Mr. Blake would straight produce a Protestant divine who inculcated the same doctrine. Sometimes Mr. Blake, not contented with acting on the defensive, would invade the enemy's territory; and if an ex-priest were tendered by Mr. Foster for cross-examination, the Popish Remembrancer of the Exchequer exhibited all his acumen and dexterity in exposing the renegade. A person of the name of Dickson, who had been a Catholic priest, was produced in order to vilify Maynooth, where he had received his eleemosynary education. Mr. Blake took hold of him, and, by a series of admirable interrogatories, eminently distinguished by astuteness and power of combination, laid this deserter of his altars bare, and tore off his apostate surplice.

But this was not the most remarkable instance in which Mr. Foster was foiled in his efforts to convert his office into the means of promoting his religious and political opinions. He had the misfortune to fall into the hands of the Provincial of the Jesuits in Ireland, the Rev. Mr. Kenny. A desire was, if I rightly recollect, expressed by Sir T. Lethbridge,* that a Jesuit should be produced at the bar of the House of Commons, in order that some sort of judgment should be formed of the peculiar nature of the ecclesiastical animal. Mr. Kenny is the most perfect specimen of this class of Catholic phenomena that could be produced. He wants, it must be confessed, some of the external attributes which should enter into the composition of the *beau ideal* of Jesuitism. He is by no means gracefully constructed; for there is a want of level about his shoulders, and his countenance, when uninvested with his spiritual expression, is rather of a forbidding and lurid cast. The eyes are of deep and fiery jet, and so disposed, that while one is bent in humility to the earth, the other is raised in inspiration to Heaven;—brows of thick and bushy black spread in straight lines above them. His rectilinear forehead is strongly indented with passion—satire sits upon his thin lips, and a livid hue is spread over a quadrangular face, the sunken cheeks of which exhibit the united effects of monastic abstinence and profound meditation. The countenance is Irish in its configuration; but Mr. Kenny was educated at Palermo, and a Sicilian suavity of manner is thrown, like a fine silken veil, over his strong Hibernian features. The beaming rays of his eye are seldom allowed to break out, for they are generally bent to the ground, and habitually concealed by lids, fringed with long dark lashes, which drop studiously over them.

Such is the outward Jesuit:—his talents and acquirements

* A county member of Parliament, bull-headed and intolerant, who, from the material of one of his garments, was usually called "Sir Thomas Leather-breeches."—M.

are of the first order, and in argumentative eloquence he has no superior in Ireland. Leslie Foster, in the spirit of theological chivalry, and having set up as a knight-errant against popery, happened to meet with this disciple of Loyala, and resolved to break a syllogism with him. Mr. Kenny was duly summoned to attend the Commissioners of Education, and upon this occasion the interposition of Mr. Blake was quite unnecessary. With a blended expression of affected humility and bitter mockery, the follower of Ignatius answered all Mr. Foster's questions, correcting the virulence of sarcasms by the softness of his mellifluous cadences, and by the religious clasping of his hands, which were raised in such a way as to touch the extremities of his chin, while he lamented, with a dolorous voice, the lamentable ignorance and delusion of the gentleman who could, in the nineteenth century, put him such preposterous interrogatories.

Leslie Foster was baffled by every response, and amid the jeers of his brother Commissioners, with Mr. Blake compassionating him on one side, and Mr. Glascot* nudging him at the other, while Frankland Lewis trod upon his toes, was at length persuaded to give up his desperate undertaking. Some of the questions put to the Jesuit were rather of an offensive character; and one of the Commissioners, when the examination had concluded, begged that he would make allowance for the imperious sense of duty which had induced Mr. Foster to commit an apparent violation of the canons of good breeding. "Holy Ignatius!" exclaimed the son of Loyola, holding his arms meekly upon his breast, "I am not offended — I never saw a more simple-minded gentleman in all my life!"

Mr. Foster, so far as the receipt of the public money is concerned, does not bear out the Jesuit's ejaculation. He has not proved himself exceedingly simple, by uniformly adopting that course of political conduct which was calculated to advance his personal interests and to better his fortune. I have already mentioned that he received large annual stipends from Govern-

* Toby Glascot was a sharp Dublin attorney, who sided with the then dominant Ascendency party. In 1829, he made a show of starting as a candidate, against O'Connell, after the Catholic Relief Bill was passed.— M.

ment as commissioner of education and of justice. His chief source of emolument, the fountain from which his Pactolus flows, is in the revenue of Ireland; and, I conceive that, in his instance, a very unqualified job has recently been effected, notwithstanding all the boasted cleansing of that Cloaca Maxima, the Customhouse. I put all levity aside, because, in my judgment, the expedient by which an annual sum of two thousand pounds sterling has been given to him calls for decided condemnation; and furthermore, I am of opinion, that he is bound to resign his seat in Parliament under the Irish statute passed in the thirty-third year of the late King.

Mr. Foster was appointed counsel to the Commissioners of Customs and Excise in April, 1818. He succeeded Sir Charles Ormsby, with a salary of one hundred pounds sterling a year, payable by the Board of Customs, with certain fees on each brief. The Irish Board of Customs was annihilated by the Consolidation Act, which abolished the employments held under their authority. The office held by Mr. Foster was abolished as never having been necessary or useful, and the Lords of the Treasury recognise that abolition. If Mr. Foster has lost his original appointment, and in lieu thereof the Crown retain him (is not every information in the name of the Crown, and is he not its counsel?) "to act as counsel to the Board, with a salary of £2000 a year," to be payable without any reference to the extent or even the existence of business, this is a new office under the Crown; and if it be, he must resign his seat, under the 33d of George III., cap. 41, in which it is enacted, by section 4, that, "if any member of the House of Commons shall accept any office of profit from the Crown, during such time as he shall continue a member, his seat shall thereupon become vacant, and a writ shall issue for a new election." The 41st of George III. virtually re-enacts these clauses. In that event, Harry Mills and the Doctor will again parade the streets of Dundalk; Leslie Foster will again wipe the cold exsudation from his forehead with an orange kerchief, but he will not again be carried in triumph through the woods of Cullen, amidst the applauses of the yeomanry, the hurras of the parson, the sexton, and the parish clerk, and the acclamations of the police.

THE CLARE ELECTION, IN 1828.

The Catholics had passed a resolution, at one of their aggregate meetings, to oppose the election of every candidate who should not pledge himself against the Duke of Wellington's Administration. This measure lay for some time a mere dead letter in the registry of the Association, and was gradually passing into oblivion, when an incident occurred which gave it an importance far greater than had originally belonged to it. Lord John Russell, flushed with the victory which had been achieved in the repeal of the Test and Corporation Acts,* and grateful to the Duke of Wellington for the part which he had taken, wrote a letter to Mr. O'Connell, in which he suggested that the conduct of his Grace had been so fair and manly toward the Dissenters as to entitle him to their gratitude; and that they would consider the reversal of the resolution which had been passed against his government as evidence of the interest which was felt in Ireland, not only in the great question peculiarly applicable to that country, but in the assertion of religious freedom through the empire. The authority of Lord John Russell is considerable, and Mr. O'Connell, under the influence of his advice, proposed that the anti-Wellington res-

* In February, 1828, Lord John Russell introduced a bill for the abolition of the Test and Corporation Acts (which subjected Dissenters to civil disabilities on account of their religious faith), and it passed into a law that session, chiefly in consequence of the feeble opposition offered to it by Peel, then Ministerial leader in the Commons. In truth, Peel was just then in a transition state, having seen that the old Tory system of intolerance could not continue, and scarcely knowing how to change it. Observant politicians judged, when relief was afforded to the Dissenters, that justice to the Catholics must follow: it did, in 1829.—M.

olution should be withdrawn. This motion was violently opposed, and Mr. O'Connell perceived that the antipathy to the Great Captain was more deeply rooted than he had originally imagined. After a long and tempestuous debate, he suggested an amendment, in which the principle of his original motion was given up, and the Catholics remained pledged to their hostility to the Duke of Wellington's Administration. Mr. O'Connell has reason to rejoice at his failure in carrying this proposition; for, if he had succeeded, no ground for opposing the return of Mr. Vesey Fitzgerald would have existed.

The promotion of that gentleman to a seat in the Cabinet created a vacancy in the representation of the county of Clare; and an opportunity was afforded to the Roman Catholic body of proving that the resolution which had been passed against the Duke of Wellington's Government was not an idle vaunt, but that it could be carried in a striking instance into effect. It was determined that all the power of the people should be put forth.* The Association looked round for a candidate, and,

* Clare Election, the unexpected result of which certainly compelled Wellington and Peel to grant Catholic Emancipation in 1829, took place under the following circumstances. The Catholic Association had resolved to oppose the election or re-election of any member of a Government hostile to the Catholic claims. On June 13, 1828 (the Duke of Wellington being Premier), Mr. Vesey Fitzgerald, who had always voted for the Catholics, was gazetted President of the Board of Trade, the holder of which office is always a Cabinet Minister. On the 16th of June, he was also appointed Treasurer to the Navy. It is a constitutional rule, in England, that no office, having emolument attached, can be conferred by the Crown on a member of the House of Commons, without his thereby vacating his seat: which explains how, on a change of Ministry, Parliamentary business is usually suspended until the new officials have gone back to their different constituencies, for re-election or rejection. Mr. Fitzgerald, who was M. P. for Clare county, therefore, had to present himself to the electors; and did so, without any anticipation of rejection. Mr. O'Connell, on becoming a candidate, pledged his professional reputation (than which none was higher) on his assertion that, if elected, he could take his seat in the House of Commons without taking the then usual oath that the Catholic religion was idolatrous. Mr. Charles Butler, the eminent Catholic barrister of London, well known as an erudite constitutional lawyer, unexpectedly backed this assertion by an elaborate argument which went to show that Mr. O'Connell's view was right. The election commenced on June 30, 1828, and proceeded as graphically related by Mr. Sheil. The entire constituency of the

without having previously consulted him, re-elected Major M'Namara, a Protestant in religion, a Catholic in politics, and a Milesian in descent. Although he is equally well known in Dublin and in Clare, his provincial is distinct from his metropolitan reputation. In Dublin he may be seen at half-past four o'clock, strolling, with a lounge of easy importance, toward Kildare-street Club-house, and dressed in exact imitation of the King [George IV.]; to whose royal whiskers the Major's are considered to bear a profusely-powdered and highly-frizzled affinity. Not contented with this single point of resemblance, he has, by the entertainment of "a score or two of tailors," and the profound study of the regal fashions, achieved a complete look of Majesty; and, by the turn of his coat, the dilation of his chest, and an aspect of egregious dignity, succeeded in producing in his person a very fine effigy of his sovereign.

With respect to his moral qualities, he belongs to the good old school of Irish gentlemen; and, from the facility of his manners, and his graceful mode of arbitrating a difference, has acquired a very eminent character as "a friend." No man is better versed in the strategies of Irish honor. He chooses the

county of Clare was eight thousand, of whom two hundred were twenty and fifty pound freeholders and rent-chargers, while the rest were forty-shilling freeholders — the class who had beaten the Beresfords, at Waterford election, in 1826, and would have been disfranchised, by one of the "wings," had the Catholic Relief Bill been passed the year before. The polling terminated on Saturday, July 5, 1828, and the result showed — for O'Connell, 2,057; for Fitzgerald, 982: majority for O'Connell, 1,075. When the state of the poll was announced, the friends of Mr. Fitzgerald presented a protest to the High-Sheriff, who was the returning-officer, claiming that Mr. F. be declared duly elected, because Mr. O'Connell was a Catholic, and had publicly declared that he would not take the usual oaths to sit in Parliament. The case was fully argued before the Sheriff and his assessor (a lawyer of eminence), and the result was that Mr. O'Connell must be returned as duly elected by a majority of votes; that the law did not disqualify a Catholic from being so elected; and that whether O'Connell would or would not refuse to take the oaths, to which he objected, could not be ascertained until his appearance in the House of Commons. So, he was declared member, and his first frank was on a letter communicating the intelligence to his wife. He exercised the privilege of franking (abolished by the penny-postage act in 1840) from the day of his election until the time after the Catholic Relief Bill was passed, when he was not allowed to take his seat without taking the *old* oaths, which he refused to do. — M.

ground with an O'Trigger eye, and by a glance over "the fifteen acres," is able to select, with an instantaneous accuracy, the finest position for the settlement of a quarrel.* In his calculation of distances, he displays a peculiarly scientific genius; and, whether it be expedient to bring down your antagonist at a long shot, or at a more embarrassed interval of feet, you may be sure of the Major's loading to a grain. In the county of Clare he does not merely enact the part of a sovereign. He is the chief of the clan of the M'Namaras, and after rehearsing the royal character at Kildare street, the moment he arrives on the coast of Clare, and visits the oyster-beds at Poldoody,† becomes "every inch a king." He possesses great influence with the people, which is founded upon far better grounds than their hereditary reverence for the Milesian nobility of Ireland. He is a most excellent magistrate. If a gentleman should endeavor to crush a poor peasant, Major M'Namara is ready to protect him, not only with the powers of his office, but at the risk of his life. This creditable solicitude for the rights and the interests of the lower orders had rendered him most deservedly popular; and, in naming him as their representative, the Association could not have made a more judicious choice.‡ He was publicly called upon to stand.

Some days elapsed, and no answer was returned by the Major. The public mind was thrown into suspense, and various conjectures went abroad as to the cause of this singular omission. Some alleged that he was gone to an island off the coast of Clare, where the proceedings of the Association had not reached him; while others suggested that he was only waiting until the clergy of the county should declare themselves more

* In Phœnix Park, the suburban residence of the Lord-Lieutenant, a particular part, called "The Fifteen Acres," was noted as the place where the Dublin duellists generally had their little "affairs of honor." Duelling is nearly extinct in Ireland now.—M.

† The Poldoody and Carlingford oysters were as popular in Ireland as the Colchester and Milton in London, or the Shrewsbury and East River in New York.—M.

‡ Major M'Namara, who was O'Connell's second in the duel with D'Esterre, in 1815, was returned to Parliament, by his Clare neighbors, after Catholic Emancipation was obtained, and usually voted with O'Connell. He died much respected by all parties, but was a very commonplace man.—M.

unequivocally favorable to him. The latter, it was said, had evinced much apathy ; and it was rumored that Dean O'Shaughnessy, who is a distant relative of Mr. Fitzgerald, had intimated a determination not to support any anti-ministerial candidate. The Major's silence, and the doubts which were entertained with regard to the allegiance of the priests, created a sort of panic at the Association. A meeting was called, and various opinions were delivered as to the propriety of engaging in a contest, the issue of which was considered exceedingly doubtful, and in which failure would be attended with such disastrous consequences. Mr. O'Connell himself did not appear exceedingly sanguine; and Mr. Purcell O'Gorman, a native of Clare, and who had a minute knowledge of the feelings of the people, expressed apprehensions.

There were, however, two gentlemen (Mr. O'Gorman Mahon and Mr. Steele), who strongly insisted that the people might be roused, and that the priests were not as lukewarm as was imagined. Upon the zeal of Dean O'Shaughnessy, however, a good deal of question was thrown. By a singular coincidence, just as his name was uttered, a gentleman entered, who, but for the peculiar locality, might have been readily mistaken for a clergyman of the Established Church. Between the priesthood of the two religions there are, in aspect and demeanor, as well as in creed and discipline, several points of affinity, and the abstract sacerdotal character is readily perceptible in both. The parson, however, in his attitude and attire, presents the evidences of superiority, and carries the mannerism of ascendency upon him. A broad-brimmed hat, composed of the smoothest and blackest material, and drawn by two silken threads into a fire-shovel configuration, a felicitous adaptation of his jerkin to the symmetries of his chest and shoulder, stockings of glossy silk, which displayed the happy proportions of a finely-swelling leg, a ruddy cheek, and a bright, authoritative eye, suggested, at first view, that the gentleman who had entered the room while the merits of Dean O'Shaughnessy were under discussion, must be a minister of the prosperous Christianity of the Established Church. It was, however, no other than Dean O'Shaughnessy himself.

He was received with a burst of applause, which indicated that, whatever surmises with respect to his fidelity had previously gone out, his appearauce before that tribunal (for it is one) was considered by the assembly as a proof of his devotion to the public interest. The Dean, however, made a very scholastic sort of oration, the gist of which it was by no means easy to arrive at. He denied that he had enlisted himself under Mr. Fitzgerald's banners, but at the same time studiously avoided giving any sort of pledge. He did not state distinctly what his opinion was with respect to the co-operation of the priests with the Association; and, when he was pressed, begged to be allowed to withhold his sentiments on the subject. The Association were not, however, dismayed; and it having been conjectured that the chief reason for Major M'Namara having omitted to return an answer was connected with pecuniary considerations, it was decided that so large a sum as five thousand pounds of the Catholic rent should be allocated to the expenses of his election.

Mr. O'Gorman Mahon and Mr. Steele were directed to proceed at once to Clare, in order that they might have a personal interview with him; and they immediately set off. After an absence of two days, Mr. O'Gorman Mahon returned, having left his colleague behind in order to arouse the people; and he at length conveyed certain intelligence with respect to the Major's determination. The obligations under which his family lay to Mr. Fitzgerald were such, that he was bound in honor not to oppose him. This information produced a feeling of deep disappointment among the Catholic body, while the Protestant party exulted in his apparent desertion of the cause, and boasted that no gentleman of the county would stoop so low as to accept of the patronage of the Association. In this emergency, and when it was universally regarded as an utterly hopeless attempt to oppose the Cabinet Minister, the public were astonished by an address from Mr. O'Connell to the freeholders of Clare, in which he offered himself as a candidate, and solicited their support.

Nothing but his subsequent success could exceed the sensation which was produced by this address, and all eyes were turned toward the field in which so remarkable a contest was to be waged. The two candidates entered the lists with signal advantages upon both sides. Mr. O'Connell had an unparalleled popularity, which the services of thirty years had secured to him. Upon the other hand, Mr. Vesey Fitzgerald presented a combination of favorable circumstances, which rendered the issue exceedingly difficult to calculate.* His father had held the office of Prime Sergeant at the Irish Bar; and, although indebted to the Government for his promotion, had the virtuous intrepidity to vote against the Union. This example of independence had rendered him a great favorite with the people. From the moment that his son had obtained access to power, he had employed his extensive influence in doing acts of kindness to the gentry of the County of Clare. He had inundated it with the overflowings of ministerial bounty. The eldest sons of the poorer gentlemen, and the younger branches of the aristocracy, had been provided for through his means; and in the army, the navy, the treasury, the Four Courts, and the Customhouse, the proofs of his political friendship were everywhere to be found.

* William Vesey Fitzgerald was the son of James Fitzgerald, once Prime Sergeant of Ireland, and Catherine Vesey, a rich co-heiress. James Fitzgerald who had held several high offices in Ireland, opposed the contemplated Legislative Union with Great Britain, and threw up his rank of Prime Sergeant, which placed him at the head of the legal profession in Ireland, whence his transition to the judicial ermine was certain. His giving up place, for the sake of his country, made him extremely popular. His eldest son entered Parliament, and successively became Privy Councillor, Chancellor of the Irish Exchequer, Paymaster of the Forces, and President of the Board of Trade. He invariably supported Catholic Emancipation, and not the less warmly because the Catholic leader defeated him at Clare. His mother was created Baroness Fitzgerald and Vesci, in 1827. On her death, in 1832, Vesey Fitzgerald succeeded to this title, as her eldest son. In January, 1835, his father went to his long and last resting-place, aged 93. In the same year, his son received an English, in addition to his Irish barony, and became a Peer of the United Kingdom. When he died in 1843 (as Lord Fitzgerald and Vesci) he was Lord Lieutenant of Clare. He was, in all respects, an accomplished gentleman, an elegant if not eloquent speaker, a tried friend of the Catholics, aad an excellent man of business. At the Clare Election, in 1828, his good temper, true courtesy, and undoubted amiability, won him "heaps of friends" even among the very men who voted against him. Mr. Sheil, in writing of him, involuntarily shows how greatly, while he opposed, he estimated him.— M.

Independently of any act of his which could be referred to his personal interest, and his anxiety to keep up his influence in the county, Mr. Fitzgerald, who is a man of very amiable disposition, had conferred many services upon his Clare acquaintances. Nor was it to Protestants that these manifestations of favor were confined. He had laid not only the Catholic proprietors, but the Catholic priesthood, under obligation. The Bishop of the diocese himself (a respectable old gentleman who drives about in a gig with a mitre upon it) is supposed not to have escaped from his bounties; and it is more than insinuated that some droppings of ministerial manna had fallen upon him. The consequence of this systematized and uniform plan of benefaction is obvious. The sense of obligation was heightened by the manners of this extensive distributer of the favors of the Crown, and converted the ordinary feeling of thankfulness into one of personal regard. To this array of very favorable circumstances, Mr. Fitzgerald brought the additional influence which arose from his recent promotion to the Cabinet; which, to those who had former benefits to return, afforded an opportunity for the exercise of that kind of prospective gratitude which has been described to consist of a lively sense of services to come. These were the comparative advantages with which the ministerial and the popular candidate engaged in this celebrated contest; and Ireland stood by to witness the encounter.

Mr. O'Connell did not immediately set off from Dublin; but, before his departure, several gentlemen were despatched from the Association in order to excite the minds of the people, and to prepare the way for him. The most active and useful of the persons who were employed upon this occasion were the two gentlemen to whom I have already referred, Mr. Steele and Mr. O'Gorman. They are both deserving of special commendation. The former is a Protestant of a respectable fortune in the County of Clare,* and who has all his life been

* The late "Tom Steele," as he was familiarly called, is supposed not to have had an enemy in the world. He was born November 3, 1788, and was a member of a Protestant family in Clare, where he succeeded to considerable landed property. He was a graduate of the Universities of Dublin and Cam-

devoted to the assertion of liberal principles. In Trinity College, he was among the foremost of the advocates of emancipation, and at that early period became the intimate associate of many Roman Catholic gentlemen who have since distin-

bridge and distinguished himself at both; a member of the London Institution of Civil Engineers (admitted for his improvements in diving machinery and sub-marine illumination); one of the defenders of Cadiz, in 1823, under the command of Sir Robert Wilson; seconded O'Connell's nomination at Clare election in 1828; was an original member of Birmingham Political Union, from its formation in 1830, and thus an instrument of the Grey Ministry in carrying the Reform Bill; threw himself, with intense earnestness, into the Emancipation anti-tithe, and Repeal movements; was O'Connell's Head Pacificator and Repeal Warden-in-Chief for all Ireland; took part in the Monster Meetings of 1843; was tried and convicted, with O'Connell and the other repealers, in 1844; suffered the like imprisonment with them, which was subsequently declared by the House of Lords to be illegal; and died in June, 1848, at Peele's Coffee-House, in London, in such extreme want, that he would have starved but for the humanity of the landlord, who kindly allowed him to want for nothing. Bitter necessity had broken his heart, and driven him to despair. His last moments were soothed by the sympathy, bounty, and personal kindness of Lord Brougham and Colonel Perceval (the Orangeman) with both of whom, as public men, he had waged political strife. How his fortune went it is hard to say. His personal expenditure was small. He disbursed a good deal in scientific investigations, and also in attempting to improve the navigation of the Shannon at his own expense — his plan has since been successfully carried out by a Parliamentary grant. In the State Trials of 1844, when he was very restless and talkative, interrupting the proceedings, Mr. Smith, then Attorney-General, turned round and said, "Steele, if you do not keep quiet, I shall certainly strike your name out of the indictment." This threat of depriving him of the honors of political persecution and martyrdom, immediately silenced Tom Steele! He was a tall, muscular, well-built man, who arrayed himself in a military blue frock, with the Repeal button. His face was full of amiability and honesty. He spoke more earnestly than eloquently. He was one of the most sincere and least selfish of public men. He had not room in his heart for one ungenerous or unmanly feeling. He loved O'Connell with a love almost passing that of woman. Ireland ought not to have allowed Tom Steele to die, almost a pauper, in a foreign land. His departure from life should have been in the country he would have died to serve, amid "troops of friends," and not to be

"By strangers honored, and by strangers mourned."

I remember when his death (and its manner) was communicated to the Londoners, how men whom I had always considered apathetic, met me in the street, pressed my hand, which had often been grasped in his, and said, in broken accents, and with moistened eyes, "Poor Tom Steele." The chivalry of his character and conduct had smitten the rock, and the fountain of feeling gushed forth, when his gallant life had passed away.— M.

guished themselves in the proceedings of their body. Being a man of independent circumstances, Mr. Steele did not devote himself to any profession, and having a zealous and active mind, he looked round for occupation. The Spanish war afforded him a field for the display of that generous enthusiasm by which he is distinguished. He joined the patriot army, and fought with a desperate valor upon the batteries of the Trocadero. It was only when Cadiz had surrendered, and the cause of Spain became utterly hopeless, that Mr. Steele relinquished this noble undertaking. He returned to England, surrounded by exiles from the unfortunate country for the liberation of which he had repeatedly exposed his life. It was impossible for a man of so much energy of character to remain in torpor; and on his arrival in Ireland, faithful to the principles by which he had been uniformly swayed, he joined the Catholic Association. There he delivered several powerful and enthusiastic declamations in favor of religious liberty. Such a man, however, was fitted for action as well as for harangue; and the moment the contest in Clare began, he threw himself into the combat with the same alacrity with which he had rushed upon the French bayonets at Cadiz. He was serviceable in various ways. He opened the political campaign by intimating his readiness to fight any landlord who should conceive himself to be aggrieved by an interference with his tenants. This was a very impressive exordium. He then proceeded to canvass for votes; and, assisted by his intimate friend Mr. O'Gorman Mahon, travelled through the country, and, by both day and night, addressed the people from the altars round which they were assembled to hear him. It is no exaggeration to say, that to him, and to his intrepid and indefatigable confederate, the success of Mr. O'Connell is greatly to be ascribed.

Mr. O'Gorman Mahon is introduced into this article as one among many figures. He would deserve to stand apart in a portrait.* Nature has been peculiarly favorable to him. He

* James O'Gorman Mahon subsequently entered Parliament, and made some good speeches on popular subjects. He was declared unseated for want of property qualification (three hundred pounds sterling for a borough, and five

has a very striking physiognomy, of the Corsair character, which the Protestant Gulnares, and the Catholic Medoras, find it equally difficult to resist. His figure is tall, and he is peculiarly free and *degagé* in all his attitudes and movements. In any other his attire would appear singularly fantastical. His manners are exceedingly frank and natural, and have a character of kindliness as well as of self-reliance imprinted upon them. He is wholly free from embarrassment and *mauvaise honte*, and carries a well-founded consciousness of his personal merit; which is, however, so well united with urbanity, that it is not in the slightest degree offensive. His talents as a popular speaker are considerable. He derives from external qualifications an influence over the multitude, which men of diminutive stature are somewhat slow of obtaining. A little man is at first view regarded by the great body of spectators with disrelish; and it is only by force of phrase, and by the charm of speech, that he can at length succeed in inducing his auditors to overlook any infelicity of configuration; but when O'Gorman Mahon throws himself out before the people, and, touching his whiskers with one hand, brandishes the other, an enthusiasm is at once produced, to which the fair portion of the spectators lend their tender contribution. Such a man was exactly adapted to the excitement of the people of Clare; and it must be admitted, that by his indefatigable exertions, his unremitting activity, and his devoted zeal, he most materially assisted in the election of Mr. O'Connell.

While Mr. Steele and Mr. O'Gorman Mahon harangued the people in one district, Mr. Lawless, who was also despatched upon a similar mission, applied his faculties of excitation in another. This gentleman has obtained deserved celebrity by his being almost the only individual among the Irish deputies who remonstrated against the sacrifice of the rights of the forty-shilling freeholders. Ever since that period he has been eminently popular; and although he may occasionally, by

hundred pounds a year for a county member) and abandoned public life for a considerable time. He again entered Parliament, in 1847, but was not re-elected in 1852 He was a remarkably handsome man, in 1828; and dressed in a showy manner.—M.

ebullitions of ill-regulated but generous enthusiasm, create a little merriment among those whose minds are not as susceptible of patriotic and disinterested emotion as his own, yet the conviction which is entertained of his honesty of purpose, confers upon him a considerable influence. "Honest Jack Lawless" is the designation by which he has been known since the "wings" were in discussion.* He has many distinguished

* To have been called "*Honest* Jack Lawless," and to have merited the name, must be considered a great distinction. John Lawless originally studied for the Irish bar, but his friendship for, and presumed connection with Robert Emmett, in 1803, caused Lord Clare to reject his application for admission. Lawless, who was full of energy, bore this with great philosophy, and, relinquishing law and precedents for malt and hops, next became partner in a brewery at Dublin. After this, he yielded to his political and literary tastes, and became editor of a newspaper in Newry, where he obtained so high a reputation for the touch-and-go talent which makes alike a light comedian and a "gentleman of the press," that he was invited to Belfast, where he established and conducted an excellent journal called "The Irishman." When the Catholic Association was founded, John Lawless became an early and eager member. In 1825, he opposed O'Connell on "The Wings." O'Connell's chief notice (though the opposition annoyed him) was a complaint of "the under-growl of Jack Lawless." After this, they soon were reconciled—a hollow truce, for, in 1832, when Lawless was defeated in a contest for the Parliamentary representation of Meath County, he was charged by O'Connell with having, "for a con-si-dera-ti-on" (as old Trapbois says), sold his chances of being elected. Judging from every one of Lawless's political and personal antecedents, this charge was unfounded. Mr. Lawless died in August, 1837.—It may be necessary to state that "The Wings" (to which Mr. Lawless and several other patriotic Irishmen were so much opposed, as then to endanger the popularity of Mr. O'Connell, who certainly did not resist them), were drawbacks with which Catholic Emancipation was to have been clogged, if the Bill brought in, by Sir Francis Burdett, in 1825, had passed into a law. They were embodied in a separate Bill, which passed through several stages, but was necessarily abandoned, when, mainly influenced by the Duke of York's "So help me God" speech, the House of Lords rejected Burdett's bill, and thus deferred Emancipation until 1829. By one "wing" the forty shilling freehold qualification, to vote at Parliamentary elections, would have been abolished, and no one allowed to vote, in counties, on less than a freehold of ten pounds sterling annual value. By the other "wing," the entire Catholic clergy of Ireland, then estimated at two thousand, who were paid by the *people*, were to be paid by the Government, at a cost of two hundred and fifty thousand pounds sterling a year, out of the public money. The matter for wonder is that any Catholic, who complained of being called upon to pay, in tithes, for the maintenance of clergymen of another faith, could not have perceived the anomaly of allowing his

qualifications as a public speaker. His voice is deep, round, and mellow, and is diversified by a great variety of rich and harmonious intonation. His action is exceedingly graceful and appropriate: he has a good figure, which, by a purposed swell and dilation of the shoulders, and an elaborate erectness, he turns to good account; and by dint of an easy fluency of good diction, a solemn visage, an aquiline nose of no vulgar dimension, eyes glaring underneath a shaggy brow with a certain fierceness of emotion, a quizzing-glass, which is gracefully dangled in any pauses of thought or suspensions of utterance, and, above all, by a certain attitude of dignity, which he assumes in the crisis of eloquence, accompanied with a flinging back of his coat, which sets his periods beautifully off, "Honest Jack" has become one of the most popular and efficient speakers at the Association.

Shortly after Mr. Lawless had been despatched, a great reinforcement to the oratorical corps was sent down in the person of the celebrated Father Maguire, or, as he is habitually designated, "Father Tom." This gentleman had been for some time a parish priest in the county of Leitrim. He lived in a remote parish, where his talents were unappreciated. Some accident brought Mr. Pope, the itinerant controversialist, into contact with him. A challenge to defend the doctrines of his religion was tendered by the wandering disputant to the priest, and the latter at once accepted it. Maguire had given no previous proof of his abilities, and the Catholic body regretted the encounter. The parties met in this strange duel of theology. The interest created by their encounter was prodigious. Not only the room where their debates were carried on was crowded, but the whole of Sackville street, where it was situated, was thronged with population. Pope brought to the combat great fluency, and a powerful declamation. Maguire was a master of scholastic logic. After several days of controversy, Pope was overthrown, and "Father Tom,"

own clergy to be paid by taxes, levied on all other creeds. For the promised two hundred and fifty thousand pounds was a small sum compared with the millions wrung out of the Catholics by the Protestant hierarchy and inferior clergy.—M.

as the champion of orthodoxy, became the object of popular adoration. A base conspiracy was got up to destroy his moral character, and by its failure raised him in the affection of the multitude. He had been under great obligations to Mr. O'Connell, for his exertions upon his trial; and from a just sentiment of gratitude, he tendered his services in Clare. His name alone was of great value; and when his coming was announced, the people everywhere rushed forward to hail the great vindicator of the national religion.* He threw fresh ingredients into the caldron, and contributed to impart to the contest that strong religious character which it is not the fault of the Association, but of the Government, that every contest of the kind must assume.

* The Reverend Thomas Maguire was an Irish Catholic priest, a dialectician of great power and ingenuity, who, shortly before the election-struggle in Clare, had greatly distinguished himself, in a public and prolonged discussion with the Reverend Mr. Pope, a Protestant clergyman. Mr. Maguire, who accepted his challenge, was scarcely known even among his own persuasion, and many apprehended defeat, not from any weakness of his cause, but from a belief that its champion, unknown and untried, was unequally opposed to a practised polemic. The discussion, which took place in Dublin, excited much interest in the religious world. Each controversialist had to defend three articles of his own and to assail as many of his adversary's faith. To the surprise of all, Mr. Maguire proved equal, at least, to his more practised opponent. As usual, both parties claimed the honor of the victory—at all events, Mr. Maguire was admitted to have most distinguished himself. It is pleasant to add, that a warm and mutual regard between Mr. Maguire and Mr. Pope sprang out of this controversy. The Orange party in Ireland, shortly after this discussion, did not discourage, if they did not assist, a conspiracy which was got up to destroy Mr. Maguire's private and clerical character. An action at law was brought by a person named M'Gerratty, to recover damages for the seduction of his daughter Ann, by the Reverend Thomas Maguire. The young woman was examined on the trial, and swore, among other things, that Mr. Maguire had seduced her under a promise of marriage, to be fulfilled on his becoming a Protestant clergyman! The jury, coupling this improbability with serious discrepancies in her evidence as to the subject-matter of the suit, with her demeanor in the witness-box, and with strong testimony of her previous bad character, acquitted Mr. Maguire, without hesitation. For the remaining twenty years of his life, he was undisturbed by slander. He was a popular preacher, and was often called upon to plead in aid of the sacred cause of charity. He died suddenly, and it was suspected that he was poisoned by two of his own servants, who desired to appropriate to themselves whatever portable property he was possessed of.—M.

"Father Tom" was employed upon a remarkable exploit. Mr. Augustine Butler, the lineal descendant of the famous Sir Toby Butler, is a proprietor in Clare: he is a liberal Protestant, but supported Mr. Vesey Fitzgerald. "Father Tom" proceeded from the town of Ennis to the county chapel where Mr. Butler's freeholders were assembled, in order to address them; and Mr. Butler, with an intrepidity which did him credit, went forward to meet him. It was a singular encounter in the house of God. The Protestant landlord called upon his freeholders not to desert him. "Father Tom" rose to address them in behalf of Mr. O'Connell. He is not greatly gifted with a command of decorated phraseology; but he is master of vigorous language, and has a power of strong and simple reasoning, which is equally intelligible to all classes. He employs the syllogism of the schools as his chief weapon in argument; but uses it with such dexterity, that his auditors of the humblest class can follow him without being aware of the technical expedient of logic by which he masters the understanding. His manner is peculiar: it is not flowery, nor declamatory, but is short, somewhat abrupt, and, to use the French phrase, is *tranchant*. His countenance is adapted to his mind, and is expressive of the reasoning and controversial faculties. A quick blue eye, a nose slightly turned up, and formed for the tossing off of an argument, a strong brow, a complexion of mountain ruddiness, and thick lips, which are better formed for rude disdain than for polished sarcasm, are his characteristics. He assailed Mr. Butler with all his powers, and overthrew him. The topic to which he addressed himself, was one which was not only calculated to move the tenants of Mr. Butler, but to stir Mr. Butler himself. He appealed to the memory of his celebrated Catholic ancestor, of which Mr. Butler is justly proud. He stated, that what Sir Toby Butler had been, Mr. O'Connell was; and he abjured him not to stand up in opposition to an individual, whom he was bound to sustain by a sort of hereditary obligation. His appeal carried the freeholders away, and one hundred and fifty votes were secured to Mr. O'Connell. Mr. Maguire was seconded in this achievement by Mr. Dominick Ronayne, a barrister of the

Association, of considerable talents, and who not only speaks the English language with eloquence, but is master of the Irish tongue;* and, throwing an educated mind into the powerful idiom of the country, wrought with uncommon power upon the passions of the people.

Mr. Sheil was employed as counsel for Mr. O'Connell before the assessor; but proceeded to the county of Clare the day before the election commenced. On his arrival, he understood that an exertion was required in the parish of Corofin, which is situate upon the estate of Sir Edward O'Brien, who had given all his interest to Mr. Vesey Fitzgerald. Sir Edward is the most opulent resident landlord in the country.† In the parish of Corofin he had no less than three hundred votes; and it was supposed that his freeholders would go with him. Mr. Sheil determined to assail him in the citadel of his strength, and proceeded, upon the Sunday before the poll commenced, to the chapel of Corofin. Sir Edward O'Brien having learned that this agitator intended this trespass upon his authority, resolved to anticipate him, and set off in his splendid equipage, drawn by four horses, to the mountains in which Corofin is situated. The whole population came down from their residences in the rocks, which are in the vicinity of the town of

* The Irish are fond of a joke, and O'Connell often indulged them. In 1843, when the Monster Meetings were proceeding, the Peel Ministry sent short-hand writers to report the speeches of O'Connell and his co-agitators. On one occasion, seeing "the gentlemen of the press" assembled on the platform, ready to record every word he uttered, O'Connell called out to know whether they had every facility and accommodation necessary. They answered, truly, that everything had been done for their ease and comfort. It was in one of the Southern counties, where the Irish language is spoken as often as the English, and O'Connell, glancing waggishly around, commenced a speech *in Irish*, to the surprise and dismay of the "Saxon" reporters. The multitude instantly entered into the humor of the joke, and shouts of laughter mingled with the usual applause. It was a great triumph thus to have baffled the Government through its reporters, and was one of the amusing episodes of a period of great personal and political excitement.—M.

† Sir E. O'Brien, of Drumoland, County of Clare, was born in 1773 and died in 1837. He was succeeded in his title by his eldest son, now Sir Lucius O'Brien. His second son, William Smith O'Brien, late M. P. for Ennis, is now (January, 1854) in New South Wales, as a transport for life, under his conviction, on a charge of high treason, in 1848.—M.

Ennis, and advanced in large bands, waving green boughs, and preceded by fifes and pipers, upon the road. Their landlord was met by them on his way. They passed him by in silence, while they hailed the demagogue with shouts, and attended him in triumph to the chapel. Sir Edward O'Brien lost his resolution at this spectacle ; and feeling that he could have no influence in such a state of excitation, instead of going to the house of Catholic worship, proceeded to the church of Corofin. He left his carriage exactly opposite the doors of the chapel, which is immediately contiguous, and thus reminded the people of his Protestantism, by a circumstance of which, of course, advantage was instantaneously taken.

Mr. Sheil arrived with a vast multitude of attendants at the chapel, which was crowded with people, who had flocked from all quarters; there a singular scene took place. Father Murphy, the parish priest, came to the entrance of the chapel dressed in his surplice. As he came forth, the multitude fell back at his command, and arranged themselves on either side, so as to form a lane for the reception of the agitator. Deep silence was imposed upon the people by the priest, who had a voice like subterraneous thunder, and appeared to hold them in absolute dominion. When Mr. Sheil had reached the threshold of the chapel, Father Murphy stretched forth his hand, and welcomed him to the performance of the good work.

The figure and attitude of the priest were remarkable. My English reader draws his ordinary notion of a Catholic clergyman from the caricatures which are contained in novels, or represented in farces upon the stage; but the Irish priest, who has lately become a politician and a scholar, has not a touch of foigardism about him; and an artist would have found in Father Murphy rather a study for the enthusiastic Macbriar, who is so powerfully delineated in "Old Mortality," than a realization of the familiar notions of a clergyman of the Church of Rome. As he stood surrounded by a dense multitude, whom he had hushed into profound silence, he presented a most imposing object. His form is tall, slender, and emaciated; but was enveloped in his long robes, that gave him a peculiarly sacerdotal aspect. The hand which he stretched forth was ample, but worn to a skinny meagritude and pallor. His face was long, sunken, and cadaverous, but was illuminated by eyes blazing with all the fire of genius, the enthusiasm of religion, and the devotedness of patriotism. His lank black hair fell down his temples, and eyebrows of the same color stretched in thick straight lines along a lofty forehead, and threw over the whole countenance a deep shadow. The sun was shining with brilliancy, and rendered his figure, attired as it was in white garments, more conspicuous. The scenery about him was in harmony; it was wild and desolate, and crags, with scarce a blade of verdure shooting through their crevices, rose everywhere around him. The interior of the chapel, at the entrance of which he stood, was visible. It was a large pile of building, consisting of bare walls, rudely thrown up, with a floor of clay, and at the extremity stood an altar made of a few boards clumsily put together.

It was on the threshold of this mountain-temple that the envoy of the Association was hailed with a solemn greeting. The priest proceeded to the altar, and commanded the people to abstain, during the divine ceremony, from all political thinking or occupation. He recited the mass with great fervency and simplicity of manner, and with all the evidences of unaffected piety. However familiar, from daily repetition, with the ritual, he pronounced it with a just emphasis, and went through the various forms which are incidental to it with singular propriety and grace. The people were deeply attentive, and it was observable that most of them could read; for they had prayer-books in their hands, which they read with a quiet devotion. Mass being finished, Father Murphy threw his vestments off, and, without laying down the priest, assumed the politician. He addressed the people in Irish, and called upon them to vote for O'Connell in the name of their country and of their religion.

It was a most extraordinary and powerful display of the externals of eloquence; and, as far as a person unacquainted with the language could form an estimate of the matter by the effects produced upon the auditory, it must have been pregnant with genuine oratory. It will be supposed that this singular priest addressed his parishioners in tones and gestures as rude as the wild dialect to which he was giving utterance. His action and attitudes were as graceful as an accomplished actor could use in delivering the speech of Antony, and his intonations were soft, pathetic, and denunciatory, and conjuring, accordingly as his theme varied, and as he had recourse to different expedients to influence the people. The general character of this strange harangue was impassioned and solemn; but he occasionally had recourse to ridicule, and his countenance at once adapted itself with a happy readiness to derision. The finest spirit of sarcasm gleamed over his features, and shouts of laughter attended his description of a miserable Catholic who should prove recreant to the great cause, by making a sacrifice of his country to his landlord. The close of his speech was peculiarly effective. He became inflamed by the power of his emotions; and while he raised himself into the loftiest attitude to which he could ascend, he laid one hand on the altar, and shook the other in the spirit of almost prophetic admonition, and as his eyes blazed and seemed to start from his forehead, thick drops fell down his face, and his voice rolled through lips livid with passion and covered with foam. It is almost unnecessary to say that such an appeal was irresistible. The multitude burst into shouts of acclamation, and would have been ready to mount a battery roaring with cannon at his command. Two days after the results were felt at the hustings; and while Sir Edward O'Brien stood aghast, Father Murphy marched into Ennis at the head of his tenantry, and polled them to a man in favor of Daniel O'Connell. But I am anticipating.

The notion which had gone abroad in Dublin, that the priests were lukewarm, was utterly unfounded. With the exception of Dean O'Shaughnessy, who is a relative of Mr. Fitzgerald (and for whom there is perhaps much excuse), and a Father Coffey, who has since been deserted by his congregation, and is paid his dues in bad halfpence, there was scarcely a clergyman in the county who did not use his utmost influence over the peasantry. On the day on which Mr. O'Connell arrived, you met a priest in every street, who assured you that the battle should be won, and pledged himself that "the man of the people" should be returned. "The man of the people" arrived in the midst of the loudest acclamations. Near thirty thousand people were crowded into the streets of Ennis, and were unceasing in their shouts. Banners were suspended from every window, and women of great beauty were everywhere seen waving handherchiefs with the figure of the patriot stamped upon them. Processions of freeholders, with their parish priests at their head, were marching like troops to different quarters of the city; and it was remarkable that not a single individual was intoxicated. The most perfect order and regularity prevailed; and the large bodies of police which had been collected in the town stood without occupation. These were evidences of organization, from which it was easy to form a conjecture as to the result.

The election opened, and the courthouse in which the Sheriff read the writ presented a very new and striking scene. On the left-hand of the Sheriff stood a Cabinet-minister, attended by the whole body of the aristocracy of the County of Clare. Their appearance indicated at once their superior rank and their profound mortification. An expression of bitterness and of wounded pride was stamped in various modifications of resentment upon their countenances; while others, who were in the interest of Mr. Fitzgerald, and who were the small Protestant proprietors, affected to look big and important, and swelled themselves into gentry upon the credit of voting for the minister. On the right-hand of the Sheriff stood Mr. O'Connell, with scarcely a single gentleman by his side; for most even of the Catholic proprietors had abandoned him, and joined the ministerial candidate. But the body of the Court presented the power of Mr. O'Connell in a mass of determined peasants, among whom black coats and sacerdotal visages were seen felicitously intermixed, outside the balustrade of the gallery on the left-hand of the Sheriff.

Before the business began, a gentleman was observed on whom every eye was turned. He had indeed chosen a most singular position; for, instead of sitting like the other auditors on the seats in the gallery, he leaped over it, and, suspending himself above the crowd, afforded what was an object of wonder to the great body of the spectators, and of indignation to the High-Sheriff. The attire of the individual who was thus perched in this dangerous position was sufficiently strange. He had a coat of Irish tabinet, with glossy trousers of the same national material; he wore no waistcoat; a blue shirt, lined with streaks of white, was open at his neck, in which the strength of Hercules and the symmetry of Antinous were combined; a broad green sash, with a medal of "the order of Liberators" at the end of it, hung conspicuously over his breast; and a profusion of black curls, curiously festooned about his temples, shadowed a very handsome and expressive countenance, a great part of which was occupied by whiskers of a busy amplitude. "Who, sir, are you?" exclaimed the High-Sheriff, in a tone of imperious melancholy, which he had acquired at Canton, where he had long resided in the service of the East India Company.

But I must pause here, and even at the hazard of breaking the regular thread of the narration—I can not resist the temptation of describing the High-Sheriff. When he stood up with his wand of office in his hand, the contrast between him and the aerial gentleman whom he was addressing was to the highest degree ludicrous. Of the latter some conception has already been given. He looked a chivalrous dandy, who, under the most fantastical apparel, carried the spirit and intrepidity of an exceedingly fine fellow. Mr. High-Sheriff had, at an early period of his life, left his native county of Clare, and had migrated to China, where, if I may judge from his manners and demeanor, he must have been in immediate communication with a Mandarin of the first class, and made a Chinese functionary his favorite model. I should conjecture that he must long have presided over the packing of Bohea, and that some tincture of that agreeable vegetable had been infused into his complexion. An oriental sedateness and gravity are spread over a countenance upon which a smile seldom presumes to trespass. He gives utterance to intonations which were originally contracted in the East, but have been since melodized by his religious habits into a puritanical chant in Ireland. The Chinese language is monosyllabic, and Mr. Molony has extended its character to the English tongue; for he breaks all his words into separate and elaborate divisions, to each of which he bestows a due quantity of deliberate intonation. Upon arriving in Ireland, he addicted himself to godliness, having previously made great gains in China, and he has so contrived as to impart the cadences of Wesley to the pronunciation of Confucius.

Such was the aspect of the great public functionary, who, rising with a peculiar magisteriality of altitude, and stretching forth the emblem of his power, inquired of the gentleman who was suspended from the gallery who he was. "My name is O'Gorman Mahon," was the reply, delivered with a firmness which clearly showed that the person who had conveyed this piece of intelligence thought very little of a High-Sheriff and a great deal of O'Gorman Mahon. The Sheriff had been offended by the general appearance of Mr. Mahon, who had distracted the public attention from his own contemplation; but he was particularly irritated by observing the insurgent symbol of "the Order of Liberators" dangling at his breast.* "I tell that gentleman," said Mr. Molony, "to take off that badge." There was a moment's pause, and then the following answer was slowly and articulately pronounced: "This gentleman" (laying his hand on his breast) "tells that gentleman" (pointing with the other to the Sheriff) "that if that gentleman presumes to touch this gentleman, this gentleman will defend himself against that gentleman, or any other gentleman, while he has got the arm of a gentleman to protect him." This ex-

* The Order of Liberators arose out of the contested election for the county of Waterford, in 1826, when Mr. Villiers Stuart (subsequently raised to the peerage) defeated Lord George Beresford, brother to the Marquis of Waterford. The forty-shilling freeholders having thus beaten down what was called "the Beresford tyranny," O'Connell instituted the Order of Liberators, of which he was Grand-Master, to commemorate the patriotic deed. Whoever, being of good character, had rendered a service to Ireland, was entitled to wear the medal, attached to a broad green riband. After Clare Election, it was resolved, at a Chapter of the Order, over which Mr. Lawless presided, that four thousand medals should be struck, for the purpose of distribution among the liberal electors of Clare. — M.

traordinary sentence was followed by a loud burst of applause from all parts of the courthouse. The High-Sheriff looked aghast. The expression of self-satisfaction and magisterial complacency passed off of his visage, and he looked utterly blank and dejected. After an interval of irresolution, down he sat. "The soul" of O'Gorman Mahon (to use Curran's expression) "walked forth in its own majesty;" he looked "redeemed, regenerated, and disenthralled." The medal of "the Order of Liberators" was pressed to his heart. O'Connell surveyed him with gratitude and admiration; and the first blow was struck, which sent dismay into the heart of the party of which the Sheriff was considered to be an adherent.

This was the opening incident of this novel drama. When the sensation which it had created had in some degree subsided, the business of the day went on. Sir Edward O'Brien proposed Mr. Vesey Fitzgerald as a proper person to serve in Parliament. Sir Edward had upon a former occasion been the vehement antagonist of Mr. Fitzgerald, and in one instance a regular battle had been fought between the tenantry of both parties. It was supposed that this feud had left some acrimonious feelings which were not quite extinct behind, and many conjectured that the zeal of Sir Edward in favor of his competitor was a little feigned. This notion was confirmed by the circumstance that Sir Edward O'Brien's son (the member for Ennis) had subscribed to the Catholic rent, was a member of the Association, and had recently made a vigorous speech in Parliament in defence of that body.* It is, however, probable

* William Smith O'Brien, of Cahermoyle, Clare county, second son of the late Sir Edward O'Brien, was born on October 17, 1803. He entered Parliament early, and soon attached himself to the popular cause. His ablest speech in Parliament was when moving for an inquiry into the state of Ireland. It was a clear and forcible statement of Irish grievances, and caused a prolonged and exciting discussion. The Repeal agitation of 1843–'4 made him a convert, and he took his seat in Conciliation Hall amid much applause, as his adhesion, delayed till then, was evidently caused by conviction. While O'Connell was in *duresse*, under illegal verdict and judgment, in 1844 his place in Conciliation Hall was supplied by Smith O'Brien, who announced that, having abandoned all hope of "justice to Ireland" from the British Parliament, he withdrew from regular attendance in the House of Commons, and would now

that the feudal pride of Sir Edward O'Brien, which was deeply mortified by the defection of his vassals, absorbed every other feeling, and that, however indifferent he might have been on Mr. Fitzgerald's account, yet that he was exceedingly irritated upon his own. He appeared at least to be profoundly moved, and had not spoken above a few minutes when tears fell from his eyes. He has a strong Irish character impressed upon him. It is said that he is lineally descended from the Irish emperor, Brian-Borue; and indeed he has some resemblance to the sign-post at a tavern near Clontarf, in which the image of that celebrated monarch is represented. He is squat, bluff, and impassioned. An expression of good-nature, rather than of good-humor, is mixed up with a certain rough consciousness of his own dignity, which in his most familiar moments he never lays aside, for the Milesian predominates in his demeanor, and his royal recollections wait perpetually upon him. He is a great favorite with the people, who are attached to the descendants of the ancient indigenous families of the county, and who see in Sir Edward O'Brien a good landlord, as well as the representative of Brian Borue.

I was not a little astonished at seeing him weep upon the hustings. It was, however, observed to me that he is given to the "melting mood," although his tears do not fall like the gum of "the Arabian tree." In the House of Commons he once produced a great effect, by bursting into tears, while he described the misery of the people of Clare, although, at the

apply his energies to the attainment of a domestic legislature for Ireland. In 1846, still declining to attend, he refused to serve on a railway committee, and was committed to confinement by the House of Commons for "contempt." After a time he was liberated, but without any concession on his part. In 1848, having ardently adopted "physical force" principles, he unsuccessfully attempted to liberate Ireland from legislative connection with Great Britain: was apprehended, committed, and tried for high-treason; convicted, sentenced to death (for which transportation for life was substituted), and hurriedly deported to Van Dieman's Land, the very worst of the penal settlements, and commonly called "Hell-upon-earth," and is now (January, 1854) a "convict" there. Marked ability and the purest motives have always distinguished this man, who loved Ireland "not wisely" (under acts of Parliament), "but too well."—M.

same time, his granaries were full. It was said that his hustings pathos was of the same quality, and arose from the peculiar susceptibility of the lacrymatory nerves, and not from any very nice fibres about the heart: still I am convinced that his emotion was genuine, and that he was profoundly touched. He complained that he had been deserted by his tenants, although he had deserved well at their hands; and exclaimed that the country was not one fit for a gentleman to reside in, when property lost all its influence, and things were brought to such a pass. The motion was seconded by Sir A. Fitzgerald in a few words.* Mr. Gore, a gentleman of very large estate, took occasion to deliver his opinions in favor of Mr. Fitzgerald; and Mr. O'Gorman Mahon and Mr. Steele proposed Mr. O'Connell.

It then fell to the rival candidates to speak; and Mr. Vesey Fitzgerald, having been first put in nomination, first addressed the freeholders. He seemed to me to be about five-and-forty years of age, his hair being slightly marked with a little edging of scarcely-perceptible silver, but the care with which it was distributed and arranged showed that the Cabinet Minister had not yet entirely dismissed his Lothario recollections. I had heard, before I had even seen Mr. Fitzgerald, that he was in great favor with the *Calistas* at Almack's; and I was not surprised at it, on a minute inspection of his aspect and deportment. It is not that he is a handsome man (though he is far from being the reverse), but that there is an air of blended sweetness and assurance, of easy intrepidity and gentle gracefulness about him, which are considered to be eminently winning. His countenance, though too fully circular, and a little tinctured with vermilion, is agreeable. The eyes are of bright hazel, and have an expression of ever-earnest frankness, which an acute observer might suspect, while his mouth is full of a strenuous solicitude to please. The moment he rose, I perceived that he was an accomplished gentleman; and, when I had heard him utter a few sentences, I was satisfied that he was a most accomplished speaker.

* Sir Augustus Fitzgerald, of Newmarket-on-Fergus, county of Clare, a Lieutenant-General in the army, was created Baronet in 1821, and died in 1834.—M.

He delivered one of the most effective and dexterous speeches which it has ever been my good fortune to hear. There were evident marks of deep pain and of fear to be traced in his features, which were not free from the haggardness of many an anxious vigil; but though he was manifestly mortified in the extreme, he studiously refrained from all exasperating sentiment or expression. He spoke at first with a graceful melancholy, rather than a tone of impassioned adjuration. He intimated that it was rather a measure of rigorous, if not unjustifiable policy, to display the power of the Association in throwing an individual out of Parliament who had been the warm and uniform advocate of the Catholic cause during his whole political life. He enumerated the instances in which he had exerted himself in behalf of that body which were now dealing with him with such severity, and referred to his services with regard to the College of Maynooth.

The part of his speech which was most powerful related to his father. The latter had opposed the Union, and had many claims upon the national gratitude. The topic was one which required to be most delicately touched, and no orator could treat it with a more exquisite nicety than Mr. Fitzgerald. He became, as he advanced, and the recollection of his father pressed itself more immediately upon his mind, more impassioned. At the moment he was speaking, his father, to whom he is most tenderly attached, and by whom he is most beloved, was lying upon a bed whence it was believed that he would never rise; and efforts had been made to conceal from the old man the contest in which his son was involved.* It is impossible to mistake genuine grief; and when Mr. Fitzgerald paused for an instant, and, turning away, wiped off the tears that came streaming from his eyes, he won the sympathies of every one about him. There were few who did not give the same evidence of emotion; and when he sat down, although the great majority of the audience were strongly opposed to him, and were enthusiasts in favor of the rival candidate, a loud and unanimous burst of acclamation shook the courthouse.

* The Right Honorable James Fitzgerald, who sacrificed place and its emoluments for his country, died in 1835, aged ninety-three. — M.

Mr. O'Connell rose to address the people in reply.* It was manifest that he considered a great exertion to be requisite in order to do away the impression which his antagonist had produced. It was clear that he was collecting all his might, to those who were acquainted with the workings of his physiognomy. Mr. O'Connell bore Mr. Fitzgerald no sort of personal aversion, but he determined, in this exigency, to have little mercy on his feelings, and to employ all the power of vituperation of which he was possessed, against him. This was absolutely necessary; for if mere dexterous fencing had been resorted to by Mr. O'Connell, many might have gone away with the opinion that, after all, Mr. Fitzgerald had been thanklessly treated by the Catholic body. It was therefore disagreeably requisite to render him, for the moment, odious. Mr. O'Connell began by awakening the passions of the multitude in an attack on Mr. Fitzgerald's allies. Mr. Gore had lauded him highly. This Mr. Gore is of Cromwellian descent, and the people detest the memory of the Protector to this day. There is a tradition (I know not whether it has the least foundation) that the ancestor of this gentleman's family was a nailer by trade in the Puritan army. Mr. O'Connell, without any direct reference to the fact, used a set of metaphors, such as "striking the nail on the head"—"putting a nail into a coffin," which at once recalled the associations which were attached to the name of Mr. Gore; and roars of laughter assailed that gentleman on every side. Mr. Gore has the character of being not only very opulent, but of bearing a re-

* O'Connell's personal appearance was greatly in his favor. He had that massiveness of mould which the populace like to witness in one who aspires to lead them. He had what singers call a *chest-voice;* deep, clear, musical, and audible even in a whisper. At the Clare Election, in 1828, he was in his fifty-third year. Prince Puckler Muscau, who visited Ireland about this time, thus described the Man of the People, in his *Tour of a German Prince:* "Daniel O'Connell, is indeed, no common man, though the man of the commonalty. His exterior is attractive, and the expression of intelligent good nature, united with determination and prudence, which marks his countenance, is extremely winning. It is impossible not to follow his powerful arguments with interest: and such is the martial dignity of his carriage, that he looks more like a general of Napoleon's than a Dublin advocate."—M.

gard to his possessions proportioned to their extent. Nothing is so unpopular as prudence in Ireland; and Mr. O'Connell rallied Mr. Gore to such a point upon this head, and that of his supposed origin, that the latter completely sunk under the attack. He next proceeded to Mr. Fitzgerald, and, having drawn a picture of the late Mr. Perceval, he turned round and asked of the rival candidate, with what face he could call himself their friend, when the first act of his political life was to enlist himself under the banners of "the bloody Perceval." This epithet (whether it be well or ill deserved is not the question) was sent into the hearts of the people with a force of expression, and a furious vehemence of voice, that created a great sensation among the crowd, and turned the tide against Mr. Fitzgerald. "This too," said Mr. O'Connell, "is the friend of Peel—the bloody Perceval, and the candid and manly Mr. Peel—and he is our friend! and he is everybody's friend! The friend of the Catholic was the friend of the bloody Perceval, and is the friend of the candid and manly Mr. Peel!"

It is unnecessary to go through Mr. O'Connell's speech. It was stamped with all his powerful characteristics,* and galled Mr. Fitzgerald to the core. That gentleman frequently muttered an interrogatory, "Is this fair?" when Mr. O'Connell was using some legitimate sophistication against him. He seemed particularly offended when his adversary said, "I never shed tears in public," which was intended as a mockery of Mr. Fitzgerald's references to his father. It will be thought by some sensitive persons that Mr. O'Connell was not quite warranted in this harsh dealing, but he had no alternative. Mr. Fitzgerald had made a very powerful speech, and the effect was to be got rid of. In such a warfare a man must not

* When O'Connell said that he "was the best-abused man in the world," he might have added that he was the *best-abusing*. However, he had ample precedents, one of which now occurs to me. Sir Archibald Macdonald (who was Chief-Baron of the English Court of Exchequer, from 1793 to 1813) once told Sir Fletcher Norton, afterward Speaker of the House of Commons, that he was "a lazy, indolent, evasive, shuffling, plausible, artful, mean, confident, cowardly, poor, pitiful, sneaking, and abject creature." This was in Parliament, where the decencies of speech are supposed to be observed!—M.

pause in the selection of his weapons, and Mr. O'Connell is not the man to hesitate in the use of the rhetorical sabre.

Nothing of any peculiar interest occurred after Mr. O'Connell's speech upon the first day. On the second the polling commenced; and on that day, in consequence of an expedient adopted by Mr. Fitzgerald's committee, the parties were nearly equal. A Catholic freeholder can not, in strictness, vote at an election without making a certain declaration, upon oath, respecting his religious opinions, and obtaining a certificate of his having done so from a magistrate. It is usual for candidates to agree to dispense with the necessity of taking this oath. It was, however, of importance to Mr. Fitzgerald to delay the election; and with that view his committee required that the declaration should be taken.* Mr. O'Connell's committee were unprepared for this form, and it was with the utmost difficulty that magistrates could be procured to attend to receive the oath. It was, therefore, impossible, on the first day, for Mr. O'Connell to bring his forces in the field, and thus the parties appeared nearly equal. To those who did not know the real cause of this circumstance, it appeared ominous, and the O'Connellites looked sufficiently blank; but the next day everything was remedied. The freeholders were sworn *en masse*. They were brought into a yard enclosed within four walls. Twenty-five were placed against each wall, and they simultaneously repeated the oath. When one batch of swearers had been disposed of, the person who administered the declaration, turned to the adjoining division, and despatched them. Thus he went through the quadrangle, and in the course of a few minutes was able to discharge one hundred patriots upon Mr. Fitzgerald.

It may be said that an oath ought to be more solemnly administered. In reply it is only necessary to observe, that

* Formerly, a County Election might occupy 15 days, in the mere polling of the voters. The Reform Bill has changed that, and County Elections can not now last more than two days (if there be a contest), exclusive of the day on which the candidates are publicly nominated, and that on which the Returning officer declares the result of the electoral strife. If there be no opposition to the candidate, the nomination, candidate's address, and declaration of the election, need not occupy an hour. I have seen it hurried through in less time.—M.

the declaration in question related principally to "the Pretender," and when "the legislature persevere in compelling the name of God to be thus taken in vain," the ritual becomes appropriately farcical, and the manner of the thing is only adapted to the ludicrous matter upon which it is legally requisite that Heaven should be attested! The oath which is imposed upon a Roman Catholic is a violation of the first precept of the decalogue! This species of machinery having been thus applied to the art of swearing, the effects upon the poll soon became manifest, and Mr. O'Connell ascended to a triumphant majority. It became clear that the landlords had lost all their power, and that their struggles were utterly hopeless. Still they persevered in dragging the few serfs whom they had under their control to the hustings, and in protracting the election. It was Mr. Fitzgerald's own wish, I believe, to abandon the contest, when its ultimate issue was already certain; but his friends insisted that the last man whom they could command should be polled out. Thus the election was procrastinated.

In ordinary cases, the interval between the first and the last day of polling is monotonous and dull; but during the Clare election so many ludicrous and extraordinary incidents were every moment occurring, as to relieve any attentive observer from every influence of ennui. The writer of this article was under the necessity of remaining during the day in the Sheriff's booth, where questions of law were chiefly discussed, but even here there was much matter for entertainment. The sheriff afforded a perpetual fund of amusement. He sat with his wand of office leaning against his shoulder, and always ready for his grasp. When there was no actual business going forward, he still preserved a magisterial dignity of deportment, and with half-closed eyelids, and throwing back his head, and forming with his chin an obtuse angle with the horizon, reproved any indulgence in illicit mirth which might chance to pass among the bar. The gentleman who were professionally engaged having discovered the chief foible of the Sheriff, which consisted in the most fantastical notions of himself, vied with each other in playing upon this weakness. "I feel that

I address myself to the first man of the county," was the usual exordium with which legal argument was opened.* The Sheriff, instead of perceiving the sneer which involuntarily played round the lips of the mocking sycophant, smiled with an air of Malvolio condescension, and bowed his head. Then came some noise from the adjoining booths, upon which the Sheriff used to start up and exclaim, "I declare I do not think that I am treated with proper respect—verily, I'll go forth and quell this tumult—I'll show them I am the first man in the county, and I'll commit somebody." With that "the first man in the county," with a step slightly accelerated by his resentment at a supposed indignity to himself, used to proceed in quest of a riot, but generally returned with a good-humored

* The Sheriff's powers exceeded those of the Magistracy. In those days, nearly every out-at-elbows Protestant, who, like Justice Shallow, could write himself "in any bill, warrant, quittance, or obligation, *armigero*," was made a magistrate, provided he had the requisite amount of Ascendency intolerance. The *vademecum* of such justices, under which they dispensed law indifferently (*very* indifferently, indeed), was MacNally's "Justice of the Peace in Ireland," which, with adaptations to the present state of the law, is yet in vogue and has long been to magistrates in Ireland, what "Burn's Justice" is to those of England. As originally published, it was full of errors, and those who acted on it, often found themselves drawn into lawsuits, as defendants. "What could make you act so?" MacNally would ask. "Faith, sir, I acted on the advice of your own book!" Not much taken aback, for such scenes were frequent, MacNally would say, "As a human work, the book has errors, no doubt—but I shall correct them all *when it comes to a second edition!*"—Leonard MacNally was very short and nearly as broad as long: his legs were of unequal length, and he had a face which no washing could clean, and he wanted one thumb. He had good eyes and an expressive countenance. He was lame, also, which made Curran say, when he entered the lawyer's corps, in 1798, that he ran a chance of being shot for disobedience of orders, for that when the adjutant would cry "march," MacNally would certainly "*halt!*" When he walked rapidly, he would take two thumping steps with the short leg, to bring up the space made by the long one, and from this the bar nicknamed him "One *pound* two." He was expelled by the bar-mess, on account of the dirtiness of his person. Once when he went to France for a month, Curran said, "He has taken a shirt and a guinea, and he'll change neither until he comes back." The well-known song, "The lass of Richmond Hill" was written by MacNally upon his sweetheart, a Miss Janson, who sympathized with him in scribbling verses and not washing her hands. They were married, lived happily, and, to the last, were economic in the use of soap!—M.

expression of face, observing: "It was only Mr. O'Connell, and I must say when I remonstrated with him, he paid me every sort of proper respect. He is quite a different person from what I had heard. But let nobody imagine that I was afraid of him. I'd commit him, or Mr. Vesey Fitzgerald, if I was not treated with proper respect; for by virtue of my office I am the first man in the county." This phrase of the Sheriff became so familiar, that a set of wags, who in the intervals of leisure, had set about practising mimicry, emulated each other in repeating it, and succeeded in producing various pleasant imitations of the "first man in the county."

A young gentleman (Mr. Nicholas Whyte) turned this talent to a very pleasant and useful account. He acted as agent to Mr. O'Connell, in a booth of which the chief officer, or Sheriff's Deputy, as he is called, was believed to be a partisan of Mr. Fitzgerald, and used to delay Mr. O'Connell's tallies. A tumult would then ensue, and the deputy would raise his voice in a menacing tone against the friends of Mr. O'Connell. The High-Sheriff himself had been accustomed to go to the entrance of the different booths and to command silence with his long-drawn and dismal ejaculations. When the deputy was bearing it with a high hand, Mr. Whyte would sometimes leave the booth, and standing at the outward edge of the crowd, just at the moment that the deputy was about to commit some partisan of Mr. O'Connell, the mimic would exclaim, in a death-bell voice, "Silence, Mr. Deputy, you are exceedingly disorderly —silence!" The deputy being enveloped by the multitude, could not see the individual who thus addressed him, and believing it to be the Sheriff, sat down confounded at the admonition, while Mr. O'Connell's tally went rapidly on, and the disputed vote was allowed.

These vagaries enlivened occupations which in their nature were sufficiently dull. But the Sheriff's booth afforded matter more deserving of note than his singularities. Charges of undue influence were occasionally brought forward, which exhibited the character of the election in its strongest colors.

One incident I particularly remember. An attorney employed by Mr. Fitzgerald rushed in and exclaimed that a priest was terrifying the voters. This accusation produced a powerful effect. The counsel for Mr. O'Connell defied the attorney to make out his charge. The assessor very properly required that the priest should attend; and behold Father Murphy of Corofin! His solemn and spectral aspect struck everybody. He advanced with fearlessness to the bar, behind which the Sheriff was seated, and inquired what the charge was which had been preferred against him, with a smile of ghastly derision. "You were looking at my voters," cries the attorney. "But I said nothing," replied the priest, "and I suppose that I am to be permitted to look at my parishioners."—"Not with such a face as that!" cried Mr. Dogherty, one of Mr. Fitzgerald's counsel. This produced a loud laugh; for, certainly, the countenance of Father Murphy was fraught with no ordinary terrors. "And this, then," exclaimed Mr. O'Connell's counsel, "is the charge you bring against the priests! Let us see if there be an act of Parliament which prescribes that a Jesuit shall wear a mask." At this instant, one of the agents of Mr. O'Connell precipitated himself into the room, and cried out, "Mr. Sheriff, we have no fair play—Mr. Singleton is frightening his tenants—he caught hold of one of them just now, and threatened vengeance against him." This accusation came admirably *apropos*. "What!" exclaimed the advocate of Mr. O'Connell, "is this to be endured? Do we live in a free country, and under a constitution? Is a landlord to commit a battery with impunity, and is a priest to be indicted for his physiognomy, and to be found guilty of a look?" Thus a valuable set-off against Father Murphy's eyebrows was obtained. After a long debate, the assessor decided that, if either a priest or a landlord actually interrupted the poll, they should be indiscriminately committed; but thought the present a case only for admonition. Father Murphy was accordingly restored to his physiognomical functions.

The matter had been scarcely disposed of, when a loud shout was heard from the multitude outside the courthouse, which had gathered in thousands, and yet generally preserved a profound tranquillity. The large window in the Sheriff's booth gave an opportunity of observing whatever took place in the square below; and, attracted by the tremendous uproar, everybody ran to see what was going on among the crowd. The tumult was produced by the arrival of some hundred freeholders from Kilrush, with their landlord, Mr. Vandeleur, at their head. He stood behind a carriage, and, with his hat off, was seen vehemently addressing the tenants who followed him. It was impossible to hear a word which he uttered, but his gesture was sufficiently significant: he stamped, and waved his hat, and shook his clinched hand. While he thus adjured them, the crowd through which they were passing assailed them with cries: "Vote for your country, boys! vote for the old religion!—Three cheers for liberty!—Down with Vesey, and hurra for O'Connell!" These were the exclamations which rent the air as they proceeded. They followed their landlord until they had reached a part of the square where Mr. O'Connell lodged, and before which a large platform had been erected, which communicated with the window of his apartment, and to which he could advance whenever it was necessary to address the people. When Mr. Vandeleur's freeholders had attained this spot, Mr. O'Connell rushed forward on the platform, and lifted up his arm. A tremendous shout succeeded, and in an instant Mr. Vandeleur was deserted by his tenants.

This platform exhibited some of the most remarkable scenes which were enacted in this strange drama of "The Clare Election." It was sustained by pillars of wood, and stretched out several feet from the wall to which it was attached. Some twenty or thirty persons could stand upon it at the same time. A large quantity of green boughs were turned about it, and, from the sort of bower which they formed, occasional orators addressed the people during the day. Mr. M'Dermot, a young gentleman from the county of Galway, of considerable fortune, and a great deal of talent as a speaker, used to harangue the multitude with great effect. Father Sheehan, a clergyman from Waterford, who had been mainly instrumental in the overthrow of the Beresfords, also displayed from this spot his eminent popular abilities. A Dr. Kenny, a Waterford surgeon, thinking that "the times were out of joint," came "to set them right." Father Maguire, Mr. Lawless, indeed the whole company of orators, performed on this theatre with indefatigable energy.

Mirth and declamation, and anecdote and grotesque delineation, and mimicry, were all blended together for the public entertainment. One of the most amusing and attractive topics was drawn from the adherence of Father Coffey to Mr. Fitzgerald. His manners, his habits, his dress, were all selected as materials for ridicule and invective; and puns, not the less effective because they were obvious, were heaped upon his name. The scorn and detestation with which he was treated by the mob clearly proved that a priest has no influence over them when he attempts to run counter to their political passions. He can hurry them on in the career into which their own feelings impel them, but he can not turn them into another course. Many incidents occurred about this rostrum, which, if matter did not crowd too fast upon me, I should stop to detail. I have not room for a minute narration of all that was interesting at this election, which would occupy a volume, and must limit myself to one, but that a very striking circumstance.

The generality of the orators were heard with loud and clamorous approbation; but, at a late hour one evening, and when it was growing rapidly dark, a priest came forward on the platform, who addressed the multitude in Irish. There was not a word uttered by the people. Ten thousand peasants were assembled before the speaker, and a profound stillness hung over the living but almost breathless mass. For minutes they continued thus deeply attentive, and seemed to be struck with awe as he proceeded. Suddenly I saw the whole multitude kneel down, in one concurrent genuflection. They were engaged in silent prayer, and when the priest arose (for he too had knelt down on the platform), they also stood up together from their orison. The movement was performed with the facility of a regimental evolution. I asked (being unacquainted with the language) what it was that had occasioned this extraordinary spectacle; and was informed that the orator had stated to the people that one of his own parishioners, who had voted for Mr. Fitzgerald, had just died; and he called upon the multitude to pray to God for the repose of his soul, and the forgiveness of the offence which he had committed in taking the bribery oath. Money, it seems, had been his inducement to give his suffrage against Mr. O'Connell. Individuals, in reading this, will exclaim, perhaps, against these expedients for the production of effect upon the popular passions. Let me observe in parenthesis, that the fault of all this (if it is to be condemned) does not lie with the Association, with the priesthood, or with the people, but with the law, which has, by its system of anomalies and alienations, rendered the national mind susceptible of such impressions.

Thus it was the day passed, and it was not until nearly nine o'clock that those who were actively engaged in the election went to dinner. There a new scene was opened. In a small room in a mean tavern, kept by a Mrs. Carmody, the whole body of leading patriots, counsellors, attorneys, and agents, with divers interloping partakers of election hospitality, were crammed and piled upon one another, while Mr. O'Connell sat at the head of the feast, almost overcome with fatigue, but yet sustained by that vitality which success produces. Enormous masses of beef, pork, mutton, turkeys, tongues, and fowl, were strewed upon the deal-boards, at which the hungry masticators proceeded to their operations. For some time nothing was heard but the clatter of the utensils of eating, interrupted by an occasional hobnobbing of "the counsellor," who, with his usual abstinence, confined himself to water.

The cravings of the stomach having been satisfied, the more intellectual season of potations succeeded. A hundred tumblers of punch, with circular slices of lemon, diffused the essence of John Barleycorn in profuse and fragrant steams. Loud cries for hot water, spoons, and materials, were everywhere heard, and huge jugs were rapidly emptied and replenished by waiters, who would have required ubiquity to satisfy all the demands upon their attention. Toasts were then proposed and speeches pronounced, and the usual "hip, hip, hurra!" with unusual accompaniments of exultation, followed. The feats of the day were then narrated: the blank looks of Ned Hickman, whose face had lost all its natural hilarity, and looked at the election like a full moon in a storm; the shroud-colored physiognomy of Mr. Sampson; and the tears of Sir Edward O'Brien, were alternately the subjects of merriment. Mr. Whyte was then called upon for an imitation of the Sheriff, when he used to ride upon an elephant at Calcutta. But in the midst of this conviviality, which was heightened by the consciousness that there was no bill to be paid by gentlemen who were the guests of their country, and long before any inebriating effect was observable, a solemn and spectral figure used to stride in, like the ghost of Hamlet, and the same deep, churchyard voice which had previously startled my ears, raised its awful peal, while it exclaimed: "The wolf, the wolf is on the walk! Shepherds of the people, what do you here? Is it meet that you should sit carousing and in joyance, while the freeholders remain unprovided, and temptation, in the shape of famine, is among them? Arise, I say, arise from your cups—the wolf, the wolf is on the walk!"

Such was the disturbing and heart-appalling adjuration of Father Murphy of Corofin, whose enthusiastic sense of duty never deserted him, and who, when the feast was unfinished, entered like the figure of Death which the Egyptians employed at their banquets. He walked round the room with a measured pace, like the envoy of another world, chasing the revellers before him, and repeating the same dismal warning—"The wolf, the wolf is on the walk!" Nothing was comparable to the aspect of Father Murphy upon these occasions, except the physiognomy of Mr. Lawless.

This gentleman, who had been usefully exerting himself during the whole day, somewhat reasonably expected that he should be permitted to enjoy the just rewards of patriotism for a few hours without any nocturnal molestation. It was about the time that he had just commenced his second tumbler, and when the exhilarating influence of his eloquent chalices was beginning to display itself, that the dismal cry was wont to come upon him. The look of piteous despair with which he surveyed this unrelenting foe to conviviality, was almost as ghastly at that of his merciless disturber; and as, like another Tantalus, he saw the draughts of pleasantness hurled away, a schoolmaster, who sat by him, and who "was abroad" during the election, used to exclaim: —

——"A labris sitiens fugientia captat
Flumina."—

It was in vain to remonstrate against Father Murphy, who insisted that the whole company should go forth to meet "the wolf upon the walk."

Upon going down stairs, the lower apartments were found thronged with freeholders and priests. To the latter had been assigned the office of providing food for such of the peasants as lived at too great a distance from the town to return immediately home; and each clergyman was empowered to give an order to the victuallers and tavern-keepers to furnish the bearer with a certain quantity of meat and beer. The use of whiskey was forbidden.

There were two remarkable features observable in the discharge of this office. The peasant, who had not tasted food perhaps for twenty-four hours, remained in perfect patience and tranquillity until his turn arrived to speak "to his reverence;" and the Catholic clergy continued with unwearied assiduity and the most amiable solicitude, though themselves quite exhausted with fatigue, in the performance of this necessary labor. There they stayed until a late hour in the morning, and until every claimant had been contented. It is not wonderful that such men, animated by such zeal, and operating upon so grateful and so energetic a peasantry, should have effected what they succeeded in accomplishing.

The poll at length closed; and, after an excellent argument delivered by the assessor, Mr. Richard Keatinge, he instructed the Sheriff to return Mr. O'Connell as duly elected.*

* The result of this election, was that the Duke of Wellington (who a few months previously had declared that "he could not comprehend the possibility of placing Roman Catholics in a Protestant legislature with any kind of safety, and whose personal knowledge told him, that no King, however Catholic, could govern his Catholic subjects without the aid of the Pope") became convinced that the choice lay between Catholic Emancipation and Civil war. He preferred the former, for which the repeal of the Test Act, in the previous year, had prepared the English mind. On the 5th February, 1829, the King's speech, at the opening of the Session recommended the suppression of the Catholic

The Courthouse was again crowded, as upon the first day, and Mr. Fitzgerald appeared at the head of the defeated aristocracy. They looked profoundly melancholy. Mr. Fitzgerald himself did not affect to disguise the deep pain which he felt, but preserved that gracefulness and perfect good temper which had characterized him during the contest, and which, at its close, disarmed hostility of all its rancor. Mr. O'Connell made a speech distinguished by just feeling and good taste, and

Association, and the subsequent consideration of Catholic disabilities, with a view to their adjustment and removal. At the instance of Mr. Sheil, supported by the Catholic Bishops, the Association dissolved itself. Mr. O'Connell, who had arrived in London, to take his seat for Clare, *as a Catholic*—which he contended he could do even under the old law—did not make the attempt, fearful lest it should embarrass a Government determined, however tardily and by compulsion, to do justice to Ireland. The Emancipation Bill became the law of the land, after much angry and personal discussion. O'Connell expected, as did the public at large, that he might take his seat under the new law. He presented himself at the bar of the House to be sworn, but declining to take the old oath (which declared the Catholic faith to be idolatrous), was directed by the Speaker to withdraw. A motion that he should take the new oaths, which were framed for the relief of Catholics, was negatived—on the ground that Mr. O'Connell was elected under the old system. He was then heard at the bar of the House, where he claimed his right to sit and vote, under the Act of Union as well as under the new Relief Bill. When the form of oath was again handed to him, he again refused to take it, saying that it contained one assertion which he knew to be not true, and another which he believed to be false. It was decided that he should not sit without taking the objectionable oath—thus making the Emancipation Act have an *ex post facto* operation. A new writ was issued for Clare. O'Connell again presented himself, and was again elected—though a certain Mr. Toby Glascock started from Dublin to oppose him, but did not reach Ennis until the election was over. On this re-election O'Connell took his seat, under the new act, and it was felt, even by the bulk of their partisans, that Ministers had done wrong to him, insult to his constituents, and injury to themselves, by refusing to extend the privileges of their own statute to Mr. O'Connell. It was a strange way to conciliate him, and they soon felt his power. Such a man, then virtually representing five millions of Irish Catholics, and endowed with rare talents, as an orator and a lawyer, speedily found his level in Parliament—and that was with the ablest and the most influential. Smarting under the sense of wrong, in this instance of asking him to swear an oath which the Legislature had just abrogated, it was only natural, when the opportunity came, that O'Connell should be found vehement and strong against Wellington and Peel. They had sowed the wind and he made them reap the whirlwind.—M.

begged that Mr. Fitzgerald would forgive him, if he had upon the first day given him any sort of offence. Mr. Fitzgerald came forward and unaffectedly assured him that whatever was said should be forgotten. He was again hailed with universal acclamation, and delivered a speech which could not surpass, in good judgment and persuasiveness, that with which he had opened the contest, but was not inferior to it. He left an impression, which hereafter will, in all probability, render his return for the County of Clare a matter of certainty; and, upon the other hand, I feel convinced that he has himself carried away from the scene of that contention — in which he sustained a defeat, but lost no honor — a conviction that not only the interests of Ireland, but the safety of the empire, require that the claims of seven millions of his fellow-citizens should be conceded. Mr. Fitzgerald, during the progress of the election, could not refrain from repeatedly intimating his astonishment at what he saw, and from indulging in melancholy forebodings of the events, of which these incidents are perhaps but the heralds. To do him justice, he appeared at moments utterly to forget himself, and to be absorbed in the melancholy presages which pressed themselves upon him. "Where is all this to end?" was a question frequently put in his presence, and from which he seemed to shrink.

At the close of the poll, Mr. Sheil delivered a speech, in which the views of the writer of this article were expressed; and as no faithful account of what he said upon that occasion appeared in the London papers, an extract from his observations will be justified, not by any merit in the composition as a piece of oratory, but by the sentiments of the speaker, which appear to me to be just, and were suggested by the scenes in which he had taken a part. The importance of the subject may give a claim to attention, which in other instances the speaker may not be entitled to command. He spoke in the following terms:—

"I own that I am anxious to avail myself of this opportunity to make reparation to Mr. Fitzgerald. Before I had the honor of hearing that gentleman, and of witnessing the mild and conciliatory demeanor by which he is distinguished, I had in another place expressed myself with regard to his political conduct, in language to which I believe that Mr. Fitzgerald referred upon the first day of the election, and which was, perhaps, too deeply tinctured with that virulence which is almost inseparable from the passions by which this country is so unhappily divided. It is but an act of justice to Mr. Fitzgerald to say, that, however we may be under the necessity of opposing him as a Member of an Administration hostile to our body, it is impossible to entertain toward him a sentiment of individual animosity; and I confess that, after having observed the admirable temper with which he encountered his antagonists, I can not but regret that, before I had the means of forming a just estimate of his personal character, I should have indulged in remarks in which too much acidity may have been infused.

"The situation in which Mr Fitzgerald was placed was peculiarly trying to his feelings. He had been long in possession of this County. Though we considered him as an inefficient friend, we were not entitled to account him as an opponent. Under these circumstances, it may have appeared harsh, and perhaps unkind, that we should have selected him as the first object for the manifestation of our power; another would have found it difficult not to give way to the language of resentment and of reproach; but, so far from doing so, his defence of himself was as strongly marked by forbearance as it was by ability. I thought it, however, not altogether impossible that, before the fate of this election was decided, Mr. Fitzgerald might have been merely practising an expedient of wily conciliation, and that, when he appeared so meek and self-controlled in the midst of a contest which would have provoked the passions of any ordinary man, he was only stifling his resentment, in the hope that he might succeed in appeasing the violence of the opposition with which he had to contend. But Mr. Fitzgerald, in the demeanor which he has preserved to-day, after the election has concluded with his defeat, has given proof that his gentleness of deportment was not affected and artificial; and, now that he has no object to gain, we can not but give him as ample credit for his sincerity, as we must give him for that persuasive gracefulness by which his manners are distinguished. Justly has he said that he has not lost a friend in this country; and he might have added, that, so far from having incurred any diminution of regard among those who were attached to him, he has appeased, to a great extent, the vehemence of that political enmity in which the associate of Mr. Peel was not very unnaturally held.

"But, Sir, while I have thus made the acknowledgment which was due to Mr. Fitzgerald, let me not disguise my own feelings of legitimate, but not, I hope, offensive exultation, at the result of this great contest, that has attracted the attention of the English people beyond all example. I am not mean enough to indulge in any contumelious vaunting over one who has sustained his defeat with so honorable a magnanimity. The victory which has been achieved has been obtained, not so much over Mr. Fitzgerald, as over the faction with which I excuse him, to a great extent, for having been allied. A great display of power has been made by the Catholic Association, and that manifestation of its influence over the national mind I regard as not only a very remarkable, but a very momentous incident. Let us consider what has taken place, in order that we may see this singular political phenomenon in its just light. It is right that we attentively survey the extraordinary facts before us, in order that we may derive from them the moral admonitions which they are calculated to supply. What then has happened? Mr. Fitzgerald was promoted to a place in the Duke of Wellington's councils, and the representation of this great County became vacant. The Catholic Association determined to oppose him, and at first view the undertaking seemed to be desperate. Not a single Protestant gentleman could be procured to enter the lists, and, in the want of any other candidate, Mr. O'Connell stood forward on behalf of the people. Mr. Vesey Fitzgerald came into the field encompassed with the most signal advantages. His father is a gentleman of large estate, and had been long and deservedly popular in Ireland. Mr. Fitzgerald himself, inheriting a portion of the popular favor with a favorite name, had for twenty years been placed in such immediate contiguity with power, that he was enabled to circulate a large portion of the influence of Government through this fortunate district. There is scarcely a single family of any significance among you which does not labor under Mr. Fitzgerald's obligations. At this moment it is only necessary to look at him, with the array of aristocracy beside him, in order to perceive upon what a high position for victory he was placed. He stands encompassed by the whole gentry of the County of Clare, who, as they stood by him in the hour of battle, come here to cover his retreat. Almost every gentleman of rank and fortune appears as his auxiliary; and the gentry, by their aspect at this instant, as well as by their devotedness during the election, furnish evidence that in his person their own cause was to be asserted.

"To this combination of favorable circumstances—to the promising friend, to the accomplished gentleman, to the eloquent advocate, at the head of all the patrician opulence of the county, what did we oppose? We opposed the power of the Catholic Association, and with that tremendous engine we have beaten the Cabinet Minister, and the phalanx of aristocracy by which he is surrounded, to the ground. Why do I mention these things? Is it for the purpose (God forbid that it should) of wounding the feelings or exasperating the passions of any man? No! but in order to exhibit the almost marvellous incidents which have taken place, in the light in which they ought to be regarded, and to present them in all their appalling magnitude. Protestants who hear me, gentlemen of the county Clare, you whom I address with boldness, perhaps, but certainly not with any purpose to give you offence, let me entreat your attention. A baronet of rank and fortune, Sir Edward O'Brien, has asked whether this was a condition of things to be endured; he has expatiated upon the extraordinary influence which has been exercised in order to effect these signal results; and, after dwelling upon many other grounds of complaint, he has with great force inveighed against the severance which we have created between the landlord and tenant.

"Let it not be imagined that I mean to deny that we have had recourse to the expedients attributed to us; on the contrary, I avow it. We have put a great engine into action, and applied the entire force of that powerful machinery which the law has placed under our control. We are masters of the passions of the people, and we have employed our dominion with a terrible effect. But, sir, do you, or any man here, imagine that we could have acquired this dreadful ability to sunder the strongest ties by which the different classes of society are fastened, unless we found the materials of excitement in the state of society itself? Do you think that Mr. Daniel O'Connell has himself, and by the single powers of his own mind, unaided by any external co-operation, brought the country to this great crisis of agitation? Mr. O'Connell, with all his talents for excitation, would have been utterly powerless and incapable, unless he had been allied with a great conspirator against the public peace; and I will tell you who that confederate is—it is the law of the land itself that has been Mr. O'Connell's main associate, and that ought to be denounced as the mighty agitator of Ireland. The rod of oppression is the wand of this potent enchanter of the passions, and the book of his spells is the Penal Code.* Break the wand of this

* It would swell these notes out of all proportion to attempt the biographies of such men as the Duke of Wellington. He was in the Irish Parliament in 1790, and voted for the extension of civil rights to the Catholics. The year after his return from India (in 1806), he was appointed Irish Secretary (his eldest son, the present Duke, was born, in Dublin, in 1807), and did not resign that office until 1809, when his active service in the Peninsula sufficiently occupied all his attention. When the war was ended, and the great soldier had to lay aside his sword, he adopted the Anti-Catholic views of the civilians with whom he was associated in the Government of the country. The result of Clare Election in 1828, showed him that concession or civil war must ensue, and he wisely adopted the former. Thomas Moore, who knew that

"Peace hath her victories, no less than War,"

introduced into one of his Irish Melodies, an address to Wellington, as prophetic as poetical:—

"And still the last crown of thy toils is remaining,
The grandest, the purest, even *thou* hast yet known;
Though proud was thy task, other nations unchaining,
Far prouder to heal the deep wounds of thy own.
At the foot of that throne, for whose weal thou hast stood,
Go, plead for the land that first cradled thy fame."

Although he granted what they desired, the Irish Catholics had little regard

political Prospero, and take from him the volume of his magic, and he will evoke the spirits which are now under his control no longer. But why should I have recourse to illustration which may be accounted fantastical, in order to elucidate what is in itself so plain and obvious?

"Protestant gentlemen, who do me the honor to listen to me, look, I pray you, a little dispassionately at the real causes of the events which have taken place among you. I beg of you to put aside your angry feelings for an instant, and believe me that I am far from thinking that you have no good ground for resentment. It must be most painful to the proprietors of this county to be stripped in an instant of all their influence; to be left destitute of all sort of sway over their dependents, and to see a few demagogues and priests usurping their natural authority. This feeling of resentment must be aggravated by the consciousness that they have not deserved such a return from their tenants; and as I know Sir Edward O'Brien to be a truly benevolent landlord, I can well conceive that the apparent ingratitude with which he was treated, has added to the pain which every landlord must experience; and I own that I was not surprised to see tears bursting at his eyes, while his face was inflamed with the emotions to which it was not in human nature that he should not give way. But let Sir Edward O'Brien and his fellow-proprietors, who are gathered about him, recollect that the facility and promptitude with which the peasantry have thrown off their allegiance, are owing not so much to any want of just moral feeling on the part of the people, as to the operation of causes for which the peo-

for "The Duke." They had got an idea that he had denied that he was an Irishman, and this was strengthened, in 1821, by his not accompanying George IV. on his visit to Ireland. The Duke of Wellington died, September 14, 1852, aged eighty-three.—It may be worth mentioning that shortly before his death, when the comparative merits of modern generals were discussed, the Duke said, "The greatest man of the lot, is Zachary Taylor, the American. In sight of the Mexicans, who had a vast superiority of men and artillery, he held a council of war, and the general opinion was that he should not risk a contest. 'Gentlemen,' said Taylor, 'I adjourn this council, until tomorrow—*after the battle.*' He won the battle against immense odds, and had great courage to run the risk, against advice. *That* was a true commander."—M.

ple are not to blame. In no other country, except in this, would such a revolution have been effected. Wherefore?—Because in no other country are the people divided by the law from their superiors, and cast into the hands of a set of men, who are supplied with the means of national excitement by the system of government under which we live.

"Surely no man can believe that such an anomalous body as the Catholic Association could exist, excepting in a community which had been alienated from the state by the state itself. The discontent and the resentment of seven millions of the population have generated that domestic government, which sways through the force of public opinion, and uses the national passions as the instruments for the execution of its will. From that body there has now been issuing, for many years, a continuous supply of exciting matter, which has overflowed the nation's mind. The lava has covered and inundated the whole country, and is still flowing, and will continue to flow, from its volcanic source. But, if I may so say, the Association is but the crater in which the fiery matter finds a vent, while its fountain is in the depth of the law itself. It would be utterly impossible, if all men were placed upon an equality of citizenship, and there was no exasperating distinctions among us, to create any artificial causes of discontent. Let men declaim for a century with far higher powers than any Catholic agitator is endowed with, and if they have no real ground of public grievance to rest upon, their harangues will be empty sound and idle air. But when what they tell the people is true—when they are sustained by substantial facts, then effects are produced, of which what has taken place at this election is only an example. The whole body of the people being previously inflamed and rendered susceptible, the moment any incident, such as this election, occurs, all the popular passions start simultaneously up, and bear down every obstacle before them. Do not, therefore, be surprised that the peasantry should thus at once throw off their allegiance to you, when they are under the operation of emotions which it would be wonderful if they could resist. The feeling by which they are now actuated, would make them not only vote against their landlords, but would make them rush into the field, scale the batteries of a fortress, and mount the breach; and, gentlemen, give me leave now to ask you, whether, after a due reflection upon the motives by which your vassals (for so they are accounted) are governed, you will be disposed to exercise any measure of severity in their regard?

"I hear it said, that before many days go by, there will be many tears shed in the hovels of your slaves, and that you will take a terrible vengeance of their treason. I trust in God that you will not, when your own passions have subsided, and your blood has had to cool, persevere in such a cruel, and, let me add, such an unjustifiable determination. Consider, gentlemen, whether a great allowance should not be made for the offence which they have committed. If they are, as you say they are, under the influence of fanaticism, I would say to you, that such an influence affords many circumstances of extenuation, and that you should forgive them, 'for they know not what they do.' They have followed their priests to the hustings, and they would follow them to the scaffold. But you will ask, wherefore should they prefer their priests to their landlords, and have purer reverence for the altars of their religion, than for the counter in which you calculate your rents? Ah, gentlemen, consider a little the relation in which the priest stands toward the peasant. Let us put the priest into one scale, and the landlord into the other, and let us see which should preponderate?

"I will take an excellent landlord and an excellent priest. The landlord shall be Sir Edward O'Brien, and the priest shall be Mr. Murphy of Corofin. Who is Sir Edward O'Brien? A gentleman who has a great fortune, who lives in a splendid mansion, and who, from the windows of a palace, looks upon possessions almost as wide as those which his ancestors beheld from the summit of their feudal towers. His tenants pay him their rent twice a-year, and they have their land at a moderate rate. So much for the landlord. I now come to Father Murphy of Corofin. Where does he reside? In an humble abode, situated at the foot of a mountain, and in the midst of dreariness and waste. He dwells in the midst of his parishioners, and is their benefactor, their friend, their father. It is not only in the actual ministry of the sacraments of religion that he stands as an object of affectionate reverence among them. I saw him, indeed, at his altar, surrounded by thousands, and felt myself the influence of his contagious and enthusiastic devotion. He addressed the people in the midst of a rude edifice, and in a language which I did not understand; but I could perceive what a command he has over the minds of his devoted followers. But it is not merely as the celebrator of the rites of Divine worship that he is dear to his flock; he is their companion, the mitigator of their calamities, the soother of their afflictions, the trustee of their hearts, the repository of their secrets, the guardian of their interests, and the sentinel of their death-beds. A peasant is dying: in the midst of the winter's night, a knock is heard at the door of the priest, and he is told that his parishioner requires his spiritual assistance: the wind is howling, the snow descends upon the hills, and the rain and storm beat against his face; yet he goes forth, hurries to the hovel of the expiring wretch, and, taking his station beside the mass of pestilence of which the bed of straw is composed, bends to receive the last whisper which unloads the heart of its guilt, though the lips of the sinner should be tainted with disease, and he should exhale mortality in his breath.

"Gentlemen, this is not the language of artificial declamation—this is not the mere extravagance of rhetorical phrase. This, every word of this, is the truth—the notorious, palpable, and unquestionable truth. You know it, every one of you know it to be true; and now let me ask you can you wonder for a moment that the people should be attached to their clergy, and should follow their ordinances as if they were the injunctions of God? Gentlemen, forgive me, if I venture to supplicate, on behalf of your poor tenants, for mercy to them. Pardon them, in the name of that God who will forgive you your offences in the same measure of compassion which you will show to the trespasses of others. Do not, in the name of that Heaven before whom every one of us, whether landlord, priest, or tenant, must at last appear—do not prosecute these poor people: don't throw their children out upon the public road—don't send them forth to starve, to shiver, and to die!

"For God's sake, Mr. Fitzgerald, and for your own sake, and as you are a gentleman and a man of honor, interpose your influence with your friends, and redeem your pledge. I address myself personally to you. On the first day of the election you declared that you would deprecate all persecution by the landlords, and that you were the last to wish that harsh and vindictive measures should be employed. I believe you; and now I call upon you to redeem that pledge of mercy, to fulfil that noble engagement, to perform that great moral promise. You will cover yourself with honor by so doing, in the same way that you will share in the ignominy that will attend upon any expedients of rigor. Before you leave this country to assume your high functions, employ yourself diligently in this work of benevolence, and enjoin your friends, with that eloquence of which you are the master, to refrain from cruelty, and not to oppress their tenants. Tell them, sir, that instead of busying themselves in the worthless occupation of revenge, it is much fitter that they should take the political condition of their country into their deep consideration. Tell them that they should address themselves to the Legislature, and implore a remedy for these frightful evils. Tell them to call upon the men, in whose hands the destiny of this great empire is placed, to adopt a system of conciliation and of peace, and to apply to Ireland the great canon of political morality which has been so powerfully expressed by the poet—'*Pacis imponere morem.*' Our manners, our habits, our laws, must be changed. The evil is to be plucked out at the root. The cancer must be cut out of the breast of the country. Let it not be imagined that any measure of disfranchisement, that any additional penalty, will afford a remedy. Things have been permitted to advance to a height from which they can not be driven back.

"Protestants, awake to a sense of your condition. Look round you. What have you seen during this election? Enough to make you feel that this is not mere local excitation, but that seven millions of Irish people are completely arrayed and organized. That which you behold in Clare, you would behold, under similar circumstances, in every county in the kingdom. Did you mark our discipline, our subordination, our good order, and that prophetic tranquillity which is far more terrible than any ordinary storm? You have seen sixty thousand men under our command, and not a hand was raised, and not a forbidden word was uttered, in that amazing multitude. You have beheld an example of our power in the almost miraculous sobriety of the people. Their lips have not touched that infuriating beverage to which they are so much attached, and their habitual propensity vanished at our command. What think you of all this? Is it meet and wise to leave us armed with such a dominion? Trust us not with it; strip us of this appalling despotism; annihilate us by concession; extinguish us with peace; disarray us by equality; instead of angry slaves, make us contented citizens: if you do not, tremble for the result!"

THE PENENDEN HEATH MEETING.

ANXIOUS to witness the great assembly of "the men of Kent," of which the High-Sheriff had called a meeting (having appointed twelve o'clock upon Friday the 24th for the immense gathering), I proceeded from Rochester to Maidstone at an early hour.* Upon my way, I saw the evidences of prodigious

* The Repeal of the Test and Corporation Acts, early in 1828, with little more than a shadow of resistance from the Wellington Ministry, was a sort of political "writing on the wall," to the Protestant Ascendency people throughout the United Kingdom. To check any further concessions, particularly as the Catholics had more and juster claims than the Dissenters, it was resolved to establish Brunswick Clubs, which were practically much the same, *minus* the secret oaths and obligations, as the Orange Lodges, put down by a prohibitory and penal statute in 1825. The Duke of Cumberland (brother of the reigning sovereign) was the patron of these associations, and Lords Winchilsea, Kenyon, and other persons of rank and property, were openly members. Clare Election, ending July 5, 1828, on the victory of O'Connell, a Catholic, excited the anger and apprehension of these ultra-Protestant agitators, who determined to hold public meetings, in defence of Protestant Ascendency in all the English counties. The first of these came off in Kent, on the 24th of October, 1828, on Penenden Heath, and from twenty thousand to thirty thousand persons were present. Mr. Sheil, whose graphic description brings the scene before us, happened in London when the meeting was about taking place, and several friends of civil and religious liberty strongly pressed him to attend, as a speaker, confident that he might thereby advance the cause which they had at heart. He consented, prepared a long and elaborate speech, obtained the small landed qualification requisite to allow him to address the meeting as a freeholder, and proceeded to Penenden Heath, where the clamor was so great that he could utter only a few sentences, though what he intended to say was printed, and distributed far and wide. The Penenden Heath Meeting, however, did not encourage similar attempts elsewhere, and Protestant Ascendency made no further public display until February, 1829, when Catholic Emancipation was proposed as a Government measure.—The newspapers of the day amused them-

exertion to call the yeomanry together, and from the summit of a hill that surmounts a beautiful valley near Maidstone, I beheld a long array of wagons moving slowly toward the spot which had been fixed by the High-Sheriff for the meeting. The morning was peculiarly fine and bright, and had a remnant of "summer's lingering bloom;" and the eye, through the pure air, and from the elevated spot on which I paused to survey the landscape, traversed an immense and glorious prospect. The fertile county of Kent, covered with all the profusion of English luxury, and exhibiting a noble spectacle of agricultural opulence, was before me; under any circumstances the scene would have attracted my attention, but, upon the occasion on which I now beheld it, it was accompanied by circumstances which greatly added to its influence, and lent to the beauty of nature a sort of moral picturesque. The whole population of an immense district seemed to have swarmed from their towns and cottages, and filled the roads and avenues which led to the great place of political rendezvous. In the distance lay Penenden Heath; and I could perceive that, long before the hour appointed by the Sheriff for the meeting, large masses had assembled upon the field, where the struggle between the two contending parties was to be carried on.

After looking upon this extraordinary spectacle, I proceeded on my journey. I passed many of "the men of Kent," who were going on foot to the meeting;* but the great majority were conveyed in those ponderous teams which are used for the purposes of conveying agricultural produce: and, indeed, "the men of Kent," who were packed up in those vehicles, seemed almost as unconscious as the ordinary burdens with which their heavy vehicles are laden. The wagons went on in their dull and monotonous rotation, filled with human beings,

selves with ridiculing Mr. Sheil's printed but unspoken oration; the public, however, perused it eagerly, and multitudes of copies were circulated all over the Kingdom. This is included in the volume of Sheil's published speeches, and is in every way worthy of his great reputation for political rhetoric.—M.

* There is a difference between Men of Kent and Kentish men. The former are locally accounted superior to the latter. A Kentish man, is a native of Kent county, born north of the river Medway; a "Man of Kent" comes from the district south of that river, which includes two thirds of that county.—M.

whose faces presented a vacant blank, in which it was impossible to trace the smallest interest or emotion. They did not exchange a word with each other, but sat in their wagons, with a half-sturdy and half-fatuitous look of apathy, listening to the sound of the bells which were attached to the horses by which they were drawn, and as careless as those animals of the events in which they were going to take a part. It was easy, however, to perceive to which faction they belonged; for poles were placed in each of these wagons, with placards attached to them, on which directions were given to the loads of freeholders to vote for their respective proprietors. I expected to have seen injunctions to vote for Emancipation, or for the Constitution, or against Popery and Slavery. These ordinances would, in all likelihood, have been above the comprehension of "the men of Kent;" and, accordingly, the more intelligible words, "Vote for Lord Winchilsea," or "Vote for Lord Darnley,"* were inscribed upon the placards.

I proceeded to my place of destination, and reached Penenden Heath. It is a gently-sloping amphitheatrical declivity, surrounded with gradually-ascending elevations of highly-cultivated ground, and presenting in the centre a wide space, exceedingly well calculated for the holding of a great popular assembly. On arriving, I found a great multitude assembled at about an hour before the meeting. A large circle was formed, with a number of wagons placed in close junction to each other, and forming an area capable of containing several thousand persons. There was an opening in the spot immediately opposite the Sheriff for the reception of the people, who were pouring into the enclosure, and had already formed a dense mass. The wagons were laden with the better class of yeomen, with the gentry at their head. A sort of hustings was

* John Stuart Bligh, fourth Earl of Darnley, was born in 1767, and died in 1831. In 1829, he claimed the Scottish Dukedom of Lennox, as next heir, in default of male issue for the last of the Stuarts. Cardinal York, who died in 1807 and was the next-of-kin (legitimate) of King Charles II., had been duly served heir to the peerage. The House of Lords have not come to a decision on this claim. The Darnley property in Kent, is Chobham Hall, near Gravesend. The Earldom is Irish, but its holder sits in the Lords, for his English barony of Clifton.—M.

raised for the Sheriff and his friends, with chairs in the front, and from this point the wagons branched off in two wings—that on the left of the Sheriff being allotted to the Protestant, and the right having been appropriated to the Catholic party. The wagons bore the names of the several persons to whom they belonged, and were designated as "Lord Winchilsea's," or "Lord Darnley's," or as "The Committee's," and ensigns were displayed from them which indicated the opinions of their respective occupiers.

The moment I ascended one of the wagons, where all persons were indiscriminately admitted, I saw that the Protestants, as they called themselves, had had the advantage in preparation, and that they were well arrayed and disciplined. Of this the effects produced by Lord Winchilsea's arrival afforded strong proof; for the moment he entered, there was a simultaneous waving of hats by his party, and the cheering was so well ordered and regulated, that it was manifest that every movement of the faction was preconcerted and arranged. The appearance of Lord Darnley, of Lord Radnor,* and the other leaders of the Catholic party, was not hailed with the same concurrence of applause from their supporters; not that the latter were not warmly zealous, but that they had not been disciplined with the same care.

I anxiously watched for the coming of Cobbett and of Hunt. I not only desired to see two persons of whom I had heard so much, but to ascertain the extent of their influence upon the public mind. Cobbett, I understood, had, before the meeting took place, succeeded in throwing discord into the ranks of the liberal party. He had intimated that he would move a petition against tithes. To this Lord Darnley vehemently objected, and asked very reasonably how he could, as a peer of

* William Pleydell Bouverie, third Earl of Radnor, was born in 1779, and sat in the House of Commons, from an early age until 1828. He was known, as a Commoner, by his courtesy title of Viscount Folkstone, during his father's life. He took a leading part, in 1809, in the investigation of the charges against the late Duke of York, of having allowed Mary Anne Clarke, his mistress, to dispose of commissions in the army, by her influence. Whither in the Upper or Lower House, the speeches and votes of Lord Radnor have generally been in aid of the liberal cause.—M.

the realm, co-operate in such a proposal. Several others, however, although they greatly disapproved of Cobbett's proposition in the abstract, were disposed to support any expedient which would have the effect of extinguishing the Brunswick faction. It had therefore been decided first, to try whether the Brunswick measure could not be got rid of without having recourse to any substitute, and, in the event of failing in that course, to sustain Cobbett's amendment. Cobbett had dined the preceding day at Maidstone, with about a hundred farmers, and had been very well received. He there gave intimations of his intended proposition against the Church. His friends said that he had devoted great care to his petition, and that he plumed himself upon it. I thought it exceedingly probable that he would succeed in carrying his measure, especially as he had obtained a signal triumph at a meeting connected with the Corn-Laws, and borne down the gentry before him. These anticipations had greatly raised my curiosity about this singular person, and I watched the effect which his coming should produce with some solicitude.

He at length arrived. Upon his entering the enclosure, I heard a cry of "Cobbett, Cobbett!" and turning my eyes to the spot from which the exclamation came, I perceived less sensation than I had expected to find.* Some twenty of the

* William Cobbett, son of a small farmer in Sussex, was born in 1762, and enlisted as a private soldier, when he was about two-and-twenty years old. He was sent with his regiment to British North America; diligently educated himself as an English scholar; was raised by his good conduct to the rank of sergeant-major; obtained his discharge (with good-service certificate) after seven years' service; returned to England, and went to France to perfect himself in French; thence came to the United States, where, writing under the *soubriquet* of "Peter Porcupine," he got into hot water; he again returned home, and supported the Government in a daily paper called the *Porcupine;* changed that publication into *Cobbett's Weekly Register,* in which he assailed the Ministry, with much continuity and force; was prosecuted, and fined repeatedly, but most heavily for comments on the illegal flogging of some militia-men at Ely, for which he had to undergo two years' imprisonment, with a fine of one thousand pounds sterling; continued his *Register,* however, during his confinement, and until what were called the "Six Acts" were passed to check him; came back to America, whence his *Register,* still published in London, was duly supplied with "copy," until his final return to England in 1819, bringing with

lowest class of freeholders made some demonstration of pleasure at his appearance, and followed him as he made his way toward a wagon on the right of the Sheriff. He was dressed in a gray frieze coat, with a red handkerchief, which gave him a very extraordinary aspect, and presented him in contrast with the body of those who occupied the wagons, who, on account of the public mourning, were dressed in black. He seemed in excellent health and spirits, for his cheeks were almost as ruddy as his neckcloth, and set off his white hair, while his eyes sparkled at the anticipation of the victory which he was confident that he should obtain. He seemed to me to

him the bones of Thomas Paine; successfully contested the representation of Coventry, in 1820, and of Preston, in 1826; warmly supported the French Revolution of July, 1830; was tried, in July, 1831, for the publication of "a libel, with intent to raise discontent in the minds of the laborers in husbandry, and to excite them to acts of violence, and to destroy cornstacks, machinery, and other property;" defended himself so ably and boldly, that the jury declined agreeing on a verdict of conviction; and thus allowed him a victory over Lord Grey's Ministry, who had prosecuted him. From that hour, his attacks on the Grey Ministry were untiring. He travelled all over the country, lecturing against them, and always with success. He continued his weekly attacks on them, in his *Register*, and his exposure of ministerial nepotism and grasping selfishness, as evidenced by "The Grey List," or schedule of places and sinecures distributed among members and connections of the family of Earl Grey, had a mighty influence in throwing that nobleman into the cold shade of unpopularity, after the Reform Bill excitement had subsided. In December, 1832, Cobbett was elected M. P. for Oldham, in Lancashire, under the Reform Bill. He was constant in his attendance, and a good man of business, but did not succeed in Parliament—a motion of his for the impeachment of Sir Robert Peel was a signal failure. The late hours and unwholesome atmosphere of the House told against one who used to boast of rising at four and going to bed at nine. In May, 1835, he was suddenly attacked with a disease of the throat, which eventuated in his death, on June 17, 1835, aged seventy-three. In July, 1852, his second son, John Morgan Cobbett, was elected member for Oldham, which he had unsuccessfully contested in July, 1835, on his father's death, as well as in July, 1847.—William Cobbett was an inconsistent politician, very much swayed by impulse and personal feeling, but, self-taught as he was, no English writer of his time was master of a purer style of writing. Southey, the poet, told me, in 1836, that since the time of Jeremy Taylor, no man had written such pure, homely, and expressive English as William Cobbett. He had a great love of the country, and some of his descriptions are landscapes in words. A curious vein of egotism ran through all nis writings, and, strangely enough, formed one of their leading attractions.—M.

mistake the following and acclamation of a few of the rabble for the applauses of the whole meeting. When, however, he ascended the wagon, and stood before the assembly, he ought to have discovered that he did not stand very high in the general favor; for while the circle about him cheered him with rather faint plaudits, the moment his tall but somewhat fantastical figure was exhibited to the meeting, he was assailed by the Brunswickers with the grossest insults, which, instead of exciting the anger, produced a burst of merriment among the Catholic party. "Down with the old bone-grubber!"—"Oh, Cobbett, have you brought Burdett along with you?"—"Where's your gridiron?"—"Will you pay Burdett out of the next crop of Indian corn?" These, and other contumelies, were lavished upon him by a set of fellows who were obviously posted in the meeting, in order to assail their antagonists and beat them down. Cobbett was so flushed with the certainty of success, and so self-deluded by his egregious notions of his own importance, that his temper was not at first disturbed, but, looking down triumphantly to those immediately about him, and drawing forth a long petition, told them that he had brought them something that should content them all. I surveyed him attentively at this moment.

Cobbett is generally represented as a man of rather a clownish-looking demeanor; and I have read, in some descriptions of him, that he could not, at first view, suggest any notion of his peculiar intellectual powers. I do not at all agree in the opinion. He has certainly a rude and rough bearing, and affects a heedlessness of form, amounting to coarseness and rusticity. But it is only requisite to look at him, in order to see in the expression of his countenance the vigorous mind with which he is endowed. The higher portion of his face is not unlike Sir Walter Scott's, to whom he bears, especially about the brow, a resemblance.* His eyes are more vivid

* There were several points of personal resemblance between Scott and Cobbett—so much so that when I first saw Cobbett, in 1830, I mistook him for Sir Walter, whose acquaintance I had made, some time before, on his visit to Ireland. Scott was taller and more erect; Cobbett looked like a plain, well-to-do farmer. The expression of Scott's face indicated shrewdness and sagacity; that

than the great author's, while the lower part of his countenance is expressive of fierce and vehement emotions. His attire and aspect certainly suggest, at first view, his early occupations, and the predilections of his later life (for he is more attached to agriculture than to politics); but whoever looks at him narrowly will see the impress of intellectual superiority upon his countenance, and perceive, under his rude bearing, the predominance of mind. When he first addressed the people, he was in exceedingly good humor; and as he snapped his fingers, and cried out, "Emancipation is all roguery!" the laugh which the recollection of his own devotedness to the Catholic cause created, was echoed by his own merriment, and he seemed to enjoy his political inconsistency as an exceeding good joke. He told the people that he was well aware that the Sheriff intended to adjourn the meeting, but that he would stay there, and hold a meeting himself.

Next to Cobbett stood the great leader of the radicals, Mr. Hunt.* A reconciliation has been recently effected between

of Cobbett's denoted more of cunning—the look of a man determined not to be taken in. Both wore very plain attire, and I never saw gloves with either. Cobbett dressed like a Surrey farmer: Scott like a Border laird.—M.

* Henry Hunt, for a long time the leader of the Radical Reform movement in England (hence the title of "Radicals"), was originally a farmer in Wiltshire. In his youth, he was such a strong loyalist, that, in 1801, when Napoleon threatened to invade England, which threat did "fright the isle out of its propriety," he offered the whole of his stock, valued at twenty thousand pounds sterling, for the use of the Government, if needed, and engaged to enter, with three of his servants all well mounted and equipped at his own cost, as volunteers into any regiment of horse that might make the first charge upon the enemy. He joined the Marlborough troop of cavalry yeomanry, but a dispute with Lord Bruce, its commander, caused him to challenge that officer, for which he was tried, fined one hundred pounds, and imprisoned for six weeks. From this time he joined the party who demanded radical reform of all abuses in Church and State. In August 16, 1819, he presided at a reform meeting in St. Peter's fields, Manchester, where the Magistrates interrupted the proceedings by sending mounted yeomanry among the unarmed multitude, shooting and sabring them in a brutal manner. This has long been called "The Massacre of Peterloo." The murdering magistrates escaped with impunity, but Hunt was indicted as the ringleader of an unlawful assembly of the people, tried, convicted, and sentenced to three years' imprisonment in Ilchester jail. He subsequently attempted to drive a trade by selling ground roasted corn, as a

them, and they stood together in the front of the same wagon before the people. I was surprised to find in Mr. Hunt, a man of an exceedingly mild and gentle aspect, with a smooth and almost youthful cheek, a bright and pleasant eye, a sweet and urbane smile, and altogether a most gentlemanlike and disarming demeanor. His voice too is exceedingly melodious, and as soft as his manners. This Gracchus of Manchester is utterly unlike the picture which the imagination is apt to form of a tribune of the people; and, indeed, I do not consider him to possess the external qualifications of a great demagogue, though he is certainly endowed with that plain and simple eloquence which is so peculiarly effective with an English multitude. Near Hunt and Cobbett, the Pylades and Orestes of radicalism, stood Counsellor French,* an Irish Catholic barrister, who is now a proselyte among the reformers, but seems to have many of the qualities necessary to constitute an apostle in the cause, and is likely one day to set up for himself.

In the wagon next that in which Cobbett, Darrel, and Hunt,

substitute for coffee, but the Excise interfered. Finally, he settled down into a large manufacturer of "Hunt's Matchless Blacking." He made several attempts to obtain a seat in Parliament, but was unsuccessful at Bristol, Westminster, and Somersetshire. At last, in the borough of Preston, in Lancashire, the potwallopers (every man who boiled a pot within its limits) elected him in 1830 and again in 1831 — the first time rejecting their previous member, Mr. Stanley (Earl of Derby, in 1854) whose family had long all but nominated the members. Mr. Hunt, a popular open air speaker, by no means made his mark in the legislature, but was quiet, and subdued, though consistent in the liberality of his votes. He was nearly sixty years old when he entered Parliament, and was too old to accommodate himself to its routine and requirements. In the election of 1832, following the enactment of the Reform Bill, the electors of "proud Preston," as the smoky place is called, did not re-elect Mr. Hunt. He died in February, 1835, aged sixty-two. In person he was tall and muscular. His oratory was singularly devoid of ornament, but he had a plain way of putting facts, argument, and assertions, before his auditory, which had immense force. He published his own Memoirs, while in prison, but their literary merit was small. At one time, he was the most popular man in England, and his summons would have collected a hundred thousand men, in the suburbs of London alone.— M.

* Counsellor French, who was a strong Catholic, held a public discussion at Hammersmith, London, on points of religious faith and practice, with a Minister of the Scotch Church, named Cumming. This was many years after Emancipation was granted. Both claimed the victory — of course.— M.

were placed, sat Mr. Sheil, the Irish demagogue. This gentleman was said, by some people, to have been sent over by the Association; while others asserted, that he had of his own accord embarked in the perilous enterprise of addressing "the Men of Kent." There was a feeling of curiosity, mingled with disrelish, produced by his appearance there. The English Catholics had endeavored to dissuade him from the undertaking; and Mr. Darrel, a gentleman of property in the county, was particularly anxious that he should not attempt to speak. Lord Darnley was also very adverse to this adventurous step, and so far from having given Mr. Sheil a freehold, had intimated, I heard, that the death-bed of the Duke of York was not yet so much forgotten, that Mr. Sheil should venture into such an assembly.* That gentleman sat in one of the wagons, apparently careless of the impression which he should produce; but his pale and bilious face, in which discontent and solicitude, mingled with a spirit of sardonic virulence, are expressed, and his restless and unquiet eye, gave indications that he was annoyed at the opprobrious epithets which were showered upon him, and that he was anxious about the event, as it should personally affect himself. There is certainly in Mr. Sheil's face and person little to bespeak the favor of a public assembly; and if he produces oratorical effects, he must be indebted to a power of phrase, and an art in delivery, of which, in the uproar in which he spoke, it was impossible in that meeting to form any estimate. Next to Mr. Sheil was the wagon appropriated to the Committee, where there were some English Catholics; and Lord Darnley's and Lord Radnor's wagons succeeded.

The opposite wing was, as I have mentioned, occupied by

* When the Duke of York was dying, two years after he had sworn, "So help me God," that he never would consent to any measure of Catholic Emancipation, Mr. Sheil endeavored "to point a moral" from the approaching funeral of him who had raised his hand to heaven against the speaker's country, and concluded by saying that, the solemn pageant ended, "the business, and pursuits, and all the frivolities of life will be resumed; and the heir to three kingdoms will be in a week forgotten; we, too, shall pardon and forget him." There was a great outcry against this speech, at this time, and the Brunswick Clubs fanned the angry flame, as best they could.—M.

the Brunswickers, of whom by far the most conspicuous was Lord Winchilsea. He is a tall, strong-built, vigorous-looking man, destitute of all dignity or grace, but with a bluff, rude, and direct nautical bearing, which reminds one of the quarter-deck, and would lead you to suppose that he was the mate of a ship (a conjecture which a black silk handkerchief tied tightly about his neck, tends to assist) rather than an hereditary Counsellor of the Crown. Whatever feelings of partiality his late conduct may have generated toward him with his own faction, he is certainly not popular in the county; for he is the terror of poachers, and is most arbitrary in the enforcement of the game laws. It is but justice to him to say, that he has, upon one or two occasions, when he has detected poachers upon his estate, given them the alternative of going to prison or fighting with him; for to his political he superadds no inconsiderable pugilistic qualifications. He seems very well qualified to lead an English mob, and possesses, in a far greater perfection than Hunt or Cobbett, the demagogic qualities of voice, which gave him, at Penenden Heath, a great advantage over his opponents.* Before the chair was taken, he was actively engaged in marshalling his troops, and cheering them on to battle, and it was manifest that he felt all the excitement of a leader engaged in a cause, upon the issue of which his own political importance was depending. I did not remark any persons of rank about him, and, indeed, the Protestant was conspicuously inferior in this particular to the Catholic wing. There were, however, on the left side, a number of persons, in whom it was easy to recognise the sacerdotal physiognomy, of far more influence than noblemen could have been; the whole body of the Kent Clergy were marshalled for the occasion; and not only the priests of the established religion, but many of the

* George Finch Hatton, tenth Earl of Winchilsea and Nottingham, was born in 1791, and succeeded to the title in 1826. His place in Kent, is Eastwell Park. He has always been much opposed, polemically and politically, to the Catholics. In 1829, having published a letter in which he imputed to the Duke of Wellington a desire to introduce popery into every department of the state, the Duke called on him to retract and apologize, and, on refusal to do so, was challenged by his Grace, and a duel ensued, in which neither combatant was hit.—In youth, from his loud voice, the Earl was called "Roaring Hatton."—M.

dissenting preachers of the Methodist school, were arrayed under the Winchilsea banners. It was easy to recognise them even amid the crowd of men habited in black, by their lugubrious and dismal expression. The clergy at the meeting were so numerous, that the Protestant side had much more a clerical than an agricultural aspect.

The different parties being thus distributed, and every wagon having been occupied, and the whole of the area within the enclosure having been filled by the dense crowd, the Sheriff, Sir T. Maryon Wilson,* appeared exactly at twelve o'clock, and took the chair. He seemed to me, from the distance at which I saw him, a young man, quite untutored in the business of public meetings; but he had beside him his sub-sheriff, Mr. Scudamore, who appeared to have all the zeal by which his employer was actuated in the cause of Protestantism, and to be perfectly well-versed in the stratagems by which an advantage may be given to one party, without affording to the other the opportunity of complaining of any very gross breach of decorum. This gentleman had a coarse, red-whiskered, and blunt face, of the Dogberry character, in which a vulgar authoritativeness was combined with those habits of submission to his superior, which are generally found in subordinate functionaries.

The High-Sheriff having taken his station, delivered a brief speech, in which he stated the object of the meeting to be the adoption of such measures as should be deemed most advisable for the support of the church establishment; and he concluded by enjoining the assembly to hear all parties, a precept which he certainly exhibited no very great solicitude to embody in his own conduct. A letter from the brother of Mr. Honeywood was then read, in which an excuse was made for that gentleman upon the ground of indisposition (it was well known that

* Sir Thomas Maryon Wilson, who, as High Sheriff of Kent, was "first man in the county" in 1828, was born in 1800; owns a property in Kent, called Charlton House; and has been chiefly noted, of late years, by his constant efforts to obtain the enactment of a Parliamentary statute allowing him to enclose, for his own use and profit, a great part of Hampstead Heath, near Highgate, which is now the common property of the London public, and is used by them for purposes of healthful recreation.—M.

he was adverse to the objects of the meeting), and then Mr. Gipps rose to move the petition. I found it difficult to ascertain exactly who he was; but thus far I learned, that he is not a man of influence or weight from property in the county, and, indeed, I could see no motive for putting him in the foreground, excepting that he has a clear and distinct voice, which, in a less clamorous assembly, would have been probably heard by a considerable part of the meeting. He dwelt upon a variety of the common topics which are pressed into the service of Anti-catholicism, but gave no novelty by any unusual display of diction to the old arguments against Popery. He seemed himself to chuckle at what he conceived to be a peculiarly jocular and picturesque representation of Mr. O'Connell, at the Clare election, bowing down to receive the benediction of a Bishop, forgetting that it was hardly stranger on the part of Mr. O'Connell to go through, what is, after all, I believe, a common form with pious Roman Catholics, than for a Duchess to print her beautiful lips on the black and bearded mouth of a coal-heaver, in order to obtain a vote for Mr. Fox.* I am surprised that this parallel was not adduced in Mr. O'Connell's defence. After Mr. Gipps had expended himself in a monotonous and wearisome diatribe against the Catholic religion, he proceeded to read a petition, which the liberal party had anticipated would have prayed distinctly against all concessions to the Roman Catholics. To their surprise, it was couched in the following words:—

* Georgiana, Duchess of Devonshire, whose [reputed?] son is the present Duke, was a very clever, charming, and (though her hair was of the color between golden and red) beautiful woman. She was a leader of the fashionable world of London, for many years. She was married at the early age of seventeen, and her house became a sort of political meeting-place for the old Whig leaders. She wrote poetry—and Coleridge eulogized the "heroic measure" of her "Passage of Mont St. Gothard." She composed music also, and patronized painters and sculptors. During the great Westminster Election, in which Fox, "the Man of the People," was a candidate, she personally canvassed for him. The story alluded to by Mr. Sheil was that having asked a coal-heaver to vote for Fox, he said, "Yes, if you will kiss me," and that, putting a guinea between her lips, she allowed him to take kiss and coin at the same time, on which he voted for Fox!—The Duchess, albeit much talked about, is believed to have been a virtuous wife. She died in 1806, aged forty-nine.—M.

"Your Petitioners beg leave to express to your Honorable House, their sense of the blessings they enjoy under the Protestant Constitution of these Kingdoms, as settled at the Revolution, viewing with the deepest regret the proceedings which have for a long time been carrying on in Ireland.

"Your Petitioners feel themselves imperatively called upon to declare their strong and inviolable attachment to those Protestant principles, which have proved to be the best security for the civil and religious liberty of these Kingdoms.

"They therefore approach your Honorable House, humbly but earnestly praying that the Protestant Constitution of the United Kingdom may be preserved entire and inviolable."

The phraseology of this petition, from its moderate character, excited some surprise; and it was justly said that no Protestant could object to the matter for which it ostensibly purported to pray. The compatibility of concession to the Catholics with the entirety and inviolability of the Protestant Church, has been always maintained, by not only the Protestant, but Catholic advocates of their claims. This subdued tone of the petition gave distinct proof that the Clubbists calculated upon a strong opposition to any more forcible interference with the legislature. The object, however, of the Clubbists was obvious, and the petition was resisted, not so much upon the ground of its containing anything in itself very objectionable, as that the intent of the petitioners themselves was avowed.

A Mr. Plumtre* seconded Mr. Gipps. It was said that he was a Calvinist, and he certainly had the aspect which we might suppose to have been worn by the founder of his religion

* In 1828, Mr. Plumtre was one of the parliamentary representatives of Kent, and ultra-illiberal in his politics and religion. He properly belonged to a small but compact body in the House of Commons, called "The Saints." He was a well-meaning, foolish-acting, absurd-speaking man — a sort of parliamentary Malvolio. — M.

when he ordered Servetus to be consumed by a slow fire. He said nothing at all worth note.

When Mr. Plumtre sat down, Lord Camden addressed the Sheriff.* He occupied a peculiar station. Instead, as was observed in one of the morning papers, of taking his place upon the right side, and bringing up his tenants in a body, he came unattended, and selected a place upon the hustings near the Sheriff. He deprecated all kinds of partisanship in the course which he took in the proceedings; and certainly his deportment and look indicated that it was with no other feeling than one of duty, and without any kind of struggle for superiority, that he had mingled in the contest. I do not know whether it was his office as Lord Lieutenant of the County that procured him a patient hearing from both sides, or whether, before their passions were strongly excited, they forbore from offering an indignity to a person who from his age and rank derived a title to universal respect. He was the only person who was heard with scarcely any interruption.

His speech was exceedingly well delivered, in a surprisingly clear, sonorous, and audible intonation. He condemned the conduct of the Catholics in the language of vehement vituperation, but at the same time pointed out the extreme violence with which their demands were resisted. The only circumstance in his speech worth recording is, that he mentioned his belief that some measure of concession was intended by Government. This attracted great attention; and it is difficult to

* The Marquis Camden deserves a passing notice, were it only to commemorate his praiseworthy conduct, as a sinecurist. He was son of the great Earl Camden, Lord Chancellor of England, 1766–'70. He was born in 1759, educated at Cambridge, entered the House of Commons in 1780; and, in the same year, was appointed one of the Tellers of the Exchequer, a lucrative sinecure. He succeeded his father in the Earldom in 1794; and soon after went, as Lord-Lieutenant of Ireland. In 1804, he became a Cabinet Minister, and quitting office on the death of Pitt, resumed it on the downfall of the Grenville administration. He was rewarded with a Marquisate in 1812, and, when an outcry was raised against sinecures, resigned for the public good about thirty thousand pounds sterling a year, out of the proceeds of his tellership. The whole amount so surrendered amounted to about two hundred and fifty thousand pounds. He was Lord-Lieutenant, custos-rotulorum, and vice-admiral of Kent, and died in 1840, aged eighty-one.—M.

conceive how a person, so prudent and so calm as Lord Camden manifestly is, would have intimated any belief of his upon the subject, unless there were some foundation on which something more substantial than a mere conjecture could be raised. Toward the end of his speech the Clubbists became exceedingly impatient, and one of them called him "an old Radical;" a term of which he protested that he was at a loss to discover the applicability, as he had never done anything to please the Radicals. This Mr. Hunt afterward controverted, and insisted that he had done much to gratify the Radicals by giving up his sinecure—a panegyric which was well merited, and was most happily pronounced.

Lord Darnley followed Lord Camden, but was received with loud and vehement hooting. This nobleman is considered to be very proud, without being arrogant, and to have as full consciousness of the dignity and rights of his order, as Lord Grey could charge any Whig disciple to entertain. He must have been deeply galled when he perceived that his rank and wealth were only turned into scoff, and when in the outset of his speech a common boor cried out, "That there fellow is an Hirishman. Tim, put a potato down his throat, and choke his d——d Hirish jaw." He was not deterred from going on by the howlings which surrounded him, and with far more intrepidity than I should have been disposed to give him credit for, he proceeded with his speech. He soon, however, received a blow, which wounded him much more than the potato proposition; for the moment he began to talk of his estate in Ireland (where he has a very large property), several people cried out, "Why don't you live on your estate, and be d——d to you, and to every other d——d absentee!" This was a thrust which it was impossible to parry. Lord Darnley endeavored to proceed; but the uproar became so terrible, that not a word which he uttered could be heard in the tumult. Whatever faults the Clubbists may have committed, any excessive deference to rank and wealth was not, on this occasion at least, among their defects; and indeed, with the exception of Cobbett and Sheil, no man was listened to with more angry impatience than the noble Earl. After speaking for about twenty minutes, he sat down with evident marks of disappointment and personal mortification.

On his resuming his place, with a determination, I should presume, never to expose himself to such an affront again, Lord Winchilsea and Mr. Sheil rose together. The competition for precedence into which the Irish demagogue was so audacious as to enter with the chief and captain of the Brunswickers, excited the fury of the latter. Mr. Sheil insisted that, as Lord Camden had—as was, I believe, the case—alluded to him, he had a right to vindicate himself; and there were many who surmised that his motive for presenting himself at this early stage of the proceedings was, that he had sent his speech to London to be printed; and he was heard to say that he did not care whether the Brunswickers listened to him, provided his arguments were read.* Whatever was his object, it was certainly not a little presumptuous in a stranger thus to enter the lists with an Earl, and to demand a prior audience. "I am an Irishman," said Mr. Sheil. "I'll be sworn you are," cried Cobbett; "you are such a d——d impudent fellow." The party on the right endeavored to support Mr. Sheil, and for a long time both Lord Winchilsea and that gentleman continued to speak together, amid a confusion in which neither could be heard.

At length the Sheriff interposed, and declared that Lord Winchilsea had first obtained his eye. That nobleman proceeded to deliver himself of a quantity of commonplace against the Catholic religion, amid the vehement plaudits of his own faction, intermingled with strong marks of disapprobation from the right. "Mushroom Lord—upstart—go mind your rabbits, and the Papists are not poachers!" were the cries of the liberal party; while the Brunswickers exclaimed,

* Mr. Sheil had prepared a long and brilliant oration, to be delivered at the Penenden Heath Meeting, and Murdo Young, of "The Sun" newspaper had it published that evening as if it had been spoken. Only a few sentences were actually spoken, but the speech, to the extent of several columns, was sent all over the United Kingdom, on the wings of the press, and produced a strong impression wherever read. I recollect that, on returning from Penenden Heath, on the evening of the meeting, Mr. Sheil supped at the "Sun" office, and I had the gratification of being one of the party.—M.

"Bravo, Winchilsea!" and waved their hats, as with the lungs of Stentor, with the gesture of a pugilist, and the frenzy of a fanatic, he proceeded. Although utterly destitute of idea, and though scarcely one distinct notion, perhaps, could be detected in his speech, yet Lord Winchilsea, by the energy of his action, and the impetuosity of his manner, and the strong evidences of rude sincerity about him, made an impression upon his auditors far greater than the cold didactic manner of Lord Camden or Lord Darnley was calculated to produce.

There can be no greater mistake than the supposition that the English people are not fond of ardent speaking, and of a vehement rhetorical enunciation. Lord Winchilsea is perfectly denuded of knowledge, reflection, or command of phrase; yet by dint of strong feeling he contrives to awaken a sympathy which a colder speaker, with all the graces of eloquence, could never attain. He seems to be in downright earnest; and although his personal vanity may be an ingredient in his sincerity, it is certain, whatever be the cause, that his ardor and vehemence are far more powerful auxiliaries to his cause, than the contemplative philosophy of the Whigs, who, contented with their cold integrity of purpose, adopted no efficient means to bring their tenants to the field, and encounter their opponents with the weapons which were so powerfully wielded against them.

After having whirled himself round, and having beaten his breast and bellowed for about half an hour, Lord Winchilsea sat down in the midst of the constitutional acclamations of the Brunswickers; and Mr. Sheil, and Mr. Shea, an English Catholic gentleman, both presented themselves to the Sheriff. The Sheriff gave a preference to Mr. Shea, who made a bold and manly speech, but was interrupted by the continued hootings of the Protestant party. The only fault committed by Mr. Shea was, that he dwelt too long on the pure blood of the English Catholics—a topic of which they are naturally but a little tediously fond: it were to be desired that this old blood of theirs did not stagnate so much in their veins, and beat a little more rapidly in its circulation. With their immense fortunes, and a little more exertion, what might they not accomplish in influencing the public mind? Excellent men in private life, they are not sufficiently ardent for politicians, and should remember that their liberty may be almost bought, and that two or three thousand pounds well applied might have turned the Kent meeting.

Mr. Shea having concluded, Lord Teynham rose; and Mr. Sheil, at the Sheriff's request, gave way to him. Lord Teynham had been a Roman Catholic.* His name is Roper, and, I believe, he is descended from Mrs. Roper, the daughter of Sir Thomas More. He was assailed with reproaches for his apostasy by the Protestants; and, though he made a very good speech, it was neutralized in its effect by his desertion of his former creed. So universal (however unjust, perhaps) is the antipathy to a renegade, that among the Brunswickers themselves, his having ceased to be a Catholic rendered him an object of scorn. "That fellow's a-going to shift his religion again!"—"Oh, my Lord, there's a man here as says that what your Lordship's saying is all a d——d Popish lie!" and other ejaculations of the same character warned my Lord Teynham that his change of creeds had not rendered him more acceptable to his audience.

Lord Teynham having sat down amid the Brunswick groans, Mr. Sheil rose among them. He was vehemently applauded on the right, and as furiously howled at from the left. "Down with him, the traitor!"—"Down with the rebel!"—"Apologize for what you said of the Duke of York!"—"Send him and O'Connell to the Tower!"—"He got his freehold last night in Maidstone!"—"Down with him!"—"Off, Sheil, off!"—"We're not the Clare freeholders!"—"See how the viper spits!"—"How the little hanimal foams at the mouth! take care of him, he'll bite you!"—"Off, Sheil, off!" were the greetings with which this gentleman was hailed by the Brunswickers, while his own party cried out, "Fair play!"—"Oh, you cowards, you are afraid to hear him!"

Of what Mr. Sheil actually said, it was impossible to give any account; and the miraculous power by which "The Sun"

* Henry Francis Roper, fourteenth Lord Teynham, born 1760, died 1842. His estate in Kent was called Linsted Lodge.—M.

newspaper of that night contrived to publish his oration in three columns, must be referred to some Hohenloe's interposition in favor of that journal. I heard but one sentence, which I afterward recognised in print, as having been spoken: "See to what conclusion you must arrive, when you denounce the advocates of Emancipation as the enemies of their country. How far will your anathema reach? It will take in one half of Westminster Abbey; and is not the very dust, into which the tongues and hearts of Pitt, and Burke, and Fox, have mouldered, better than the living hearts and tongues of those who have survived them? If you were to try the question by the authorities of the illustrious dead, and by those voices which may be said to issue from the grave, how would you determine? If, instead of counting votes in St. Stephen's Chapel, you were to count monuments in the mausoleum beside it, how would the division of the great departed stand? Enter the aisles which contain the ashes of your greatest legislators, and ask yourselves as you pass how they felt and spoke, when they had utterance and emotion, in that senate where they are heard no more: write '*Emancipation*' upon the tomb of every advocate, and its counter-epitaph on that of every opponent of the peace of Ireland, and shall we not have a majority of sepulchres in our favor?" With this exception, I do not think that the Irish demagogue uttered one word of what appeared in the shape of an elaborate essay in the newspapers."

After having stamped, and fretted, and entreated, and menaced the Brunswickers for half an hour, during which he sustained a continued volley of execrations, Mr. Sheil thought it prudent to retreat, and was succeeded by Mr. Larkin, an auctioneer from Rochester, who delivered a very clever speech in favor of radicalism, but had the prudence to keep clear of Emancipation. His occupation afforded a fine scope for Brunswick wit. "Knock him down—going, going, gone!" and similar reminiscences, exhibited the aristocracy of the mob. Mr. Larkin was not at all disturbed, but, with an almost unparalleled *sang-froid,* drew a flask from his pocket, and refreshed himself for the next sentence, when the uproar was at its height.

When he had finished, Sir Edward Knatchbull, the member for the county, and Cobbett, who had been railing for hours at the long speeches, got up together. The Sheriff preferred Sir Edward, upon which Cobbett got into a fit of vehement indignation. He accused the Sheriff of gross partiality, and, while Sir Edward Knatchbull was going on, shook his hand repeatedly at him, and exhibited the utmost savageness of demeanor and of aspect. His face became inflamed with rage, and his mouth was contorted into a ferocious grin. He grasped a large pole, with a placard at the head of it in favor of Liberty, and, standing with this apparatus of popularity, which assisted him in supporting himself at the verge of the wagon, he hurled out his denunciations against the Sheriff. The Brunswickers roared at him, and showered contumely of all kinds upon his head, but with an undaunted spirit he persevered. Sir Edward Knatchbull was but indistinctly heard in the tumult which his own party had got up to put Cobbett down. He seems a proud, obstinate, dogged sort of Squire, with an infinite notion of his own importance as an English county member, and a corresponding contempt for seven millions of his fellow-citizens. He has in his face and bearing many of the disagreeable qualities of John Bullism, without any of its frankness and plain dealing. He is rude without being honest, and offensive without being sincere.* Cobbett was almost justified in complaining that such a man should be preferred to him.

When he had terminated a speech, in which it was evident that he was thinking of the next election, at which the Deerings intended to dispute the county with him, Cobbett was allowed by the Sheriff to proceed. His hilarity was restored for a little while, and holding out his petition against tithes, he set about abusing both parties. In a letter published in the Morning Herald, he takes care, in his account of the meet-

* Sir Edward Knatchbull, of Mersham Hatch, Kent (which his family have owned since the time of Henry II.), was born in 1781, and succeeded to the title in 1819. He eventually abandoned much of his intolerance, was Paymaster of the Forces, in Peel's last Ministry, and continued comparatively liberal until his death.—M.

ing, to record the opprobrious language applied by the multitude to others; but he omits all mention of what was said of himself. "Down with the old Bone-grubber!"—"Roast him on his gridiron;"—"D—n him and his Indian corn;" were shouted from all quarters. He was not, however, much discomposed at first, for he was confident of carrying his petition, and retorted with a good deal of force and some good humor on those who were inveighing against him. "You cry out too weakly, my bucks!" said he, snapping his fingers at them. "You cry like women in the family-way. There's a rascal there, that is squeaking at me, like a parson's tithe-pig."

These sallies amused everybody; but still the roar against him continued, and I was astonished to see what little influence he had with even the lower orders by whom he was surrounded. The Catholic party looked upon him as an enemy, who came to divide them, and the Brunswickers treated him with mingled execrations and scorn. At length he perceived that the day was going against him, and his eyes opened to his own want of power over the people. Though he afterward vaunted that the great majority were with him, he appeared not to have above a dozen or two to support his proposition, and when he sat down, evident symptoms of mortification and of rage against all parties appeared in his countenance. Altogether, he acquitted himself as badly as can be well imagined; and it seems to me as clear that he is a most inefficient and powerless speaker, as that he is a great and vigorous writer.

Hunt got up to second him, and was received almost as badly as his predecessor, though his conduct and manner were quite opposite, and he did everything he could, by gentleness and persuasiveness, to allay the fury of the Brunswick party, But, after he had begun, Sir Edward Knatchbull interrupted him in a most improper and offensive manner, which induced Lord Radnor to stand up and reprobate Sir Edward's conduct as a most gross violation of decorum. Mr. Hunt went on; but, whatever may be his sway with public assemblies on other occasions, he certainly showed few evidences of omnipotence upon this. He seemed to be crest-fallen, and to have quailed under the force which was brought to bear against him. One story he told well, of Sir Edward Knatchbull having refused to pay him for four gallons of beer, when he was a brewer at Bristol, because he had sold him a less quantity than that prescribed by the law: altogether, his speech, if it might be so called, when he was not allowed to utter a connected sentence, was a complete failure; but I am convinced that no estimate of his ability can be formed from this specimen of him, as his voice was stifled by the faction to which he was opposed. Indeed both parties seemed to repudiate Cobbett and Hunt, as their common enemies.

Before Hunt had finished, there was a tremendous and seemingly a preconcerted cry of "question" from the Brunswickers; Hunt went on speaking, and immense confusion took place. Mr. Calcraft interfered in vain. Mr. Hodges and Lord Radnor then moved an amendment, declaring that the measure should be left to the discretion of the legislature; and amid a tumult, to which I never witnessed anything at all comparable, the Sheriff put the question. It has been stated in the newspapers that the Brunswickers had a great majority; the impression of a vast number of persons was quite the reverse. They were indeed so well disciplined, that their show of hats was simultaneous, while the liberal party hardly knew what what was going forward. The Sheriff omitted to put Cobbett's amendment, which seemed to be forgotten by every one but himself; and having announced that there was a large majority for the petition moved by Mr. Gipps, retired from the chair. The acclamations of the Brunswickers were reiterated; the whole body waved their hats, and lifted up their voices; the parsons shook hands with each other: the Methodists smiled with a look of ghastly satisfaction; and Lord Winchilsea, losing all decency and self-restraint, was thrown into convulsions of joy, and leaped, shouted, and roared, in a state of almost insane exultation. The whole party then joined in singing "God save the King," in one howl of appropriate discord, and the assembly broke up.

Thus terminated the great Kent meeting; to which, however, I conceive that more importance, as it affects the Catholic question, is attached than it deserves. I have not room left for many comments, but a few brief observations on this striking incident are necessary. The triumph of Protestantism is not complete. The whole body of the clergy, who are in Kent exceedingly numerous, were not only present, but used all their influence to procure an attendance, and the utmost exertions were employed to bring the tenantry of the anti-Catholic proprietors to the field. No exertion was made upon the other side. Lord Camden boasted that he had not interfered with a single individual; yet it is admitted that at least one third of the assembly were favorable to the Catholics. The spirit of Lord George Gordon may, by the metempsychosis of faction, have migrated into Lord Winchilsea; but, while he is as well qualified in intellect and in passion to conduct a multitude of fanatics, his troops are of a very different character. Will the legislature shrink before him? Or will it not rather exclaim, "*Contempsi Catilinæ gladios, non partimescam tuos?*" Will the Government permit such precedents of popular excitation to be held up?" and does it never occur to the Tory party that the time may not be far distant when republicanism may choose Protestantism for its model, and, by rallying the people, act upon the same principle of intimidation? If the Catholics are to be put down by these means, may not the aristocracy be one day put down by similar expedients? Will the House of Lords stand by and allow all the opulence and the rank of a large county to be trampled upon by the multitude? for it must occur to everybody, that Lord Winchilsea was the only nobleman on the side of the petitioners, while the rest of the Peerage were marshalled on the other. Do the patricians of England desire to see a renewal of scenes in which the nobles of the land were treated with utter scorn, and the feet of peasants trod upon their heads? Let statesmen reflect upon these very obvious subjects of grave meditation, and determine whether Ireland is to be infuriated by oppression, and England is to be maddened with fanaticism; whether they are not preparing the way for the speedy convulsion of one country, and the ultimate revolution of the other.

LORD-CHANCELLOR BROUGHAM'S LEVEE.

Unfeigned respect for, and a slight personal acquaintance with, the noble person who now holds the Seals, led me to attend his last levee.* This could not be done without some inconvenience; and not the least of it was the necessity of being equipped in full court-apparel. I do not object to this dress—indeed, I much approve of it in those who mingle in the gorgeousness of courts; but plainer attire would have more befitted the taste of an humble *incognito.* I mention this fact, lest it might be supposed that I was guilty of the not improbable gothicism of appearing in a garb fit for the funeral, but not the levee of a Lord-Chancellor. The practice of receiving the respects of the public on one or two stated occasions is sufficiently ancient, but I have understood was discontinued, or not much observed, in the latter days of Lord Eldon. It was revived with somewhat greater splendor by Lord Lyndhurst, but still it attracted little public notice. His Lordship never secured any very considerable share of general favor. As a lawyer, he was not at the head, though among the chief of his profession. For my own part, I do not regard his secondary eminence in the law as detracting much from his eminence as a public character, when it is recollected that Brougham him-

* This sketch was published in No. 1 of the *Metropolitan Magazine* (May, 1831), which was started by Thomas Campbell, the poet, after he had retired from the Editorship of the *New Monthly Magazine,* which he had held for a period of ten years. Lord Brougham's first levee would probably have been in Hilary Term, 1831, and the second, described by Mr. Sheil, at the commencement of the following Easter Term, or in April, 1831.—M.

self ranked much below Gurney,* Pollock, Campbell, and several others, whose distinction is derived from law alone—the lowest basis on which the fame of a public man can rest. In politics his career had not been such as to command respect. He was uniformly the supporter of the most profitable opinion.†

* The late Sir John Gurney, long known as one of the best cross-examiners at the bar, was made a puisne judge, and in that capacity, no one could say of him,

"Even his failings leaned to *mercy's* side,"

for he was most severe in his judgments. Sir Frederick Pollock and Lord Campbell are yet alive—the first, is Chief Baron of the Exchequer; the other, is Lord Chief Justice of England, and obtained a peerage in June, 1841, by the scandalous job (already referred to in my notes on the sketch of Plunket) of being made Irish Chancellor, for a few days, to obtain the retiring pension of four thousand pounds sterling, when the Melbourne Ministry, whose first law-officer he was, had no other means of quartering him on the public.—M.

† Lord Lyndhurst, who has been Lord Chancellor of England under five Administrations, is American by birth, having been born at Boston, May 21, 1772. His grandfather, Richard Copley, was an Irishman who emigrated to America; John Singleton Copley, this man's son, born in Boston in 1738, showed great natural taste for painting, which he adopted as a profession. He went to England, where his fine historical painting, the death of Lord Chatham, gave him high reputation. He painted several other subject-pictures, which caused him to be elected a Royal Academician. He died in 1815, having lived to see the dawning success of his son. The future Chancellor having eminently distinguished himself at Cambridge University, was called to the English bar in 1804, and, at first was remarkable for his ultra-liberal politics. He soon became leader of his circuit, entered Parliament, adopted Tory views, and was rewarded by the Government, with the Chief Justice of Chester in 1818. He was made Solicitor-General, and knighted, in 1819, became Attorney-General in 1824; was made Master of the Rolls in 1826; and was raised to the rank of Lord Chancellor, with a peerage, as Lord Lyndhurst, when Lord Eldon and five of his colleagues simultaneously resigned, with a view to embarrass Canning, the new Premier, in 1827. Lord Lyndhurst was continued in the office of Chancellor under the brief administration of Lord Goderich, and was retained, from 1827 to November, 1828, by the Duke of Wellington, under whom, in 1829, the pliant lawyer advocated Catholic Emancipation, as strongly as he had assailed it before. In November, 1830, when the Duke's Cabinet broke up, Lyndhurst had to resign, and was succeeded by Brougham. In 1831, Lord Lyndhurst was made Chief Baron of the Exchequer, which he resigned, in December, 1834, again to become Lord Chancellor. But Peel's Ministry, of which he was one, was compelled to resign in April, 1835. From this time, until the autumn of 1841, Lord Lyndhurst held no official station, but received his retiring pension of five thousand pounds sterling. He made a speech, for several

In early life a flagrant Whig, as opening up the best field for talent; in a more advanced stage, the bitter enemy of the Catholics, so long as the star of Lord Eldon, the great dispenser of legal favor, was in the ascendant; and finally, when office had secured him, the advocate of the Catholics on what was called the constitutional ground, when all favor was in the giving of the Duke of Wellington.*

It is not remarkable that the levees of Lord Lyndhurst should have passed off in quietness. I do not remember to have heard that the ceremonial was observed by his Lordship, although, from the known display of this fashionable lawyer, there is no doubt that it was not neglected. If, however, his levees had been attended by the magnificent, it is equally certain that the fact must have attracted public notoriety. I incline to think that it was reserved for Brougham to illustrate the ancient custom, by the splendor of those who chose to be dutiful to the Lord-Chancellor. The fashion of going to court

subsequent years, at the close of each Parliamentary Session, in which he ably and unmercifully exposed the "sayings and doings" of the Melbourne Ministry. When Peel again became Premier, in 1841, Lord Lyndhurst, for the fifth time, was made Lord Chancellor, and continued in office, until June, 1846, when the Peel Ministry was broken up. It is said that he was offered the Great Seal, for the *sixth* time, in 1852, by Lord Derby, but declined on the plea of advanced years—having then reached the age of seventy. As a politician, Lord Lyndhurst has been inconsistent and flexible; as a parliamentary speaker, severe and sarcastic; as an advocate, powerful and effective; as a judge, acute and shrewd. In common law, he has had few superiors; and though his bar-practice was not in the Chancery courts, sagacity and great common sense marked his decisions in equity. He still attends to his parliamentary duties [January, 1854], but seldom speaks.—M.

* War, to which Wellington owed his celebrity, rank, and fortune, has usually been an expensive luxury to John Bull. In the last four years of the contest with France, the cost to the British nation was—1812, £103,421,538; 1813, £120,952,657; 1814, £116,843,889; 1815, £116,491,051. The expenditure during the war, from 1803 to 1815 inclusive, was £1,159,729,256. It was stated after the battle of Waterloo, that young men in the United Kingdom (such as usually enlist) were so generally killed off that it would have been impossible to raise another army. I have heard Doctor Buckland, the geologist, state (in a course of lectures which I attended when at Oxford), that the present French soldiery owe their stunted appearance to the conscription in the time of Napoleon, which drew away the manhood of the country, leaving the population to spring from immature youths or exhausted *vieill*[illegible]

is such, that it infers little personal respect to the individual monarch; but the practice of attending the levee of an inferior personage is to be ascribed to the respect which individual eminence commands.

When Lord Brougham announced his levees, it could not be known whether he should receive the homage of the aristocracy, to whom it was not supposed that his Lordship's politics were very amicable. It was, moreover, thought that the republican, or, to speak more guardedly, the Whig Lord-Chancellor, would care little for a custom in which there was no manifest utility. He had declared that the gewgaws of office delighted him not; and I dare say he would fain bring his mind to believe that all ceremonial was idle, perhaps contemptible. But it is the greatest mistake to suppose that Lord Brougham is inattentive to the ceremonies with which his high place is surrounded. A careful observer will see clearly that imposing forms are perfectly agreeable to his mind; nobody could ridicule form better, so long as he held no situation which required the observance of customary rules: but, elevated to his present distinction, it is plain that he enjoys all the little peculiarities of his office. Somebody said that he presided in the House of Lords in a bar-wig, and instanced the fact as a proof of his reforming temper; but it was not true. Accident may have obliged him to take his seat in this ungainly form, but he had no purpose of deviating from the ancient full-bottom, and he is now to be seen in all the amplitude of the olden fleece. In like manner he observes the strict *regime*, so fantastical to a stranger, of causing counsel to be shouted for from without, although they are actually present, and he adds to the oddness of this custom by receiving them with a most imposing mien, and putting on his *chapeau* as they advance. This is a form for which the model is not to be found in the practice of his immediate predecessors. It is possible, however, that his extensive and minute reading may have made him aware that Wolsey, peradventure, or some great Chancellor of old, had the fancy to be covered when the suppliants approached. Let any one observe with what studied dignity he performs the duty of announcing the royal assent to acts of Parliament; he assumes a solemnity of tone for which his voice is not ill fitted, but which is unusual with him. These small circumstances, and many such which might be mentioned, show that state is not uncongenial to his mind. Why should it? His weakness consists in the unreal contempt for what is not really contemptible.

With his high notions of office, I should have been surprised if he had foregone the levee; and assuredly he has not reckoned without reason; for a more splendid or flattering pageant could not be witnessed than that which his rooms exhibited. Unquestionably the most remarkable man in the empire at this moment, it is his fortune to attract the honorable regards of all who are distinguished as his compeers. It is not my intention to offer any estimate of what I conceive to be his genuine worth, as he may be appreciated in a more dispassionate time; I speak of him only as a great man filling a very large space in the consideration of the empire. Judging from the throng of all classes upon this occasion, whose favor is desirable, no man is more popular.*

* To us, looking back upon public events, it may now appear singular that there could have been any doubt, on the part of the Whigs, on taking office, in November, 1830, of Brougham's claim to participate in "the spoils." For nearly twenty years, he had been one of the leaders of the liberal party in the House of Commons. In that capacity none had more ably or consistently advocated education, and parliamentary, and law reform. On Queen Caroline's trial, he distinguished himself above all others, and his advocacy of her cause, while it precluded him from Court favor, greatly endeared him to the public. In 1827, he strongly supported Canning's Ministry, but declined, it is said, the office of Master of the Rolls, vacant by Lord Lyndhurst's elevation to the Woolsack. At the general election in 1830, on the accession of William IV., the great County of York returned him, without his competitor's risking a contest, as one of its representatives. He pledged himself to introduce a measure of Parliamentary Reform, and the day being fixed for its introduction, the Wellington Cabinet was beaten into resignation, whereupon Lord Grey was empowered to construct a liberal Government. The post of Attorney-General (which is not held by one of the Executive) was offered to Brougham and declined. It was an inferior post, for Lord Grey actually was afraid of the great genius of the man who had emphatically become "the observed of all observers." Afraid that Brougham's plan of Parliamentary Reform would be bolder and better than that promised by the Whigs, the highest office was offered him and accepted. On November 22, 1834, he took his seat in the House of Lords,

His levee is held on a Saturday evening, at the unsuitable hour of ten o'clock. It was rather late before I could come up, and I found the whole square in the vicinity of his residence crowded with carriages. Threading one's way amid many obstructions, I reached the house, and which (to observe on a matter so small) I should remark is not very suitable for the residence of either its former (Earl Grey) or present occupant. It is expected that a noble aristocrat should be found in ample halls, surrounded by suitable magnificence, but this is not the house in which the lordly capital of the peers should be lodged. The principal rooms are of moderate dimensions, and the suite consists only of two. It was not surely in this house that Lord Byron found the family of Lord Grey, when he formed the very exalted opinion of their patrician accomplishments to which he gives expression in one of his letters.

The preparations for announcement were those which are usually observed. The Chancellor took his place at a corner of the room, backed by his chaplain, and was soon encircled by the visitants; his dress remarkably plain, being a simple suit of velvet in the court cut. The names were announced from the bottom of the stairs, and each person as he entered walked up to the Chancellor and offered his respects. The numbers were so great, that it was impossible to devote any marked attention to each; as soon, therefore, as the visiter had made his bow, he retired into the throng, or took his departure through the adjoining room. I was not present at the first of the levees which were held, and at which the attendance was very distinguished; but a friend who was, spoke very highly of the manner in which the Chancellor performed his noviciate.

The Archbishop of Canterbury came early, and was very kindly received. He was followed by the Archbishop of York and several other bishops, whose attendance gave proof that, differ as they might from Lord Brougham, they surely did not

as Baron Brougham and Vaux, and Lord High-Chancellor of England. He held this office for four years, namely, until November, 1834. While Lord Erskine's Chancery Judgments are laughed at as "the Apocryphal Volume," those of Lord Brougham, collected and edited by Charles Purton Cooper, the eminent Chancery barrister, are constantly referred to, as authority.—M.

consider him an enemy to the Church.* There is something uncommonly bland in the appearance and expression of the Primate; he is the very reverse of the full-blown dignitary who is commonly seen in high places. One's notions of a bishop are apt to be those which we entertain of a high-feeding drone —with little duty that is of much real consequence, but with a most exalted notion of such duty as he is called on to discharge. Not so the present Archbishop of Canterbury: I mistake his character extremely if he is not a meek as well as a highly-accomplished servant of his Master. I know not how he ascended to the primacy, but I am sure that it is not dishonored in his hands. Brougham evidently likes his Grace.

The most remarkable visiter of that evening was the Duke of Wellington. The crowd was astonished, and I dare say the Chancellor himself was surprised, when his name was sent up. I doubt if they had ever met in the same room before. Their political lives, with the exception of the Catholic question, were one unvarying course of opposition, if not enmity. I suspect that for a time the Duke despised the talk of the lawyer; and, on the other hand, Brougham had often declared that the respect which he entertained for military glory was not very lofty. Some of his bitterest tirades were levelled at the Duke personally. No one will deny that it was high-minded in the Duke to lay aside resentment of every sort, and offer this mark of respect as well to the man as the office. The Chancellor was flattered by the attention, and shook the Duke by the hand very cordially. There is not much heartiness of manner about the Duke, whatever may be the reality; and his dry features, thinned by the great labors in which his life has been passed, do not easily or readily relax into a smile; but on this occasion it was remarked that his countenance was more expressive of good-will than usual.† He engaged in con-

* Dr. Howley, Archbishop of Canterbury, died in 1848.—Dr. Harcourt, Archbishop of York, died in 1847.—M.

† Brougham and Wellington subsequently became intimate friends. On one occasion, Brougham publicly described Wellington as "the most magnanimous of men."—M.

versation for a minute or two with the Chancellor, and then gave place to the subsequent visiters who pressed for audience. His Grace immediately joined some military friends who had previously been received.

Not the least remarkable personage in the room was the Lord-Advocate of Scotland.* Brougham and he are very old friends, and have been much engaged in the same species of literature. Lord Brougham was his predecessor in the editorship of the "Edinburgh Review"—a fact which is not generally known, but which is certain. Brougham was not the first editor, having filled that office for a short time after Sydney Smith withdrew from the situation. Jeffrey appeared extremely *petit* in his court-dress, and did not seem very much at home; he was acquainted with but few of his fellow-visiters, and had too much good taste to occupy much of the Chancellor's attention. They did not seem to hold any conversation beyond the usual commonplace inquiries.

Ascending the stairs, I was met by a hobbling old Lord—Carnarvon by name. There is nothing very courtly or dignified in the appearance of this nobleman.† He has been a Whig the greater part of his life, but affects to be greatly dismayed at the Reform Bill; and has more than once run a tilt against the Ministers, but with no very marked success. Arm-in-arm with Lord Carnarvon came the gay and the good-look-

* Francis Jeffrey, was born in 1773, and was one of Sir Walter Scott's contemporaries and early associates. Called to the bar in 1794, he soon obtained a high reputation for eloquence, and gradually got into practice, but was chiefly eminent, during nearly thirty years, for his connection with the *Edinburgh Review*, as contributor and editor. The first number appeared October 25, 1802, and three editions were exhausted in as many weeks. It soon became, what it has ceased to be, the able and recognised organ of the liberal party in Great Britain. In 1829, when the profession chose him Dean of the Faculty (of law), Jeffrey retired from the *Review*. In 1830, he was appointed Lord-Advocate of Scotland, under the Grey Ministry, and entered Parliament, where he by no means distinguished himself. In 1834, he was promoted to the Scottish bench, where, applying all the great powers of his mind to the task, he became one of the best Judges that ever adorned that high station. He died in 1850.—M.

† Henry George Herbert, second Earl of Carnarvon, born in 1772, died in 1833, aged sixty-one. His son and successor, then Lord Porchester, had distinguished himself as the author of "The Moor," and other poems.—M.

ing Earl of Errol,* blooming with the most healthful roseate; and immediately behind followed Sir Robert Wilson. Time and hard service have made little impression on a set of not very extraordinary features. There is a buoyancy about this historic soldier which bespeaks a good heart.† He seems to have lost much of his fancy for senatorial display; and, truth to tell, Parliament is not the place of all others in which he has been destined to shine. He is one of the few whose hard fortune in less auspicious times has stood him in good part in later days.

On entering the room, I was struck by the superior brilliancy of the military costumes, always the most prominent at such times. Military rank is both common and honorable, and its apparel seems to be in favor with all classes. Hence it is that many, such as the lieutenants of counties, whose duty is exclusively of a civil nature, adopt the fashions of the army. There were half a dozen Lords-Lieutenant in the room, among whom I particularly observed the Duke of Argyle.‡ I am told that his Grace is a man of talent; and his fine features, the remains of what rendered the Marquis of Lorn one of the most eminently handsome men of his time, are now thoughtful and melancholy. The present Administration has given the Great Seal of Scotland to the Duke of Argyle; and in duty he is found

* The late Lord Errol (whose Earldom was created in 1453), was Hereditary Lord High Constable of Scotland, which is the highest hereditary distinction in the United Kingdom, after those of the Royal Family. He married one of the illegitimate daughters of William IV. and Mrs. Jordan, the actress, and died in 1846, aged forty-five.—M.

† Sir Robert Wilson, who much distinguished himself by his military services from 1793 to 1815, aided in the escape of Lavalette, from Paris, in the latter year. In 1821, for taking the popular side, at the funeral of Queen Caroline, he was dismissed from the British army. A public subscription indemnified him from the pecuniary loss, and he was reinstated some years after. From 1818 to 1831 he represented Southwark in Parliament. In 1841, he was raised to the rank of full General. In 1842, he was appointed Governor of Gibraltar, and had just returned from that post, after seven years' of command, when he died suddenly, May, 1849, aged seventy-two.—M.

‡ The sixth Duke of Argyle, born in 1768, married Lady Caroline Villiers (who had previously been the wife of, and had obtained a divorce from, the Marquis of Anglesey), and died in October, 1839.—M.

at the levee of its Chancellor. Along with his Grace were several other peers of ducal rank, but whose fortunes were no way interesting to me.

After I had paid my respects to the Chancellor, there came tripping up the Marquis of Bristol* with a springy step, which he must surely have acquired at the old court of France; for I am sure that no such movement could be attained on English ground. The elasticity of this noble Lord was such that, when once put in motion, he continued to spring up and down in the manner of the Chinese figures which are hawked by the Italian toy-venders. Had I been told that the head of the house of Newry was a dancing-master, who had not yet learned the present modes, I should certainly have believed the story without scruple if I had met him anywhere else.

He had no sooner left the Chancellor, than he was laid hold of by a fidgetty solicitor,† who was the only member of his class in the room, and who, I understand, is a sort of favorite of the Chancellor. The obsequious grin and the affected ease of this worthy do not convey any very favorable impression on his behalf. He was solicitor for the Queen, and in this capacity had formed an intimacy with her chief counsel, which an ill-natured person would perhaps think makes him now forget in some measure the great disparity between their present condition. The Chancellor gave no discouragement to his familiarity.

A certain Sir Something Noel came up immediately afterward, of whom nothing more remarkable could be told than that he was the relative of Lady Byron; and is, I suppose, the same person of whom Byron expresses himself favorably when a temporary illness of his lady shortly after their marriage

* Nephew of the celebrated Earl of Bristol, Bishop of Derry, of whom mention has already been made. In June, 1826, he was created Marquis. He is yet alive (January, 1854), and is aged eighty-four.—M.

† This "fidgetty Solicitor" was William Vizard, subsequently made Secretary of Bankrupts by Lord Brougham, in 1832, a post worth twelve hundred pounds sterling a year, which he occupied for twenty years (until 1852), and then contrived to get appointed, on its abolition, to an office equally valuable, which he retains. His connection with the Queen's trial made William Vizard's fortune, and he is now a large landed proprietor in Gloucestershire.—M.

looked rather gestatory.* A variety of lords, squires, generals, *ossa innominata*, followed, for whom the Chancellor cared perhaps about as much as I did.

At length Sir James Scarlett was announced, and the Chancellor left his place to meet him. His welcome was very hearty. Brougham was doubtless gratified by this token of respect from a man who was indisputably his leader in the courts,† and for whose forensic abilities it is known that he entertains, and has often expressed, the highest admiration. The position of the two men was singular, and to the ex-attorney not very enviable. Scarlett was in high practice before Brougham was even called to the bar. He kept ahead of him in their profession throughout; and twice he had filled the first places at the bar, when the respective attainments of these eminent persons were such, that if Brougham had been placed before him, Scarlett would have had just ground of complaint, and the bar would have unanimously decried the appointment. Now, however, by one of those cross-accidents which will occur in the most fortunate lives, Scarlett was, with strict justice and universal acquiescence, placed below his former competitor, and in direct opposition to all the early friends with whom he

* Sir Ralph Milbanke's wife was sister of Viscount Wentworth, and she succeeded to the estates, on condition that her name should be changed to Noel. Her daughter was married to Lord Byron, who prefixed the name of Noel to his own, on his mother-in-law's death. Sir Ralph Noel died in 1825, and Mr. Sheil alludes to his relative and successor, Sir John Peneston Milbanke, who dropped the name of Noel altogether.—M.

† Perhaps this is the place where I should state the cost of the administration of justice, which forms an important item in the national expenditure of Great Britain. In 1852, as appears by Parliamentary returns, the whole amount was £2,104,196, of which £645,243 was for Courts of Justice (including salaries of Judges and other officials), £891,542 for police and criminal prosecution, and £567,411 for correction. In October, 1853, the Reverend Mr. Clay, chaplain of the House of Correction in Preston (England) in his annual report to the magistrates, estimates the loss caused to the public by fifteen pickpockets, whose career he has traced, including the value of the property stolen, expenses of prosecution, and maintenance in jail, at £26,500. That is to say, England was at an expense of £1,766 for each of these worthies—a sum, one tithe of which, if judiciously applied at the proper time, would probably have sufficed to make them useful members of society.—M.

commenced his political career.* It was matter of necessity and of course that he should go out when his employers were obliged to surrender office; and no man could complain that Brougham should then be elevated to a distinction, which in other circumstances Scarlett might have thought his own by indisputable right. The Chancellor remained longer in conversation with Sir James than any of the other distinguished persons who appeared. Indeed, his anxiety to show this attention produced rather awkward effects. While they were closely together, Jocky Bell, as he is commonly called, the very eminent Chancery barrister, came in sight; but he was suffered to waddle about for some time before he caught the eye of the Chancellor.† Before the conversation with Sir James was finished, there were a good many others in the same unreceived plight, and the Chancellor was obliged to give them a hasty discharge.

The Speaker of the House of Commons was then announced. Brougham and he met as warm friends, though certainly men having little in kindred. In point of talent there is no ground of comparison; yet it may be doubted whether they are not nearly as great in their own way. I have no notion of the place which the Speaker held in Parliament before he was elected to the chair, and I know few situations which require

* It was said that Scarlett, afterward Lord Abinger, "ratted" at the wrong time. He had been liberal in politics up to 1828 (and had been Canning's Attorney-General in 1827), but took office with the Duke of Wellington, then an avowed Tory, and was as intolerant as renegades, whether political or religious, usually are. In 1830, when the Whigs came into power, Scarlett had to resign office. But, in December, 1834, when the post of Chief-Baron of the Exchequer became vacant by Lord Lyndhurst's taking the Great Seal, Scarlett was appointed, receiving a peerage shortly after, and continued Judge until his death in 1844.—Had he remained with the Whig party, he would probably have been appointed their Lord-Chancellor in 1830.—M.

† "Jock Bell," as he was called, was a friend and contemporary of Lord Eldon's. He was notorious for writing so badly that it was said he wrote three hands; one, which nobody but himself could read; a second (that in which he gave his opinion on cases) which none but his clerk could decipher, and a third which neither himself nor clerk could make out. It is a fact, and the foundation of a passage in "Pickwick," that Jock Bell's clerk realized a large income by making readable copies of his employer's opinions, which were greatly in request, on account of their ability.—M.

more tact and management. In these qualifications the present Speaker is signally gifted.* He brings a degree of good-nature to the office which no event, however untoward, can ruffle: his calmness never forsakes him; he is the same easy, dignified chairman at all times. The Commons are a truly turbulent body, but they are not impatient of his sway. In all emergencies he is vigorously supported: in his hands, the authority of his office, though rarely exercised, has lost none of its force. Brougham himself was one of the most fiery spirits in this hot region; but a word from the Speaker would calm him in an instant. Among other qualifications for command, he is possessed of a fine, mellow, deep-toned voice, which, while it powerfully enunciates "Order," frees the command from all harshness or severity. As the first commoner in the land, and a truly estimable gentleman, he was entitled to be well received. But I doubt, if deprived of his chair, whether he could insure much regard on the score of his talents. Let me not, however, shade the picture which I have already drawn; it is manifest that Mr. Sutton is a general favorite. Every one was eager to pass a minute or two with him. I was much pleased to witness a frank greeting between him and old William Smith, who is not now in the House of Commons; but who, before he left it, enjoyed the patriarchal rank of being the father of the body.† The Speaker told him that they had not much mended since he left. Longer speeches — more of them — later hours, and fewer divisions — were the characteristics of the session, compared with its predecessors.

Lord Farnham,‡ a bluff, weather-beaten old Irish Lord — the unflinching enemy of the Catholics, and the equally-deter-

* Charles Manners Sutton, speaker of the House of Commons from 1817 to 1834; created Viscount Canterbury in 1835; and died July, 1845. He was very popular as speaker, and allowed himself to be re-elected (after the Reform Bill was passed in 1832) at the especial request of the Grey Ministry.— M.

† This William Smith, who had a seat in Parliament for forty-six years, was latterly Member for Norwich. He attacked Southey, in Parliament, as a "rancorous renegade," and was replied to by the poet in nervous and indignant prose. William Smith was ultra-liberal in politics. He died in 1835, aged seventy-nine.— M.

‡ John Barry Maxwell, fifth Lord Farnham, born in 1767, died in 1838.— M.

mined enemy of Reform — got hold of the Speaker; and, in the course of a brief conversation, the latter informed him that for eight entire days and nights he had never been from under the roof of the House of Commons. The House had been sitting from three o'clock in the afternoon till three and four o'clock in the morning; and then the business of the committees commenced at ten o'clock, to which he was obliged to give a good deal of attention. He spoke of the labor as being greater than any physical strength could endure. When this fact is known, it ceases to be wonderful that he should be anxious, as has been long reported, to exchange the conspicuous and most honorable situation which he now holds, for that of the youngest peerage, and become second to such insignificancies as Bexley and Sidmouth.* Leaving Farnham, the Speaker was engaged for a short time with Lord Nugent and the Marquis of Clanricarde.† Both of these noble Lords appeared in the splendid costume which I believe is characteristic of the diplomatic corps. Nugent is evidently a person of the most accomplished manners. The perpetual play of good-humor on his agreeable features shows that the severity of his politics does not arise from any harshness of disposition. It will be recollected that he was the subject of one of Canning's pleasantries in regard to the Portuguese expedition; which, however, had little point, unless his Lordship had been a very stout man — but this is not the fact. A much larger person than Lord Nugent would have occasioned no inconvenience to

* The late Nicholas Vansittart, Chancellor of the Exchequer, from 1812 to 1823, was created Baron Bexley. Henry Addington, successively Speaker, Premier, and Home Secretary, was created Viscount Sidmouth in 1805, and died in 1844.—M.

† Lord Nugent, born in 1789, sat in Parliament over twenty years; was Lord-Commissioner of the Ionian Islands from 1832 to 1835; and died in November, 1850. His politics were liberal, and he had considerable literary taste.—The Marquis of Clanricarde, Canning's son-in-law, was born in 1802, represents the De Burgh or Burke family, and claims to be descended from Charlemagne. He has been Ambassador to Russia, and Postmaster-General. Before 1831, there was a good deal of town-talk about a young man of property having been "pigeoned" at cards, at Richmond, near London, and it was said that Lord Clanricarde was one of the party; but the scandal blew over, and no proof was given of the imputations on "the noble Marquis."—M.

the heavy Falmouth van. Lord Clanricarde is only remarkable for his connection with Canning. His countenance is anything but pleasing: his fondness for play is well known, and had at one time placed him in a disagreeable dilemma.

The last person of note who arrived, before I departed, was Sir Thomas Denman.* The Chancellor was engaged with some one at the moment, and nothing passed between them but an exchange of bows. It was nearly ten years since I had seen Brougham and Denman together: the Queen's trial was then the all-engrossing topic of public consideration. Who could then have foretold that these men would have in so short a space won the confidence of a sovereign, whom they attacked with a degree of virulence which, even in those days of party violence, was generally condemned? The change in feeling is creditable alike to all.

* Thomas Denman, born in February, 1779, and created Baron Denman, of Dovedale, in the County Derby, in March, 1834, was son of a physician in London. He was called to the bar in 1806; went the Midland circuit, entered Parliament in 1818; became Solicitor-General to Queen Caroline in 1820; was elected Common Sergeant of London, in 1822; was made King's Counsel, with a patent of precedency, in 1826; was made Attorney-General, under the Grey Ministry in 1830; was made Chief Justice of England in 1832; raised to the peerage in 1834; and compelled, under Lord John Russell's Ministry, in 1850, to resign, on the plea of advanced years, to make room for Lord Campbell (only two years his junior), for whom a job of the same character had been perpetrated, in 1841, when Lord Plunket was literally turned out of the Irish Chancellorship, in order to give Lord Campbell a legal claim to a life-pension of four thousand pounds sterling. As an advocate, Denman was bold and eloquent; his denunciation, on the Queen's trial, of the Duke of Clarence (afterward William IV.) as a "royal slanderer," was decided and fearless—ten years afterward, this prince, as Sovereign, accepted Denman as his first law officer. As a judge, he was just and constitutional. In politics, he has always been liberal. In Parliament, he was a ready debater. During the Reform Bill discussions, Sir C. Wetherell compared Old Sarum (for which three men elected two members) to Macedon. "Yes," replied Denman, "Macedon was ruled by an Alexander:"—an East India Director, named Alexander, being one of the (so-called) representatives of this nominal borough, with one house, three voters, and two Members, while Manchester, population four hundred thousand, was wholly unrepresented.—M.

STATE OF PARTIES IN DUBLIN, IN 1831.

On the 5th of this month of May [1831], my business led me into the Four Courts, Dublin; and on the way, by a train of associations too obvious to require to be analyzed, my mind involuntarily reverted to the past, and took note of the vicissitudes produced since I last wrote. But it was only when I found myself in that emporium of law, and politics, and gossip — the Hall of the Four Courts — that I felt in all their force the variety and extent of those mutations. The scene and the majority of the actors were still the same, and the general resemblance, at the first view, appeared unimpaired; but, upon a nearer scrutiny, how striking and singular had been the changes!

Of these actors, for instance, one of the first that attracted my attention was Mr. William Bellew, a Roman Catholic barrister of great personal respectability, and of just repute in certain departments of his profession. In his general aspect there was little perceptible alteration. Time, as if from a kindly feeling toward an old acquaintance, seemed to have spared him more than younger men. I found the same spire-like altitude of frame; the same solemn, spectral stride; the same grave and somewhat querulous, but not undignified cast of feature. "In his own proper person," in face and form, Mr. Bellew was such as I had seen him in his penal days; but what a transfiguration had been accomplished in his gown! How omnipotent must have been that act of Parliament which had substituted his present rustling silk attire for the dingy, tattered fustian, in which I had so often seen him haunting the precincts of the Court of Chancery, and which he had vowed to wear while a rag of it remained, as an ensign of reproach to the presiding bigot of the court! But Lord Manners and his tenets had passed away, and Mr. Bellew's epitaph may state that he too, in his generation, was one of his Majesty's counsel-at-law.

My eye, turning from Mr. Bellew, soon rested upon several other barristers of his creed, who, like him, had been taking the benefit of the statute. Among them, and apparently the youngest of the group, was Mr. O'Loghlin, upon whom Emancipation had fortunately come just at a period of his career when promotion, being possible, was inevitable. He is already one of the three sergeants, and, if the orisons of the public can confer length of days, the highest judicial office is his certain destination.

But the most singular of those metamorphoses, which, when I last addressed you, it would have been maniacal to have predicted, was exhibited in the personal identity and present official attributes of the worthy ex-Secretary of the ex-Catholic Association, Mr. Nicholas Purcel O'Gorman. This excellent and best-tempered of organized beings, who, during a life devoted to the angry politics of Ireland, has made as many friends as another would have created enemies—who was ever frank and fearless in the expression of his opinions, even though one of those opinions was and is that "St. Paul was a decided Orangeman"—now stood before me, transformed into nothing less than a public functionary, by title Cursitor, of that very court in which Mr. Saurin had pleaded and Lord Manners had presided. The selection, I am bound to add, has been pronounced by the public, from whose discernment in such matters there is no appeal, to have been worthy of the exalted person to whom, fortunately for Ireland, higher functions than the extension of mere acts of considerateness toward meritorious individuals have been again committed.

I approached the group, to whom Mr. O'Gorman, who had been recently sworn in, was detailing with humorous exaggeration the weighty responsibilities that had descended upon his rather Atlantean shoulders. The Cursitor's office, I collected from him, was one of the great fountain-heads of justice, whence litigation flowed in streams or torrents through the land. It was emphatically the *officina brevium*, the inner temple of original writs, and the Cursitor the high-priest, without whose signature, now written with majestic brevity, "O'Gorman," those sacred documents would want their legal potency. I was gratified, however, to hear Mr. O'Gorman add, which he did with a glance of no doubtful meaning at one of his auditors, who had been an unsuccessful expectant under the old *régime*, that his hierarchal cares were in some measure soothed by sundry daily and not unwelcome offerings from the devotees at the shrine over which he had been appointed to preside. It was an office of trust coupled with emolument, a coincidence which Mr. O'Gorman, though a stanch reformer, very justly pronounced to be not incongruous.

These are single instances of the changes which the surface presented, but I could multiply them without number; wherever I looked around, I found abundant evidences, had I otherwise been unaware of the fact, that the genius of Mr. Gregory,* no longer presided in the government of Ireland. Religious peace, and never was a peace more just and necessary, had been proclaimed; and, after it, had followed in due course the gradual decline of as hateful a faction as had ever desolated and insulted a devoted country. There was, however, no want of excitement. It had changed its character, but was as active in its way as in those dreary times when Mr. Lefroy's theology and Master Ellis's statesmanship found favor at the Castle. The groups of animated bustlers in the Hall were no longer discussing the divided allegiance of the Catholics, or holding a drum-head inquiry over Mr. Sheil's last speech at the Association, but much was said of schedule A—of its multiform abominations by the smaller and more hopeless politicians—of its wisdom and necessity by others, and among them not a few who conceived it to be both wise and necessary to declare their opinions in favor of reform. But I soon discovered that

* Of William Gregory (who was Privy Councillor and under-Secretary for Ireland) mention has already been made in one of the notes on Lord Norbury, page 36, in this volume. Mr. Gregory was a "Protestant Ascendency" man. His son represented Dublin, in Parliament, for a time.—M.

the buzz around me turned upon a matter of a still more immediate interest; an active canvass was going forward. The Dublin election was fixed for the following day; and the popular party, in perfect accordance upon this occasion with the wishes of the Government, had determined upon attempting a decisive blow. Committees had been sitting; subscription-lists opened; Mr. William Murphy sent for; an earnest but amicable conflict of opinion had ensued: Mr. Murphy, with the caution of long experience, was strenuous in his advice that they should run no risks, but, by concentrating their forces, secure the return of one member. "*Delenda est Carthago,*" was the cry of Sergeant O'Loghlin and Mr. Blake, and the bolder counsel had prevailed: two reform candidates had been started against the corporation of Dublin.

The competitors upon this stirring occasion were the late members, Messrs. Moore and Shaw, who rested their pretensions on their love of corporations, and their hatred of reform; Mr. (now Sir Robert) Harty,* the Lord-Mayor of Dublin, and Mr. Louis Perrin, an eminent member of the Irish bar. The two latter announced themselves as sturdy reformers.

Of Mr. George Moore I can not tell you much, for I only know of him what the public knows.† He is, I should suppose, between fifty and sixty years of age. There is nothing remarkable in his face or person. He is a man of mild manners and violent opinions; can make a long speech on most subjects, either in or out of Parliament; is the proprietor of an ample sinecure in one of our courts; and much regarded by his personal acquaintances. The only singular events in the history of his life that I have heard recorded were, his first return for the city of Dublin, and an incident connected with it. The day preceding that fixed for the election had closed, and the corporation, still in search of a fit and proper nominee,

* Sir Robert Harty, who was made a Baronet in September, 1831, was a liberal in politics. He was an Alderman of the old Dublin Corporation, and was Lord-Mayor in 1830–'1. Though he and Mr. Perrin were elected, as stated by Mr. Sheil, their triumph was short-lived, for they were unseated on petition.—M.

† Mr. George Ogle Moore, who was M. P. for Dublin, for a short time, was one of the most undistinguished men in Parliament.—M.

continued their deliberations through the night. Mr. Moore, as yet unthought of, retired at his accustomed hour to repose. At midnight, as the story goes, he was suddenly awakened, and saw at his bedside the portly form of Master Ellis, deputed from the still-sitting committee, to know if he would consent to be returned to Parliament from his native city. Mr. Moore rubbed his eyes, pressed the Master's hand more closely, to ascertain that it was a hand of flesh and blood; saw visions of Parliamentary renown start up before him, and thinking that *now* he surely could not be dreaming, gave his assent. The next day he was the member for Dublin: the "Mirror of Parliament" tells the rest.

Mr. Frederick Shaw is a much younger man than Mr. Moore. He was called to the bar in the year 1822, and for the first five years gave no signs of his subsequent prosperity.* He was assiduous, but in no way distinguished. The first occasion upon which the courts became familiar with his name was in 1827, upon the arrival of Sir Anthony Hart as the Lord Chancellor of Ireland. Sir William M'Mahon, the Master of the Rolls, conceived that in him was vested the power of appointing a particular officer of his own court. Former Chancellors, however, had claimed and exercised the right of appointment, and Sir Anthony Hart announced that he would follow their example. The Master of the Rolls, desirous that the question should undergo a solemn discussion and adjudication, nominated his relative, Mr. Shaw, to the office in dispute. Mr. Shaw presented a petition to the Lord-Chancellor, praying to be admitted to the performance of the duties, and the perception of the profits, and Mr. Saurin appeared as the leading counsel in support of the claim.

The matter, in itself, was one of no sort of public interest: it was a mere question of patronage between two judicial dig-

* Frederick Shaw, whose early appointment to the Recordership of Dublin excited much discussion at the time, probably owed his preferment to the fact that his aunt was wife of the late Sir William M'Mahon, then Master of the Rolls in Ireland. Mr. Shaw, where politics did not bias him, gave satisfaction as a judge. He was a Privy Councillor and represented the University of Dublin in several Parliaments.— M.

nitaries; yet wondrous was the interest, or at least the curiosity, with which the proceedings were watched, and the result conjectured. It had the novelty of being the first case in any way peculiar, and that one relating to himself individually, upon which the newly-imported Chancellor was to be called upon to decide. It was expected by sundry shrewd solicitors that litigation, even between two such high contending parties, would produce the usual feelings of personal estrangement, and, as a profitable result, that appeals from the Rolls to the Chancellor would not fail to be multiplied; while others, who had been often made to smart under Sir William's inexorable rules and orders, were delighted to find that his Honor for once had a prospect of feeling in his own purse what it was to have the prayer of a petition refused with costs.

These were the effusions of the mere idle gossip of the Hall, and excited nothing but amusement; but pending the discussion, an incident occurred which sent a profounder feeling through the courts and the country. In the course of his argument, Mr. Saurin, for the moment oblivious of the recent change of Chancellors, implored of the Court to recollect the seditious spirit that was abroad, and the factious disposition daily manifested to bring even the highest public functionaries into contempt—a disposition which "the continuance of the present litigation would not fail to foster and gratify." This was a topic to which Lord Manners would have listened with all the nervous attention of a weak mind overawed by the horrors of a phantom-story. The healthier intellect of Sir Anthony saw in it nothing but its inappropriateness. He interposed, saying: "If there be any spirit abroad which would lead persons to degrade the higher authorities of the country, my opinion is, that that spirit can only be met and counteracted by those who hold such high situations having their motives and their actions exposed to the fullest public scrutiny. When these motives and that conduct are properly placed before the world, they may be satisfied that both will be rightly appreciated by the public: and so much, Mr. Saurin, for that topic." The effect of these few simple words in the Irish Court of Chancery was electrical. Mr. Saurin was disconcerted; his Brunswick friends beside him panic-struck; Sergeant Lefroy looked first up to heaven, and then full in the face of his valued friend Mr. Henchy; Mr. Henchy responded with a look at once historical and prophetic; a buzz of perturbation passed along the benches of the outer bar; while Mr. Eccles Cuthbert (almost the sole surviving Whig of the olden time) rushed forth from the Court toward the Hall, and, standing at the top of the Chancery-steps, proclaimed to a group that he beckoned round him the joyful tidings that "if he" (Mr. Cuthbert) "could interpret the signs of the times—and he thought he could—the influence of Saurin and his party was gone for ever."

But, to return to Mr. Shaw—the decision of the Chancellor was against him, but he was quickly consoled for the disappointment. The Recordership of Dublin becoming vacant, he had the good fortune to be elected to the office. The public were at first dissatisfied with the selection—chiefly, however, because it had fallen upon so juvenile a person; but it is only justice to Mr. Shaw to state that he has proved himself perfectly competent to the discharge of the judicial functions that were thus rather prematurely cast upon him. As the Recorder of Dublin, he is an assiduous and excellent public officer. I would further say that this is the very office for which he is peculiarly adapted. He performs the substantial duties efficiently, and wants not the leading ornamental requisites for those matters of municipal ceremony in which he is called upon, *virtute officii*, to bear a prominent part. His aspect may still be over-youthful; in fact, when he appears at a civic festival attired in his legal costume, his smooth and pallid face and rather feminine features present a strong similitude to Portia in the scene where she holds a brief against Shylock; but ample compensation for this deficiency (if it be one) is made in the proportions of his frame, which possess all the necessary corporate massiveness and rotundity for the scenic business of a Lord-Mayor's day. I have seen him perform on such occasions with much effect, and with the bearing of an actor that liked his part. As the Recorder of an ancient and loyal corporation, Mr. Frederick Shaw is just where he ought to be. He has no unseemly contempt for pageantry; and, for city purposes, is a most discreet and emphatic orator. He can descant, with suitable amplitude of phrase, upon the sanctity of chartered rights, and can deliver the prescriptive lecture to an incoming Lord-Mayor, upon his civic responsibilities, in terms of the most stately and appropriate commonplace. To such duties he is equal, and not above them.—I pass on to the other candidates.

Sir Robert Harty is a citizen of Dublin, who has risen by his industry to considerable affluence. In the corporation, of which he has long been one of the most influential members, he has been noted for his attachment to liberal principles. He is the brother-in-law of Alderman M'Kenny, who in his year of mayoralty (1819) had the courage to convene a general meeting of the Protestants of Dublin, to petition in favor of Catholic Emancipation. Sir Robert Harty's civic career has been marked by an official act—less conspicuous, it is true, but of similar boldness. When the Roman Catholic delegates were prosecuted by the Government in 1812, he was one of the Sheriffs of Dublin, and empanelled an impartial jury for their trial. This gave great offence, and both in and out of the corporation the honest Sheriff had much to endure for having done his duty; but he has fortunately lived to find that sentence of condemnation in those times now forms one of his most valid titles to public confidence. So great was the imagined strength of the corporation of Dublin, that for some days Sir Robert Harty was the solitary candidate upon reform principles. More than one of the commercial body of Dublin, though strongly urged by the popular party to become his colleague, had declined. The bar was then resorted to. A union of the most important qualifications was found in Mr. Perrin, who, after repeated solicitations, consented to give the public the use of his name and character for the advancement of the great imperial measure.

Mr. Perrin was called to the bar in 1806. There was nothing sudden or brilliant in his ascent to professional distinction. He was patient and persevering; and in his deportment, whether in or out of court, simple and unobtrusive. Even after the extension of his character for learning and ability had brought him into full practice, there was so little forensic display in his manner—what he said upon each occasion was always so much to the purpose, and consequently so short and direct—that a stranger to his professional repute would have principally inferred, from the frequency of his appearances in court, that he was already high among the most eminent counsel of his day.*

Mr. Perrin is, I believe, universally admitted to be the best common-law lawyer of the Irish bar. It is probably to be attributed in some degree to early accidents that his studies and practice should have been exclusively confined to this department; but I apprehend that an original peculiarity of his mind had also much to do in keeping him out of the courts of equity. I have heard it related of him that, from the commencement of his legal studies, he felt a deep and unconquerable distaste to equity-pleading—to that system under which, as a matter of ordinary routine, fifty false charges may be made against a miserable defendant on the chance of eliciting a single truth, and under which the same defendant, if knavishly disposed, and aided by a dexterous pleader, may resort to as many devices to evade a direct and intelligible reply. I can easily conceive that a mind like Mr. Perrin's, always seeking accuracy of thought and brevity of expression, should have turned with disgust from the farrago of long-winded fictions, and endless repetitions, and wordy superfluities, which form the staple of Chancery pleadings; but whatever the motive, he has, almost from the outset of his career, confined himself to the common-law courts; among them the King's Bench has been the principal theatre of his exertions. Assiduous application and long experience have rendered him familiar with all the great branches of the law that are brought into discussion before that tribunal; and, to an intimate knowledge of his subject, he unites logical powers of the highest order. His diction, though clear and vigorous, is not always fluent; but the occa-

* Louis Perrin, one of the most able and honest of the Irish bar, was promoted, in due course, when the Liberal party were in power, and is now (January, 1854) third judge of the Court of Queen's Bench, Ireland. In Parliament he was a useful and laborious, rather than an oratorical member.—M.

sional tardiness of phrase to which I allude, and which detracts little from the force or effect of his reasonings, appears to be very much the result of acquired habits of mastery over the most important operations of his mind. If he sometimes pauses for a moment, it is not that he is in want of matter or of words, but that he is determined and able to retain and exercise a control over both; it is that, even while his mind is hurrying along a rapid chain of reasoning, he still preserves the power of arresting a thought in its progress from conception to expression, and of ascertaining its fitness for his purpose before he allows it irrevocably to pass his lips; and the result of the enforcement of this inward discipline is, that, though his language may be rendered less continuous, his argument is sure of being better for the delay. If Mr. Perrin could consent to be a less cautious and accurate reasoner, he would, I am satisfied, become at once a more fluent speaker; but he reasons everything, abhorring all flashy declamation, and guided by a special instinct against the use of words for talking-sake.

Having thus shortly referred to Mr. Perrin's professional qualifications, I need hardly add that he has for many years commanded the leading business of the Court of King's Bench. Among the cases constantly occurring on the criminal side of that court, there is one class in which he appears to have established a sort of personal property (for he is never omitted): I allude to appeals from convictions by magistrates under penal statutes, particularly those relating to the customs and excise. In such cases the offending party has usually a twofold chance of escape—in the blunders of the legislator, and in those of the convicting magistrates. The leaning of the court is always to uphold such convictions; but Mr. Perrin, with his sagacity, and pertinacious logic, and adroit application of authorities that bear, or appear to bear, upon the point, seldom fails to demonstrate to the full satisfaction of every mind in court (except perhaps his own) that something, in substance or in form, has been wanting to legalize the proceedings from which his clients have appealed.

The subject-matter of such discussions is in general devoid of popular interest; but they sometimes acquire from incidental circumstances no small degree of scenic effect. I remember, for instance, to have seen some years since one of the side-galleries of the Court of King's Bench occupied by an entire ship's crew of Dutch smugglers, brought up, under writs of *habeas corpus*, from one of the prisons on the southern coast of Ireland; and while Mr. Perrin, as their counsel, was moving that they should be discharged from illegal custody, and pressing the court with arguments and cases, it was curious to observe his weather-beaten clients, with their bluff figures and contraband visages, how intently they looked on as their fate was debated in (to them) an unknown tongue, and with what a singular promptness they appeared to discover, from mere external signs—from the looks and gestures of the Judges or the auditors—that their counsel was making way with the court. Their deliverance, I recollect, was effected; and if they and the hundreds of others of their trade and country, whom Mr. Perrin has similarly rescued from an Irish prison, have any gratitude, his must be a well-known and popular name in the Dutch ports.

Mr. Perrin's professional eminence was not his sole ground of claim to the honor of representing the city of Dublin in Parliament: he had a further and stronger recommendation to the public confidence in the vigor and integrity of his personal character. The political principles which he avows have now, in the circle of events, become the reigning doctrine of the day, and the merit may be small of professing such principles at the present moment. Mr. Perrin's praise is, that what he now is, he has always been; that under circumstances the most adverse to professional advancement, he entered into no compromise between his interests and opinions, but in every stage of his progress asserted himself and the dignity of his profession by an erect and independent bearing; he did so in a temper and spirit the most remote from faction, but he met with little mercy. He had incurred the virtue of public spirit, and was marked for discouragement—even the poor distinction of a silk-gown was delayed until Lord Manners's last general levee of King's counsel; and even then it was understood that Mr. Perrin would have been designedly omitted, had not the Lord

Chief-Justice, to whose better spirit what is just and manly is always familiar, peremptorily interposed his authority, as the head of the common-law bar, against an act of such unworthy partisanship.

I fear that I am trespassing on the ground of the "Sketches of the Irish Bar;" but, as I have gone so far,* let me say a word of Mr. Perrin's personal appearance. It is not so remarkable as to attract examination; but when you examine it, you find its unostentatious simplicity to be strikingly accordant with his mind and character. His figure is about the middle size, and slightly approaching to corpulence. He has black hair, a dark complexion, and regular Roman features. Though no one has a quicker perception of mirth, or enjoys it more heartily, the habitual expression of his countenance is graveness, even perhaps to a touch of sadness; the latter, however,

* Mr. Perrin was worthy of a distinct place in these "Sketches," for few lawyers had so much to contend with, on account of particular family circumstances (of no interest to the public), which, for a time clouded his prospects. The touch of sadness upon his countenance was caused, I doubt not, by the misconduct of a near relative, which met with exemplary punishment from the law. The Irish attorneys, among whom this person had once been enrolled, considered it hard that an innocent man should suffer, from a sort of reflected cloud, and generously showed their sympathy, by throwing as much business into Mr. Perrin's hands as they safely could. In a short time, proving equal to the labor, his great ability obtained, as a right, that practice which, at first had been conceded as a favor. In customs and excise cases, he was unapproached, almost from the first.—As I am on a legal question, and have arrived at the close of this work, let me add, in reference to the conviction of John Scanlan, at Limerick, in 1820, for murder on the Shannon (as detailed in the sketch called "An Irish Circuit," in the first volume), that Mr. Sheil treating of the facts, and Gerald Griffin, working them up into romantic fiction, strangely omitted two strong points. The first, as to *motive.* Sullivan confessed to Scanlan's desire to get rid, by murder, of the poor young creature whom he had seduced (by mock marriage), "because she kept calling him her husband." The second, showing the *malice prepense,* was that the crime was delayed until Scanlan had purchased a boat, in which the victim was to be carried out of sight of land, and there "done to death," and until a blacksmith had made a chain and collar to tie round her neck, attached to a heavy stone, to sink the body. I have read the report of the trial, since I annotated Mr. Sheil's detail of facts, but only in time to put the statement into this place.—At this last moment, too, I perceive that the Marchioness Wellesley (the heroine of the Dublin Tabinet Ball, Vol. I.) died at Hampton Court Palace, near London, on December 17, 1853.—M.

I apprehend to be nothing more than the mere trace of the laborious occupations in which his life has been passed. On the whole, I would say of his exterior, including face, and form, and apparel, that it was individualized by a certain republican homeliness, intimating a natural, careless manliness of taste, and not without its peculiar dignity.

I intended, when I sat down, to have entered upon some of the details of the Dublin election and its sequel; but the subject, I find, would carry me too far: let me therefore for the present merely say that, after an obstinate struggle, the corporation, that cumbrous excrescence upon our institutions, was fairly prostrated, and the popular candidates returned. The triumph was celebrated with all due rites and solemnities. I witnessed the chairing from a window in Grafton street. The sun shone brightly on the procession as it passed — but not more brightly than the countenance of our venerable and patriotic veteran, Mr. Peter Burrowes, who had taken his station at an opposite balcony, and looked down (as his friend Louis Perrin was wafted along) with a smile of joyous and ineffable thanksgiving, that he had been spared to see that day.

INDEX.

THE END.

www.ingramcontent.com/pod-product-compliance
Lightning Source LLC
LaVergne TN
LVHW020127110826
845151LV00001B/304

* 9 7 8 1 4 2 5 5 4 0 7 8 4 *